AMERICA'S MAJOR WARS:

CRUSADERS, CRITICS, AND SCHOLARS, 1775–1972

VOLUME 2: 1866–1972

Leslie E. Decker
and
Robert Seager II
Editors

ADDISON-WESLEY PUBLISHING COMPANY
Reading, Massachusetts · Menlo Park, California · London
Don Mills, Ontario

This book is in the Addison-Wesley
SERIES IN HISTORY

Consulting Editor
Robin W. Winks

DO

For Eva—

and Caroline too—

"If many empires have been destroyed by war,
by war also have many risen from nothing."

POLYBIUS—

CONTENTS

WORLD WAR II 141

I
THE CRUSADERS AND THE SCHOLARS: AMERICAN

II
THE CRUSADERS: GERMAN AND JAPANESE

INTRODUCTION

WAR, TECHNOLOGY, AND AMERICAN GROWTH

It was long the fashion, and it has become so again, to consider human violence in general and war in particular as unnatural and irrational aberrations. In the light of history, such a view is nonsense. Violence is a transcendent theme of human behavior, and socially organized violence in the form of war or revolution has always been a dynamic force in the evolution of cultures, nations, and states. No people has developed a sophisticated social organization without the impetus of one or more major wars. The United States of America is no exception. Nor is American society. It may be a sad fact; but it is nonetheless true.

America was discovered and settled by inquisitive and combative men who were variously motivated by political idealism and escapism, religious and racial chauvinism, and pragmatic greed. No wonder, then, that America's subsequent history through more than 150 years of colonial dependence and through nearly 200 years of separate national existence consistently involved the violent subjugation of aboriginal cultures and peoples. Particularly was this true during the extension of the nation's sway across the continent and beyond. This subjugation also included the equally violent assimilation of immigrants into the ethnic potpourri that became the American population. The whole process was invariably accompanied by violence of one sort or another, either against those at home who remained outside the popular concept of the American destiny or in reaction to violence perpetrated by foreign states and princes against American dreams, hopes, or ambitions.

A great deal of the violence was unorganized and "private," that is to say, it was perpetrated by or against individuals; for America was a wilderness, a violent land. No small amount was organized and "public"; that is, it was violence superintended by American governments, whether colonial assemblies, territorial legislatures, individual states, alliances of states, or a central federal authority. These governments launched countless minor wars against Indians, Blacks, and immigrant Orientals, and against such home-grown dissenters as the Mormons and the nascent labor unions. In addition, Americans have fought seven major wars against other nation-states and coalitions of states, and one major war against themselves.

All this has been closely related to the development of a modern, powerful nation. Innovations in civil government as well as major shifts in military policy and in military and civilian technology, are the normal, one might almost say the necessary, results of major wars. The American Constitution, with its peculiar balance of powers and its indeterminate location of sovereignty, was perhaps the greatest of all American innovations. It was a direct outgrowth of the Revolution, America's first major war. The second major war, the War of 1812, was in many ways a continuation of the first. It was made necessary in large part by the continuing evolution of commercial and industrial technology and, in larger part, by the evolution of the institution of war in Europe into world-wide and semi-modernized struggles between France and England for imperial domination. Out of the War of 1812 came the beginnings of American national unification. But that goal would be achieved only as the result of two more wars, one in 1846 to gain for the United states its "manifestly destined" continental boundaries, the other in 1861 to establish the sway of one notion of government and one cultural norm throughout the whole nation. In principle, the Civil War was as much a war for national unification as were those taking place in Italy and Germany at the same time.

Together with the Mexican War and the Civil War came the technological revolution that later ushered the United States and the world into the twentieth century, a century in which the connection between administration, technology, and war became clear to even the most obtuse observers. Fundamental shifts in the structure of government, begun in preceding wars and mightily influenced by war-stimulated technological developments, took place at an accelerating rate. The enhancement of the power of the executive was an immediate and obvious result of this, as was the waxing strength of the federal government and the waning power of state and local government. The centralization of power into one government and the shrinking of the decision-making power within that government into fewer and fewer hands was a major political fact of the twentieth century, at least up to the three-quarter mark. The Spanish-American War to a lesser degree, the two world wars to a greater degree, and the Cold War to the greatest degree, vastly accelerated and shaped this centralizing trend.

The relationship of war to technological change also became increasingly apparent in the twentieth century. The evolution of transportation and communication, and the interrelation of both to the health of the national economy might be mentioned in this regard. As war became increasingly technical, it became more and more an administrators' and engineers' function and less and less a question of the skill and prowess of individual fighting men and units. The application of military principles to industrial production became increasingly common; and the adaptation of military innovation to civilian economic development became a normal dimension of change. From the Civil War forward, various politicians, businessmen, and military leaders saw and capitalized upon these developing economic and technological relationships. The growth of the American railroad system, the telegraph and telephone systems, the merchant marine, extensive highway systems, air transportation, radio systems, and nuclear power have had distinct military implications. Military contingency planning and the accelerating rate of obsolescence of the tools of war increasingly served as stimulants to the national economy, or to what has been called "the warfare state." During both world wars and in the world-wide depressions that followed them, poverty or prosperity for whole areas of the United States and for whole segments of the world came substantially to depend on the locus and vigor of these military-technological developments. It was no surprise that the new era of technological revolution also marked an era of international tensions and related programs of military preparedness among America's enemies as well as in the camp of America and its allies.

The role of the executive in foreign affairs and the constitutional role of Congress in making war, questions casually considered and virtually dismissed by the Founding Fathers, became matters of central concern to students and critics of American government in the twentieth century.

WAR AND THE CONSTITUTION

The Constitution in Article I, Section 8, assigns to the Congress the power to

> declare War, grant letters of Marque and Reprisal, and make Rules concerning Captures on Land and Water; To raise and support Armies, but no Appropriation of Money to that Use shall be for a longer Term than two Years; To provide and maintain a Navy; To make Rules for the Government and Regulation of the land and naval Forces; To provide for calling forth the Militia to execute the Laws of the Union, suppress Insurrections and repel Invasions. . . .

On the surface that delegation of power seems clear enough. Unfortunately, it is not clear at all. There is nothing in the Constitution to prevent the President, in his capacity as Commander in Chief of the armed forces (Article II, Section 2), from employing American forces in being in warlike or war-related activities and operations without a formal declaration of hostilities. Nor could the Founding Fathers, students as they were of the neatly formalized balance-of-power system of the eighteenth century, visualize a disorderly world in which belligerent activity between nations and within nations would take a variety of military forms wholly foreign to the experience of the civilized European nations of 1787.

Among the various warlike activities practiced by the United States (and other nations) in the nineteenth and twentieth centuries, have been full-scale punitive expeditions (Korea, 1871; Mexico, 1916); the "hot pursuit" of hostile forces across international frontiers (Spanish Florida, 1818); preventive "surgical strikes" against enemy forces located across international boundaries or on the high seas (Barbary Coast, 1801–1805; Cambodia, 1970); numerous naval chastisements of port towns interfering with America trade (Quallah Batoo, 1832; Greytown, 1854); frequent landing of troops abroad to protect American lives and property (Vera Cruz, 1914; Haiti, 1915; Dominican Republic, 1965); participation in international punitive operations (North China, 1854; 1900); intervention in foreign civil wars (Texas, 1836; Siberia, 1918–1919; China, 1946–1948); employment of foreign mercenaries in overt and covert operations against hostile states (Cuba, 1961; Indochina, 1961–1972; subversion of hostile governments by paramilitary means (Iran, 1953; Guatemala, 1954); and the dispatch of military supplies and combat-training cadres to various allies, actual and potential (Cold War, 1947–1972). Between 1899 and 1903, the United States also fought a major war against the Filipinos that was as undeclared as it was bloody.

The waging of punitive war, limited war, vicarious war, subversive war, cold war, and other forms of undeclared war has often demanded a speed, secrecy, and decisiveness of action best achieved by executive order or executive encouragement without prior reference to Congress or literal adherence to Article I, Section 8.

Any evaluation of the Constitution as a guide to the subsequent history of war and peace in the United States must take into consideration the fact that America in 1787 was essentially a maritime nation. Because of this, the commerce-conscious Founding Fathers specifically assigned to the Congress, rather than to the President, the power to "grant Letters of Marque and Reprisal." In so doing, however, they recognized and accepted the practice of privateering, the only cold war activity generally endorsed by civilized nations of the eighteenth century. And in prosecuting the Undeclared Naval War against France, 1798–1800, the infant United States early embraced the modern notion of fighting a war that was neither legally nor technically a war.

The Constitution does not require that wars be *declared*. For this reason, among others, the numerous wars against the American Indian nations were invariably undeclared. In the minds of their congressional and executive progenitors, these military operations against the Indians were usually regarded as little more than legitimate and necessary exercises of an American police power. But like the frequent naval punitive expeditions of the nineteenth century against more distant enemies, they were wars nonetheless. The crucial point is that Americans of that era saw no constitutional problems inherent in the prosecution of such limited wars; nor in those days were there agonized appeals to what the Founding Fathers may have *intended* when they drafted Article I, Section 8, and Article II, Section 2, of the Constitution.

A surprising feature of the debates in the Constitutional Convention at Philadelphia in 1787 is that so little attention was paid to the question of the war-making power. In a document notable for its imaginative system of checks and balances, virtually no attention was given to the problems inherent in the dichotomy between the war-making powers of the Congress and the primary obligation of the President to "preserve, protect and defend the Constitution of the United States." Nor do the surviving records of the debates indicate that the Founders were aware that a contradiction in function was likely to develop in the legislative-executive relationship in this sensitive area.

Certainly, the possible martial dimensions of the role of the executive were not clearly defined. Save for a minor difference of opinion on whether the President as Commander in Chief should be empowered to command American troops in the field, there was little disposition to place restraints on his role in directing military operations once launched. As Maryland delegate Luther Martin later reported to his state legislature, "it was wished to be so far restrained that he should not command in person; but this could not be obtained."[1]

The war-making question was first brought up in the debate of May 29, 1787, four days after the deliberations had begun. On that occasion Edmund Randolph of Virginia introduced the problem with the oblique observation that any revision of the Confederation system ought, among other things, "to secure against foreign invasion." According to James Madison's notes of Randoph's speech, the Virginian charged that Congress under the Articles of Confederation had

> produced no security against foreign invasion; congress not being permitted to prevent a war nor to support it by their own authority ... that they could not cause infractions of treaties or of the law of nations, to be punished: that particular states might by their conduct provide war without controul; and that neither militia nor draughts being fit for defence on such occasions, enlistments only could be successful, and these could not be executed without money.[2]

James McHenry's recollections of Randolph's remarks on this occasion were more detailed if not more revealing:

> If [argued Randolph] a State acts against a foreign power contrary to the laws of nations or violates a treaty, it [the Con-

---

1 Max Farrand, Ed., *The Records of the Federal Convention of 1787*, revised edition, 4 vols. New Haven: Yale University Press, 1966, III, 218. See also I, 244, 247; III, 624.

2 *Ibid.*, I, 18–19 (Madison Notes).

federation Congress] cannot punish that State, or compel its obedience to the treaty. It can only leave the offending State to the operations of the offended power. It therefore cannot prevent a war. If the rights of an ambassador be invaded by any citizen it is only in a few States that any laws exist to punish the offender. A State may encroach on foreign possessions in its neighbourhood and Congress cannot prevent it. Disputes that respect naturalization cannot be adjusted. None of the judges in the several States is under the obligation of an oath made to yield to State constitutions. Imbecility of the Confederation equally conspicuous when called upon to support a war. The journals of Congress a history of expedients. . . . What reason to expect that the treasury will be better filled in the future, or that money can be obtained under the present powers of Congress to support a war. *Volunteers* not to be depended on for such a purpose. *Militia* difficult to be collected and almost impossible to be kept in the field. *Draughts* stretch the strings of government too violently to be adopted. Nothing short of a regular military force will answer the end of war, and this only to be created and supported by money.[3]

Randolph, it seems clear, was not so much concerned with the war-making power of the legislature versus that of the executive (on that crucial point he was silent) as he was with the international embarrassments inherent in the war-making power conferred on the individual states by the Articles of Confederation and the need to shift the financial burden of war from the backs of those states onto the back of the new nation.

Charles Pinckney of South Carolina approached the issue from a different viewpoint. Madison tells us that on June 1, 1787, "Mr. Pinkney was for a vigorous Executive but was afraid the Executive powers of Congress might extend to peace & war, etc. which would render the Executive a Monarchy, of the worst kind, to wit an elective one."[4] But after this promising beginning of a genuine debate on the war-making issue, the subject was abruptly and inexplicably changed, and turned instead to whether the executive should be singular or plural.

---

3 *Ibid.*, 24–25 (McHenry Notes).
4 *Ibid.*, 64–65 (Madison Notes).

Recent critics of what has been called "executive usurpation" of the war-making powers of Congress by various Cold War presidents have been quick to cite Pinckney's remark about the dangers of "monarchy" in the war-making area. Just what Pinckney had in mind, however, is not clear, and his somewhat obscure observation would seem a weak peg on which to hang an argument of executive usurpation.

Similarly, George Mason of Virginia declared on June 6 that the purse and sword must not be in the same hands and that the Legislature should not be permitted to raise revenues and also make and direct war.[5] Again, neither a strong anti-legislature nor a clear pro-executive case on the war-making power can be made by citing Mason.

Hamilton was much clearer in his thinking on the matter, although his views did not prevail. On June 18, in a six-hour speech to the delegates, an address which Gouverneur Morris said was the most able and impressive he had ever heard, Hamilton argued in passing (the war-making issue was always argued in passing) that the Senate should have "the sole power of declaring war, the power of advising and approving all treaties." In fine, Hamilton would have linked the war-making power with the treaty-making power and put both in the hands of a body that was not to be elected directly by the people.[6] Hamilton also maintained that the Executive should "have the power . . . to make war or peace, with the advice of the senate—to make treaties with their advice, but to have the sole direction of all military operations, and to send ambassadors and appoint all military officers." . . .[7]

The inconclusive debate on the war-making power came to an end on August 17, 1787. On that date John Dickinson of Delaware moved to vest the full legislature, rather than the executive alone or the Senate alone, with the power "to make war." The following (and final) exchange on the the issue then took place:

Mr. Pinckney opposed the vesting this power in the Legislature. Its proceedings were too slow. It wd. meet but once a year. The Hs. of Reps. would be too numerous for such deliberations. The Senate would be the best depositary, being more acquainted with foreign affairs, and most capable of proper resolutions. If the States are equally represented in Senate, so as to give no

---

5 *Ibid.*, 144 (Rufus King Notes).

6 *Ibid.*, 292 (Madison Notes); 300 (Robert Yates Notes).

7 *Ibid.*, 300 (Yates Notes); see also Madison Notes on the Hamilton speech for June 19, 1787 in *ibid.*, 316.

advantage to large States, the power will notwithstanding be safe, as the small have their all at stake in such cases as well as the large States. It would be singular for one authority to make war, and another peace.

Mr. Butler.[8] The Objections agst the Legislature lie in a great degree agst the Senate. He was for vesting the power in the President, who will have all the requisite qualities, and will not make war but when the Nation will support it.

Mr. M[adison] and Mr. Gerry[9] moved to insert "*declare*," striking out "*make*" war; leaving to the Executive the power to repel sudden attacks.

Mr. Sharman[10] thought it stood very well. The Executive shd. be able to repel and not to commence war. "Make" better than "declare" the latter narrowing the power too much.

Mr. Gerry never expected to hear in a republic a motion to empower the Executive alone to declare war.

Mr. Elseworth.[11] There is a material difference between the cases of making *war*, and making *peace*. It shd. be more easy to get out of war, than into it. War also is a simple and overt declaration. Peace attended with intricate & secret negociations.

Mr. Mason was agst giving the power of war to the Executive because not [safely] to be trusted with it; or to the Senate, because not so constructed as to be entitled to it. He was for clogging rather than facilitating war; but for facilitating peace. He preferred "*declare*" to "*make*."

On the motion to insert *declare*—in place of *make*, (it was agreed to.)

N.H. no. Mas. abst. Cont. no. Pa. ay. Del. ay. Md. ay. Va. ay. N.C. ay. S.C. ay. Geo. ay. (Ayes—7; noes—2; absent—1.) [On the remark by Mr. King that "make" war might be understood to "conduct" it which was an Executive function, Mr. Elseworth gave up his objection (and the vote of Cont. was changed to—ay).]

Mr. Pinkney's motion to strike out whole clause, disagd. to without call of States.

---

8 Pierce Butler of South Carolina.
9 Elbridge Gerry of Massachusetts.
10 Roger Sherman of Connecticut.
11 Oliver Elseworth of Connecticut.

Mr. Butler moved to give the Legislature power of peace, as they were to have that of war.

Mr. Gerry 2ds. him. 8 Senators may possibly exercise the power if vested in that body, and 14 if all should be present; and may consequently give up part of the U. States. The Senate are more liable to be corrupted by an Enemy than the whole Legislature.

On the motion for adding "and peace" after "war." N.H. no. Mas. no. Ct. no. Pa. no. Del. no. Md. no. Va. no. N.C. (no. S.C. no. Geo. no. (Ayes—O; noes—10.)

Adjourned.[12]

There was more than semantic subtlety involved in the discussion of permitting the Congress to "declare" rather than to "make" war. The word *declare*, as Roger Sherman of Connecticut pointed out, narrowed the scope of the legislature's function in this regard. *Declare* also had about it a less martial ring than *make*. Further, the actual *making* of war, that is, its physical prosecution once it had been declared, was to be left to the President as Commander in Chief. There was also concern that the legislature might well become too large and unwieldly a body to act quickly and decisively in the face of a crisis. Hence the decision to leave "to the Executive the power to repel sudden attacks." At what distance, in what form, and in what manner these attacks might legitimately be repelled was not, however, spelled out in the final wording of the Constitution. Therein lies the rub.

The war-declaring clause was passed by a revised vote of 8 to 1, Massachusetts not voting. Ironically, a motion to add to that clause the power of the combined House and Senate jointly to declare peace was defeated 10 to 0. That function was to be left to the Senate as part of its treaty-making power. Or, put another way, the power to declare war was put on a broader democratic basis than the power to make peace—presumably for those reasons of "intricate & secret negociations" to which Oliver Ellsworth called attention in the August 17 debate.

So it was that the final result of these peripheral and intermittent exchanges of view on war and peace at the Philadelphia Convention was a compromise. The war-making clause assigned the power to declare war to the House and Senate jointly; the treaty-making (and peace-declaring) power was given solely to the Senate; and the President became the

---

12 Farrand, *op. cit.*, II, 318–319 (Madison Notes).

Commander in Chief of the armed forces. As in most compromises, there remained (and still remains) a number of shadowy interrelationships and unspecified functions.

Nevertheless, presidents have invariably gone to the Congress to ask that war be declared; or, more accurately, to ask that a war thrust upon the United States by the perfidious behavior of an enemy be accepted and prosecuted. Indeed, presidential acceptance of the constitutional requirement to go to the Congress has generated a series of unusual and interesting state papers, the War Messages of the Presidents.[13] In these documents, the presidents have spelled out to Congress their arguments for war and in so doing have made their appeals to heaven and to history. To these importunities the Congress has always given its consent.

What presidents have not always done is to consult Congress *prior* to taking measures that had warlike implications and required the speedy use and deployment of the armed forces on a limited basis for specific and compelling reasons. It was to this point that Professor Henry Steele Commager addressed himself in testimony before the Senate Foreign Relations Committee in March 1971, when he argued for legislation that would "require congressional approval for extended military action except in an emergency."[14] How "emergency" was to be defined in this context he did not make clear. Such restraining legislation, Commager insisted, would serve to "reassert and vindicate the constitutional role of the Senate in the war making and treaty making powers, and to curb the pretensions of the executive in those areas."

At the time of his testimony, Commager was clearly concerned with the earlier deployment of American forces in Vietnam without a formal declaration of war. But most of the lengthy list of nineteenth century examples he offered to deplore that deployment and to support a proposal "to curb the pretensions of the executive" were unrelated to the Vietnam problem; and they were not responsive historically to the dilemmas built into the war-making clause of the Constitution. Indeed, his guilt-by-equation of the executive decision in, for example, the naval bombardment of Greytown in 1854 with the executive decision sharply to escalate the intervention in Vietnam in 1965 was to blur the focus

---

13 These are printed herein in Volume I which treats the American Revolution, the War of 1812, the Mexican War and the Civil War; and in Volume II which deals with the Spanish-American-Philippine War, World War I, World War II and the Cold War.

14 Professor Commager's testimony is reprinted in part in Volume II.

of the traditional punitive function of the executive. The situations were quite different. Nor was it instructive to make a constitutional distinction, as Commager did, between the relative acceptability of nineteenth century punitive actions that were continental or hemispheric, and the total unacceptability of twentieth century "military operations that were in fact acts of war, that were on a large scale, that were in distant parts of the globe, and that constituted 'commitments' whose vindication threatened the integrity of our political and constitution system.". . . Neither the demur of "emergency" (however that word might be defined), nor the geographical location of a war, nor the scale of violence of a given military action is pertinent to the larger constitutional question.

On the punitive function the Constitution is silent, although tradition and usage have long permitted the President to exercise his judgment in this regard without prior reference to Congress when American interests, lives, and property abroad were thought to be threatened by foreign forces. To be sure, such judgments have been subsequently questioned and criticized by various legislators; but in every major instance the President, usually the leader of the majority party, has been upheld by the Congress. The growth of tradition has not been unrelated to partisan political considerations.

What has happened over the years, especially in the twentieth century, and more specifically since the Cold War period began in 1947, is that the traditional executive use of the punitive power has crept toward executive decision-making in war. Much of this can be traced to the fact that the Founding Fathers could not visualize the so-called "wars of national liberation" being fought today. The Constitution did not provide for swift, decisive, and uncomplicated responses to the sort of seeping, subtle, and pervasive aggression that characterized the many-faceted North Vietnamese attack on South Vietnam in the 1960s. Oliver Ellsworth in 1787 saw the making of war as the result of "a simple and overt declaration." It no longer necessarily is. Therefore the executive has moved steadily into the gray area between punitive action and war-making. He is now caught somewhere between exercising his powers as Commander in Chief in relatively neat, traditional wars (as were World War II and the conflict in Korea) and agonizing over the extent of his punitive or war-making powers in responing to an aggressive "war of national liberation" (as was the conflict in Vietnam).

The problem today does not, therefore, stem from the fact that Cold

War presidents have been conspiratorial, power-mad, or bloodthirsty men. Both Truman and Nixon, in fact, limited the full employment of America's conventional military might in combat situations that were extremely difficult and dangerous—Truman in Korea and Nixon in Indochina. The problem stems partly from the fact that the Constitution provides little guidance to a president in modern, military decision-making situations. The issue has not been so much one of the abuse of executive power in this area as it has been the inability or the unwillingness of an unwieldly Congress to adapt itself to the unique challenges of contemporary war-making. In 1787 Elbridge Gerry "never expected to hear in a republic a motion to empower the Executive alone to declare war." And John Dickinson felt that "Secresy, vigor & Dispatch are not the properties of Republics."[15] But the America of Gerry and Dickinson, and the eighteenth century conception of war that the Founding Fathers understood, bears little resemblance to the America of today and to the phenomenon that is the Cold War.

If the charge of "executive usurpation" is to be accepted as valid, the Constitution will have to be amended and made more responsive to the realities and requirements of the world military and political situation. How this can be done short of an improbable shift to a plural executive or the adoption of a Fortress America conception of national interests is not clear. Various proposals to amend the Constitution to provide for referenda on war (such as the Ludlow Resolution of 1938) and to bind the President more closely to the will of the legislature in the execution of American foreign policy (such as the proposed Bricker Amendment of 1953) have failed because of a general feeling that the elements of time and maneuverability in modern military decision-making require that the President have great flexibility of action and a broad range of responses to potential danger. However, demands have been voiced recently that the President be required to ask Congress for its approval *after* commitment of the armed forces abroad; specifically, that the Constitution be amended to permit the President to exercise his war powers or punitive powers without restraint for a period of no more than thirty to sixty days, after which time the President would be required to ask Congress for support of his decision. Failing to receive this, the war would stop, since a hostile Congress would presumably cut off the funds with which further to sustain it. Aside from its probable political un-

---

15 Farrand, *op. cit.*, I, 144.

workability, the thirty-day deductible approach to military decision-making appeals to some critics of executive usurpation.

Congress can indeed constitutionally reverse the trend of executive escalation of power in the war-making process by denying funds for the prosecution of a particular war or punitive action. This blunt tactic would, however, have severe political, emotional, and psychological repercussions, especially if American soldiers were already engaged in combat operations, and more especially if it was clear that a military decision had been made in swift response to overt aggression against the United States or against those of its citizens legally residing abroad. Failure to respond militarily to aggression of that sort, or to overt or covert aggression against allies with which the United States has mutual defense treaty obligations, would mean nothing less than America's ceasing to be a credible twentieth-century power. It is not likely that a majority of Americans, in Congress or out, would choose that alternative to "executive usurpation." The medicine would be worse than the disease.

PATTERNS OF ASSENT AND DISSENT ON WAR

Throughout their history, Americans have vigorously disagreed about each and every march to war. Dissent has always been the foundation stone of the American way of doing things politically, and disagreement over such a basic act as participation in a major war has been both normal and necessary for most Americans. It is with advocacy and opposition in these instances that this collection of statements, essays, and documents is largely concerned. These volumes deal with the United States and its enemies, "foreign and domestic," on those eight traumatic occasions in the American experience when the normal violence quotient of the nation was so intensified as to take on fundamental significance in the creation and maintenance of the independence, prestige, or vital interests of the United States. On those eight occasions all qualities of American life—including its theoretical bent, its moral certitude, and its commitment to the obligation to dissent—have been tested, brought into focus, and related anew to America's historical *raison d'être*.

It seems clear, too, that these ideological struggles among Americans have produced a persistent pattern of American advocacy and dissent about the nation's wars. With historically appropriate variations in the arguments they have employed, Americans have declared, conducted, and opposed their major wars in a remarkably consistent manner. It is this pattern which the pages that follow seek to illustrate. The reader is urged, in the words of *The Book of Common Prayer*, to "read, mark, learn, and inwardly digest"—and, of course, to dissent if that seems proper.

In broadest terms, the pattern revealed herein has to do with the analyses of four major groupings of war participants, three contemporary and one after the fact. The contemporaries are the war crusaders, the spokesmen for the enemies against whom America fought, and the anti-war critics. The participants after the fact are those scholars who later attempted to reconstruct and interpret the relationships among the contemporaries. Hence the subtitle to these volumes: Crusaders, Critics, and Scholars.

American crusaders have almost always been constrained to cast their arguments for war in transcendent ideological terms, sometimes religious, usually idealistic, and always moral. It has never been possible for such Americans to launch and conduct a major war on grounds frankly stated to be material self-interest or candidly to refer to the realities of international power politics, however real those considerations actually were at the time. American war-makers have preferred to see themselves reluctantly responding to the provocations or outrages of an enemy. These Americans do not declare war; they courageously accept war thrust upon them from abroad.

American war critics, on the other hand, have sprung from many sources and traditions, but have two readily discernible intellectual origins: an abstract and broadly conceived humanist or religious opposition to violence in general and war in particular; and a more narrowly expressed opposition to the specific mode of gaining the material or ideological ends sought by the crusaders in the war being urged. In other words, criticism has sprung from opposition to all war or opposition to the political, diplomatic, or economic mechanics of launching a particular war. Neither form of opposition has failed to produce critics of eloquence and power with whom the crusaders have been forced strenuously to contend.

At the same time, neither the critics nor the crusaders have been able to gainsay the fact that war does not take place in a vacuum. There is always an enemy; and *his* views, reactions, ambitions, and interests significantly influence the course of domestic debate over war or peace. To judge better the course of the debate, the reader should have some awareness of events on "The Other Side of the Hill"—at least to the extent of recognizing that the enemy of the moment has his crusaders and his critics. He also has *his enemy*—the United States of America.

Why, then, have we, the editors of these volumes, undertaken this work? We are Americans and historians ourselves and are subject to the same pressures and biases as are other scholars. Part of the answer lies in two qualities we feel to be unique in the organization and presentation of these materials. One is our consideration of the enemy's conception of the origin and nature of his war against the United States. This area of concern is usually a *terra incognita* to American readers. While the dimensions of the domestic debate over war or peace are certainly instructive, it may be more instructive to know what the enemy was doing, or what Americans thought he was doing, at the time. The other quality is the manner of presentation. We have not consciously assessed the rightness or wrongness of the opinions expressed by the participants. We have attempted only to select and present representative examples of these opinions for the reader to evaluate.

In doing this, we have had two ends in view. One is the elementary goal of helping make Americans aware that these pro-war and anti-war behavior patterns have occurred and recurred for nearly two centuries, and that none of the current agonizing about America's role in the contemporary world is novel. We have passed this way before, and it is always worth remembering that, in the words of George Santyana, "he who is unaware of his own history is condemned to repeat it." The other end sought here turns on our conviction that the best way Americans can help preserve what we believe is "the last, best hope of earth" is for each generation to consider anew and act intelligently upon the realities of America's past and present values, traditions, and ambitions as these have been related to war and peace throughout American history.

HISTORY AND THE HUMAN ANIMAL

What, then, is the student of American advocacy and dissent in war—or the American advocate or dissenter in recent American wars—to conclude from his study of the essays and documents that follow? The cynic, the skeptic, the lazy or preoccupied recruit to the Now Generation might conclude that they mean nothing and go about his business, ignoring the past, convinced that the personal problems he currently faces are the only ones that count, and that the dusty records of bygone days will serve only further to confuse him. Or he might, like the author of Ecclesiastes, assert that there is no new thing under the sun and conclude that history does not matter anyhow. Such an American, we believe, takes either course at his personal peril and at the mortal peril of the United States.

This belief is based on the premise that while it is obvious that men have changed little in the two hundred years since Lexington and Concord, it is equally obvious that in the same two centuries the world of men has changed almost beyond recognition. This conviction is not the sole reason, but it is certainly the main reason, for our conclusion that the study of the past does more than satisfy intellectual curiosity; it teaches us some of the rules by which men live and have lived.

The effect of human experience is, or should be, cumulative. Hence a knowledge of history may help some Americans cope realistically and intelligently with seemingly insoluble contemporary problems. To find parallels between Corwin's hostility toward Polk's policy in Mexico, Bryan's cynical view of McKinley's policy in the Philippines, and Fulbright's criticism of Johnson's policy in Southeast Asia is to recognize at the very least that patterns of dissent do exist.

At the same time, one must also recognize that American war critics have invariably had a deep and abiding concern for the preservation of liberty at home and abroad, and have not always rejected what they considered legitimate war aims or the expenditure of American blood and treasure to achieve such aims. Opposition to a specific war is not necessarily opposition to all war; nor is opposition to war necessarily opposition to a "just" war. It is also important to understand that war crusaders from Sam Adams, Madison, and Lincoln to Wilson, Franklin Roosevelt and Kennedy have served the national interest by couching practical ambitions in moralist-idealist terms. In so doing they have not necessarily undermined moralism or idealism. They have merely translated overriding ideological commitments into practical terms— into what a recent President called "the art of the possible." Conversely, to apply to the contemporary scene the experience of such war dissenters as John Randolph, Joshua Giddings, Robert M. LaFollette, Charles A. Lindberg, or Henry A. Wallace—without repeating their tactical or analytical mistakes—would avoid the pitfalls of presentmindedness and help make future dissent more effective, potent, and lasting.

Vicarious historical experience with the phenomenon of war has yet another dimension: the realization that two hundred years of American national history—like the thousands of years of recorded human history that went before—shows rather conclusively that war has been an anvil on which much of the modern world has been shaped and that there have always been irrational and imponderable grounds upon which men willingly, even eagerly, fight and die. Men have never required either concrete material ends or definable intellectual goals to persuade them to risk their lives, their fortunes, or their sacred honor on a field of battle.

The ultimate truth about men and violence is that with the one there has always been the other, and this for the simple reason that man is only partly a rational animal. His powers of reason leave much to be desired; he is not completely educable. True, belief in his ability to reason is the prime justification for formal education; and education, particularly the study of history, may well demonstrate that war is not a reasonable way for men to solve their problems. But men have relied on the organized and directed violence that is war throughout their history to solve their problems, real or imagined. They have before and they will again. There is no persuasive evidence in recorded history to suggest otherwise. Measured on the clock of human existence, men have been out of the trees but a few minutes and out of caves but a few seconds. This is the problem.

THE
SPANISH–AMERICAN–
PHILIPPINE WAR

The Spanish-American War was launched in April, 1898, to free the people of Cuba from the thraldom of Spanish colonial maladministration. Or so President McKinley argued in perhaps the most idealistically worded of all the presidential war messages. America was marching to war to liberate an oppressed neighboring people who were fighting for the same independence Americans had fought for in 1775–1783. True, there were admitted motives of national self-interest, but McKinley viewed these as peripheral to the larger humanitarian and idealistic concerns of the United States government in Cuba.

The fact that the Madrid government had attempted to avoid war with the United States by a policy of appeasement and had capitulated to American demands in the matter a few days earlier was barely mentioned by the President in his War Message. On April 20, Congress by joint resolution enthusiastically endorsed war, adding a pledge—the famous self-denying ordinance that was the Teller Amendment—that the United States had absolutely no territorial ambitions in Cuba, that Cuba was indeed to be free. *Cuba Libre!*

The war was a swift and decisive affair. So hopelessly inept were Spanish land and naval forces in Cuba and in the Philippines that the unequal contest was over in three months. If there were doubts about the morality of the war in the minds of some Americans, those doubts had too little incubation time to hatch into a full-fledged peace movement during the conflict. On the other hand, if the United States had viewed the war in April, 1898, in terms of selfless humanitarianism, the decisiveness of the victory soon suggested to some Americans an insistence on peace terms more ambitious than mere *Cuba Libre*. McKinley's instructions to his peace commissioners in mid-September indicated that the war to free Cuba had somehow become a war for American empire in the Pacific. It was this unexpected development that launched the anti-imperialist movement.

Within a few months after the Spanish surrender, as the annexation of the Philippine Islands was being debated in the Senate, Filipino insurgents under the leadership of Emilio Aguinaldo commenced military operations against their American liberators in Luzon. They had no desire to exchange one set of masters for another. What had thus commenced as a "splendid little war" against Spain quickly metastasized, after February 1899, into a Philippine war of national liberation against the United States. As Senator Henry Cabot Lodge ruefully admitted, "I think the situation is unique in the fact that the people whom we liberated down there have turned against us."¹ Lodge, a leading imperialist, then explained to a somewhat bewildered Senate the background of Aguinaldo's uprising against the American army of occupation, wholly absolving the United States of any moral responsibility for the onset of hostilities. Aguinaldo, he maintained, was little more than a bandit. Similarly, Senator Albert J. Beveridge placed Philippine annexation in a broader national and imperialist context and urged a vigorous prosecution of the struggle against the ingrate Filipinos. "Reluctantly and only from a sense of duty am I forced to say that American opposition to the war has been the chief factor in prolonging it," he charged. So long did it drag on, and so unorthodox did it become as a military problem to the frustrated American military commanders in the field, that Brigadier General J. F. Bell finally issued, in December, 1901, a tough policy statement to his officers and men on how to deal with enemy guerrilla forces and the atrocities inherent in guerrilla tactics.

Aguinaldo, meanwhile, had couched his own War Message in the loftiest of nationalistic and patriotic terms. He also proclaimed the independence of the Philippine Republic from the United States (as he had earlier proclaimed it from Spain) and listed the grievances that had reluctantly impelled a Filipino resort to arms—all in words reminiscent of the American Declaration of Independence. Propaganda leaflets distributed to Filipino guerrilla forces in the jungles and to civilians in the villages vowed a fight to the finish against the American aggressors. These leaflets had a curiously contemporary ring: Yankee Go Home.

It was a ring that sounded like a Filipino Liberty Bell to many American critics of McKinley and the imperialists. No sooner had the war with Spain ended than Professor Charles Eliot Norton of Harvard belatedly attacked the morality of American participation in it and lamented the resulting end of American isolationism. Senator Benjamin Tillman of South Carolina saw the subsequent uprising in the Philippines as a genuine patriotic movement and counselled speedy American withdrawal from the Islands. And William Jennings Bryan, leading anti-imperialist spokesman and Democratic Party politician, summed up the Republican arguments for imperialist expansion, refuted them to his own satisfaction, and promised that were he elected President in November, 1900, the war in the Philippines would end and the Filipino

---

1 *Congressional Record.* Senate, 55th Congress, 3rd Session (February 7, 1899), p. 1531.

people would soon receive their independence under an American protectorate.

Bryan and the Democrats were routed in the election and opposition to United States war policy in the Philippines increasingly took the form of attacks on Army atrocities in the field. That some atrocities occurred could not be denied—as Senator Charles A. Culberson of Texas demonstrated with testimony supplied by Pvt. Andrew K. Weir of the Fourth Cavalry. That the perpetration of atrocities was a conscious dimension of American military policy in the Islands, a charge made by some Administration critics in 1901–1902, was another matter entirely. It remained unproven. On the other hand, the critics of the Army were reluctant to admit that the Filipinos also committed atrocities. Actually, it was a dirty little bushwacking war on both sides.

The atrocity question indicated, however, that the United States Army was clearly unprepared to fight a guerrilla war in the Philippines in 1899–1902. It certainly could not bring operations against Aguinaldo to the swift and neat conclusion that had characterized the victory in Cuba and in Manila during the summer of 1898. As casualties mounted in the jungles of Luzon and Samar, so too did criticism of American military and political policy in the Islands. Fortunately, for crusaders and critics alike, the fortuitous capture of Aguinaldo on March 23, 1901, broke the back of organized Filipino resistance. By mid-1902 the war had sputtered to an end, American casualties had ceased, and the concern over Army atrocities evaporated as quickly as it had risen.

It should be noted that the American-Philippine War was the third war of national liberation in which the United States had participated in its history. The War of the American Revolution and the War for Southern Independence were clearly wars of this sort. Because of their intense ideological and emotional quality—involving nothing less than demands for freedom and political independence—the debates on the issues in these wars were particularly bitter. Indeed, such wars have had a tendency to produce, on both sides, large numbers of what Eric Hoffer has called "true believers." Perhaps this is why critics of established national policy is such conflicts often find themselves in particularly awkward, indeed "subversive," situations as both the philosophical certitudes and the military casualties mount.

It is also true that critics on the eve of war and during wartime have invariably been viewed as "un-American" by the warmakers. It was so with the Loyalists in 1775–1782, the Francophile Democrats in 1798–

1800, the Anglophile Federalists in 1812–1815, the Abolitionist Whigs in 1846–1848, the Copperheads in 1861–1865, and the Anti-Imperialists in 1898–1902. The sentiments of these critics, however sincere philosophically, have usually been identified with support of the enemy cause by the war crusaders. Conversely, the warmakers have often been viewed by the peacemakers as parties to a conscious conspiracy against the real and best interests of America. Such "conspirators" have ranged from the Radical Rebels of 1774–1782 and the Aggressive Slavocracy of 1846–1861 to the Wall Street Imperialists of 1914–1972.

Conspiracy thesis has thus been a consistent and concomitant dimension of antiwar dissidence in America. So too has been the persistent and related theme that various presidents have lied, manipulated, or otherwise maneuvered the United States into unnecessary wars by unconstitutional usurpations of executive power—that Congress and the people have been regularly duped by unscrupulous chief executives bent on political aggrandizement or personal glory. These interpretations, crude as they have been historically, can be traced to the fact that the theses of conspiracy or manipulation best flourish in the extravagance of emotion and absence of common sense that accompanies war.

Whatever the reason for this phenomenon, critics of America's five major wars in the 1775–1902 period were branded variously as traitors, enemy agents, cowards, confused muddleheads, arrant subversives, or dupes of foreign propaganda. Undoubtedly some were. The larger point, however, is that antiwar dissidence has been too frequently and casually identified with unpatriotism and treason. It was so in 1776, 1812, 1846, 1861 and in 1898. It would be so again in 1917, and it has certainly been so during the Cold War (1947–1972).

The historian is thus tempted to argue that charges of treason and un-Americanism have been the one historical constant in antiwar activity since the founding of the Republic—just as prowar activity has often been characterized as conspiratorial and manipulative. As in chess, a standard "traitor" opening seems to demand a standard "conspiracy" defense.

THE
SPANISH-AMERICAN-PHILIPPINE
WAR

I
THE CRUSADERS:
AMERICAN

A

THE WAR MESSAGE: PRESIDENT WILLIAM MCKINLEY
APRIL 11, 1898

*"The forcible intervention of the United States as a neutral to stop
the war, according to the large dictates of humanity and following
many historical precedents where neighboring states have interfered
to check the hopeless sacrifices of life by internecine conflicts beyond
their borders, is justifiable on rational grounds."*

Obedient to that precept of the Constitution which commands the President to give from time to time to the Congress information of the state of the Union and to recommend to their consideration such measures as he shall judge necessary and expedient, it becomes my duty to now address your body with regard to the grave crisis that has arisen in the relations of the United States to Spain by reason of the warfare that for more than three years has raged in the neighboring island of Cuba.

I do so because of the intimate connection of the Cuban question with the state of our own Union and the grave relation the course which it is now incumbent upon the nation to adopt must needs bear to the traditional policy of our Government if it is to accord with the precepts laid

---

James D. Richardson, Ed., *Messages and Papers of the Presidents*. Washington: Bureau of National Literature and Art, 1910, IX, 6281–6292.

down by the founders of the Republic and religiously observed by succeeding Administrations to the present day.

The present revolution is but the successor of other similar insurrections which have occurred in Cuba against the dominion of Spain, extending over a period of nearly half a century, each of which during its progress has subjected the United States to great effort and expense in enforcing its neutrality laws, caused enormous losses to American trade and commerce, caused irritation, annoyance, and disturbance among our citizens, and, by the exercise of cruel, barbarous, and uncivilized practices of warfare, shocked the sensibilities and offended the humane sympathies of our people.

Since the present revolution began, in February, 1895, this country has seen the fertile domain at our threshold ravaged by fire and sword in the course of a struggle unequaled in the history of the island and rarely paralleled as to the numbers of the combatants and the bitterness of the contest by any revolution of modern times where a dependent people striving to be free have been opposed by the power of the sovereign state.

Our people have beheld a once prosperous community reduced to comparative want, its lucrative commerce virtually paralyzed, its exceptional productiveness diminished, its fields laid waste, its mills in ruins, and its people perishing by tens of thousands from hunger and destitution. We have found ourselves constrained, in the observance of that strict neutrality which our laws enjoin and which the law of nations commands, to police our own waters and watch our own seaports in prevention of any unlawful act in aid of the Cubans.

Our trade has suffered, the capital invested by our citizens in Cuba has been largely lost, and the temper and forbearance of our people have been so sorely tried as to beget a perilous unrest among our own citizens, which has inevitably found its expression from time to time in the National Legislature, so that issues wholly external to our own body politic engross attention and stand in the way of that close devotion to domestic advancement that becomes a self-contained commonwealth whose primal maxim has been the avoidance of all foreign entanglements. All this must needs awaken, and has, indeed, aroused, the utmost concern on the part of this Government, as well during my predecessor's term as in my own.

In April, 1896, the evils from which our country suffered through the Cuban war became so onerous that my predecessor made an effort to bring about a peace through the mediation of this Government in any way that might tend to an honorable adjustment of the contest between

Spain and her revolted colony, on the basis of some effective scheme of self-government for Cuba under the flag and sovereignty of Spain. It failed through the refusal of the Spanish government then in power to consider any form of mediation or, indeed, any plan of settlement which did not begin with the actual submission of the insurgents to the mother country, and then only on such terms as Spain herself might see fit to grant. The war continued unabated. The resistance of the insurgents was in no wise diminished.

The efforts of Spain were increased, both by the dispatch of fresh levies to Cuba and by the addition to the horrors of the strife of a new and inhuman phase happily unprecedented in the modern history of civilized Christian peoples. The policy of devastation and concentration, inaugurated by the Captain-General's *bando* of October 21, 1896, in the Province of Pinar del Rio was thence extended to embrace all of the island to which the power of the Spanish arms was able to reach by occupation or by military operations. The peasantry, including all dwelling in the open agricultural interior, were driven into the garrison towns or isolated places held by the troops.

The raising and movement of provisions of all kinds were interdicted. The fields were laid waste, dwellings unroofed and fired, mills destroyed, and, in short, everything that could desolate the land and render it unfit for human habitation or support was commanded by one or the other of the contending parties and executed by all the powers at their disposal.

By the time the present Administration took office, a year ago, reconcentration (so called) had been made effective over the better part of the four central and western provinces—Santa Clara, Matanzas, Havana, and Pinar del Rio.

The agricultural population to the estimated number of 300,000 or more was herded within the towns and their immediate vicinage, deprived of the means of support, rendered destitute of shelter, left poorly clad, and exposed to the most unsanitary conditions. As the scarcity of food increased with the devastation of the depopulated areas of production, destitution and want became misery and starvation. Month by month the death rate increased in an alarming ratio. By March, 1897, according to conservative estimates from official Spanish sources, the mortality among the reconcentrados from starvation and the diseases thereto incident exceeded 50 per cent of their total number.

No practical relief was accorded to the destitute. The overburdened towns, already suffering from the general dearth, could give no aid. So-called "zones of cultivation" established within the immediate areas of effective military control about the cities and fortified camps proved illusory as a remedy for the suffering. The unfortunates, being for the most part women and children, with aged and helpless men, enfeebled by disease and hunger, could not have tilled the soil without tools, seed, or shelter for their own support or for the supply of the cities. Reconcentration, adopted avowedly as a war measure in order to cut off the resources of the insurgents, worked its predestined result. As I said in my message of last December, it was not civilized warfare; it was extermination. The only peace it could beget was that of the wilderness and the grave. . . .

In this state of affairs my Administration found itself confronted with the grave problem of its duty. My message of last December reviewed the situation and narrated the steps taken with a view to relieving its acuteness and opening the way to some form of honorable settlement. The assassination of the prime minister, Canovas, led to a change of government in Spain. The former administration, pledged to subjugation without concession, gave place to that of a more liberal party, committed long in advance to a policy of reform involving the wider principle of home rule for Cuba and Puerto Rico.

The overtures of this Government made through its new envoy, General Woodford, and looking to an immediate and effective amelioration of the condition of the island, although not accepted to the extent of admitted mediation in any shape, were met by assurances that home rule in an advanced phase would be forthwith offered to Cuba, without waiting for the war to end, and that more humane methods should thenceforth prevail in the conduct of hostilities. Coincidentally with these declarations the new government of Spain continued and completed the policy, already begun by its predecessor, of testifying friendly regard for this nation by releasing American citizens held under one charge or another connected with the insurrection, so that by the end of November not a single person entitled in any way to our national protection remained in a Spanish prison. . . .

On the 24th of December last I caused to be issued an appeal to the American people inviting contributions in money or in kind for the succor of the starving sufferers in Cuba. . . .

Thousands of lives have already been saved. The necessity for a change in the condition of the reconcentrados is recognized by the Spanish Government. Within a few days past the orders of General Weyler have been revoked. The reconcentrados, it is said, are to be permitted to return to their homes and aided to resume the self-supporting pursuits of peace. Public works have been ordered to give them employment and a sum of $600,000 has been appropriated for their relief.

The war in Cuba is of such a nature that, short of subjugation or extermination, a final military victory for either side seems impracticable. The alternative lies in the physical exhaustion of the one or the other party, or perhaps of both—a condition which in effect ended the ten years' war by the truce of Zanjon. The prospect of such a protraction and conclusion of the present strife is a contingency hardly to be contemplated with equanimity by the civilized world, and least of all by the United States, affected and injured as we are, deeply and intimately, by its very existence.

Realizing this, it appeared to be my duty, in a spirit of true friendliness, no less to Spain than to the Cubans, who have so much to lose by the prolongation of the struggle, to seek to bring about an immediate termination of the war. To this end I submitted on the 27th ultimo, as a result of much representation and correspondence, through the United States minister at Madrid, propositions to the Spanish Government looking to an armistice until October 1 for the negotiation of peace with the good offices of the President.

In addition I asked the immediate revocation of the order of reconcentration, so as to permit the people to return to their farms and the needy to be relieved with provisions and supplies from the United States, cooperating with the Spanish authorities, so as to afford full relief.

The reply of the Spanish cabinet was received on the night of the 31st ultimo. It offered, as the means to bring about peace in Cuba, to confide the preparation thereof to the insular parliament, inasmuch as the concurrence of that body would be necessary to reach a final result, it being, however, understood that the powers reserved by the constitution to the central Government are not lessened or diminished. As the Cuban parliament does not meet until the 4th of May next, the Spanish Government would not object for its part to accept at once a suspension of hostilities if asked for by the insurgents from the general in chief, to whom it would pertain in such case to determine the duration and conditions of the armistice.

The propositions submitted by General Woodford and the reply of the Spanish Government were both in the form of brief memoranda, the texts of which are before me and are substantially in the language above given. The function of the Cuban parliament in the matter of "preparing" peace and the manner of its doing so are not expressed in the Spanish memorandum, but from General Woodford's explanatory reports of preliminary discussions preceding the final conference it is understood that the Spanish Government stands ready to give the insular congress full powers to settle the terms of peace with the insurgents, whether by direct negotiation or indirectly by means of legislation does not appear. . . .

Nor from the standpoint of expediency do I think it would be wise or prudent for this Government to recognize at the present time the independence of the so-called Cuban Republic. Such recognition is not necessary in order to enable the United States to intervene and pacify the island. To commit this country now to the recognition of any particular government in Cuba might subject us to embarrassing conditions of international obligation toward the organization so recognized. In case of intervention our conduct would be subject to the approval or disapproval of such government. We would be required to submit to its direction and to assume to it the mere relation of a friendly ally.

When it shall appear hereafter that there is within the island a government capable of performing the duties and discharging the functions of a separate nation, and having as a matter of fact the proper forms and attributes of nationality, such government can be promptly and readily recognized and the relations and interests of the United States with such nation adjusted.

There remain the alternative forms of intervention to end the war, either as an impartial neutral, by imposing a rational compromise between the contestants, or as the active ally of the one party or the other.

As to the first, it is not to be forgotten that during the last few months the relation of the United States has virtually been one of friendly intervention in many ways, each not of itself conclusive, but all tending to the exertion of a potential influence toward an ultimate pacific result, just and honorable to all interests concerned. The spirit of all our acts hitherto has been an earnest, unselfish desire for peace and prosperity in Cuba, untarnished by differences between us and Spain and unstained by the blood of American citizens.

The forcible intervention of the United States as a neutral to stop the war, according to the large dictates of humanity and following many historical precedents where neighboring states have interfered to check the hopeless sacrifices of life by internecine conflicts beyond their borders, is justifiable on rational grounds. It involves, however, hostile constraint upon both the parties to the contest, as well to enforce a truce as to guide the eventual settlement.

The grounds for such intervention may be briefly summarized as follows:

First. In the cause of humanity and to put an end to the barbarities, bloodshed, starvation, and horrible miseries now existing there, and which the parties to the conflict are either unable, or unwilling to stop or mitigate. It is no answer to say this is all in another country, belonging to another nation, and is therefore none of our business. It is specially our duty, for it is right at our door.

Second. We owe it to our citizens in Cuba to afford them that protection and indemnity for life and property which no government there can or will afford, and to that end to terminate the conditions that deprive them of legal protection.

Third. The right to intervene may be justified by the very serious injury to the commerce, trade, and business of our people and by the wanton destruction of property and devastation of the island.

Fourth, and which is of the utmost importance. The present condition of affairs in Cuba is a constant menace to our peace and entails upon this Government an enormous expense. With such a conflict waged for years in an island so near us and with which our people have such trade and business relations, when the lives and liberty of our citizens are in constant danger and their property destroyed and themselves ruined, where our trading vessels are liable to seizure and are seized at our very door by war ships of a foreign nation; the expeditions of filibustering that we are powerless to prevent altogether, and the irritating questions and entanglements thus arising—all these and others that I need not mention, with the resulting strained relations, are a constant menace to our peace and compel us to keep on a semi war footing with a nation with which we are at peace.

These elements of danger and disorder already pointed out have been strikingly illustrated by a tragic event which has deeply and justly moved the American people. I have already transmitted to Congress the report of the naval court of inquiry on the destruction of the battle ship *Maine* in the harbor of Havana during the night of the 15th of February. The destruction of that noble vessel has filled the national heart with inexpressible horror. Two hundred and fifty-eight brave sailors and marines and two officers of our Navy, reposing in the fancied security of a friend-ly harbor, have been hurled to death, grief and want brought to their homes and sorrow to the nation.

The naval court of inquiry, which, it is needless to say, commands the unqualified confidence of the Government, was unanimous in its con-clusion that the destruction of the *Maine* was caused by an exterior explosion—that of a submarine mine. It did not assume to place the responsibility. That remains to be fixed.

In any event, the destruction of the *Maine*, by whatever exterior cause, is a patent and impressive proof of a state of things in Cuba that is intolerable. That condition is thus shown to be such that the Spanish Government can not assure safety and security to a vessel of the Ameri-can Navy in the harbor of Havana on a mission of peace, and rightfully there. . . .

The long trial has proved that the object for which Spain has waged the war can not be attained. The fire of insurrection may flame or may smolder with varying seasons, but it has not been and it is plain that it can not be extinguished by present methods. The only hope of relief and repose from a condition which can no longer be endured is the enforced pacification of Cuba. In the name of humanity, in the name of civiliza-tion, in behalf of endangered American interests which give us the right and the duty to speak and to act, the war in Cuba must stop.

In view of these facts and of these considerations I ask the Congress to authorize and empower the President to take measures to secure a full and final termination of hostilities between the Government of Spain and the people of Cuba, and to secure in the island the establishment of a stable government, capable of maintaining order and observing its inter-national obligations, insuring peace and tranquillity and the security of its citizens as well as our own, and to use the military and naval forces of the United States as may be necessary for these purposes.

And in the interest of humanity and to aid in preserving the lives of the starving people of the island I recommend that the distribution of food and supplies be continued and that an appropriation be made out of the public Treasury to supplement the charity of our citizens.

The issue is now with the Congress. It is a solemn responsibility. I have exhausted every effort to relieve the intolerable condition of affairs which is at our doors. Prepared to execute every obligation imposed upon me by the Constitution and the law, I await your action.

Yesterday, and since the preparation of the foregoing message, official information was received by me that the latest decree of the Queen Regent of Spain directs General Blanco, in order to prepare and facilitate peace, to proclaim a suspension of hostilities, the duration and details of which have not yet been communicated to me.

This fact, with every other pertinent consideration, will, I am sure, have your just and careful attention in the solemn deliberations upon which you are about to enter. If this measure attains a successful result, then our aspirations as a Christian, peace-loving people will be realized. If it fails, it will be only another justification for our contemplated action.

B
PRESIDENT MCKINLEY'S INSTRUCTIONS TO THE AMERICAN PEACE COMMISSIONERS
SEPTEMBER 16, 1898

"We took up arms only in obedience to the dictates of humanity and in the fulfillment of high public and moral obligations. We had no design of aggrandizement and no ambition of conquest. . . . In view of what has been stated, the United States can not accept less than the cession in full right and sovereignty of the island of Luzon. . . ."

. . . I have appointed you as Commissioners on the part of the United States to meet and confer with Commissioners on the part of Spain.

As an essential preliminary to the agreement to appoint Commissioners to treat of peace, this Government required of that of Spain the unqualified concession of the following precise demands:

(1) The relinquishment of all claim of sovereignty over and title to Cuba.

(2) The cession to the United States of Porto Rico and other islands under Spanish sovereignty in the West Indies.

(3) The cession of an island in the Ladrones, to be selected by the United States.

Papers Relating to the Foreign Relations of the United States . . . 1898. Washington: Government Printing Office, 1901, 904–908.

(4) The immediate evacuation by Spain of Cuba, Porto Rico, and other Spanish islands in the West Indies.

(5) The occupation by the United States of the city, bay, and harbor of Manila pending the conclusion of a treaty of peace which should determine the control, disposition, and government of the Philippines.

These demands were conceded by Spain, and their concession was, as you will perceive, solemnly recorded in the protocol of the 12th of August. . . .

By article 6 of the protocol it was agreed that hostilities between the two countries should be suspended, and that notice to that effect should be given as soon as possible by each Government to the commanders of its military and naval forces. Such notice was given by the Government of the United States immediately after the signature of the protocol, the forms of the necessary orders having previously been prepared. But before notice could reach the commanders of the military and naval forces of the United States in the Philippines they captured and took possession by conquest of the city of Manila and its suburbs, which are therefore held by the United States by conquest as well as by virtue of the protocol.

In view of what has taken place it is necessary now to determine what shall be our future relations to the Philippines. Before giving you specific instructions on this subject it is my desire to present certain general considerations.

It is my wish that throughout the negotiations intrusted to the Commission the purpose and spirit with which the United States accepted the unwelcome necessity of war should be kept constantly in view. We took up arms only in obedience to the dictates of humanity and in the fulfillment of high public and moral obligations. We had no design of aggrandizement and no ambition of conquest. Through the long course of repeated representations which preceded and aimed to avert the struggle, and in the final arbitrament of force, this country was impelled solely by the purpose of relieving grievous wrongs and removing long-existing conditions which disturbed its tranquillity, which shocked the moral sense of mankind, and which could no longer be endured.

It is my earnest wish that the United States in making peace should follow the same high rule of conduct which guided it in facing war. It should be as scrupulous and magnanimous in the concluding settlement as it was just and humane in its original action. The luster and the moral strength attaching to a cause which can be confidently rested upon the considerate judgment of the world should not under any illusion of the hour be dimmed by ulterior designs which might tempt us into excessive demands or into an adventurous departure on untried paths. It is believed that the true glory and the enduring interests of the country will most surely be served if an unselfish duty conscientiously accepted and a signal triumph honorably achieved shall be crowned by such an example of moderation, restraint, and reason in victory as best comports with the traditions and character of our enlightened Republic.

Our aim in the adjustment of peace should be directed to lasting results and to the achievement of the common good under the demands of civilization, rather than to ambitious designs. The terms of the protocol were framed upon this consideration. The abandonment of the Western Hemisphere by Spain was an imperative necessity. In presenting that requirement, we only fulfilled a duty universally acknowledged. It involves no ungenerous reference to our recent foe, but simply a recognition of the plain teachings of history, to say that it was not compatible with the assurance of permanent peace on and near our own territory that the Spanish flag should remain on this side of the sea. This lesson of events and of reason left no alternative as to Cuba, Porto Rico, and the other islands belonging to Spain in this hemisphere.

The Philippines stand upon a different basis. It is none the less true, however, that, without any original thought of complete or even partial acquisition, the presence and success of our arms at Manila imposes upon us obligations which we can not disregard. The march of events rules and overrules human action. Avowing unreservedly the purpose which has animated all our effort, and still solicitous to adhere to it, we can not be unmindful that, without any desire or design on our part, the war has brought us new duties and responsibilities which we must meet and discharge as becomes a great nation on whose growth and career from the beginning the Ruler of Nations has plainly written the high command and pledge of civilization.

Incidental to our tenure in the Philippines is the commercial opportunity to which American statemanship can not be indifferent. It is just to use every legitimate means for the enlargement of American trade; but we seek no advantages in the Orient which are not common to all. Asking only the open door for ourselves, we are ready to accord the open door to others. The commercial opportunity which is naturally and inevitably associated with this new opening depends less on large territorial possession than upon an adequate commercial basis and upon broad and equal privileges.

It is believed that in the practical application of these guiding principles the present interests of our country and the proper measure of its duty, its welfare in the future, and the consideration of its exemption from unknown perils will be found in full accord with the just, moral, and humane purpose which was invoked as our justification in accepting the war.

In view of what has been stated, the United States can not accept less than the cession in full right and sovereignty of the island of Luzon. . . .

C

SENATOR HENRY CABOT LODGE EXPLAINS THE ORIGIN OF THE AMERICAN-PHILIPPINE WAR AND ABSOLVES THE UNITED STATES OF WRONGDOING
FEBRUARY 7, 1899

"But . . . knowing all that, the Filipinos deliberately precipitated this attack upon the American forces in Manila, where our army had a right to be. They precipitated an attack upon the forces of the country which had given them their existence as a fighting force, upon the forces of the country which had liberated them from the power of Spain. . . . Therefore I do not think that this is the moment to flatter or to coddle or to praise them."

There was an insurrection in the Philippines under the lead of Aguinaldo. The insurrection was dealt with ruthlessly by the Spaniards and was substantially put down. They made an agreement with Aguinaldo and the other chiefs by which on the payment of a certain sum of money and the establishment of certain reforms the chiefs were to withdraw and the insurrection come to an end. In a perfectly characteristic manner, in fact just as they behaved in Cuba in 1878, after the chiefs had yielded and the

---

Congressional Record, 55th Congress, 3rd Session (February 7, 1899), 1533.

insurrection was substantially over, the Spaniards failed to make the reforms and paid only half the money. With that money Aguinaldo and his chiefs retired to Hongkong, and, although there was guerrilla warfare here and there in the outlying districts, the insurgent Filipinos were absolutely at the mercy of the Spaniards and the Spanish authority was complete as it always had been over those islands. There was no other sovereignty there. There was no belligerent there.

Aguinaldo was brought to the islands on the 19th of May in the steamer *Nanshaw*, under American auspices. There was at that time no organized Filipino force. At first the results of his appeal were so discouraging that he was disinclined to continue. But he did remain, on representations of support made by our commanders. Then the Filipinos began to come in. They found a very great difference between the situation when they had last faced it and the situation after Admiral Dewey's destruction of the Spanish fleet. So long as there were Spanish ships of war in Manila Bay it was absolutely hopeless for the insurgents to think for one moment of besieging the city or of making any effective attack upon the capital which was the center of the whole Philippine system. But with the Spanish fleet destroyed, with the bay in the hands of the American fleet, they were enabled to draw their forces gradually about the city, and they did so. When Aguinaldo first came into connection with our consuls he said to them that his desire was for annexation to the United States and for freedom from the Spanish rule. After he had got over again to Luzon and found how much the situation had changed, he gradually began to increase his ideas of his own importance. He had never adjusted his own relations to the universe, and they remain unadjusted, I think, at the present time.

But the essential point I desire to make is simply this: The insurgent force, as an effective force, and the insurgent rebellion, as an effective rebellion, existed solely because of the victory of Admiral Dewey, and the Admiral, as you may see by reading his dispatches, said to our Government, "I have been extremely careful in all my dealings with these people. I have never made them the allies of the United States. I have never recognized them. I have simply aided them because they were fighting the common foe." Admiral Dewey can be trusted, I think, to manage a matter of that sort without committing the United States to any position to which it should not be committed.

Now, to-day we are there in the city of Manila rightfully by all the

laws of war and by all international law. We hold it, as we have a right to
hold it, under the agreement with Spain. There was no sovereignty there
whatever except the sovereignty of Spain, and we succeeded to that
sovereignty in the city of Manila and its suburbs. There has never been
an act of oppression against the Filipinos by any American soldier or by
the American forces of any kind in the Philippine Islands. Those patriots
have never been oppressed by any American in the active service of the
country, or by any American act. Their oppression exists solely in
speeches in the United States Senate. They have been treated with the
utmost consideration and the utmost kindness, and, after the fashion of
Orientals, they have mistaken kindness for timidity.

Now, Mr. President, there were the American forces in Manila,
where they had a right to be, and, more than that, stringent orders had
gone from the President of the United States to General Otis and Admiral
Dewey that under no circumstances whatever should any attack be made
upon the Filipinos. More than that, Mr. President, over a fortnight ago
Aguinaldo was informed officially by General Otis that the President of
the United States had ordered him not to attack the Filipinos, so that he
knew we had no intention of attacking him. He knew it a fortnight ago.

This idea that he had no notion of our intentions, Mr. President,
is a totally mistaken one. He knew absolutely and officially what the intentions of the United States Government were. He knew what the orders
of the President of the United States were to the General and Admiral.

But, Mr. President, knowing all that, the Filipinos deliberately
precipitated this attack upon the American forces in Manila, where our
army had a right to be. They precipitated an attack upon the forces of
the country which had given them their existence as a fighting force,
upon the forces of the country which had liberated them from the power
of Spain. They did it in the face of the declared intention of the United
States, conveyed to them from the President by the officers in command
of the army and navy.

What caused them to make that attack, what encouraged them to
do it, I do not know; but I do know that their representative here fled
from this city to Canada and started on the flight before any news had
reached this city of an attack at Manila. He knew that that attack was
coming, and his flight was a confession that he knew it, and I believe
that he incited and advised it. He knew the dispatches that he had sent,
and whatever reason they may have had for making the attack, they
believed they were going to produce a great effect in this country

and upon the fate of the treaty by assailing the troops and the ships of the United States.

Now, Mr. President, the Filipinos made that assault upon our troops, upon the friendly nation, upon people who had never oppressed them, and the attack was met as American soldiers and sailors will always meet every attack. And while they are there in arms assailing American troops, when they have shed American blood, I do not think it is the time to help or to encourage them either by speech or in any other way. Let us bring them back to order and to peace. When they return to their senses, when they have learned their lesson, when they are ready to meet us in the spirit in which we went to them, then will be the time to negotiate and deal with them.

But when they attack American troops, attack them with an attempted surprise, attack without one reason or a single provocation for doing so, while that state of things continues, while they, as Spanish subjects, have broken the truce that exists between this country and Spain, and put themselves in the light of public enemies of the United States, there is to my mind but one thing to do, and that is to sustain our Army and Navy. When they return to the ways of peace, then we can deal with them in the ways of peace; but when they of their own motion attack us in the ways of war, then there is but one way to deal with them, and that is by the way of war. They are in collusion with Spain. Spanish soldiers, as General Otis reports, served their guns, and they have been met, as they deserved to be met, with swift and overwhelming punishment.

But the one point I desired to make above all others, Mr. President, and which I now repeat, was that the Filipinos and Aguinaldo knew the generous and peaceful intentions of the United States. They knew that the President had given orders not to attack them, and under those circumstances they themselves made the attack, and made it wantonly. Therefore I do not think that this is the moment to flatter or to coddle or to praise them.

D

SENATOR ALBERT J. BEVERIDGE SUPPORTS
IMPERIALISM AND A VIGOROUS PROSECUTION
OF THE PHILIPPINE WAR
JANUARY 9, 1900

*"The Pacific is our ocean. . . . China is our natural customer. . . .
The Philippines give us a base at the door of all the East. . . .
Aguinaldo is a clever, popular leader, able, brave, resourceful,
cunning, ambitious, unscrupulous, and masterful. . . . He is a
natural dictator. His ideas of government are absolute orders,
implicit obedience, or immediate death. He understands the
character of his countrymen. He is a Malay Sylla; not a Filipino
Washington."*

. . . Mr. President, I address the Senate at this time because Senators
and Members of the House on both sides have asked that I give to Congress and country my observations in the Philippines and the far East,
and the conclusions which those observations compel; and because of
hurtful resolutions introduced and utterances made in the Senate, every
word of which will cost and is costing the lives of American soldiers.

Mr. President, the times call for candor. The Philippines are ours
forever, "territory belonging to the United States," as the Constitution
calls them. And just beyond the Philippines are China's illimitable markets. We will not retreat from either. We will not repudiate our duty in
the archipelago. We will not abandon our opportunity in the Orient.
We will not renounce our part in the mission of our race, trustee, under
God, of the civilization of the world. And we will move forward to our
work, not howling out regrets like slaves whipped to their burdens, but
with gratitude for a task worthy of our strength, and thanksgiving to
Almighty God that He has marked us as His chosen people, henceforth to
lead in the regeneration of the world.

This island empire is the last land left in all the oceans. If it should
prove a mistake to abandon it, the blunder once made would be irre-

---

Congressional Record, 56th Congress, 1st Session (January 9, 1900), 704–705;
707–708.

trievable. If it proves a mistake to hold it, the error can be corrected when we will. Every other progressive nation stands ready to relieve us.

But to hold it will be no mistake. Our largest trade henceforth must be with Asia. The Pacific is our ocean. More and more Europe will manufacture the most it needs, secure from its colonies the most it consumes. Where shall we turn for consumers of our surplus? Geography answers the question. China is our natural customer. She is nearer to us than to England, Germany, or Russia, the commercial powers of the present and the future. They have moved nearer to China by securing permanent bases on her borders. The Philippines give us a base at the door of all the East.

Lines of navigation from our ports to the Orient and Australia; from the Isthmian Canal to Asia; from all Oriental ports to Australia, converge at and separate from the Philippines. They are a self-supporting, dividend-paying fleet, permanently anchored at a spot selected by the strategy of Providence, commanding the Pacific. And the Pacific is the ocean of the commerce of the future. Most future wars will be conflicts for commerce. The power that rules the Pacific, therefore, is the power that rules the world. And, with the Philippines, that power is and will forever be the American Republic.

China's trade is the mightiest commercial fact in our future. Her foreign commerce was $285,738,300 in 1807, of which we her neighbor, had less than 9 per cent, of which only a little more than half was merchandise sold to China by us. We ought to have 50 per cent, and we will. . . .

The Philippines command the commercial situation of the entire East. Can America best trade with China from San Francisco or New York? From San Francisco, of course. But if San Francisco were closer to China than New York is to Pittsburg, what then? And Manila is nearer Hongkong than Habana is to Washington. And yet American statesmen plan to surrender this commercial throne of the Orient where Providence and our soldiers' lives have placed us. When history comes to write the story of that suggested treason to American supremacy and therefore to the spread of American civilization, let her in mercy write that those who so proposed were merely blind and nothing more.

But if they did not command China, India, the Orient, the whole Pacific for purposes of offense, defense, and trade, the Philippines are so valuable in themselves that we should hold them. I have cruised more than 2,000 miles through the archipelago, every moment a surprise at its loveliness and wealth. I have ridden hundreds of miles on the islands, every foot of the way a revelation of vegetable and mineral riches. . . .

It will be hard for Americans who have not studied them to understand the people. They are a barbarous race, modified by three centuries of contact with a decadent race. The Filipino is the South Sea Malay, put through a process of three hundred years of superstition in religion, dishonesty in dealing, disorder in habits of industry, and cruelty, caprice, and corruption in government. It is barely possible that 1,000 men in all the archipelago are capable of self-government in the Anglo-Saxon sense.

My own belief is that there are not 100 men among them who comprehend what Anglo-Saxon self-government even means, and there are over 5,000,000 people to be governed. I know many clever and highly educated men among them, but there are only three commanding intellects and characters—Arellano, Mabini, and Aguinaldo. Arellano, the chief justice of our supreme court, is a profound lawyer and a brave and incorruptible man. Mabini, who, before his capture, was the literary and diplomatic associate of Aguinaldo, is the highest type of subtlety and the most constructive mind that race has yet produced. Aguinaldo is a clever, popular leader, able, brave, resourceful, cunning, ambitious, unscrupulous, and masterful. He is full of decision, initiative, and authority, and had the confidence of the masses. He is a natural dictator. His ideas of government are absolute orders, implicit obedience, or immediate death. He understands the character of his countrymen. He is a Malay Sylla; not a Filipino Washington. . . .

The military situation, past, present, and prospective, is no reason for abandonment. Our campaign has been as perfect as possible with the force at hand. We have been delayed, first, by a failure to comprehend the immensity of our acquisition; and, second, by insufficient force; and, third, by our efforts for peace. In February, after the treaty of peace, General Otis had only 3,722 officers and men whom he had a legal right to order into battle. The terms of enlistment of the rest of his troops had expired, and they fought voluntarily and not on legal military compulsion. It was one of the noblest examples of patriotic devotion to duty in the history of the world.

Those who complain do so in ignorance of the real situation. We attempted a great task with insufficient means; we became impatient that it was not finished before it could fairly be commenced; and I pray we may not add that other element of disaster, pausing in the work before it is thoroughly and forever done. That is the gravest mistake we could possibly make, and that is the only danger before us. Our Indian wars would have been shortened, the lives of soldiers and settlers saved, and the Indians themselves benefited had we made continuous and decisive war; and any other kind of war is criminal because ineffective. We acted toward the Indians as though we feared them, loved them, hated them— a mingling of foolish sentiment, inaccurate thought, and paralytic purpose. Let us now be instructed by our own experience.

This, too, has been Spain's course in the Philippines. I have studied Spain's painful military history in these islands. Never sufficient troops; never vigorous action, pushed to conclusive results and a permanent peace; always treating with the rebels while they fought them; always cruel and corrupt when a spurious peace was arranged. This has been Spain's way for three hundred years, until insurrection has become a Filipino habit. Never since Magellan landed did Spain put enough troops in these islands for complete and final action in war; never did she intelligently, justly, firmly, administer government in peace.

At the outbreak of the last insurrection, in August, 1806, Spain had only 1,500 Spanish soldiers in all the Philippines, and 700 of these were in Manila. In November of that year she had only 10,000 men. The generals in command of these were criticised and assailed in Spain. It is characteristic of Spain that the people at home do not support, but criticise their generals in the field. The Spanish method has always been a mixed policy of peace and war, a contradiction of terms, an impossible combination, rendering war ineffectice and peace impossible. This was Compo's plan. It was Blanco's plan. Those who would make it our plan will inherit Blanco's fate and failure.

Mr. President, that must not be our plan. This war is like all other wars. It needs to be finished before it is stopped. I am prepared to vote either to make our work thorough or even now to abandon it. A lasting peace can be secured only by overwhelming forces in ceaseless action until universal and absolutely final defeat is inflicted on the enemy. To halt before every armed force, every guerrilla band, opposing us is dispersed or exterminated will prolong hostilities and leave alive the seeds of perpetual insurrection.

Even then we should not treat. To treat at all is to admit that we are wrong. And any quiet so secured will be delusive and fleeting. And a false peace will betray us; a sham truce will curse us. It is not to serve the purposes of the hour, it is not to salve a present situation, that peace should be established. It is for the tranquillity of the archipelago forever. It is for an orderly government for the Filipinos for all the future. It is to give this problem to posterity solved and settled not vexed and involved. It is to establish the supremacy of the American Republic over the Pacific and throughout the East till the end of time.

It has been charged that our conduct of the war has been cruel. Senators, it has been the reverse. I have been in our hospitals and seen the Filipino wounded as carefully, tenderly cared for as our own. Within our lines they may plow and sow and reap and go about the affairs of peace with absolute liberty. And yet all this kindness was misunderstood, or rather not understood. Senators must remember that we are not dealing with Americans or Europeans. We are dealing with Orientals. We are dealing with Orientals who are Malays. We are dealing with Malays instructed in Spanish methods. They mistake kindness for weakness, forbearance for fear. . . .

Our mistake has not been cruelty; it has been kindness. It has been the application to Spanish Malays of methods appropriate to New England. Every device of mercy, every method of conciliation, has been employed by the peace-loving President of the American Republic, to the amazement of nations experienced in oriental revolt. . . .

We smiled at intolerable insult and insolence until the lips of every native in Manila were curling in ridicule for the cowardly Americans. We refrained from all violence until their armed bravos crossed the lines in violation of agreement. Then our sentry shot the offender, and he should have been court-martialed had he failed to shoot. That shot was the most fortunate of the war. For there is every reason to believe that Aguinaldo had planned the attack upon us for some nights later. Our sentry's shot brought this attack prematurely on. He arranged for an uprising in Manila to massacre all Americans, the plans for which, in a responsible officer's handwriting, are in our possession. This shot and its results made that awful scheme impossible. We did not strike till they attacked us in force, without provocation. This left us no alternative but war or evacuation. . . .

The news that 60,000 American soldiers have crossed the Pacific; that, if necessary, the American Congress will make it 100,000 or 200,000 men; that, at any cost we will establish peace and govern the islands, will do more to end the war than the soldiers themselves. But the report that we even discuss the withdrawal of a single soldier at the present time and that we even debate the possibility of not administering government throughout the archipelago ourselves will be misunderstood and misrepresented and will blow into a flame once more the fires our soldiers' blood has almost quenched.

Mr. President, reluctantly and only from a sense of duty am I forced to say that American opposition to the war has been the chief factor in prolonging it. Had Aguinaldo not understood that in America, even in the American Congress, even here in the Senate, he and his cause were supported; had he not known that it was proclaimed on the stump and in the press of a faction in the United States that every shot his misguided followers fired into the breasts of American soldiers was like the volleys fired by Washington's men against the soldiers of King George his insurrection would have dissolved before it entirely crystallized.

The utterances of American opponents of the war are read to the ignorant soldiers of Aguinaldo and repeated in exaggerated form among the common people. Attempts have been made by wretches claiming American citizenship to ship arms and ammunition from Asiatic ports to the Filipinos, and these acts of infamy were coupled by the Malays with American assaults on our Government at home. The Filipinos do not understand free speech, and therefore our tolerance of American assaults on the American President and the American Government means to them that our President is in the minority or he would not permit what appears to them such treasonable criticism. It is believed and stated in Luzon, Panay, and Cebu that the Filipinos have only to fight, harass, retreat, break up into small parties, if necessary, as they are doing now, but by any means hold out until the next Presidential election, and our forces will be withdrawn.

All this has aided the enemy more than climate, arms, and battle. Senators, I have heard these reports myself; I have talked with the people; I have seen our mangled boys in the hospital and field; I have stood on the firing line and beheld our dead soldiers, their faces turned to the pitiless southern sky, and in sorrow rather than anger I say to those whose voices in America have cheered those misguided natives on to shoot our soldiers down, that the blood of those dead and wounded boys of ours is on their hands, and the flood of all the years can never wash that stain away. In sorrow rather than anger I say these words, for I earnestly believe that our brothers knew not what they did.

But, Senators, it would be better to abandon this combined garden and Gibraltar of the Pacific, and count our blood and treasure already spent a profitable loss, than to apply any academic arrangement of self-government to these children. They are not capable of self-government. How could they be? They are not of a self-governing race. They are Orientals, Malays, instructed by Spaniards in the latter's worst estate. . . .

E
BRIGADIER GENERAL J. F. BELL ON THE PROBLEMS OF GUERRILLA TACTICS AND WARFARE IN THE PHILIPPINES DECEMBER 13, 1901

"We consequently find ourselves operating in a thoroughly occupied terrain against the entire population, united in a hopeless struggle, using, conniving at, or tolerating barbarous methods which almost reach the limit in outraging the laws and usages of legitimate warfare."

BATANGAS, P. I., December 13, 1901.

To all station commanders:

The United States Government, disregarding many provocations to do otherwise, has for three years exercised an extraordinary forbearance and patiently adhered to a magnanimous and benevolent policy toward the inhabitants of the territory garrisoned by this brigade. Notwithstanding this fact, opposition to the Government has been persistently continued throughout this entire period of a majority of its inhabitants. The enemy, long realizing their inability to maintain themselves without the unanimous cooperation and support of the entire population, have, in order to keep up their useless struggle, established a reign of terror by resorting to atrocities and expedients which violate the well-known laws and usages of war as announced in General Orders, No. 100, Adjutant-General's Office, 1863, approved and published by order of President Lincoln, for the government of the armies of the United States in the field.

Senate Documents, Volume 24, 57th Congress, 1st Session (December 13, 1901), 1612–1614.

First. They have accepted local offices from the Government and taken the oath of allegiance solely for the purpose of improving their opportunities and facilities for deceiving American officials and treacherously aiding and assisting the cause of the insurrection, in violation of section 26.

Second. They have with bolos and other weapons killed helpless prisoners and soldiers lying on the ground, wholly disabled by wounds which prevented their defending themselves in any way, in violation of sections 49, 56, 61, and 71.

Third. In order to confuse their identity, and thereby be able the more safely to conduct their skulking operations, they have adopted the uniform of our Army and native troops without any plain, striking, and uniform mark of distinction of their own, in violation of section 63.

Fourth. They have improvised and secreted in the vicinity of roads and trails rudely constructed infernal machines propelling poisoned arrows or darts, in violation of section 70, thus placing themselves beyond the pale of the laws and usages of war.

Fifth. Men and squads of men without commission, without being part or portion of the regularly organized hostile army, without sharing continuously in the war, but with intermittent returns to their homes and avocations, and with frequent assumption of the semblance of peaceful pursuits, divesting themselves of the character and appearance of soldiers, have committed hostilities by fighting and making raids of various kinds, after which, concealing their arms, they have returned, posing as peaceful citizens, and secretly lived in the same towns with garrisons of our troops, in violation of section 82.

Sixth. Armed prowlers have stolen within the lines of our Army to cut telegraph wires and destroy bridges. Armed assassins, designated and controlled by the enemy, have come, disguised as peaceful citizens, into the very presence of our garrisons and have assassinated, in broad daylight in crowded market places, persons unlawfully condemned to death by the enemy for being friendly to or assisting the legitimately organized government—the fear, sympathy, or cooperation of the entire population effectually preventing our apprehension and punishment of the assassin. This in violation of section 84.

Seventh. The apparently pacific inhabitants of towns occupied by the American Army have treacherously risen in arms against it, in violation of section 85.

Eighth. A large percentage of the population, though owing

allegiance to the American Government under the provisions of section 26, have acted as spies and war traitors, in violation of the provisions of sections 88, 90, and 92.

Ninth. A very great number of insurgent officials, soldiers, and other aiders and abettors of the insurrection, after voluntarily surrendering and after having been captured, have been pardoned and released from confinement upon taking the oath of allegiance or giving paroles, and have subsequently violated their oaths or paroles without scruple by again entering the service of the insurgent army or aiding or assisting the same, in violation of sections 26, 124, and 130.

Against but one of these flagrant violations of the laws of war, namely, murder, has the United States Government ever adjudged or executed the severe penalties authorized by the sections of the law above cited, in the vain hope that, by this exercise of forbearance and generosity, the people might be conciliated and become reconciled to and convinced of the benevolent purposes of the Government. Instead of having had the desired effect, however, this policy in the provinces of Batangas and Laguna has apparently failed to appeal to even the keenest and most appreciative intellects. On the contrary, it has been interpreted by many as an evidence of weakness and fear, and puffed up by a childish and ignorant conceit over what they are pleased to consider successful resistance of our power, the people have become so arrogant that they look down upon our Government and scorn its kindliest efforts at pacification. We consequently find ourselves operating in a thoroughly occupied terrain against the entire population, united in a hopeless struggle, using, conniving at, or tolerating barbarous methods which almost reach the limit in outraging the laws and usages of legitimate warfare.

The reckless expedients adopted by the enemy, especially the policy of intimidation and assassination, leaves to the brigade commander no other means of protecting either the lives of his subordinates, or those of peaceful or friendly citizens, or the interests of his Government against the repetition of barbarous outrage except the enforcement of the penalties authorized by the above cited laws of war, and he has reluctantly concluded it to be absolutely necessary to avail himself of the right of retaliation under the provisions of sections 59 and 148, whenever the duly and carefully ascertained conditions and circumstances warrant the same under the restrictions prescribed in section 28.

The brigade commander therefore announces for the information of all concerned that wherever prisoners or unarmed or defenseless Americans or natives friendly to the United States Government are murdered or assassinated for political reasons, and this fact can be established, it is his purpose to execute a prisoner of war under the authority contained in sections 59 and 148. This prisoner of war will be selected by lot from among the officers or prominent citizens held as prisoners of war, and will be chosen when practicable from those who belong to the town where the murder or assassination occurred.

It is also his purpose to severely punish, in the same or a lesser degree, the commission of other acts denounced by the aforementioned articles. In this connection the attention of all American officers is invited to the last paragraph of section 29 and to the provisions of section 134. Commanding officers are authorized to enforce the provisions of this latter section whenever they may deem it just and practicable.

J. F. BELL,
Brigadier-General, Commanding.

THE
SPANISH–AMERICAN–
PHILIPPINE WAR

II
THE CRUSADERS:
FILIPINO

A

THE WAR MESSAGE: PRESIDENT EMILIO AGUINALDO
FEBRUARY 4, 1899

*"But it is my unavoidable duty to maintain the integrity
of the national honor and that of the army so unjustly attacked by
those who, posing as our friends and liberators, attempted to
dominate us in place of the Spaniards. . . ."*

[Malolos, February 4, 1899]

GENERAL ORDER TO THE PHILIPPINE ARMY

Nine o'clock p.m., this date, I received from Caloocan station a message
communicated to me that the American forces, without prior notification
or any just motive, attacked our camp at San Juan del Monte and our
forces garrisoning the blockhouses around the outskirts of Manila,
causing losses among our soldiers, who, in view of this unexpected aggression and of the decided attack of the aggressors, were obliged to
defend themselves until the firing became general all along the line.

No one can deplore more than I this rupture of hostilities. I have a
clear conscience that I have endeavored to avoid it at all costs, using
all my efforts to preserve friendship with the army of occupation, even
at the cost of not a few humiliations and many sacrificed rights.

Senate Document 208, 56th Congress, 1st Session (February 4, 1899), 104.

But it is my unavoidable duty to maintain the integrity of the national honor and that of the army so unjustly attacked by those who, posing as our friends and liberators, attempted to dominate us in place of the Spaniards, as is shown by the grievances enumerated in my manifest of January 8 last; such as the continued outrages and violent exactions committed against the people of Manila, the useless conferences, and all my frustrated efforts in favor of peace and concord.

Summoned by this unexpected provocation, urged by the duties imposed upon me by honor and patriotism and for the defense of the nation intrusted to me, calling on God as a witness of my good faith and the uprightness of my intentions—

I order and command:

1. Peace and friendly relations between the Philippine forces and the American forces of occupation are broken, and the latter will be treated as enemies, with the limits prescribed by the laws of war.

2. American soldiers who may be captured by the Philippine forces will be treated as prisoners of war.

3. This proclamation shall be communicated to the accredited consuls of Manila, and to congress, in order that it may accord the suspension of the constitutional guaranties and the resulting declaration of war.

Given at Malolos February 4, 1899.

EMILIO AGUINALDO,
General in Chief.

B
PRESIDENT EMILIO AGUINALDO ON WHY THE
PHILIPPINE REPUBLIC MUST FIGHT
FEBRUARY 5, 1899

"Be not discouraged. Our independence has been watered by the generous blood of our martyrs. Blood which may be shed in the future will strengthen it. Nature has never despised generous sacrifices."

[Malolos, February 5, 1899]

To the Philippine People:

By my proclamation of yesterday I have published the outbreak of hostilities between the Philippine forces and the American forces of occupation in Manila, unjustly and unexpectedly provoked by the latter.

In my manifest of January 8 last I published the grievances suffered by the Philippine forces at the hands of the army of occupation. The constant outrages and taunts, which have caused the misery of the people of Manila, and, finally, the useless conferences and the contempt shown the Philippine government prove the premeditated transgression of justice and liberty.

I know that war has always produced great losses; I know that the Philippine people have not yet recovered from past losses and are not in the condition to endure others. But I also know by experience how bitter is slavery, and by experience I know that we should sacrifice all on the altar of our honor and of the national integrity so unjustly attacked.

I have tried to avoid, as far as it has been possible for me to do so, armed conflict, in my endeavors to assure our independence by pacific means and to avoid more costly sacrifices. But all my efforts have been useless against the measureless pride of the American Government and of its representatives in these islands, who have treated me as a rebel because I defend the sacred interests of my country and do not make myself an instrument of their dastardly intentions.

Past campaigns will have convinced you that the people are strong when they wish to be so. Without arms we have driven from our beloved country our ancient masters, and without arms we can repulse the

---

Senate Document 208, 56th Congress, 1st Session (February 5, 1899), 105.

foreign invasion as long as we wish to do so. Providence always has means in reserve and prompt help for the weak in order that they may not be annihilated by the strong; that justice may be done and humanity progress.

Be not discouraged. Our independence has been watered by the generous blood of our martyrs. Blood which may be shed in the future will strengthen it. Nature has never despised generous sacrifices.

But remember that in order that our efforts may not be wasted, that our vows may be listened to, that our ends may be gained, it is indispensable that we adjust our actions to the rules of law and of right, learning to triumph over our enemies and to conquer our own evil passions.

EMILIO AGUINALDO,
President of the Philippine Republic.

C

PROPAGANDA LEAFLET DISTRIBUTED BY THE PHILIPPINE GOVERNMENT TO FILIPINO SOLDIERS AND CIVILIANS FEBRUARY 24, 1899

"Away with the wretches. Destruction to the Americans. Down with the United States."

Major Tirona to the Secretary of War.

To-day at 8 a.m. the citizen Perfecto, commissioner, passed, stating that he left Tondo at 2 in the morning of to-day. States that there is firing going on on Calle Azcarraga from Mariano Ponce's troops of Tondo militia. First fire Oriente factory, afterwards Tondo, caused by our troops. Firing also on General Pio's line. Sending messenger that office. This leaf for free distribution.

COUNTRYMEN:

Let us rejoice that the men of North America showed themselves in their true light, for if it had not been so we might have been sunk in

---

Senate Document 208, 56th Congress, 1st Session (February 24, 1899), 105–106.

the mire; let us therefore thank God who has willed the war. Nothing good can be expected from these people, who, on the contrary, can teach us all the evil we wish to learn from them; the proof is that of the barbarities inflicted on our brethern in Manila. These men watch for a lack of care, an unprotected house, and then attack it.

In order to give free rein to their infernal desires, the principles of morality are nothing to them and can not hold them back. They have outdone the savage of the North, and have not an iota of shame or decency. They thrust their hands into dishes and take what they want, without even asking permission, or even, after taking what they want, say thanks. If they find the family sleeping the siesta they enter the room without permission from anyone, as if it were a forest. In the stores they take what they want, and, if the owner tries to collect from them, they shoot him. It seems almost impossible to believe it, and our hands tremble in recording such abominations. These deeds are a shame on the nation which gives them birth. History records no more hateful deeds, even committed by a savage. Various cases have occurred where women have been handled all over their persons, and their money taken from them, as well as anything else they may have, and if this happens in out-of-way places they strip their clothing from them. Are these the deeds of an honest people? Is this the people who was to teach us decency and morality? Are these to be our teachers? Such acts as these are committed by no other people on the globe. This is the nation of unrestrained liberty. This is the nation which does not know how to teach women to become mothers! This is the nation where honor is yet unknown, in a word, is a nation hated by all other nations! A nation which knows not honor, has not an atom of feeling. Are these our protectors? Better death be related to a people whose evil is inborn. Away with the wretches. Destruction to the Americans. Down with the United States.

THE
SPANISH–AMERICAN–PHILIPPINE
WAR

III
THE CRITICS:
AMERICAN

A
ANTI–IMPERIALIST PROFESSOR CHARLES ELIOT NORTON
CONDEMNS THE WAR WITH SPAIN AND LAMENTS
THE ENDING OF AMERICAN ISOLATIONISM
AUGUST 25, 1898

"Whatever disposition may be made of the Philippines, we are already ... brought into entangling relations with the nations of the Old World .... It is, indeed, a momentous revolution."

... Our hearts have been heavy with new weight of care, and the very brightness of the sunshine has but deepened by contrast the cloud of our sorrowful thoughts—sorrowful that our Nation should have turned its back upon its old ideals, and standing at the parting of the ways, should have chosen that ancient path, familiar to the old world, worn by the bloody feet of hapless generations, and which has never led to anything but ill—the path of aggressive war, of foreign conquest, of alien territorial aggrandisement, the path that leads from trouble to trouble. "For what can war but endless war still breed?"

The black and brutal visage of war has, indeed, been lighted up from time to time during the Summer by the gallant deeds of our men in service and by the good conduct and marvelous good fortune of our navy, and by the general temper of humanity displayed so soon as the actual

---

New York *Times*, August 26, 1898. Reprinted by permission.

fight was over by both officers and men. But it has taken on a deeper shade of gloom from the needless sufferings which our brave soldiers have had to endure from the lack of due provision for their needs, alike in camp, on field, and in hospital. It has been a miserable spectacle of incompetency, for which account must be rendered and penalty exacted.

Of all our privileges and blessings none was greater than our exemption from the fear of war. We were set apart for peace. We should have held ourselves consecrated to it, for we professed to be a Christian Nation, and, as followers of the Prince of Peace, to hold war in abhorrence. We professed that our constantly increasing National power rested on a moral foundation.

There have indeed of late been many threatening indications that these professions had not the force of principles; that safety, prosperity, and ignorance had corrupted the moral sense of the Nation and weakened its sense of responsibility; that there were vast numbers of our people too unacquainted with the teachings of history to get a right value on our peculiar and priceless National privileges; that there were others, including many men of more than average intelligence and virtue, who had no absolute conviction of the wickedness of war, and others still, including a large body of politicians, so indifferent to right and wrong as to be eager to force the Nation into war, if by so doing their personal or partisan interests could be promoted.

Flinging common sense and moral principles alike to the winds, under the influence of hysterical emotion, without decent deliberation, without due preparation, the representatives of the people rushed with childish precipitancy into war, and, what is worse, forced war upon a weak nation which, whatever it had done to provoke it, showed itself finally ready to make every reasonable effort to avert it and to meet every legitimate demand of the United States. Even if the good faith of Spain were to be questioned, we put ourselves in the wrong by refusing to test it. No attention was paid to her repeated offer of armistice in Cuba, of an international commission to determine the responsibility for the destruction of the *Maine*, of the grant of practical autonomy to Cuba.

The President and our Minister to Spain, both presumably better informed of the conditions than any other men, declared their belief that the ends we had a right to seek could be secured by negotiation, and urged that the attempt thus to obtain them should not be abandoned. But Congress, representing the Nation, refused to listen to the counsels of prudence, patience, and of peace.

The worst of war is, indeed, that its results can never be fully foreseen, and that they may turn out far worse than the actual calamity of its course. The United States went to war fancying that a comparatively simple, easy, and brief task was before it. Peace has nominally come. The actual conflict has ended; but less than one hundred days of war has resulted in revolution in the United States. The foundations on which the Republic has rested have been unsettled; the principles upon which the Government depends have been violated; we have undertaken obligations which neither our institutions nor our National character enable us properly to discharge.

Whatever disposition may be made of the Philippines, we are already, through holding them and claiming the right to dispose of them, brought into entangling relations with the nations of the Old World and run the risk of losing the inestimable boon, which has hitherto been ours, of freedom from the complications of the international politics of the Old World, and of remaining the independent masters of our own fortunes. It is, indeed, a momentous revolution.

B

SENATOR BENJAMIN TILLMAN VIEWS THE PHILIPPINE WAR
AS A FILIPINO STRUGGLE FOR LIBERTY
FEBRUARY 7, 1899

"We may say they are rebels, and in strict legal interpretation they may be rebels, but, Mr. President, let this war terminate how it will, history will declare that they are to-day patriots striving for what we fought for in our struggle with Great Britain in the last century. . . ."

As I understand the legal status the ratification of the treaty will bring about this result: That in the eye of the law the Philippine Islands are ours and the inhabitants thereof are to-day rebels; they are now ours by right of cession from Spain, ratified yesterday by this body, and to be ratified soon by the Spanish Government; they are American subjects;

Congressional Record, 55th Congress, 3rd Session (February 7, 1899), 1530–1532

and since they have fired upon the flag they are "rebels." That is the law
of the situation as we see it and possibly as the world sees it.

Now, considering the fact, which can not be denied—for our
consul, Mr. Williams, reported the fact as far back as February,
1898, before Dewey sailed into Manila Bay—that there was a rebellion against Spain: that the Filipino army was lying outside of the
city of Manila and hostilities were active; considering the fact that
they organized a government as far back as last June; considering
the fact that they have been actively engaged in collecting munitions
of war and have recruited their army until, as this officer told me,
they have not less than 40,000 men outside of Manila to-day, we are
brought face to face with the consideration as to whether it was not
wise and proper and the best thing from their point of view for the
Filipinos to make the attack which they did, or which it is said they
did, on Saturday night last.

If they went to war with the United States before the United States
had a title to those islands in law, what is their legal status in international law? They can not be called rebels to us except from the
extreme standpoint of legal technicality. We had no right in Manila
so far as they were concerned; we only had rights there so far as Spain
was concerned; and if, after they had their representative here pleading
and begging for some word of comfort, some promise as to our policy,
or some dim outline even as to the purpose of recognizing their right
to local self-government, they grew desperate at last and fired upon
our troops, the firing upon those troops before we had any legal title
must give them the right of belligerents in war, although they have
been subjects of Spain, because by the cession to us we simply fall heir
to Spain's residuary title in those islands, subject to the rights of the
natives who were struggling for freedom before we went to war with
Spain on an entirely different issue.

We may say they are rebels, and in strict legal interpretation they
may be rebels, but, Mr. President, let this war terminate how it will,
history will declare that they are to-day patriots striving for what we
fought for in our struggle with Great Britain in the last century; and
we can not escape from the condition at least of doubt as to the course
we ought to follow when we consider this fact. They were fighting for
their freedom against Spanish tyranny two years ago, and they continued
to fight up to the time when Aguinaldo left the islands and went to
Singapore; they continued the fight, as our own consul said, after he

left; they never did cease, some of them; there never was peace; and now the question which addresses itself to every American who loves his flag and loves his great country and loves the great principle upon which that flag rests and that country is founded is this: Are we to take the place of Spain as their taskmasters and oppressors? Do "governments derive their just powers from the consent of the governed"? . . .

We can send troops enough to Manila to kill, as the Senator from Montana [Mr. CARTER] said the other day, "to shoot them to death," if need be, to make them respect our flag and our authority. We can do it. Nobody doubts that. The question is ought we to do it? Is it honorable to do it? Is it right to do it? . . .

The report of the battle claims that we lost only 75 killed and a hundred and odd wounded; but the first skirmish has carried with it what anguish, what desolation, to homes in a dozen States! How many more victims are we to offer up on this altar of Mammon or national greed? When those regiments march back, if they return with decimated ranks, as they are bound to come, if we have to send thousands and tens of thousands of reinforcements there to press onward until we have subdued those ten millions, at whose door will lie these lives—their blood shed for what? An idea. If a man fires upon the American flag, shoot the last man and kill him, no matter how many Americans have to be shot to do it.

The city of Manila is surrounded by swamps and marshes, I am told. A few miles back lie the woods and jungles and mountains. These people are used to the climate. They know how to get about, and if they mean to have their liberties, as they appear to do, at what sacrifice will the American domination be placed over them? . . .

Those peoples are not suited to our institutions. They are not ready for liberty as we understand it. They do not want it. Why are we bent on forcing upon them a civilization not suited to them and which only means in their view degradation and a loss of self-respect, which is worse than the loss of life itself? . . . .

C
DEMOCRATIC PRESIDENTIAL CANDIDATE
WILLIAM JENNINGS BRYAN AND THE
CASE AGAINST IMPERIALISM
AUGUST 8, 1900

"Imperialism finds no warrant in the Bible. The command, 'Go ye into all the world and preach the gospel to every creature,' has no Gatling gun attachment."

... The principal arguments advanced by those who enter upon a defense of imperialism are:

First—That we must improve the present opportunity to become a world power and enter into international politics.

Second—That our commercial interests in the Philippine Islands and in the Orient make it necessary for us to hold the islands permanently.

Third—That the spread of the Christian religion will be facilitated by a colonial policy.

Fourth—That there is no honorable retreat from the position which the nation has taken.

The first argument is addrest to the nation's pride and the second to the nation's pocket-book. The third is intended for the church member and the fourth for the partizan.

It is sufficient answer to the first argument to say that for more than a century this nation has been a world power. For ten decades it has been the most potent influence in the world. Not only has it been a world power, but it has done more to shape the politics of the human race than all the other nations of the world combined. ...

The permanent chairman of the last Republican National Convention presented the pecuniary argument in all its baldness when he said:

We make no hypocritical pretense of being interested in the Philippines solely on account of others. While we regard the welfare of those people as a sacred trust, we regard the welfare

William Jennings Bryan, Ed., *Speeches of William Jennings Bryan*. New York: Funk and Wagnalls, 1913, II, 17–49.

of the American people first. We see our duty to ourselves as well as to others. We believe in trade expansion. By every legitimate means within the province of government and constitution we mean to stimulate the expansion of our trade and open new markets.

This is the commercial argument. It is based upon the theory that war can be rightly waged for pecuniary advantage, and that it is profitable to purchase trade by force and violence.... The Democratic party is in favor of the expansion of trade. It would extend our trade by every legitimate and peaceful means; but it is not willing to make merchandise of human blood.

But a war of conquest is as unwise as it is unrighteous. A harbor and coaling station in the Philippines would answer every trade and military necessity and such a concession could have been secured at any time without difficulty.

It is not necessary to own people in order to trade with them. We carry on trade today with every part of the world, and our commerce has expanded more rapidly than the commerce of any European empire....

When trade is secured by force, the cost of securing it and retaining it must be taken out of the profits, and the profits are never large enough to cover the expense. Such a system would never be defended but for the fact that the expense is borne by all the people, while the profits are enjoyed by a few.

Imperialism would be profitable to the army contractors; it would be profitable to the ship owners, who would carry live soldiers to the Philippines and bring dead soldiers back; it would be profitable to those who would seize upon the franchises, and it would be profitable to the officials whose salaries would be fixt here and paid over there; but to the farmer, to the laboring man and to the vast majority of those engaged in other occupations it would bring expenditure without return and risk without reward....

The pecuniary argument, tho more effective with certain classes, is not likely to be used so often or presented with so much enthusiasm as the religious argument. If what has been termed the "gunpowder gospel" were urged against the Filipinos only it would be a sufficient answer to say that a majority of the Filipinos are now members of one branch of the Christian church; but the principle involved is one of much wider application and challenges serious consideration.

The religious argument varies in positiveness from a passive belief that Providence delivered the Filipinos into our hands, for their good and our glory, to the exultation of the minister who said that we ought to "thrash the natives (Filipinos) until they understand who we are," and that "every bullet sent, every cannon shot and every flag waved means righteousness." . . .

If true Christianity consists in carrying out in our daily lives the teachings of Christ, who will say that we are commanded to civilize with dynamite and proselyte with the sword? He who would declare the divine will must prove his authority either by Holy Writ or by evidence of a special dispensation.

Imperialism finds no warrant in the Bible. The command, "Go ye into all the world and preach the gospel to every creature," has no Gatling gun attachment. . . .

There is an easy, honest, honorable solution of the Philippine question. It is set forth in the Democratic platform and it is submitted with confidence to the American people. This plan I unreservedly indorse. If elected, I will convene Congress in extraordinary session as soon as inaugurated and recommend an immediate declaration of the nation's purpose, first, to establish a stable form of government in the Philippine Islands, just as we are now establishing a stable form of government in Cuba; second, to give independence to the Filipinos as we have promised to give independence to the Cubans; third, to protect the Filipinos from outside interference while they work out their destiny, just as we have protected the republics of Central and South America, and are, by the Monroe doctrine, pledged to protect Cuba.

A European protectorate often results in the plundering of the ward by the guardian. An American protectorate gives to the nation protected the advantage of our strength, without making it the victim of our greed. For three-quarters of a century the Monroe doctrine has been a shield to neighboring republics and yet it has imposed no pecuniary burden upon us. After the Filipinos had aided us in the war against Spain, we could not honorably turn them over to their former masters; we could not leave them to be the victims of the ambitious designs of European nations, and since we do not desire to make them a part of us or to hold them as subjects, we propose the only alternative, namely, to give them independence and guard them against molestation from without.

When our opponents are unable to defend their position by argument they fall back upon the assertion that it is destiny, and insist that we must submit to it, no matter how much it violates our moral precepts and our principles of government. This is a complacent philosophy. It obliterates the distinction between right and wrong and makes individuals and nations the helpless victims of circumstance.

Destiny is the subterfuge of the invertebrate, who, lacking the courage to oppose error, seeks some plausible excuse for supporting it. . . .

D

SENATOR CHARLES A. CULBERSON ON ARMY ATROCITIES IN THE PHILIPPINES: TESTIMONY OF PVT. ANDREW K. WEIR
JUNE 3, 1902

"I have something to inform you about. It is the terrible cruelty practiced upon Filipino prisoners by American soldiers in these islands. . . . We soldiers are representatives of a civilized nation sent out to these islands to 'civilize' a so-called lot of savages. These people are not nearly so uncivilized as is supposed. You probably have read about some of our men being put to death by horrible torture, but what can you expect when we do equally as bad to our prisoners?"

Mr. CULBERSON. Mr. President, on the 22nd of May I introduced a resolution directing the Secretary of War to send to the Senate copies of the charges that had been preferred by Private Andrew K. Weir, of the Fourth Cavalry, against Lieutenant Arnold and Sergeant Edwards, of that regiment. The resolution went over from day to day for three or four days on objections made by the Senators from Wisconsin [Mr. SPOONER] and Massachusetts [Mr. LODGE], they stating that they desired to make inquiry as to whether or not a court-martial had been ordered.

Congressional Record, 57th Congress, 1st Session, Vol. 35 (June 3, 1902), 6220–6222.

During that period I asked the Senator from Massachusetts [Mr. LODGE], who stated that a court-martial had been ordered, when the court-martial had been ordered. He answered that he was unable to state, because he did not know, and I suggested that I had no objection to the resolution going over if the information as to when the court-martial was ordered would be given the next day in a communication from the Secretary of War, and so it went over.

Subsequently, Mr. President, on the 27th of May, the Senator from Massachusetts [Mr. LODGE] presented to the Senate a letter from the Secretary of War stating, without giving the date of the order, that a court-martial had been ordered in the case of Sergeant Edwards, but none in the case of Lieutenant Arnold, the charges as to that officer being still, as I understood it, under investigation. The resolution was then referred by vote to the Committee on the Philippines. . . .

In view of all the circumstances as they have come into my possession since the resolution was introduced, I desire to have read by the Secretary a copy of the charges made by Private Andrew K. Weir and a copy of the report of Capt. P. W. West thereon. The first paper I will ask to have read is a copy of the charges. . . .

BALAYAN, BATANGAS PROVINCE, LUZON, P. I., *April 10, 1901.*

MY DEAR UNCLE: You are a free American citizen, and as such you are entitled to know how our government is carried on. I have something to inform you about. It is the terrible cruelty practiced upon Filipino prisoners by American soldiers in these islands. First, I want to know if the Constitution of the United States and international law does not prohibit torture.

We soldiers are representatives of a civilized nation sent out to these islands to "civilize" a so-called lot of savages. These people are not nearly so uncivilized as is supposed. You probably have read about some of our men being put to death by horrible torture, but what can you expect when we do equally as bad to our prisoners?

Has any court the right to force any prisoner to confess, no matter how many crimes the prisoner is supposed to have committed? When I say force I mean to force by torture. The Army of the United States in the Philippines is representing the law of the United States. But whether or not it is proper to torture a man it is done anyway, and under the orders of commissioned officers.

I have heard men of other regiments make their boasts of how they have made captured insurgents tell where their arms were, but never witnessed the torture once.

The instance that I have reference to occurred about two months ago. I told the officer that he had to stop it or I would report him to higher authority. He said he would not practice it any more, so I never informed on him; but now I have information about him doing the same, and even worse, nearly every day.

While I was one of a detachment of 24 men doing garrison duty in the town of Pasay, 3 miles from Manila, a native man about 21 years of age was arrested and accused of being a murderer, highway robber, and accused of rape. Now, whether the man was guilty or not I do not know, but anyway Lieut. F. T. Arnold, for he was the officer in command, gave orders to Sergeant Edwards, both of Troop H, Fourth Cavalry, to take the man to the basement of our quarters and get what information he could out of the man.

So Edwards took the man and asked him if he had any information to give. The man had none. Edwards said to the rest of the soldiers who had congregated to witness the "fun" that he would have to commence operations. The prisoner was stripped naked and laid on his back on the bare floor. He was then given the "water cure." A rough stick about 8 inches long and a half inch in diameter was put between the man's jaws. A soldier held the man's head down by pressing on the ends of the stick. Another sat on the man's stomach, and still another sat on the man's legs. Edwards had a bucket of water at hand. Water was poured down the man until it was vomited up. It was then repeated.

This water cure must be a terrible torture alone. The man heaved and begged for mercy, but to no avail. While down he was whipped and beaten unmercifully. He was then stood up and asked to confess. He did not. He was then beaten and clubbed again. I do not think that a square inch of the man's body was left untouched. He was kicked. A rope was then thrown across a beam. The man was strung up by the thumbs. Another rope was tied to his ankles and his foot jerked from under him. While up he was beaten.

All this time I was a looker on. I hoped that the punishment would stop. I dared not interfere. But when the man was strung up by the neck I could stand it no longer, so I went to the lieutenant. Before I went to him I did not know that he had given orders to Edwards to torture the man if he did not confess. I told Arnold that I was an American and that there was something going on at the quarters that I could not stand. He jumped all over me and asked if I was not making myself very busy. I said I was not; that such carryings on were against all law.

He said, in a very sarcastic manner, that I knew such a lot about law. He said that a lot of men in the Army, especially volunteers, think that they know how to run an army, but they do not. He said: "Now, when I give a man to Sergeant Edwards, I want information. I do not know how he gets it, but he gets the information anyway." He said that these people have no feelings other than physical and should not be treated as human beings. I told Arnold that I did not come to get any-one in trouble, but merely to have the torture stopped, that if it were not stopped I would report the matter to higher authority.

I was then threatened with court-martial for insubordination. About this time Edwards came in and said that he had succeeded in making the man tell where the money was. Arnold told Edwards to take the man with him and get the money.

I told Arnold that as the torture was finished I would not report the matter if it were not repeated. He promised not to do it again. I then left him.

The prisoner did not show where the money was. He had only said that he would show the hiding place to have the torture stopped. Three weeks later the prisoner was released. Now, that was criminal of Arnold. If the man was guilty he should not be released. If guilty he should not be tortured anyway.

The rest of the time that I was with the detachment under Arnold no torture was committed that I know of.

Now, Arnold has a detachment of 20 men at Calaca, 7 miles from here. Men that are under him now have told me that Arnold is having men tortured the same as before and other ways besides. This is one of his new ways: A strip of flesh is cut just above the ankle of the prisoner; it is then attached to a stick; the stick is coiled with the strip of flesh. Imagine the torture the poor man must endure! I am told that when Arnold is out looking for some criminal or suspected insurgent he will grab, or have his men grab, any native and ask for information.

If the man gives no information, he is put to all kinds of torture. I saw the man that was cut at the ankle. I was over at Calaca the other day. He had his leg all bound up and was out in the road with other prisoners working.

Last week a part of this troop, a part of the Calaca detachment, and some of the soldiers from Taal were out in the mountains. I was not along, but have been told by several men that Arnold had his men take an old man to a stream and keep him under water until the man was unconscious. This was because the old man did not give certain information that he was supposed to possess.

Men of H Troop have told me that they have known Arnold to have a man tied to a saddled horse. A few feet of slack was allowed. A man was then mounted on the horse and told to gallop down the road for a mile and then back. If the prisoner could run as fast as the horse, it was all well, but if he could not he had to drag. Arnold has had this done several times, and more than once the prisoner was dragged.

Now, I have witnesses for all that I have written about, and should there ever be an investigation of this I will be perfectly willing to be put upon the stand. I know other men that would be willing to do the same.

I believe that most of the officers and enlisted men in the Army are humane, but those that practice what Arnold has should be brought to justice.

It would do me no good to report this matter through Army channels, as it would only be hushed up and then I would get the worst of it.

Now, I am writing this letter to you; you are a close relation of mine, and for that reason I believe I can write anything. I think that you should bring this before the proper persons.

Lieut. Frederick T. Arnold was appointed to West Point from Iowa in 1893. He graduated from West Point in 1897 and was commissioned a second lieutenant in the Sixth Cavalry. He is now second lieutenant of Troop H, Fourth Cavalry.

I hope that the proper people of the United States will take hold of this case and have all torture in these islands stopped.

Well, my dear uncle, as I have already written so much on this subject, I will not write about other subjects. I am in fine health, and hope you are the same. Give my love to all.

I remain, your loving nephew,

ANDREW K. WEIR, JR.,
Troop C, Fourth United States Cavalry, Balayan, P. I. . . . .

OFFICE OF THE INSPECTOR-GENERAL,
DEPARTMENT OF NORTHERN LUZON,
Manila, P. I., August 27, 1901.

The ADJUTANT-GENERAL DEPARTMENT OF NORTHERN LUZON.

SIR: I have the honor to submit the following report of the investigation made by me into the complaint of Private Andrew K. Weir, Troop C, Fourth Cavalry, against Lieut. F. T. Arnold, Fourth Cavalry, in regard to the cruelties practiced by Lieutenant Arnold upon native prisoners at Pasay and Calaca, Luzon:

Sergt. George Schurman, Troop B. Fourth Cavalry, stated that he had witnessed the punishment of the prisoner at Pasay and that the facts were correctly stated in Private Weir's letter to his uncle. The prisoner was choked, beaten, hung up by the thumbs, and then by the neck, and given the water cure, and was whipped with rattans, this whipping being so severe as to bring blood on the prisoners legs. That this punishment was all inflicted by Sergeant Edwards and three native policemen.

Private George Bowers, Troop B, Fourth Cavalry, stated that he had only heard of the punishment of the prisoner at Pasay. I believe this man knows more about the cruel treatment of prisoners at Pasay and Calaca than he stated, but the departure of his troop for the United States prevented me from examining him thoroughly.

Private James B. Barry, Third Cavalry, formerly of Troop B, Fourth Cavalry, stated that he witnessed the treatment of the prisoner at Pasay and that it was brutal. He corroborated the statement of Private Weir in regard to this prisoner's treatment.

He stated that Sergeant Edwards often talked of the way he had beaten native prisoners. He stated that while corporal of the guard near Taal he had charge of about 50 native prisoners and that he had orders to turn them over to Sergeant Edwards whenever he wanted them, and that Lieutenant Arnold told Sergeant Edwards in his (Barry's) presence that he could take them out whenever he wanted to and to get what information he could out of them, and that Sergeant Edwards and the native scouts frequently took out one or two prisoners and would keep them out from half an hour to an hour. He did not know whether or not they were badly treated while out with Sergeant Edwards.

Corpl. George E. West, Troop B, Fourth Cavalry, stated that while corporal of the guard at Calaca he had seen native prisoners brought to the guard-house whose shins looked like they had been rubbed with a stick, but he did not know how they got in this condition.

Corpl. S. J. Peterson, Troop B, Fourth Cavalry, stated that he did not know personally that native prisoners had been cruelly treated, but the general impression among the men at Calaca was that Sergeant Edwards was torturing these prisoners, and had Lieutenant Arnold's permission to do so.

Corpl. Charles Austin, Troop B. Fourth Cavalry, stated that he was stationed with the detachment at Calaca under command of Lieutenant Arnold, and that his (Austin's) quarters were very near where the scouts under command of Sergeant Edwards lived; that he had seen Sergeant Edwards take native prisoners from the guardhouse to the scouts' quarters and shortly thereafter heard cries and groans coming from these quarters; that he saw them take one prisoner from the guardhouse to the scouts' quarters, and when he was returned to the guardhouse his shins looked as though they had been scraped with a stick. He did not know whether or not Lieutenant Arnold knew that prisoners were being badly treated, but the impression was that he knew all about it.

Private John Tuck, Troop B, Fourth Cavalry, states that while stationed at Calaca he had seen, through the windows of the scouts' quarters, prisoners being whipped with rattans by Sergeant Edwards and the scouts, that while on detached service near Calaca with Sergeant Edwards and the scouts he saw them abuse and beat an old man and made them stop it; that Sergeant Edwards took the prisoner off into the brush after this, and he (Tuck) heard two shots, and then Sergeant Edwards came back without the prisoner and stated that he had had a fight with the prisoner and showed where he had been bitten on the arm and said "He will be down there a long time." Private Tuck did not know if the prisoner had been killed nor whether Lieutenant Arnold knew about the prisoners being badly treated.

Private James M. Whitney, Troop B, Fourth Cavalry, stated that he was a member of the detachment at Calaca under command of Lieutenant Arnold, and that while in the scouts' quarters one day he saw a native prisoner on the floor, and that the prisoner was bucked and the scouts, in the presence of Sergeant Edwards, were rubbing the prisoner's legs with a broomstick, and that this treatment was brutal; that while on detached service with Sergeant Edwards and the scouts near Calaca he saw them beat a native in a brutal manner; that Sergeant Edwards told him that Lieutenant Arnold knew all about the way the natives were being treated. Private Whitney stated that Privates Reeves and Graham, of Troop C, Fourth Cavalry, could tell all about the inhuman treatment of prisoners at Calaca.

I was informed that Privates Fielding, St. Clair, and Taylor, of "B" Troop, Fourth Cavalry, could also give testimony on this subject, but the departure of the troop for the United States prevented me from finishing this investigation.

I believe that a thorough investigation into this matter will substantiate the charges made by Private Weir, that prisoners were treated in a cruel and harsh manner and that Lieutenant Arnold winked at this treatment.

Very respectfully,

P. W. WEST,
Captain, Fifth Cavalry, Inspector-General Department of Northern Luzon. . . .

Mr. ALLISON. These charges made by a private soldier against two officers of the Army, a commissioned officer and a noncommissioned officer, seem to have been made largely upon hearsay, and the statement of the inspector, Captain West, is largely hearsay.

I do not know whether this matter has been pursued beyond the report of Captain West. I observe that Lieutenant Arnold is a resident of my State. I know nothing of him or about him, except I have a general idea that a young man reared in Iowa and educated at West Point is not very likely to be guilty of the brutality that is charged here.

I wish to express the hope that the Senator from Texas [Culberson] will pursue his inquiry so far as to give Lieutenant Arnold an opportunity of defending his honor and his character somewhere, and that these charges, put in the RECORD against him while he is in the service of his country in a distant region, will not injure him, in the opinion, at least, of those who are his near friends and relatives without an opportunity being given somewhere for an investigation. I have no doubt that the Secretary of War is making such an investigation. I do not discuss the propriety of spreading upon the RECORD this fragment against an officer of the Army. I can only say that as a Senator on this floor if this presentation had been made to me I would not have given it the publicity which the Senator from Texas has given it. . . .

WORLD WAR I

The First World War found the United States intervening in a European conflict that had been raging for nearly three years. World War I was truly a modern war in that the technological advances of the second Industrial Revolution were applied on a large scale to the weapons and techniques of war. The submarine, the airplane, the tank, the machine gun, quick-firing artillery, poison gas, and vast armies of civilian conscripts had already been introduced on the fighting fronts prior to America's entry in April, 1917. The ratio of civilian and military casualties to total populations far exceeded anything experienced by mankind in the history of warfare. America, therefore, entered onto a scene of unequaled human misery.

The conflict was modern also in the fact that both sides waged open warfare on noncombatant civilians. The chief weapon in this phase of the fighting was the calculated starvation of entire national populations—starvation by maritime blockades. These were effected by British and French surface fleets, by the laying of extensive minefields, and by German U-Boats. Starvation as a tactic had been tried in the Napoleonic Wars when Bonaparte matched his Continental System against Britain's blockading Royal Navy. But by 1914–1917 the new machines of war at sea had rendered the strategy of victory-through-starvation both feasible and technologically achievable. It was this dimension of the conflict that ultimately involved the United States in the fighting.

As had been their experience in the years immediately preceding the War of 1812, Americans in 1914–1917 found that the war in Europe both complicated and stimulated the profitable export of American products to European ports. And as it was in 1812, the issue of the maritime rights of neutrals in wartime again became a major concern of American foreign policy. Indeed, Wilson in his War Message emphasized the violation of America's maritime neutral rights by Germany as the primary reason for the entry of the United States on the Allied side. A comparison of Madison's War Message in 1812 with Wilson's in 1917 is instructive in this regard. In 1812 there was also the problem of whether to declare war solely against Britain or to include France in a joint declaration. Similarly, the issue in 1914–1917 was which belligerent, Germany or Britain, was more culpable in violating what America conceived to be its legitimate rights on the high seas, it being generally agreed by American crusaders and critics alike that both nations were guilty of serious violations.

Nor is there substantial disagreement among scholars today that the Wilson Administration's evolving policy of "differential neutrality" had much to do with involving the United States in the war. The point here is that Wilson, for various reasons, held the German Government to "strict accountability" for the safety of American citizens traveling on belligerent ships to Europe and for American ships carrying cargoes to Britain and France; at the same time, he tolerated British interference with American ships and cargoes bound to Germany or to neutral ports in Europe from which such cargoes might be transshipped to Germany. Further, substantial American loans, economic assistance, and general encouragement went to Britain from the very beginning of the war. Germany, on the other hand, was widely regarded in the United States as having "started" or "caused" the war; and there was much more American sympathy for Anglo-French "democracy" than there was for the so-called "autocracy" and "militarism" of the Central Powers. Nevertheless, it was the unevenly applied concept of strict accountability at sea that steadily reduced the President's decision-making options and ultimately placed the decision for war or peace in hands other than his own. As Wilson confessed during the presidential campaign of 1916, "Any little German lieutenant can put us into the war at any time by some calculated outrage."[1]

This being so, the question was not that Wilson pursued a policy of differential neutrality that discriminated against Germany. He clearly did. The question is why he did this and what factors persuaded him to do so. It was therefore on the *why* of Wilson's policy that American crusaders and critics clashed in 1914—1917 and on which scholars have since debated.

Wilson's War Message on April 2, 1917 reviewed the recent history of Berlin's violations of American maritime rights and presented transcendent, ideological reasons for entering a war forced on the United States by an authoritarian and militarist Germany. The famous and much-quoted line, "the world must be made safe for democracy," was but a passing sentence in a detailed explanation of why Wilson felt America had to throw its weight onto the scales against the inhumanitarian political principles for which Germany was presumed to stand. Three days later, on April 5, Representative John J. Rogers of Massachusetts spelled out in greater detail those German outrages against

---

1 Ray Stannard Baker, *Woodrow Wilson: Life and Letters*. New York: Doubleday, Page; Doubleday, Doran, 1927–1939, VI, 258.

the United States that had forced America into the fight. "I believe," he concluded, "that it is a war not of aggression or for conquest or power, or even for expansion of trade, but a war of self-defense; a war for humanity; a war for Christianity itself."

The ideological certainties of the April 2 War Message were much less obvious to Wilson in the weeks that preceded his final decision for war. As one historian has put it, it was a period of "spiritual agony" for the President.[2] Certainly, it was not an easy or off-the-cuff decision for Wilson to make; and because it was a complex decision there have since been numerous scholarly interpretations of Wilson's motives in finally calling for war. Professor Richard W. Leopold has skillfully surveyed the controversial historiography of the "Why We Fought" issue, a controversy still alive among students of the period.

The Germans had their decision-making problems too. At a Crown Council Meeting at Pless on January 9, 1917, the High Command discussed in the Kaiser's presence the advantages and disadvantages of the resumption of unrestricted submarine warfare. In this exchange, the High Command was not of one mind or of one will. Chancellor Theobald von Bethmann-Hollweg, in particular, saw that such an announcement would very likely bring the United States into the war. Nevertheless, the decision was made to accept the military implications of that near-certainty in return for expected strategic and tactical advantages that would ensure an early German victory against the Allies. The fateful announcement was thus made. Professor Ernest R. May has analyzed the various political and military factors that Bethmann-Hollweg had to consider as he weighed the need for a speedy German victory against America's probable entry into the war in response to a resumption of unrestricted submarine warfare. Like those on Wilson, the psychological pressures on Bethmann-Hollweg were intense. In the final decision to unleash their U-Boats the Germans gambled, as perhaps they had to; and they lost.

American critics of Wilson's decision to respond with force to the German decision for U-Boat war were numerous and vocal. Senator Robert M. LaFollette of Wisconsin charged that it was little more than a rich man's war and a poor man's fight, and demanded that Wilson submit the question to a popular referendum prior to any formal declaration.

---

2 Arthur S. Link, *Woodrow Wilson and the Progressive Era, 1910–1917*. New York: Harper, 1954, 272–281.

LaFollette also felt that the march to war was the direct result of Wilson's skewed policy of differential neutrality and argued that noxious British influences had helped maneuver America into a war in which the nation had neither great stake nor legitimate interest. Senator George W. Norris of Nebraska saw the issue in pseudo-Marxist terms, as a Wall Street plot against the American people: "I would like to say to this war god, You shall not coin into gold the lifeblood of my brethren.... we are about to put the dollar sign upon the American flag." Representative Fred A. Britten of Illinois took still another tack in his plea for the continuation of noninvolvement and in his fear that amateur American troops would be cut to ribbons by professional Prussian soldiers. "It is like throwing a fine greyhound into a pit for a death struggle with a trained bulldog who has seen many victories" he said. Together, the antiwar critics made a powerful if belated case against the Wilson administration. But in indirectly attacking the Allied cause they opened themselves to the charge that they were basically and unpatriotically pro-German in sentiment.

The role of the traditional American pacifist was indeed an awkward one as Americans marched to war. Prior to the entry of the United States, arguments for American neutrality served to identify the peacemakers with German-American extremists who preached neutrality because they sincerely wanted to see the old Fatherland bring "perfidious Albion" to her knees. These particular German-Americans knew full well that American entry on the British side would render a German victory unlikely. On the same side of the neutrality argument with the extremist German-Americans and the pacifists were those socialists of one persuasion or another who saw the European war as a capitalist conspiracy against the oppressed proletariat from which the World Revolution would surely derive. The socialists urged strict American noninvolvement in the mechanics of this historical law.

It was true that many of the noninterventionists were either German-Americans, pacifists, or Marxists. Some were various combinations of these. But the German-American-Marxist-Pacifist linkage thoughtlessly (or malevolently) effected by interventionist and pro-war spokesmen was clearly a gratuitous one. It also helped confuse the motives and goals of the 1914–1917 peace movement by making it difficult for many Americans to separate the genuine peacemakers from those noninterventionists who were either pro-German or who saw the war as a major step toward world revolution. For the Anglophile war crus-

aders in the United States this confusion encouraged a shrewd and successful exercise in guilt-by-association that seriously undermined pacifist
influence on Wilson's decision for war in 1917.[3]

As Jane Addams later pointed out, the position of antiwar Americans
became especially isolated and dangerous after the United States actually
entered the fray. The role of the dissenter in 1917–1918 was not an
enviable one; nor was the wave of wartime emotionalism and patriotism conducive to the maintenance of his basic civil liberties. On the
contrary, the years 1917–1920 represent one of the low periods in the
checkered history of civil liberties in America. As Wilson had promised
in his War Message, "If there should be disloyalty, it will be dealt with
with a firm hand of stern repression." Of repression there was much; of
disloyalty there was little, although dissent of any sort was often so
regarded.

---

3 Robert Seager II, *The Progressives and American Foreign Policy, 1898–1917*.
Unpublished Ph.D. Dissertation, The Ohio State University, 1956, 253–412.

WORLD WAR I

I

THE CRUSADERS AND THE SCHOLARS: AMERICAN

A

THE WAR MESSAGE:
PRESIDENT WOODROW WILSON
APRIL 2, 1917

*". . . we shall fight for the things which we have always carried near-
est our hearts—for democracy, for the right of those who submit to
authority to have a voice in their own governments, for the rights
and liberties of small nations, for a universal dominion of right by
such a concert of free peoples as shall bring peace and safety to all
nations and make the world itself at last free."*

On the third of February last I officially laid before you the extraordinary announcement of the Imperial German Government that on
and after the first day of February it was its purpose to put aside all
restraints of law or of humanity and use its submarines to sink every
vessel that sought to approach either the ports of Great Britain and
Ireland or the western coasts of Europe or any of the ports controlled
by the enemies of Germany within the Mediterranean. That had seemed
to be the object of the German submarine warfare earlier in the war,
but since April of last year the Imperial Government had somewhat
restrained the commanders of its undersea craft in conformity with its
promise then given to us that passenger boats should not be sunk and that
due warning would be given to all other vessels which its submarines
might seek to destroy, when no resistance was offered or escape attempted, and care taken that their crews were given at least a fair chance

---

Congressional Record, Senate, 65th Congress, 1st Session, Vol. 55, (April 2, 1917),
102–104.

to save their lives in their open boats. The precautions taken were meagre and haphazard enough, as was proved in distressing instance after instance in the progress of the cruel and unmanly business, but a certain degree of restraint was observed. The new policy has swept every restriction aside. Vessels of every kind, whatever their flag, their character, their cargo, their destination, their errand, have been ruthlessly sent to the bottom without warning and without thought of help or mercy for those on board, the vessels of friendly neutrals along with those of belligerents. Even hospital ships and ships carrying relief to the sorely bereaved and stricken people of Belgium, though the latter were provided with safe conduct through the prescribed areas by the German Government itself and were distinguished by unmistakable marks of identity, have been sunk with the same reckless lack of compassion or of principle.

I was for a little while unable to believe that such things would in fact be done by any government that had hitherto subscribed to the humane practices of civilized nations. International law had its origin in the attempt to set up some law which would be respected and observed upon the seas, where no nation had right of dominion and where lay the free highways of the world. By painful stage after stage has that law been built up, with meagre enough results, indeed, after all was accomplished that could be accomplished, but always with a clear view, at least, of what the heart and conscience of mankind demanded. This minimum of right the German Government has swept aside under the plea of retaliation and necessity and because it had no weapons which it could use at sea except these which it is impossible to employ as it is employing them without throwing to the winds all scruples of humanity or of respect for the understandings that were supposed to underlie the intercourse of the world. I am not now thinking of the loss of property involved, immense and serious as that is, but only of the wanton and wholesale destruction of the lives of noncombatants, men, women, and children, engaged in pursuits which have always, even in the darkest periods of modern history, been deemed innocent and legitimate. Property can be paid for; the lives of peaceful and innocent people cannot be. The present German submarine warfare against commerce is a warfare against mankind.

It is a war against all nations. American ships have been sunk, American lives taken, in ways which it has stirred us very deeply to learn of, but the ships and people of other neutral and friendly nations have been sunk and overwhelmed in the waters in the same way. There has been no discrimination. The challenge is to all mankind. Each nation must decide for itself how it will meet it. The choice we make for ourselves must be made with a moderation of counsel and a temperateness of judgment befitting our character and our motives as a nation. We must put excited feeling away. Our motive will not be revenge or the victorious assertion of the physical might of the nation, but only the vindication of right, of human right, of which we are only a single champion. . . .

With a profound sense of the solemn and even tragical character of the step I am taking and of the grave responsibilities which it involves, but in unhesitating obedience to what I deem my constitutional duty, I advise that the Congress declare the recent course of the Imperial German Government to be in fact nothing less than war against the government and people of the United States; that it formally accept the status of belligerent which has thus been thrust upon it; and that it take immediate steps not only to put the country in a more thorough state of defense but also to exert all its power and employ all its resources to bring the Government of the German Empire to terms and end the war. . . .

While we do these things, these deeply momentous things, let us be very clear, and make very clear to all the world what our motives and our objects are. My own thought has not been driven from its habitual and normal course by the unhappy events of the last two months, and I do not believe that the thought of the nation has been altered or clouded by them. I have exactly the same things in mind now that I had in mind when I addressed the Senate on the twenty-second of January last; the same that I had in mind when I addressed the Congress on the third of February and on the twenty-sixth of February. Our object now, as then, is to vindicate the principles of peace and justice in the life of the world as against selfish and autocratic power and to set up amongst the really free and self-governed peoples of the world such a concert of purpose and of action as will henceforth ensure the observance of those principles. Neutrality is no longer feasible or desirable where the peace of the world is involved and the freedom of its peoples, and the menace to that peace and freedom lies in the existence of autocratic governments backed by organized force which is controlled wholly by their will, not by the will of their people. We have seen the last of neutrality in such circumstances. We are at the beginning of an age in which it will be insisted that the same standards of conduct and of responsibility for wrong done shall be

observed among nations and their governments that are observed among
the individual citizens of civilized states.

We have no quarrel with the German people. We have no feeling
towards them but one of sympathy and friendship. It was not upon their
impulse that their government acted in entering this war. It was not with
their previous knowledge or approval. It was a war determined upon as
wars used to be determined upon in the old, unhappy days when peoples
were nowhere consulted by their rulers and wars were provoked and
waged in the interest of dynasties or of little groups of ambitious men
who were accustomed to use their fellow men as pawns and tools. Self-
governed nations do not fill their neighbour states with spies or set the
course of intrigue to bring about some critical posture of affairs which
will give them an opportunity to strike and make conquest. Such designs
can be successfully worked out only under cover and where no one has
the right to ask questions. Cunningly contrived plans of deception or
aggression, carried, it may be, from generation to generation, can be
worked out and kept from the light only within the privacy of courts or
behind the carefully guarded confidences of a narrow and privileged
class. They are happily impossible where public opinion commands and
insists upon full information concerning all the nation's affairs.

A steadfast concert for peace can never be maintained except by a
partnership of democratic nations. No autocratic government could be
trusted to keep faith within it or observe its covenants. It must be a
league of honour, a partnership of opinion. Intrigue would eat its vitals
away; the plottings of inner circles who could plan what they would and
render account to no one would be a corruption seated at its very heart.
Only free peoples can hold their purpose and their honour steady to a
common end and prefer the interests of mankind to any narrow interest
of their own.

Does not every American feel that assurance has been added to our
hope for the future peace of the world by the wonderful and heartening
things that have been happening within the last few weeks in Russia?
Russia was known by those who knew it best to have been always in fact
democratic at heart, in all the vital habits of her thought, in all the intimate relationships of her people that spoke their natural instinct, their
habitual attitude towards life. The autocracy that crowned the summit
of her political structure, long as it had stood and terrible as was the
reality of its power, was not in fact Russian in origin, character, or
purpose; and now it has been shaken off and the great, generous Russian

people have been added in all their naive majesty and might to the forces that are fighting for freedom in the world, for justice, and for peace. Here is a fit partner for a League of Honour.

One of the things that has served to convince us that the Prussian autocracy was not and could never be our friend is that from the very outset of the present war it has filled our unsuspecting communities and even our offices of government with spies and set criminal intrigues everywhere afoot against our national unity of counsel, our peace within and without, our industries and our commerce. Indeed it is now evident that its spies were here even before the war began; and it is unhappily not a matter of conjecture but a fact proved in our courts of justice that the intrigues which have more than once come perilously near to disturbing the peace and dislocating the industries of the country have been carried on at the instigation, with the support, and even under the personal direction of official agents of the Imperial Government accredited to the Government of the United States. Even in checking these things and trying to extirpate them we have sought to put the most generous interpretation possible upon them because we knew that their source lay, not in any hostile feelings or purpose of the German people towards us (who were, no doubt as ignorant of them as we ourselves were), but only in the selfish designs of a Government that did what it pleased and told its people nothing. But they have played their part in serving to convince us at last that that Government entertains no real friendship for us and means to act against our peace and security at its convenience. That it means to stir up enemies against us at our very doors the intercepted note to the German Minister at Mexico City is eloquent evidence.

We are accepting this challenge of hostile purpose because we know that in such a government, following such methods, we can never have a friend; and that in the presence of its organized power, always lying in wait to accomplish we know not what purpose, there can be no assured security for the democratic governments of the world. We are now about to accept gauge of battle with this natural foe to liberty and shall, if necessary, spend the whole force of the nation to check and nullify its pretensions and its power. We are glad, now that we see the facts with no veil of false pretence about them, to fight thus for the ultimate peace of the world and for the liberation of its peoples, the German peoples included; for the rights of nations great and small and the privilege of men everywhere to choose their way of life and of obedience. The world must be made safe for democracy. Its peace must be planted upon the tested foundations of political liberty. We have no selfish ends to serve. We desire no conquest, no dominion. We seek no indemnities for ourselves, no material compensation for the sacrifices we shall freely make. We are but one of the champions of the rights of mankind. We shall be satisfied when those rights have been made as secure as the faith and the freedom of nations can make them. . . . We enter this war only where we are clearly forced into it because there are no other means of defending our rights.

It will be all the easier for us to conduct ourselves as belligerents in a high spirit of right and fairness because we act without animus, not in enmity towards a people or with the desire to bring any injury or disadvantage upon them, but only in armed opposition to an irresponsible government which has thrown aside all considerations of humanity and of right and is running amuck. We are, let me say again, the sincere friends of the German people, and shall desire nothing so much as the early re-establishment of intimate relations of mutual advantage between us,—however hard it may be for them, for the time being, to believe that this is spoken from our hearts. We have borne with their present government through all these bitter months because of that friendship,—exercising a patience and forbearance which would otherwise have been impossible. We shall, happily, still have an opportunity to prove that friendship in our daily attitude and actions towards the millions of men and women of German birth and native sympathy who live amongst us and share our life, and we shall be proud to prove it towards all who are in fact loyal to their neighbours and to the Government in the hour of test. They are, most of them, as true and loyal Americans as if they had never known any other fealty or allegiance. They will be prompt to stand with us in rebuking and restraining the few who may be of a different mind and purpose. If there should be disloyalty, it will be dealt with with a firm hand of stern repression; but, if it lifts its head at all, it will lift it only here and there and without countenance except from a lawless and malignant few.

It is a distressing and oppressive duty, Gentlemen of the Congress, which I have performed in thus addressing you. There are, it may be, many months of fiery trial and sacrifice ahead of us. It is a fearful thing to lead this great peaceful people into war, into the most terrible and disastrous of all wars, civilization itself seeming to be in the balance. But the right is more precious than peace, and we shall fight for the things which we have always carried nearest our hearts,—for democracy, for the right of those who submit to authority to have a voice in their own governments, for the rights and liberties of small nations, for a universal dominion of right by such a concert of free people as shall bring peace and safety to all nations and make the world itself at last free. To such a task we can dedicate our lives and our fortunes, everything that we are and everything that we have, with the pride of those who know that the day has come when America is privileged to spend her blood, and her might for the principles that gave her birth and happiness and the peace which she has treasured. God helping her, she can do no other.

B
REPRESENTATIVE JOHN JACOB ROGERS VIEWS THE WAR
AS A GREAT CRUSADE FOR CHRISTIANITY AND DECENCY
APRIL 5, 1917

". . . I confess myself amazed at the moderation and forbearance of the United States. I doubt if there has ever been in the history of the world a case where so much patience has been exhibited by one nation toward another. As we consider the language of our own communications to Germany — 'strict accountability' . . . and so forth — what must be our conclusion? Surely if men are ever again to believe that we mean what we say we must make good those ringing and patriotic declarations."

Mr. ROGERS. Mr. Chairman, I am unreservedly in favor of the pending resolution. I had the honor of voting to report it out of the Committee on Foreign Affairs, and I shall have the honor of voting to pass it through the House. And yet I realize, as every man must, the gravity and importance of the step which the Congress of the United States is taking to-day. War is at all times a frightful thing, and science and invention have combined in these recent months and years to make it doubly frightful. The toll of men, the flower of our Nation, may well be great as a

---

Congressional Record, House, 65th Congress, 1st Session, Vol. 55, (April 5, 1917), 333–335.

result of this step; the drain upon our resources and the burden of taxation upon us will certainly be severe beyond precedent. This is a solemn hour; it is no time for heroics or hysterics, and yet, as I view the situation, no patriot can hesitate to cast his vote—and it makes no difference whether his vote be cast as a Member of this body or as a member of our body politic—in favor of a vigorous prosecution of the war against Germany.

Frankly, I do not believe that the question whether Germany has given us a cause for war is arguable. For nearly two and a half years she has in the most deliberate and often in the most contemptuous way disregarded the fundamental and sacred rights of American citizens and the American Nation both at home and abroad. Almost daily for long periods of time has Germany committed at least one act against the peace and safety of the United States which was an abundant cause for war. I can not conceive how any thinking and even moderately informed man, whether in the United States or in Germany, can fail to agree that there is ample justification—that for more than two years there has at all times been ample justification—for the United States to take the step which she is taking to-day. The only possible argument, even on the part of those who are pacifists or pro-Germans, must be as to whether the present declaration that a state of war exists is hastily taken or premature. . . .

After the *Lusitania* sinking, Mr. Bryan, as Secretary of State, on May 13, 1915, addressed another communication to Germany, in which he again stated that the United States—

> can not admit the adoption of such measures or such a warning of danger to operate as in any degree an abbreviation of the rights of American shipmasters or of American citizens bound on lawful errands as passengers on merchant ships of belligerent nationality; and that it must hold the Imperial German Government to a strict accountability for any infringement of those rights, intentional or incidental. . . . The lives of noncombatants, whether they be of neutral citizenship or citizens of one of the nations at war, can not lawfully or rightfully be put in jeopardy by the capture or destruction of an unarmed merchantman. . . . The Imperial German Government will not expect the Government of the United States to omit any word or any act necessary to the performance of its sacred duty of maintaining

the rights of the United States and its citizens and of safeguarding their free exercise and enjoyment.

Here again, over the signature of the pacific Mr. Bryan, we have the "strict accountability" phrase. We also have the positive and emphatic statement that the United States will not "omit any word, or any act" necessary to protect the rights of the Nation or its citizens. This, again, was about two years ago. If we are to take words in their usual and literal significance, can we to-day feel that the German Government has not been fully advised of the course and purpose of the United States?

Thereafter the submarine war was prosecuted by Germany with fluctuating success for about a year. Time and time again during that period acts were committed which clearly infringed and invaded our American rights. Yet the American Nation gritted its teeth and, in spite of the strong words of the two notes which I have quoted, did nothing very definite. To many of us it seemed as if the Nation was becoming benumbed to indignity and outrage. It seemed as if prosperity had overbalanced and removed from view every consideration not of the purely material sort. Notes were exchanged now and then, but very little of a substantive nature seemed to result from the procedure.

The next high light occurred on April 19, 1916, when, for the first time, the President addressed Congress upon the subject of submarine warfare. In the course of his address, he said:

I have deemed it my duty, therefore, to say to the Imperial German Government that if it is still its purpose to prosecute relentless and indiscriminate warfare against vessels of commerce by the use of submarines, notwithstanding the now demonstrated impossibility of conducting that warfare in accordance with what the Government of the United States must consider the sacred and indisputable rules of international law and the universally recognized dicates of humanity, the Government of the United States is at last forced to the conclusion that there is but one course it can pursue; and that unless the Imperial German Government should now immediately declare and effect an abandonment of its present methods of warfare against passenger and freight carrying vessels this Government can have no choice but to sever diplomatic relations with the Government of the German Empire altogether.

Again there was a period of nearly a year of delays. Our citizens were drowned and our rights invaded, usually by retail and not by wholesale. At all events, no definite steps were taken during the period by the United States Government.

On January 31 of the present year Germany announced that on the following day a great war zone, surrounding Great Britain, France, and Italy, and applying also in the eastern Mediterranean, would be established, and stating that she would forcibly prevent all navigation in that zone, including that of neutrals. "All ships met within the zone will be sunk." President Wilson on February 3 again came before Congress and announced that he had severed diplomatic relations between the United States and the German Empire and had caused to be handed to the German ambassador his passports.

Germany persisted in this course, and in the next two or three weeks sank at least two American ships—the *Housatonic* and the *Lyman M. Law.* Many other ships she also sank with Americans on board, whose lives were lost as a result. Accordingly, on February 26, President Wilson came before Congress and said:

> Since it is unhappily proved impossible to safeguard our neutral rights by diplomatic means against the unwarranted infringement they are suffering at the hands of Germany, there may be no recourse but to armed neutrality, which we shall know how to maintain and for which there is abundant American precedent. . . . I request that you will authorize me to supply our merchant ships with defensive arms, should that become necessary, and with the means of using them, and to employ any other instrumentalities or methods that may be necessary and adequate to protect our ships and our people in their legitimate and peaceful pursuits on the seas.

Germany, nevertheless, made no modification of her program of frightfulness, and for the last six weeks has been proceeding with a ruthlessness not previously approached. . . .

It is sufficient in this connection to say that during the submarine warfare of Germany 226 American lives have been taken without justification and in direct subversion of the most elementary principles of law and of morality. And I am leaving to other speakers the recital of German outrages upon the American Continent—outrages upon the persons and property of United States citizens.

Mr. Chairman, whatever the verdict of history may be, I am satisfied that it will acquit this Government and the American people of the charge that they acted with rashness or precipitation. As I review in my own mind the dastardly career of Germany in its relation with the United States, I confess myself amazed at the moderation and forbearance of the United States. I doubt if there has ever been in the history of the world a case where so much patience has been exhibited by one nation toward another. As we consider the language of our own communications to Germany—"strict accountability," "omit no word nor act," and so forth—what must be our conclusion? Surely if men are ever again to believe that we mean what we say we must make good those ringing and patriotic declarations.

There is no question that Germany itself has been astounded that it has not long ago been at war with the United States. Its responsible officers have been unable to understand how the German program could result in any other course. They could not see how any self-respecting nation could refrain from accepting the gauntlet which time and time again they have cast at the feet of the United States. Take, for example, the famous Zimmermann letter of instructions to the German minister in Mexico, dated January 10 of the present year. The letter reads, in part:

> On the 1st of February we intend to begin submarine war-
> fare unrestricted.... You are instructed to inform the President
> of Mexico of the above in the greatest confidence as soon as it
> is certain that there will be an outbreak of war with the United
> States.

"As soon as it is certain that there will be an outbreak of war with the United States." There was no suggestion of doubt in the mind of the Imperial German minister, who was very well informed as to the senti-ment of this country, whether or not war would result from ruthless submarine warfare. It was perfectly clear to him on the 19th of January, two weeks before the announcement of February 1 was made, that that announcement must inevitably bring about war between the United States and Germany. He knew, of course, that there was a man in the White House who had been reelected upon a peace program, a man who stood for peace. He knew that the people of the United States desired peace, and, indeed, yearned for peace, and yet he thought it too clear for argument that war would follow the declaration of February 1.

The United States to-day is doing the inevitable thing. It is taking up arms against the pirate and the desperado of nations, which, as President Wilson said the other evening, is running amuck. It is because we are lovers of peace that we are forced to take this step. Only thus can an enduring peace be achieved. Mr. Chairman, in entering upon this conflict we are fighting the battle of democracy against autocracy, of liberty against despotism, of freedom against enslavement, of civilization against barbarism. . . .

April has been a momentous month in the history of our Nation. In April, 1775, the embattled farmers of Lexington and Concord struck the first blow for liberty; in April, 1812, the Congress of the United States began to voice those protests against the invasion by England of our American rights at sea, which resulted in the war sometimes called the second war of independence. In April, 1861, the first blood was shed by men of Lowell in defense of the Union; in April, 1898, Congress passed the resolution declaring that the people of Cuba should be free, thereby reaching the climax in the relations between Spain and the United States, prior to the actual declaration of war. In April, 1916, the President made the first declaration to Germany to the effect that the patience of the American Government had been exhausted. Whenever on these occasions the United States has taken up arms it has been for a righteous cause. I believe, with all my heart, that our course to-day is righteous—that it is the only course open to an honorable and self-respecting nation. I believe that it is a war not of aggression or for conquest or power, or even for expansion of trade, but a war of self-defense; a war for humanity; a war for Christianity itself. God grant that the issue be decided in accordance with the dictates of right and of humanity, and that our entrance into war to-day may aid in the wiping of wars for all time from the face of the earth. [Applause.]

C

PROFESSOR RICHARD LEOPOLD ON
HISTORICAL INTERPRETATIONS OF
AMERICAN INTERVENTION IN 1917

*"Every war President . . . has been accused at some time of having
needlessly led his people to Armageddon. . . . So long as men strive
to eliminate war, historians will scrutinize its causes and the revisionists will themselves be periodically revised."*

It is a truism, long recognized, that every generation writes its own
history. It is a fact, widely conceded, that complete historical objectivity
will forever remain, in the words of the late Charles A. Beard, "that
noble dream." And nowhere is the cycle of changing interpretations
better illustrated or the pitfalls of subjectivity better evidenced than in
the literature of the wars in which the United States has engaged. Every
war President, for example, has been accused at some time of having
needlessly led his people to Armageddon. One has only to think of the
ink spilled over Madison and the Henry letters, Polk and the despatch
of Taylor to the Rio Grande, Lincoln and Fort Sumter, McKinley and
the so-called last-minute concessions of Spain, Wilson and the House-
Grey Memorandum, or Franklin Roosevelt and the alleged ultimatum of
November 26, 1941. So long as men strive to eliminate war, historians
will scrutinize its causes and the revisionists will themselves be periodically revised. . . .

In dealing with the problem of American intervention, historians
have been greatly affected by their own personal convictions and by the
availability of source materials at the time they wrote. Obviously every
author has been influenced by his views on war in general, by his estimate of the wisdom of our participation in 1917, and by the course of
American foreign policy since that date. Divergent opinions of why we
fought date from Wilson's message of April 2. The first accounts by
scholars, men like John B. McMaster and John S. Bassett, supported
the Presidential contention that war had been forced upon us by

Richard W. Leopold, "The Problem of American Intervention, 1917: An Historical
Retrospect," *World Politics*, II (October, 1949–July, 1950), 405–425. Reprinted by
permission.

Germany. Dissent, however, was instantly voiced by journalists like Randolph Bourne and Scott Nearing or by legislators like George Norris and Robert La Follette. Dissent turned to disillusionment as wartime infringements upon civil rights infuriated liberals everywhere and as the bright hopes for a peace without victory had to be compromised with the realities of world politics at Paris. Disillusionment grew apace during the 'twenties, aided by the *Kriegsschuldfrage*, and reached its peak after 1934 when a new holocaust loomed on the horizon....

Given a belated availability of primary sources, professional historians in the 'twenties tended to avoid the problem of American intervention. The subject provoked no controversy in learned circles comparable to the question of war guilt in 1914. Not until 1933 did the journals carry articles based upon the *Foreign Relations Supplements*. The field was thus left to a small group of so-called revisionists, men who would revise the Wilsonian version of why we fought, men who committed their views to paper even though complete documentation was not at their disposal.

The earliest revisionists were, with one exception, journalists. The first was John Kenneth Turner whose polemical *Shall It Be Again?* appeared from the press of B. W. Huebsch in May 1922. The forty-four-year-old Turner was a veteran Socialist writer who had exposed the Diaz regime in the pages of the muckraking *American Magazine*, who had personally assisted the Mexican rebels, and who had gone on record as a bitter foe of the Versailles Treaty. *Shall It Be Again?* categorically denied that we had intervened in 1917 to protect American commerce and lives or to uphold national honor and international law. Rather it argued through over four hundred pages that we had gone to war at the command of a profit-crazed Wall Street that was aided and abetted by the broken pledges and executive usurpations of the pseudo-liberal in the White House. Despite its vitriolic tone (or because of it) and frequent diversionary attacks upon American imperialism in the Caribbean, the book went through four printings and may have sold as many as eight thousand copies.

The second important revisionist was Professor Harry Elmer Barnes. In a sixty-page chapter in his *Genesis of the World War* (1926) Barnes contended that American intervention had been an unmitigated disaster for the world and for ourselves. It was due, he said, to a cowardly acquiescence in British illegal actions and to a misguided desire to save the Entente from certain defeat. Much the same view was expressed by

Frederick Bausman, a West Coast jurist, who had already contributed an indictment of France to the war guilt question. In *Facing Europe* (1926) Bausman turned his fire on both England and the Wilson administration. Ostensibly a criticism of the British war debt policy, his volume provided the fullest and latest discussion thus far on the infringements of our neutral rights and on the allegedly unpatriotic diplomacy of Page and House. Like Turner and Barnes, Bausman regarded American intervention as a national calamity; like the other revisionists, he succumbed to the German wartime plea that she had been surrounded by hostile states and had resorted to the submarine only to avoid starvation at home. In the retrospect of a quarter-century all three writers seem guilty of considerable naiveté and much oversimplification. . . .

A more scholarly statement of revisionism appeared on Armistice Day, 1929, in C. Hartley Grattan's *Why We Fought*. The twenty-seven-year-old Grattan, a former student of Barnes's at Clark University, had gone beyond his master in probing the origins of our entry and had already produced several articles in addition to his books. *Why We Fought* was, in fact, only one of three books he published in 1929. It was a solid four-hundred-page volume that sought "to get behind the rationalizations . . . and try to discover the real forces" that led to war. Carefully annotated and replete with bibliography, it was soberly written and only occasionally lapsed into sarcasm or half-truths. It was blunt and sincere. Yet nowhere does Grattan explicitly state why we fought. It is apparent that he believed that economic entanglements, propaganda, and inept statesmanship created a bogus neutrality that gave Germany no choice but to counter with the submarine. Two long chapters on propaganda and economic forces, comprising a third of the text, were achievements in their day, but on both topics subsequent scholarship has modified or superseded Grattan's findings. The book ignored strategic considerations and the treatment of Congress was scanty. A creditable performance in 1929, *Why We Fought* is now remembered as the first documented narrative of the road to war and as an early thoughtful analysis of the role of commerce and finance. . . .

The first historian's history of intervention was Charles Seymour's *American Diplomacy during the World War* (1934). Seymour seemed the logical man for the task. An early student of European diplomacy, he had served under Wilson, had contributed a volume on the era to the *Chronicles of America* series, had edited *The Intimate Papers of Colonel House,* and had in numerous articles and reviews explored and assessed the literature of the subject. Now, working from a thorough knowledge of the sources, with access to unprinted House material, and aided by comments from surviving participants, Seymour fashioned a first-rate account that bore all the hallmarks of ripe scholarship. His main thesis was, of course, that Germany's use of the submarine was the primary cause of our intervention, that we fought for sentimental reasons, not political or economic ones. Seymour exploded the idea that the U-boat campaign was simply retaliation, and he argued persuasively that no neutral plans or pleas for a peace without victory ever had a chance of success. Within the limits Seymour set for himself, it was an excellent job. As such, it was loudly hailed in the historical journals, and its immediate influence upon subsequent writing was marked.

Time, however, has dimmed some of the luster of Seymour's achievement. For one thing, the limits he set for himself were too narrow. By rigidly excluding propaganda and public opinion, preparedness and the peace movement, by concentrating on the White House and ignoring Congress, he betrayed the venerable fault of discussing diplomacy in a vacuum. In the second place, a vast array of new sources was made available soon after Seymour wrote. Some of these indicated that economic considerations were more in the mind of Wilson and his advisers than Seymour would concede. Seymour's later writings reveal no essential modification of the views expressed in 1934. It is fair to say that few historians today accept *American Diplomacy during the World War* as a complete explanation of why we fought.

The next full-length account was the fascinating *Road to War: America, 1914–1917* by Walter Millis. Son of an army officer, a Yale graduate and editorial writer for the *New York Herald Tribune*, Millis had already produced the *The Martial Spirit*, a satirical narrative of the war with Spain that emphasized the ludicrous. Millis presumably spent the better part of four years, aided by his English-born wife, in reading the more obvious printed sources of the neutrality years. Published in May 1935, the *Road to War* was quickly chosen as a Book-of-the-Month Club selection and has since sold over twenty thousand copies.

Although often regarded as a popularization of Grattan, the *Road to War* was an independent study. There is a difference in emphasis, purpose, and proportion. But whatever its historical merit may have been, and it was considerable, the book alienated the professionals by its proclivity for debunking and by a lack of sustained analysis. Like Grattan, Millis nowhere clearly stated why we fought. He implied that we stumbled and blundered into war unwittingly, aided by an unneutrality (that is never defined), by propaganda, and by a quest for lucrative trade. At times the reader is made to feel that involvement was avoidable; at other times he receives the impression that involvement was inevitable. Thus we are told that by 1917 Americans had become the prisoners of their own policies, of fate, and of human limitations. An absorbing tale, grounded on the conviction that force accomplishes nothing, the *Road to War* suffered from excessive sarcasm and the author's reluctance to say just what he meant.

Actually Millis was perfectly competent to analyze the causes of our intervention. In a forgotten article in July 1935, he brilliantly dissected the exact nature of the economic pressures for war, examined the problem of multiple causation, and sagely noted that the issue of the future was not how to stay out of war but rather should we stay out of war. This and other soberly written essays, however, passed unnoticed by the profession. Generally speaking, Millis received rough going from his reviewers, especially Charles Seymour, although a few scholars had some words of praise. For the specialist who can discount the debunking and dismiss the sarcasm, the *Road to War* is still of value today. Its chronological approach points up better than any other treatment the interrelationship of the various crises at home and abroad. It is full of shrewd, if fleeting, remarks on psychological forces. The description of the preparedness movement has not yet been improved upon. And the space allotted to Congress and to the two months after the rupture of relations with Germany is more generous, and properly so, than in any other account.

The *Road to War*, anticipating by a few months the most sensational publicity of the Nye Committee and the enactment of the first Neutrality Law, let loose during 1935–1939 a flood of writings. Most, being polemical or specialized in nature, can be ignored here or disposed of briefly. Robert Lansing's posthumous *War Memoirs* (1935), anonymously edited from a longer manuscript, seemed to confirm the suspicions of his worst enemies; but several scholars have questioned the representative character of the document. Newton D. Baker, another ex-cabinet member, eloquently restated the Wilsonian argument in *Why We Went to War* (1936), but he said nothing historians did not already know. Charles Seymour, aroused by the antics of Senators Nye and Clark, countered dogmatically in *American Neutrality* (1935), a group of essays that destroyed Congressional straw men rather than satisfied specialists. As one authority observed, the chapter "American Opinion on the Eve of War" was based largely on German sources. Grattan replied for the revisionists in a scathing review, and in his *Preface to Chaos* (1936) he tried to fit American intervention into this rigid formula:

> Economic entanglements with the Allied powers in the First World War made the participation of the United States in it on the side of the Allies possible, logical, and in the end necessary for the health of private capitalism; the wartime policies of the United States Government made participation inevitable.

Less contentious were the many useful articles and monographs of the five years 1935–1939. To their pioneer efforts of 1933, Thomas A. Bailey and Richard W. Van Alstyne added discussions of the blacklist, the Declaration of London, and the sinking of the *Lusitania*. Ralph Lutz and Schuyler Foster tackled the problems of propaganda and news dissemination, while J. V. Fuller and Clifton Child emphasized the munitions traffic and attempts to check it. Paul Birdsall's stimulating essay on economic pressures is still the best short discussion of the subject. At book length, James D. Squires's *British Propaganda at Home and in the United States* (1935) was a model of restrained scholarship; H. C. Peterson, spreading his net more widely in *Propaganda for War* (1939) seemed unduly influenced by the Nye Committee disclosures. A chapter in Merle Curti's *Peace or War* (1936) skillfully outlined the pacifist dilemma, while one phase was pursued in Marie L. Degen's *History of the Woman's Peace Party* (1939). Carl Wittke broke new ground with his *German-Americans and the World War* (1935); equally competent was Clifton J. Child's *German-Americans in Politics, 1914–1917* (1939). Harley Notter carried *The Origins of the Foreign Policy of Woodrow Wilson* (1937) down to 1917; and Alice M. Morrissey produced a concise unpretentious, but legalistic summary of *The American Defense of Neutral Rights* (1939). Alex M. Arnett's *Claude Kitchin and the Wilson War Policies* (1937) underscored the significance of Congressional leaders, but he claimed too much for his hero. Samuel F. Bemis's *Diplomatic History of the United States* (1936) contained a masterly summary of recent literature, marred only, in the opinion of some, by two unscholarly speculations on the torpedoing of the *Lusitania* and the *Sussex*.

Two other special works must be mentioned before examining the longer general accounts. One is Charles A. Beard's *The Devil Theory of War* (1936), an expansion of three articles that had been prompted by the Nye Committee hearings. Beard's slender volume did two things. First, it flatly rejected both the narrow economic determinism of Gerald Nye and the single cause argument of Charles Seymour. Beard expounded lucidly the virtues of multiple causation, and he contributed the analogy of a chemist mixing reagents in a test tube, a figure popularized in the Bemis textbook. Secondly, Beard spelled out for the first time, though with melodramatic overtones, Wilson's changing policy on loans and credits. He intimated that Bryan's ban on loans of August 1914 was circumvented behind his back by a Wall Street-minded, if not dominated, Lansing. Then within three months Beard took it all back. New evidence satisfied him that Bryan not only consented to the reversal of his own policy before Lansing acted but also pursued a disingenuous and hypocritical course in demanding that his inconsistency be kept secret. Somewhat chastened, Beard confessed that the Great Commoner, the hero of the revisionists, also had feet of clay. Wryly he concluded: "Verily, writing history is a dangerous trade."

A second special study to influence future authors was the crisply written, cogently argued *Neutrality for the United States* (1937) by Edwin Borchard and W. P. Lage. Borchard, a disciple of John Bassett Moore, had long been critical of our wartime diplomacy. Now with Lage he attributed our involvement primarily to the blundering failure of Wilson and his advisers to follow recognized rules of neutrality. The two men stressed particularly the novel claim of immunity for American citizens who traveled on armed belligerent merchantmen as a factor in our intervention. They found the acme of ineptitude in the "strict accountability" note of February 10, 1915 and in the State Department memorandum of March 4, 1916, justifying the withdrawal of the Lansing compromise. Few reviewers have dared to challenge this legal brief, although several have insisted that it did not tell the whole story. Dissenters from—or, better, qualifiers of—the Borchard thesis deplored the cavalier dismissal of economic and emotional forces. They argued that we cannot prove that acceptance of the Lansing formula would have ended the sinking of unarmed ships, belligerent or neutral; they rejected the book's assumption that an embargo by the United States or the closing of our ports to armed ships would have solved all difficulties. Nevertheless, the Borchard influence can be detected in the later works of Tansill, Morrissey, and Bailey.

Of the three general accounts published after Millis from 1935 to 1939, the first to appear was Frederic L. Paxson's *Pre-War Years, 1914–*

1917 (1936). Like Seymour, Paxson had long specialized in the period; but his volume was unenthusiastically received by the profession, perhaps because it offered no novel interpretation, perhaps because it lacked documentation, perhaps because its jerky style and kaleidoscopic presentation recalled McMaster. Yet Paxson's skillful mingling of domestic and foreign affairs was just what most revisionists had failed to achieve. The tone of the book, moreover, was excellent and the objectivity commendable. Paxson avoided sarcasm, innuendo, second-guessing and devil-hunting. He did not demolish straw men to prove his erudition. He was especially good at saying a lot in a few words, at stripping complex matters to essentials. Very praiseworthy were his summaries of pressure groups, of the debates in Congress and of the election of 1916. He was the first to expose the revisionist distortion of the "He Kept Us Out of War" campaign. Paxson also suggested, but did not develop, the global implications of the First World War. In short, his is a difficult but perceptive book, one that merits rereading, one that the specialist can best appreciate.

A second general account can be pieced together from the fifth and sixth volumes of Ray Stannard Baker's *Woodrow Wilson: Life and Letters* (1935, 1937). Baker, too, was fitted by past experience to undertake the task. Although not a trained historian and too dependent on research assistants, he did attempt a scholarly work. He was the first to use the Wilson Papers. Baker was the authorized biographer but not an hagiographer. He retained his dignity and that of his subject throughout. He did not ridicule or impugn motives. He agreed with Seymour that the resumption of submarine warfare was the occasion of our intervention, but he recognized that economic considerations governed several momentous White House decisions. Baker paid close attention to related domestic problems. He frequently insisted that political isolation was impossible in a world of economic unity. Since the Wilson story contains elements of Greek tragedy, his volumes possess a dramatic quality.

But the Baker biography also has its defects. The Wilson manuscripts seemed to reveal surprisingly little that was new, and some suspect there is more to be found. The remaining research was narrow. No other personal papers were examined and only one newspaper was consulted. Wilson's untenable position on armed merchantmen was not emphasized. The treatment of House was unsatisfactory and unfair; echoes of Paris in 1919 could still be heard. Lastly, the portrait of Wilson was blurred. At times he was depicted as a strong, confident executive; at others, he appeared dependent upon and misled by his advisers. The author did not enhance the President's prestige by attributing his mistakes to House or Lansing. All in all, the Baker version is adequate, but there is every reason to anticipate a decided improvement from Arthur Link.

The last general account of these years was Charles C. Tansill's *America Goes to War* (1938). In some ways any discussion of intervention in 1917 should begin and end with Professor Tansill, for it is against his volume that all future work will be judged. Tansill devoted ten years to the enterprise and even resigned his teaching position so he could finish the task. No other writer has even come close to matching his extensive research. Tansill was the first to exploit the Lansing manuscripts, the minutes of the Neutrality Board, and selected data from the archives of the German Foreign Office and Admiralty. He squeezed more out of the Bryan Papers than did Curti, more out of the Kitchin Papers than did Arnett. Only the Wilson Collection was closed to him, and Baker's sixth volume appeared too late to use. Tansill was a multiple causationist; he offered no single, simple explanation of why we fought. He insisted in his preface that he had no thesis to prove or crusades to win. On subjects he chose to discuss, his treatment was exhaustive and his facts accurate. Allan Nevins declared that "at many points [it] approaches finality." Henry Commager called it "one of the notable achievements of historical scholarship of this generation." The total sale must have been about five thousand copies.

Yet, as some dissenting reviewers observed, it may be doubted that even for this generation Tansill's is the last word. For one thing, it was traditional diplomatic history with little attention to public opinion, pressure groups, Congress, or strategic factors. Tansill did allot one chapter to American sentiment in August 1914, but he did not carry the topic onward. He was disappointingly brief on preparedness, pacifism, and propaganda. He was not interested in popular writings about the war or about America's role in world affairs. He ignored the issue of American security. There was not a word on the global aspects of the war: our fears in the Caribbean and South America, the question of independence for the Philippines or the Japanese advance in China and the western Pacific. Tansill did almost nothing, save for the Gore-McLemore resolutions, with Congressional debates and alignments; and the election of 1916 was barely mentioned. The twelve pages devoted to the critical weeks after February 4, 1917 are wholly inadequate. The account of economic entanglements is very detailed but, as Paul Birdsall has said, "almost totally lacking in interpretative treatment and completely lacking in synthesis." In short, one can, in retrospect, doubt that Tansill considered the problem of American intervention in its broadest terms.

In the second place, the volume was predicated on an assumption which many historians do not now share. Professor Tansill regarded our entry into the war as a mistake. He believed that a German victory would have been a lesser evil than our participation. We shall never know; but we ought to recognize that his conviction, right or wrong, colored the book. One senses that the German case is treated more sympathetically than the Allied. German newspapers were read but not the British. The harsh Allied peace terms of January 10, 1917 were mentioned in the text, but the equally severe German ones escaped in a footnote. Tansill was hostile to, not just critical of, all who sincerely believed we must fight. He made no attempt to understand Roosevelt or Lodge. His handling of House and Lansing was devil-hunting of the grossest sort. He impugned motives without proof, such as Lansing's zeal for promotion. He indulged in sarcasm and insinuation that do not belong in a scholarly work. Even the portrait of Wilson, ostensibly friendly, recalls Henry Adams' depiction of Jefferson. Adams repeatedly asserted that Jefferson was a great man and then took four volumes to show that he was not.

A third criticism of *America Goes to War* has to do with organization. Can a topical presentation, such as Tansill employs, properly convey the intricate connections, diplomatic and domestic, of the neutrality years? When Tansill describes American yielding to British illegalities in 1914–15, the reader is still unaware of the simultaneous disputes with Germany over the submarine. By the time the author gets around to the House mission of 1915, the events that called it forth are three hundred pages back.

Finally, Tansill occasionally seemed to strain the evidence to fit his ideas. Bryan is a hero. The Nye documents revealed a flattering pattern of consistency on loans and credits. But when Beard offered new data to destroy the picture, Tansill cited the article but minimized the conclusion. The basic portrait of Bryan was left unchanged. House is an evil genius. The thesis of an entire chapter, "Colonel House Blocks a Path to Peace," rested on a single cablegram of February 14, 1916. Certainly the German declaration of February 8, and the mounting

Republican protest (as manifested by the Sterling resolution and speeches by Root and Lodge— none of which Tansill mentioned) must share with that sole cablegram the explanation of the Wilson-Lansing retreat from the proposal of January 18. And certainly there is slight evidence for the frequent speculations and numerous "might have beens" that dot the pages and inevitably lead the reader where he should not be led. . . .

In the ten years since 1939 historians have written relatively little on the problem of intervention. There have been three monographs on public opinion in single states, Ruhl Bartlett's excellent *League to Enforce Peace* (1944), Outten Clinard's suggestive but inconclusive study on Japan, and a few articles on the newspaper press. But no full-length story has been attempted, and the best-rounded recent accounts must be sought in our textbooks in diplomatic history. These texts have shown a tendency to soften certain criticisms prominent in the late 'thirties, as a comparison of the three editions of Bailey's work will show. In general, the submarine is still regarded as the immediate cause of our intervention. Since Borchard wrote, more attention has been paid to the armed merchantmen issue. Less emphasis is now placed on the persuasiveness of British propaganda. Walter Millis has called for a fresh study of the whole problem, while between 1940 and 1942 Bailey markedly modified his position. Few today would deny the importance of trade and finance in making our participation more likely; but it is now agreed that the entire nation, not a selfish few, benefited from wartime commerce and that Wilson's final casting of the die was not governed by material considerations. The economic motive was not uppermost in the American decision for war, but it was a decisive factor in Germany's renewal of the U-boat campaign.

The one new interpretation stressed since 1939 is that the United States intervened in 1917 to safeguard its security. A more restricted version is that we sought to maintain Anglo-American control of the Atlantic. This security idea naturally appealed to many when Nazi legions bestrode the Continent and threatened England and the Royal Navy. It is not surprising that it was popularized by two newspapermen, Walter Lippmann and Forrest Davis, in the year of decision, 1941. Very few specialists have wholly accepted the Lippmann-Davis thesis, but all agree that strategic concepts merit closer scrutiny. Van Alstyne has asserted that though some Americans in 1917 thought in terms of security "at no time during the First World War was the United States conscious of fighting a war for survival." Edward M. Earle has said that our motive in 1917 should have been to redress the European balance of power; "but no evidence, conclusive beyond reasonable doubt, has been brought to light to show that Wilson ... was consciously influenced by such considerations or by fear that a German victory might jeopardize American security." Bailey has insisted that security became the objective of our intervention but that it was never the cause. John Hicks has quoted Davis approvingly; while Dexter Perkins, after manifesting some hesitation, has urged further study of the problem. ...

It is to be hoped that future studies will take a broader view of the neutrality years. It is imperative that future historians treat American intervention in 1917 as but a single step, albeit an important one, in the transition of the United States from a role of relative indifference to world affairs to one of active participation. Perhaps when that point is grasped, they will be more tolerant than their predecessors of the hesitations, inconsistencies, and even mistakes of those who steered the ship of state in 1914. They may even come to concede that Wilson and his advisers were men genuinely puzzled and perplexed by a changing world order—the outlines of which a few but dimly glimpsed—rather than clumsy bunglers, exponents of double talk, or traitorous tools of the Allies. The witch-hunting tactics of the early revisionists and their followers should be avoided. Not until then shall we possess, with the perspective of another global upheaval, a more rounded and more realistic understanding of the problem of American intervention in 1917.

WORLD WAR I

II
THE CRUSADERS AND THE CRITICS: GERMAN

A

THE GERMAN CROWN COUNCIL DEBATES RESUMPTION OF
UNRESTRICTED SUBMARINE WARFARE
AUGUST 31, 1916; AND JANUARY 9, 1917

". . . time is working against us; the blockade of Germany is
becoming more and more oppressive. . . . If His Majesty commands
that a ruthless U-boat war shall be launched, the Chancellor will
endeavor to succeed in keeping America 'out of it.' For this purpose,
certain concessions already taken up previously with the Admiralty
Staff would have to be made. But we will have to calculate upon
America's entrance into the war against us."

[Pless Castle, August 31, 1916]

Admiral v. HOLTZENDORFF, after reading an official comment concerning the present determination of the U-boat question, said: According to the general military situation, we are placed in a situation of
defense; the continuation of the war on the part of our opponents is
completely dependent upon England's attitude; it is therefore necessary
for us to prevent England, by the use of all means in our power, from
continuing to carry on the war, and the destruction of England's ocean
commerce will accomplish this purpose; the last memorial of the
Admiralty Staff sets out plainly what the result of this destruction would
be.

Carnegie Endowment for International Peace, *Official German Documents Relating
to the World War*, 2 Vols. New York & London: Carnegie Endowment for International
Peace, 1923, II, 1317–1321. Reprinted by permission.

The reaction of the United States and the remaining neutral Powers is used as an argument against carrying on the unrestricted U-boat warfare; that in such case the entire shipping space of the world would be made available to England; that Russia's incapacity to carry out a third winter campaign and its necessity for peace are also arguments against the taking up of the U-boat war at an early date.

In the meanwhile, time is working against us; the blockade of Germany is becoming more and more oppressive; as the result of a good harvest we will be less dependent upon imports, and, speaking from the military standpoint, we can maintain an effective defensive.

So far as the neutrals are concerned, Holland will attack the first one to put foot upon her territory; the entrance of Denmark into the war is very improbable; England will not be able to gain in freight space; no freight space will be placed at its disposal by any action of the United States; nor is this likely to be the case with regard to the South American States, since they themselves are suffering from a shortage of tonnage; the tonnage of those of our ships which are in the possession of the enemy is negligible; it is within our power to break England's determination to carry on the war to the end of the year; to put off commencing the U-boat war would put off the results in question; in this connection the question must be well considered as to whether our allies will be able to hold out any longer; if we renounce the use of the U-boat weapon we may have reason to believe that this means *finis Germaniae.*

Secretary of State v. JAGOW: Unrestricted U-boat war would in any event mean the breaking of diplomatic relations with the United States, and, if American lives are lost, would finally lead to war; if the last neutral world Power were to take the side of the Entente, the smaller neutral States would be left with no choice other than to work with us or against us. (Here follow comments about the European neutral Powers.) If we take up unrestricted U-boat warfare, the attitude of all neutral Powers will be changed against us and we shall have to calculate upon establishing new fronts. Germany will in such case be looked upon as a mad dog against whom the hand of every man will be raised for the purpose of finally bringing about peace....

Secretary of State [Karl] HELFFERICH: It is to be admitted that the situation both here and in England for launching a U-boat war is more favorable now than it was a year ago or in the spring, because at that time the mere blockade on the part of the neutrals would have been sufficient to starve us. Our harvest is notably better than it was last year, but at the same time we shall be pinched, and every importation would be welcome by us. . . .

The reactions of the U-boat war from the political and economic standpoint must not be underestimated. Everybody is perfectly convinced that a break with the United States and a war with the United States would be unavoidable. The assumption that the hostile attitude of the United States can not reach a higher pitch so far as we are concerned, is erroneous. Up to the present time, the Allies have received from the United States in the way of loans $1,250,000,000. In the case of war, America will stand ready with all of its reserves available for the cause of the Allies, which will then become the cause of the United States. America will desire to win the war as quickly as possible and will summon all its energies for putting this wish into execution. Acting in cooperation with England, the very strongest kind of pressure can be exerted upon the neutral Powers to join the Entente. Since Denmark and Holland are dependent upon imports by water, they will be utterly unable to oppose it. We have no means of exerting pressure to avoid this result. Our need for iron is now so urgent that we are already at the point at which we can release no more. Holland can obtain from England, with limitations, whatever she needs in the way of coal. I see nothing but catastrophe following the application of the U-boat weapon at this time. A method which will lead us out of one serious situation only into the toils of another more serious, is not practical if we are not able to adopt counter-measures for the purpose of rendering the otherwise disadvantageous result ineffectual. . . .

Imperial Chancelor v. BETHMANN-HOLLWEG notes a reservation with regard to the report of his views contained in the written comment which was read by Admiral v. Holtzendorff, and continues as follows: I take the stand that the decision of the U-boat question must depend very greatly on the estimate of the military situation made by the Supreme High Command. According to the view of Field Marshal v. Hindenburg, with whom I have had a preliminary conference, no decision, either *pro* or *con*, can be reached as long as the military situation resulting from the participation of Roumania is not clear. According to my personal opinion the declaration of a U-boat war would be looked upon as an act of desperation both by the hostile and neutral world, as well as by a great portion of our own people. It would be very inadvisable to label such an undertaking from the very outset as an act of desperation.

If we combine the results of the statements made yesterday and today, no one will doubt that we shall be able to rely upon the destruction of, roughly speaking, 4 million tons of British shipping within from four to six months. The Admiralty Staff is of the opinion that England will then be ready to conclude peace. This opinion is considered by other gentlemen, for instance, by Secretary of State Helfferich, as of doubtful correctness, and nobody can prove that the hoped-for success will really come about. I, too, believe that this is merely an assumption. It is certain that a complete blockade from and to England can not be carried out, because U-boats can undertake nothing in the night time. We can lay down no iron ring around England, and, moreover, our blockade can be broken by the accompaniment of transports by war-ships. I have understood Admiral v. Holtzendorff to say that intercourse to and from Holland and Denmark can be stopped. Will it be possible to do this if, at the same time, we are carrying on an intensive U-boat war against the English coast?

We must realize that the break with the United States will certainly follow the launching of the U-boat war. . . .

I believe that a decision with regard to the launching of the U-boat war without an understanding with our allies is out of the question. We must calculate, in this connection, on the contingency that Turkey will be alienated from us. . . . Nor can we involve Austria-Hungary in a war with the remaining neutral Powers without asking her opinion in the matter. If the Roumanian war were to turn out unfavorably for us, the U-boat war would avail us nothing; if Austria-Hungary falls to pieces, I do not know whether we shall be able to put up any further opposition. For these reasons, a final decision seems to me to be possible only after a clearing up of the military situation. . . .

[Pless Castle, January 9, 1917]

The CHANCELOR: If His Majesty commands that a ruthless U-boat war shall be launched, the Chancelor will endeavor to succeed in keeping America "out of it." For this purpose, certain concessions already taken up previously with the Admiralty Staff would have to be made. But we will have to calculate upon America's entrance into the war against us.

The Chancelor feels more assurance about the attitude of the European neutrals. Our peace note has brought good results. Holland and Denmark will not enter the war, at least not as long as they do not see that the U-boat war brings us no success.

With regard to Switzerland, we shall have to bear in mind the possibility that the Entente will bring pressure to bear on Switzerland if food becomes scarce in that country, to make it possible for French armies to march through or even for Switzerland to join the cause of the Entente.

Denmark will possibly lay up its shipping.

The Chancelor requests that the military measures which are to be taken with regard to the neutral boundaries, and particularly with regard to the Danish boundary, be such as not to carry the implication of excessive menace.

GENERAL LUDENDORFF: The purpose is just to detail a few regiments of cavalry to the borders.

CHANCELOR: The determination to launch the unrestricted U-boat war depends, then, upon the results which we may expect. Admiral v. Holtzendorff assumes that we will have England on her knees by the next harvest. The experiences of the U-boats during the last few months, the increased number of U-boats, and England's bad economic situation, will at least increase our chances of success.

On the whole, the prospects for the unrestricted U-boat war are very favorable.

Of course, it must be admitted that those prospects are not capable of being demonstrated by proof.

We should be perfectly certain that, so far as the military situation is concerned, great military strokes are insufficient as such to win the war.

The U-boat war is the "last card." A very serious decision. "But if the military authorities consider the U-boat war essential, I am not in a position to contradict them."

FIELD MARSHAL: We are ready to meet all eventualities and to meet America, Denmark, Holland, and Switzerland too.

The restricted U-boat war on commerce will only bring a slight increase in the results reached up to this time. We need the most energetic, ruthless methods which can be adopted. For this reason, we need the ruthless U-boat war to start from February 1, 1917.

The war must be brought to an end rapidly, although we would be able to hold out still longer, but haste is needed on account of our allies.

CHANCELOR: It may be imagined that the U-boat war might postpone the end of hostilities.

GENERAL LUDENDORFF: The U-boat war will also bring our armies into a different and a better situation. Through the lack of wood needed for mining purposes and for lack of coal, the production of ammunition is hard pressed. It means that there will be some relief for the western front. We must spare the troops a second battle of the Somme. That this relief will come about will be proved by our own situation and the effects of our transportation crisis.

And, too, Russia's power of initiative will be detrimentally affected by the lack of ammunition which will result from shortage in tonnage. The Siberian railroad alone will not be sufficient for Russia's needs.

CHANCELOR: America's assistance, in case she enters the war, will consist in the delivery of food supplies to England, financial support, delivery of airplanes and the dispatching of corps of volunteers.

FIELD MARSHAL: We can take care of that. The opportunity for the U-boat war is such that it can perhaps never become as favorable again; we can carry it on and we must carry it on.

CHANCELOR: Of course, if success beckons, we must follow.

FIELD MARSHAL: We would reproach ourselves later if we let the opportunity pass by.

CHANCELOR: The situation is certainly better than it was in September.

GENERAL LUDENDORFF: The measures of security taken against the neutrals will have nothing about them in the nature of a challenge; they will be purely defensive measures.

CHANCELOR: And suppose Switzerland came into the war, or that the French were to come through Switzerland.

FIELD MARSHAL: That would not be unfavorable from a military standpoint.

B
GERMANY ANNOUNCES THE RESUMPTION OF
UNRESTRICTED SUBMARINE WARFARE
JANUARY 31, 1917

"In waging war with such aims, the Entente allies are violating
all rules of international law, as they prevent the legitimate trade
of neutrals with the Central powers, and of the neutrals among
themselves. . . . Germany is unable further to forego the full use of
her submarines. . . . The Imperial Government is confident that
this measure will result in a speedy termination of the war and in
the restoration of peace which the Goverment of the United States
has so much at heart."

WASHINGTON, *January 31, 1917.*
MR. SECRETARY OF STATE: . . . Enclosing two memoranda regarding
the details of the contemplated military measures at sea, I remain [etc.]
J. BERNSTORFF

MEMORANDUM

After bluntly refusing Germany's peace offer, the Entente powers stated
in their note addressed to the American Government that they are
determined to continue the war in order to deprive Germany of German
provinces in the West and the East, to destroy Austria-Hungary, and
to annihilate Turkey. In waging war with such aims, the Entente allies
are violating all rules of international law, as they prevent the legitimate
trade of neutrals with the Central powers, and of the neutrals among
themselves. Germany has, so far, not made unrestricted use of the
weapon which she possesses in her submarines. Since the Entente
powers, however, have made it impossible to come to an understanding
based upon equality of rights of all nations, as proposed by the Central
powers, and have instead declared only such a peace to be possible which
shall be dictated by the Entente allies and shall result in the destruction

Papers Relating to the Foreign Relations of the United States, 1917, Supplement I,
The World War. Washington: Government Printing Office, 1931, 97; 100–102.

and humiliation of the Central powers, Germany is unable further to forego the full use of her submarines. The Imperial Government, therefore, does not doubt that the Government of the United States will understand the situation thus forced upon Germany by the Entente allies' brutal methods of war and by their determination to destroy the Central powers, and that the Government of the United States will further realize that the now openly disclosed intentions of the Entente allies give back to Germany the freedom of action which she reserved in her note addressed to the Government of the United States on May 4, 1916.

Under these circumstances Germany will meet the illegal measures of her enemies by forcibly preventing after February 1, 1917, in a zone around Great Britain, France, Italy, and in the eastern Mediterranean all navigation, that of neutrals included, from and to England and from and to France, etc., etc. All ships met within that zone will be sunk.

The Imperial Government is confident that this measure will result in a speedy termination of the war and in the restoration of peace which the Government of the United States has so much at heart. Like the Government of the United States, Germany and her allies had hoped to reach this goal by negotiations. Now that the war, through the fault of Germany's enemies, has to be continued, the Imperial Government feels sure that the Government of the United States will understand the necessity of adopting such measures as are destined to bring about a speedy end of the horrible and useless bloodshed. The Imperial Government hopes all the more for such an understanding of her position, as the neutrals have under the pressure of the Entente powers, suffered great losses, being forced by them either to give up their entire trade or to limit it according to conditions arbitrarily determined by Germany's enemies in violation of international law.

MEMORANDUM

From February 1, 1917, all sea traffic will be stopped with every available weapon and without further notice in the following blockade zones around Great Britain, France, Italy, and in the Eastern Mediterranean. . . .

Sailing of regular American passenger steamers may continue undisturbed after February 1, 1917, if—

(*a*)   the port of destination is Falmouth.

(*b*)   sailing to or coming from that port course is taken via the Scilly Islands and a point 50°N. 20°W.

(*c*)   the steamers are marked in the following way which must not be allowed to other vessels in American ports: On ship's hull and superstructure 3 vertical stripes 1 meter wide each to be painted alternately white and red. Each mast should show a large flag checkered white and red, and the stern the American national flag.

Care should be taken that, during dark, national flag and painted marks are easily recognizable from a distance and that the boats are well lighted throughout.

(*d*)   one steamer a week sails in each direction with arrival at Falmouth on Sunday and departs from Falmouth on Wednesday.

(*e*)   the United States Government guarantees that no contraband (according to German contraband list) is carried by those steamers.

C
PROFESSOR ERNEST R. MAY ON THE DILEMMAS OF GERMAN CHANCELLOR BETHMANN-HOLLWEG

"To temporize was, of course, Bethmann's way. He was scarcely a figure of fire and granite. But circumstances made it literally impossible for him to choose one of the drastic alternatives. He could not decide to abandon the submarine permanently. . . . Nor, on the other hand, could Bethmann bring himself to opt for an unrestricted U-boat campaign. Neither his conscience nor his political judgment would allow him to do so."

After the spring of 1915, the burden of choice between war and peace lay upon the German government. Wilson had apparently threatened

Ernest R. May, *The World and American Isolation, 1914–1917.* Chicago: Quadrangle Paperbacks, 1966, pp. 197–203; 387; 393–394; 404–405; 409–415. Reprinted by permission.

war if U-boats were allowed to attack passenger liners. By declaring that his demands on Germany were quite independent of any made upon Britain, he encouraged no hope that the threat might be lifted. Germany had to deny herself the use of the weapon in order to keep the peace or else strike at England and risk war. Chancellor Bethmann Hollweg had no doubt that the more important aim was to keep America neutral, and he was prepared to sacrifice the U-boat campaign or any part of it in order to keep the peace. Neither the Navy Ministry nor the Naval Staff agreed with him; the admirals insisted that the submarine weapon should be used to the full, come what might, and their pleas were supported by powerful blocs among the Reichstag and the public. It was necessarily Germany's policy, therefore, to carry on the U-boat war at whatever pitch the United States would allow. The result, both internationally and internally, was a rising rhythm of lull and crisis.

To temporize was, of course, Bethmann's way. He was scarcely a figure of fire and granite. But circumstances made it literally impossible for him to choose one of the drastic alternatives. He could not decide to abandon the submarine permanently. The Kaiser probably could not have been brought to approve such a policy, and, in any case, the decision would have shaken the unity of the nation, cut the Chancellor off from the Reichstag and the country, and perhaps imperiled the foundations of the Empire. Nor, on the other hand could Bethmann bring himself to opt for an unrestricted U-boat campaign. Neither his conscience nor his political judgment would allow him to do so.

He was convinced that the submarine could not achieve decisive results in the war with England. "A peace forced upon England by the U-boat war," he wrote, "would be equivalent to public acknowledgment that England's supremacy at sea had been destroyed by Germany's sea power. Before England would make up her mind to make such an acknowledgment, she would sacrifice the last man and the last penny." The best impartial advice given him was to the effect that, in the first place, the submarines could stop only a fraction of Britain's imports and, in the second place, that ruthlessness on Germany's part merely intensified the English will to fight.

He was also certain that an all-out U-boat campaign would bring the United States into the war, with disastrous results for Germany. "It is absolutely beyond doubt," he said to the Reichstag budget committee, "that if today I proclaim a ruthless U-boat war, tomorrow

America will have broken with us." The effect of such a break, he believed, would be to bring all the European neutrals into the war on the Allied side. . . .

Quite apart from its effect on European neutrals, the intervention of the United States would in itself, Bethmann thought, have cataclysmic results for Germany. There is a memorandum in the Secret File of the Foreign Ministry Archives which, if not Bethmann's, at least reflects his views. Itemizing the probable results of armed intervention by the United States, it mentions the financing of Germany's enemies, a doubling of their munitions imports, a reinforcement of Allied armies by the enlistment of American volunteers, "liquidation of the Balkans," and privations for Germany herself. Intervention by the United States, the Chancellor did assert, would prolong the war by two years, and unlimited U-boat war was therefore the *ultima ratio*. "It represents such a challenge," he declared in 1916, "that it [could] . . . signify *finis Germaniae*."

Holding such views, Bethmann could not bring himself to sanction a defiant submarine campaign. Although he was temperamentally disinclined to battle for convictions, he could not allow the admirals to ignore political considerations, to bet on their optimistic estimates of the U-boat's capabilities, and to make war on the United States. He felt obliged to fight with every resource against a decision in favor of an unlimited U-boat campaign.

At the same time, he was almost incapable of forcing a decision to abandon the weapon. The admirals would not accept his reasoning. Tirpitz and the successive Chiefs of the Naval Staff staked their experience and professional reputations upon the prediction that an all-out campaign would bring England to her knees before American intervention could affect the outcome for the war. Bethmann could caution the admirals of dangers, but he could not change their minds. He was continually in the position of seeming to place political ahead of military considerations.

As one result, he depended very heavily on the support of the army, although the army did not accept all his premises. Falkenhayn thought the navy's proposals untimely rather than pernicious. Eager to believe the admirals' prophecies, he said repeatedly that submarine commanders should be given their freedom as soon as the military situation permitted. The general did not share Bethmann's dread of the United States herself. . . .

Outside imperial councils, moreover, a decision to give up the U-boat would have met opposition in the Reichstag and among the public. The right-wing parties were fanatical in their enthusiasm for unrestricted U-boat war. Not only did they disagree with the Chancellor's reasoning, but they chafed at his temporizing policy and criticized it as openly as the *Burgfrieden* and the German political tradition permitted. In this attitude they were supported by a large segment of the *Zentrum* and even by Progressives.

The right-wing press challenged all the Chancellor's premises. It insisted, in the first place, that the U-boat could bring England to her knees. When a retired admiral published an article declaring that the submarine could not win the war, the journals that deigned to notice it commented with derision. The Hamburg Chamber of Commerce passed a resolution of condemnation, and two of the city's newspapers, the *Nachrichten* and the *Fremdenblatt*, denounced such writing as treasonable. When Captain Persius, the respected naval expert of the *Berliner Tageblatt*, suggested that the claims of U-boat enthusiasts might be exaggerated, even this modest warning provoked scorn and anger. Conservatives, Free Conservatives, National Liberals, and right Centrists would hear no denial of the U-boat's effectiveness.

They insisted, too, that no serious consequences were to be feared from war with the United States. At the time of the strict accountability note the *Berliner Zeitung* declared of America, "She has no army, and her fleet would not dare to approach nearer our shores than does the English. The expulsion of Germans from America would mean her ruin. America's threats are simply ridiculous, and it is more than ridiculous to take them in earnest." The conservative *Tägliche Rundschau* declared that Germany had nothing to lose except the nice new ships sitting idle in American harbors, and a writer in *Der Tag* pointed out contemptuously that the United states had shown herself too feeble even to deal with Mexico.

Nor was such comment confined to journals of the far right. The *Kölnische Volkszeitung*, a Centrist organ, declared that Americans would not go to war because they lacked the martial virtues, and war "requires so many sacrifices and destroys business." The Progressive *Vossische Zeitung* printed an article by the eminent classical scholar, Eduard Meyer, asserting that Wilson would not be able to go to war if he wanted to. Even the Social Democratic *Vorwärts*, which commented skeptically on Meyer's prediction, suggested that American pacifism was probably powerful enough to prevent armed retaliation against a German U-boat campaign. And challenges to this complacency were usually either mild, like the *Münchener Neueste Nachrichten's* observation that Germany should keep the peace in order to protect German-Americans. . . .

Confronted with such a state of parliamentary and public opinion, Bethmann could not easily carry a proposal to abandon the submarine weapon. He felt obliged, indeed, to make a public pretense of sympathy with the U-boat enthusiasts. . . .

The four weeks from December 12, 1916, to January 9, 1917, brought the tragic climax to Bethmann's long struggle for peace with America. He offered to end the war. Had he succeeded, the German-American issue would have dissolved. Had he even been able to link his own peace hopes with Wilson's, he might have looosened the knots in German-American relations. But his peace effort failed not only to close the war but even to prevent a break with the United States. It was over-taken by a decision in favor of unrestricted U-boat war. . . .

Bethmann's decision to offer peace can only be understood as an act of despair. Not that he assumed Germany to be beaten; he knew the military and economic plight of the Allies to be no better than that of the Central Powers. What made him desperate was an expectation that Germany's situation would get no better, that the Austrian and Turkish allies were losing heart, and that the German government, over which he was fast losing control, would eventually commit suicide with the U-boat weapon. It was not in order to prepare the way for a submarine decision that Bethmann offered to make peace; it was to prevent that decision.

The Chancellor must also have been prompted, of course, by a recognition of his own weakening power. The new Supreme Command was gradually substituting its authority for his. The *Zentrum* resolution had demonstrated that the Chancellor no longer commanded the Reichstag. If peace negotiations were to begin, however, his words would once again become weightier than Hindenburg's, not only with the Kaiser but with the Reichstag as well. The U-boat bloc would break up. On the issue of moderate as opposed to annexationist terms, it seemed as if he could reunite his left and center support. The socialist peace manifesto, letters to the Chancellor from Progressive deputies, and editorials in the Centrist *Germania* foreshadowed the peace resolution majority of the succeeding year. The opening of peace negotiations must have seemed to Bethmann the sole means of saving Germany from her own madness and of rescuing himself and the imperial constitution that he symbolized. . . .

Even while the Chancellor awaited responses to his appeal, the decisive moment for German-American relations arrived. The Supreme Command, which had been threatening to do so for months, resolved in favor of unrestricted U-boat war. The Chancellor, having lost control of the Reichstag, also lost command over the Kaiser. He found himself unable to resist.

A test with the Supreme Command had been impending ever since Hindenburg and Ludendorff succeeded Falkenhayn. At their very first conference, it will be remembered, the generals had dismayed Bethmann by declaring that as soon as the military situation altered they would have to resort to a U-boat campaign. Bethmann's uneasiness at this declaration had been reflected two days later when he made his first genuine solicitation of an American peace move.

The likelihood of an early option for the U-boat by the Supreme Command had appeared at the time when the peace move was first decided upon. When Bethmann secured the Kaiser's approval of an overture through Bernstorff, he suggested warning mildly of a possible necessity for resuming submarine warfare. It was Ludendorff who insisted that the message should begin with a ringing affirmation of confidence in victory and that it should say, "the Imperial fleet promises that swift success will follow the unrestricted participation of an increased number of U-boats. . . . For this reason, the Supreme Command must take the unrestricted U-boat war into consideration in the course of their calculations, in order to relieve the situation at the Somme front." Ludendorff had desired, indeed, that the message declare unequivocally, "we must regain the freedom of action which we reserved for ourselves" in the *Sussex* pledge. . . .

As soon as the peace offer had been made, Ludendorff returned to the attack. He left the conference at Pless to visit the Somme front. There he became even more convinced that it was necessary to cut off the enemy's supplies across the Channel. He may also have regarded the evident lack of enthusiasm on the part of German troops as a partial result of the peace proposal itself. Seizing upon almost the first excuse, at any rate, he telegraphed Berlin that the Chancellor's effort had failed. The evidence that he cited was Lloyd George's preliminary speech to the House of Commons, the one quoting Lincoln against peace without victory. "Since Lloyd George has rejected our peace proposal . . . ," he declared, "I am of the opinion that ... the U-boat war should now be launched with the greatest vigor." Although the Chancellor protested that his note had not even been answered as yet, Ludendorff would not retreat. He threatened a cabinet crisis, declaring "that the Field Marshal would no longer be able to shoulder the responsibility of the campaign in case the government should not agree."

There resulted a direct clash between the Chancellor and the Supreme Command. The question, Bethmann wrote to Hindenburg, is one "of foreign policy for which I have to bear the sole responsibility, a responsibility which is constitutional and can not be delegated." The Chancellor promised, it is true, to take full account of the Supreme Command's views. He volunteered to approve a campaign against armed merchant vessels as soon as the Allies formally answered his peace note, and he offered to discuss the issue of unrestricted warfare "as soon as our peace move has been brought to a definite conclusion as the result of the answer which the Entente will make." But Ludendorff would not be put off. Over Hindenburg's signature the Chancellor was warned that the majority of the German people regarded the Supreme Command as sharing responsibility. If their views were rejected, the generals would have to announce their disagreement publicly.

Bethmann hurried to Pless on December 29 for a confrontation with the generals. Judging from his past tactics and from the sparse evidence available, it can be inferred that he hoped to outmaneuver the generals. The question of a limited campaign, directed only against armed vessels, had been under discussion since the previous October. Bethmann had approved it in principle but insisted that no order be issued until the peace proposal bore fruit and until the American government had been prepared for it.... With regard to the U-boat matter, he had no choice but to set forth his views fully:

> Never have I sought ... to restrain the Supreme Command. It is not now possible ... for them independently to command a ruthless U-boat war. First we have to take back the promises we have made to America. That is a political act, for which constitutionally I alone bear responsibility.... Since the retraction of our promises could mean war with America, my responsibility in the question is a fateful one. Obviously the opinion of the Supreme Command would have the greatest weight with me, and it is my strongest hope to bring about com-

plete understanding between us. Should that, contrary to my
hopes, prove impossible, then a combined audience before the
Kaiser will have to decide.

When he attempted to draw the generals into debate on the issues of a
limited campaign, they declined to argue. They accepted his conten-
tions but asserted that the real question still remained. Instead of discussing it, they turned to other matters. . . .

Barely a week later he found himself challenged once again. In
that short time his position had materially weakened. The Allied answer
to his peace note had been published. The Kaiser had angrily declared
that Germany now needed to fight on, that Belgium would have to be annexed, and that there could be no understanding with France. The
Emperor was no longer to be held in check by warnings against endan-
gering the peace move. Nor could the Chancellor any longer command
a peace bloc in the Reichstag. Even the majority socialists admitted in
their newspapers that the Allied reply killed all chances of immediate
negotiations. Progressive journals meanwhile sidled toward advocacy
of a U-boat campaign, and Progressive deputies were heard declaring
that the people would never forgive the government if it failed to use
all weapons to the full. Just as the Chancellor saw his grip loosening
over both the Kaiser and the country, he received from Hindenburg a
terse telegram declaring, "the military situation is such that unrestricted
U-boat warfare can begin on the 1st February and for that very reason
should begin."

Bethmann hurried once again to Pless. The decisive audience before
the Kaiser was scheduled to occur on the evening of January 9. He had
less than thirty hours in which to prepare for it. Although he talked
earnestly with Zimmermann and Helfferich before leaving Berlin,
neither could accompany him. Helfferich did sit up all night, however,
preparing an exhaustive memorandum which the Chancellor would
receive by telegraph. At Pless Bethmann found himself in for a lonely
struggle. Müller evidently offered him no help, saying simply that the
Kaiser's mind was already made up. Although Valentini still resolutely
opposed a U-boat campaign, he was confined to his bed. The Chancellor
did arrange that the final audience should be held in the chambers of
the Civil Cabinet chief. But he first had to meet Hindenburg and Ludendorff alone.

He spent the entire morning debating with the generals. There is no record of the arguments he employed, but they cannot have been much different from those he had advanced again and again. If he commented on the danger of drawing Holland and Denmark into the war, the generals replied that they were ready. The western front had been reinforced, and three cavalry brigades stood on the Danish frontier. The key problem was, of course, the United States. Bethmann still felt that a U-boat campaign would unquestionably bring America into the war and that her intervention would mean, at the very least, an interminable prolongation of hostilities. But Hindenburg had said to Holtzendorff on the previous day, "We are counting on the possibility of war with the United States, and have made all preparations to meet it. Things can not be worse than they are now." Ludendorff was to explain a few days later to the Austrian chief of staff that he did not believe the United States could supply more shipping or war material to the Allies, that money was of no importance, and that American contributions of manpower would be slow in arriving. Since Ludendorff was already convinced that he could not "work with" Bethmann, it is doubtful that he made any concessions at all. The Chancellor returned to Valentini's room at 1 o'clock grey and exhausted.

He realized that the issue was decided. Holtzendorff had prepared the Kaiser on the previous day. Müller would not stand out against the Supreme Command. When the Chancellor and the generals assembled before the throne in the evening, as Valentini has described:

> Everyone stood around a large table, on which the Kaiser, pale and excited, leaned his hand. Holtzendorff spoke first, and, from the standpoint of the navy, both well and above all in confidence of victory. England will lie on the ground in at most six months, before a single American has set foot on the continent; the American danger does not disturb him at all. Hindenburg spoke very briefly, observing only that from the measure a reduction in American munitions exports had to be expected. Bethmann finally, with a visible inner excitement, set forth once again the reasons that had led him in the past to cast an opposing vote against a U-boat war beyond the limits of cruiser warfare, namely concern about the prompt entry of America into the ranks of our enemies, with all the ensuing consequences, but he closed by saying that in view of the recently altered stand of the Supreme Command and the categorical de-

clarations of the admirals as to the success of the measure, he wished to withdraw his opposition. The Kaiser followed his statements with every sign of impatience and opposition and declared in closing that the unrestricted U-boat war was therefore decided.

The decision was final. . . .

WORLD WAR I

III
THE CRITICS:
AMERICAN

A

SENATOR ROBERT M. LAFOLLETTE
VIEWS AMERICAN ENTRY INTO THE WAR
AS A PLOT AGAINST THE POOR AND A DEFEAT FOR
DEMOCRACY
APRIL 4, 1917

"The poor, sir, who are the ones called upon to rot in the trenches,
have no organized power, have no press to voice their will upon this
question of peace or war; but, oh, Mr. President, at some time they
will be heard. I hope and I believe they will be heard in an orderly
and peaceful way. . . . Will the President and the supporters of this
war bill submit it to a vote of the people before the declaration of
war goes into effect?"

. . . The poor, sir, who are the ones called upon to rot in the trenches,
have no organized power, have no press to voice their will upon this
question of peace or war; but, oh, Mr. President, at some time they will
be heard. I hope and I believe they will be heard in an orderly and a
peaceful way. I think they may be heard from before long. I think, sir, if
we take this step, when the people to-day who are staggering under the
burden of supporting families at the present prices of the necessaries of
life find those prices multiplied, when they are raised a hundred per cent,
or 200 per cent, as they will be quickly, aye, sir, when beyond that those
who pay taxes come to have their taxes doubled and again doubled to pay
the interest on the nontaxable bonds held by Morgan and his combinations, which have been issued to meet this war, there will come an

Congressional Record, Senate, 65th Congress, 1st Session, Vol. 55, (April 4, 1917),
225–234.

awakening; they will have their day and they will be heard. It will be as certain and as inevitable as the return of the tides, and as resistless, too. . . .

Just a word of comment more upon one of the points in the President's address. He says that this is a war "for the things which we have always carried nearest to our hearts—for democracy, for the right of those who submit to authority to have a voice in their own government." In many places throughout the address is this exalted sentiment given expression.

It is a sentiment peculiarly calculated to appeal to American hearts and, when accompanied by acts consistent with it, is certain to receive our support; but in this same connection, and strangely enough, the President says that we have become convinced that the German Government as it now exists—"Prussian autocracy" he calls it—can never again maintain friendly relations with us. His expression is that "Prussian autocracy was not and could never be our friend," and repeatedly throughout the address the suggestion is made that if the German people would overturn their Government it would probably be the way to peace. So true is this that the dispatches from London all hailed the message of the President as sounding the death knell of Germany's Government.

But the President proposes alliance with Great Britain, which, however liberty-loving its people, is a hereditary monarchy, with a hereditary ruler, with a hereditary House of Lords, with a hereditary landed system, with a limited and restricted suffrage for one class and a multiplied suffrage power for another, and with grinding industrial conditions for all the wageworkers. The President has not suggested that we make our support of Great Britain conditional to her granting home rule to Ireland, or Egypt, or India. We rejoice in the establishment of a democracy in Russia, but it will hardly be contended that if Russia was still an autocratic Government, we would not be asked to enter this alliance with her just the same. Italy and the lesser powers of Europe, Japan in the Orient; in fact, all of the countries with whom we are to enter into alliance, except France and newly revolutionized Russia, are still of the old order—and it will be generally conceded that no one of them has done as much for its people in the solution of municipal problems and in securing social and industrial reforms as Germany.

Is it not a remarkable democracy which leagues itself with allies already far overmatching in strength the German nation and holds out to such beleaguered nation the hope of peace only at the price of giving up their Government? I am not talking now of the merits or demerits of any government, but I am speaking of a profession of democracy that is linked in action with the most brutal and domineering use of autocratic power. Are the people of this country being so well represented in this war movement that we need to go abroad to give other people control of their governments? Will the President and the supporters of this war bill submit it to a vote of the people before the declaration of war goes into effect? Until we are willing to do that, it illy becomes us to offer as an excuse for our entry into the war the unsupported claim that this war was forced upon the German people by their Government "without their previous knowledge or approval."

Who has registered the knowledge or approval of the American people of the course this Congress is called upon to take in declaring war upon Germany? Submit the question to the people, you who support it. You who support it dare not do it, for you know that by a vote of more than ten to one the American people as a body would register their declaration against it.

In the sense that this war is being forced upon our people without their knowing why and without their approval, and that wars are usually forced upon all peoples in the same way, there is some truth in the statement; but I venture to say that the response which the German people have made to the demands of this war shows that it has a degree of popular support which the war upon which we are entering has not and never will have among our people. The espionage bills, the conscription bills, and other forcible military measures which we understand are being ground out of the war machine in this country is the complete proof that those responsible for this war fear that it has no popular support and that armies sufficient to satisfy the demand of the entente allies can not be recruited by voluntary enlistments. . . .

B

SENATOR GEORGE W. NORRIS
SEES AMERICAN INVOLVEMENT
IN THE WAR AS A WALL STREET CONSPIRACY
APRIL 4, 1917

"Their object in having war and in preparing for war is to make money. Human suffering and the sacrifice of human life are necessary, but Wall Street considers only the dollars and the cents. . . . We are about to do the bidding of wealth's terrible mandate. . . . I feel that we are about to put the dollar sign upon the American flag."

. . . Mr. President, while I am most emphatically and sincerely opposed to taking any step that will force our country into the useless and senseless war now being waged in Europe, yet if this resolution passes I shall not permit my feeling of opposition to its passage to interfere in any way with my duty either as a Senator or as a citizen in bringing success and victory to American arms. I am bitterly opposed to my country entering the war, but if, notwithstanding my opposition, we do enter it, all of my energy and all of my power will be behind our flag in carrying it on to victory. . . .

There are a great many American citizens who feel that we owe it as a duty to humanity to take part in this war. Many instances of cruelty and inhumanity can be found on both sides. Men are often biased in their judgment on account of their sympathy and their interests. To my mind, what we ought to have maintained from the beginning was the strictest neutrality. If we had done this I do not believe we would have been on the verge of war at the present time. We had a right as a nation, if we desired, to cease at any time to be neutral. We had a technical right to respect the English war zone and to disregard the German war zone, but we could not do that and be neutral. I have no quarrel to find with the man who does not desire our country to remain neutral. While many such people are moved by selfish motives and hopes of gain, I have no doubt but that in a great many instances, through what I believe to be a misunderstanding of the real condition, there are many honest, patriotic

Congressional Record, Senate, 65th Congress, 1st Session, Vol. 55, (April 4, 1917), 212–214.

citizens who think we ought to engage in this war and who are behind the President in his demand that we should declare war against Germany. I think such people err in judgment and to a great extent have been misled as to the real history and the true facts by the almost unanimous demand of the great combination of wealth that has a direct financial interest in our participation in the war. We have loaned many hundreds of millions of dollars to the allies in this controversy. While such action was legal and countenanced by international law, there is no doubt in my mind but the enormous amount of money loaned to the allies in this country has been instrumental in bringing about a public sentiment in favor of our country taking a course that would make every bond worth a hundred cents on the dollar and making the payment of every debt certain and sure. Through this instrumentality and also through the instrumentality of others who have not only made millions out of the war in the manufacture of munitions, etc., and who would expect to make millions more if our country can be drawn into the catastrophe, a large number of the great newspapers and news agencies of the country have been controlled and enlisted in the greatest propaganda that the world has ever known, to manufacture sentiment in favor of war. It is now demanded that the American citizens shall be used as insurance policies to guarantee the safe delivery of munitions of war to belligerent nations. The enormous profits of munition manufacturers, stockbrokers, and bond dealers must be still further increased by our entrance into the war. This has brought us to the present moment, when Congress, urged by the President and backed by the artificial sentiment, is about to de-clare war and engulf our country in the greatest holocaust that the world has ever known.

In showing the position of the bondholder and the stockbroker I desire to read an extract from a letter written by a member of the New York Stock Exchange to his customers. This writer says:

> Regarding the war as inevitable, Wall Street believes that it would be preferable to this uncertainty about the actual date of its commencement. Canada and Japan are at war, and are more prosperous than ever before. The popular view is that stocks would have a quick, clear, sharp reaction immediately upon outbreak of hostilities, and that then they would enjoy an old-fashioned bull market such as followed the outbreak of war with Spain in 1898. The advent of peace would force a read-

justment of commodity prices and would probably mean a post-
ponement of new enterprises. As peace negotiations would be
long drawn out, the period of waiting and uncertainty for
business would be long. If the United States does not go to war it
is nevertheless good opinion that the preparedness program will
compensate in good measure for the loss of the stimulus of
actual war.

Here we have the Wall Street view. Here we have the man representing the class of people who will be made prosperous should we become entangled in the present war, who have already made millions of
dollars, and who will make many hundreds of millions more if we
get into the war. Here we have the cold-blooded proposition that war
brings prosperity to the class of people who are within the viewpoint
of this writer. He expresses the view, undoubtedly, of Wall Street, and of
thousands of men elsewhere, who see only dollars coming to them
through the handling of stocks and bonds that will be necessary in case
of war. "Canada and Japan," he says, "are at war, and are more prosperous than ever before."

To whom does war bring prosperity? Not to the soldier who for the
munificent compensation of $16 per month shoulders his musket and
goes into the trench, there to shed his blood and to die if necessary; not
to the broken-hearted widow who waits for the return of the mangled
body of her husband; not to the mother who weeps at the death of her
brave boy; not to the little children who shiver with cold; not to the babe
who suffers from hunger; nor to the millions of mothers and daughters
who carry broken hearts to their graves. War brings no prosperity to the
great mass of common and patriotic citizens. It increases the cost of
living of those who toil and those who already must strain every effort
to keep soul and body together. War brings prosperity to the stock gam-
bler on Wall Street—to those who are already in possession of more
wealth than can be realized or enjoyed. Again this writer says that if we
can not get war, "it is nevertheless good opinion that the preparedness
program will compensate in good measure for the loss of the stimulus
of actual war." That is, if we can not get war, let us go as far in that direction as possible. If we can not get war, let us cry for additional ships,
additional guns, additional munitions, and everything else that will
have a tendency to bring us as near as possible to the verge of war. And
if war comes do such men as these shoulder the musket and go into the
trenches?

Their object in having war and in preparing for war is to make money. Human suffering and the sacrifice of human life are necessary, but Wall Street considers only the dollars and the cents. The men who do the fighting, the people who make the sacrifices, are the ones who will not be counted in the measure of this great prosperity that he depicts. The stock brokers would not, of course, go to war, because the very object they have in bringing on the war is profit, and therefore they must remain in their Wall Street offices in order to share in that great prosperity which they say war will bring. The volunteer officer, even the drafting officer, will not find them. They will be concealed in their palatial offices on Wall Street, sitting behind mahogany desks, covered up with clipped coupons—coupons soiled with the sweat of honest toil, coupons stained with mothers' tears, coupons dyed in the lifeblood of their fellow men.

We are taking a step to-day that is fraught with untold danger. We are going into war upon the command of gold. We are going to run the risk of sacrificing millions of our countrymen's lives in order that other countrymen may coin their lifeblood into money. And even if we do not cross the Atlantic and go into the trenches, we are going to pile up a debt that the toiling masses that shall come many generations after us will have to pay. Unborn millions will bend their backs in toil in order to pay for the terrible step we are now about to take. We are about to do the bidding of wealth's terrible mandate. By our act we will make millions of our countrymen suffer, and the consequences of it may well be that millions of our brethren must shed their lifeblood, millions of broken-hearted women must weep, millions of children must suffer with cold, and millions of babes must die from hunger, and all because we want to preserve the commercial right of American citizens to deliver munitions of war to belligerent nations. . . .

I know that I am powerless to stop it. I know that this war madness has taken possession of the financial and political powers of our country. I know that nothing I can say will stay the blow that is soon to fall. I feel that we are committing a sin against humanity and against our countrymen. I would like to say to this war god, You shall not coin into gold the lifeblood of my brethren. I would like to prevent this terrible catastrophe from falling upon my people. I would be willing to surrender my own life if I could cause this awful cup to pass. I charge no man here with a wrong motive, but it seems to me that this war craze has robbed us of our judgment. I wish we might delay our action until reason could again be enthroned in the brain of man. I feel that we are about to put the dollar sign upon the American flag.

I have no sympathy with the military spirit that dominates the Kaiser and his advisers. I do not believe that they represent the heart of the great German people. I have no more sympathy with the submarine policy of Germany than I have with the mine-laying policy of England. I have heard with rejoicing of the overthrow of the Czar of Russia and the movement in that great country toward the establishment of a government where the common people will have their rights, liberty, and freedom respected. I hope and pray that a similar revolution may take place in Germany, that the Kaiser may be overthrown, and that on the ruins of his military despotism may be established a German republic, where the great German people may work out their world destiny. The working out of that problem is not an American burden. We ought to remember the advice of the Father of our Country and keep out of entangling alliances. Let Europe solve her problems as we have solved ours. Let Europe bear her burdens as we have borne ours. In the greatest war of our history and at the time it occurred, the greatest war in the world's history, we were engaged in solving an American problem. We settled the question of human slavery and washed our flag clean by the sacrifice of human blood. It was a great problem and a great burden, but we solved it ourselves. Never once did we think of asking Europe to take part in its solution. Never once did any European nation undertake to settle the great question. We solved it, and history has rendered a unanimous verdict that we solved it right. The troubles of Europe ought to be settled by Europe, and wherever our sympathies may lie, disagreeing as we do, we ought to remain absolutely neutral and permit them to settle their questions without our interference. We are now the greatest neutral nation. Upon the passage of this resolution we will have joined Europe in the great catastrophe and taken America into entanglements that will not end with this war, but will live and bring their evil influences upon many generations yet unborn.

C

REPRESENTATIVE FRED A. BRITTEN ON THE HORRORS OF WAR AND THE CERTAIN NEED FOR CONSCRIPTION APRIL 5, 1917

"You and I do not want our boys to go up against that liquid fire, noxious gasses, and a trench warfare that has made wild animals out of human beings, just because our administration has convinced itself that the future safety of our country will be more secure in the defeat of Germany than in the defeat of England."

Mr. Chairman, I was much impressed with the statement of my good friend from Mississippi [Mr. HARRISON] a few minutes ago, and particularly so when he referred to the patriotism of our scattered forces at Valley Forge. He forgot to remind the House that those forces were brought together by a German general, Von Steuben, who was largely responsible for their organization and success. He might also have referred to the German regiment at Brandywine and at Princeton, and to the 53 men and 14 officers who comprised Washington's bodyguard, every one of them a German, selected because they were Germans. . . .

I am not a pacifist in any sense, but am firm in the belief that this resolution is being jammed through Congress against the wishes of a great majority of people all over the country.

I do not believe that the great masses of our people are in favor of a declaration of war, and I am certain that they are opposed to the use of our militia in the bloody trench warfare which has already annihilated the flower of the youth of the most civilized countries on earth.

The wrongs of Germany, England, and all of the other belligerents which have been heaped upon us will not justify the loss of untold thousands of lives, the crippling and maiming of our American boys, nor the suffering and anguish which is bound to follow our flag to Europe.

It is not yet too late to diplomatically consider the differences between Germany and ourselves, and I am sure that a sincere effort in

Congressional Record, House, 65th Congress, 1st Session, Vol. 55, (April 5, 1971), 317–318; 397.

this direction would prove more valuable and creditable to the country than a declaration of war.

Let Congress immediately pass a bill for universal military service, which will give the country not less than a million real soldiers in 12 months from now, and let us leave nothing undone to bring our Navy up to the equal at least of the second great naval power just as quickly as possible, and we will then be in position to command the respect not only of Germany but of every country on earth.

Let us arm our whole Nation for its own defense and keep clear of any entangling alliances with European and Asiatic Governments.

By maintaining an attitude of armed neutrality we can rest secure until additional revolutions in Europe have done their work, and we can then assist in establishing a condition of universal peace. . . .

The truth of the matter is that 90 per cent of your people and mine do not want this declaration of war, and are distinctly opposed to our going into that bloody mire on the other side. There is something in the air, gentlemen, and I do not know what it is, whether it be the hand of destiny, or some superhuman movement, something stronger than you and I can realize or resist, that seems to be picking us up bodily and literally forcing us to vote for this declaration of war when away down deep in our hearts we are just as opposed to it as are our people back home. . . .

You and I do not want our boys to go up against that liquid fire, noxious gases, and a trench warfare that has made wild animals out of human beings, just because our administration has convinced itself that the future safety of our country will be more secure in the defeat of Germany than in the defeat of England.

But let us not deceive ourselves that we are going into this war in the interest of humanity. The man who deceives himself is a fool. We are being dragged into this because our administration is firm in the belief, and has been for a long time, that the future safety of our country will be more secure in the defeat of Germany than in the defeat of England, and every one of you who votes for this resolution without amendment will feel its effects a year from now when the sisters, widows, and mothers of your district come to you and say, "Mr. Congressman, my boy is my only support; he is just 22, or he is just 21; are you going to send him to the trenches in France or in Salonika?" That is what your vote to-day will mean. You will be putting your young man with probably one year's training up against a lot of seasoned warriors who will cripple him and send him home to live the balance of his life as a public charge or dependent upon his relatives. . . .

The President said, "We would not choose the path of submission." Is it not a peculiar fact that our submission has ceased only in one direction? England has violated international law and our treaty rights a thousand times during the last three years, and we have submitted as though we were her dependent colonies. They have opened our mail and we have submitted. They established a black list against our citizens—your manufacturers and mine—telling them that they could not ship their own goods out of an American port. In many instances they deliberately blacklist in order that they may steal American business, and in other instances permits have been withheld by the British foreign office at London until the business might be stolen by British concerns. Did we submit? Certainly we did.

Mr. Chairman, Japan has violated her sacred treaties with us as though they were "scraps of paper," just as Germany did with the other powers. Did we submit? Certainly we did. After the House had passed the last immigration bill and its phraseology did not suit the Japanese foreign office, did we change it when the Japanese Embassy had sent word to that effect to our Secretary of State? I should say we did! When the Japanese foreign office told us that certain State laws objectionable to them were being enacted, did we tell them that was our business? No; we apologized and promised to be good.

Mr. Chairman, have we submitted to Mexico? Our men, women, and children have been murdered and butchered with the sanction of the de facto government of Mexico and our soldiers deliberately shot down by Mexican troops, shot down willfully. Did we submit? Certainly we did, by writing a letter to Gen. Carranza and asking him if his men really meant to kill ours. That is exactly what we did in the Carrizal affair, after our soldiers were shot down by American machine guns in the hands of the Carranza troops. . . .

Mr. Chairman, what do you suppose England would do with one of our ships if we insisted upon taking foodstuffs and other peaceful commerce into Germany? She would sink the ship, would she not? But, my dear friends, we are not even permitted to negotiate peaceful commerce with neutral countries without British consent, and still "we claim to have been neutral." It is because of these facts that I had hoped we might keep out of that terrible slaughter even though we did have to "submit" to violations of international law and our rights a little longer.

We ourselves are largely responsible for being drawn into this war. Our lack of firmness and failure to deal with England, Italy, France, and Japan just as we would deal with Austria and Germany has brought about the condition of to-day. We have failed to deal with a firm hand with all of the belligerents alike, and I maintain that even a man like Roosevelt, with all his military valor and desire, would have kept us out of this declaration of war, because he would have treated alike all of the belligerents and made them respect that flag [pointing], which they have not done up to the present time. [Applause.]. . . .

I voted for the armed neutrality bill recently recommended by the President, because I felt that this step would keep us out of something more terrible. Is it not remarkable that just 28 days after the President has referred to that "little group of willful men" in the Senate he comes to us and says that armed neutrality has been a failure? That "little group of willful men" have been cartooned and criticized all over the United States for carrying on a filibuster against a bill which in 28 days is declared a failure, impracticable, by its maker, the President. . . .

Mr. Chairman, I offer an amendment. . . .

> *Provided, however*, That no part of the military forces of the United States shall be ordered to do land duty in any part of Europe, Asia, or Africa until so directed by act of Congress, excepting those troops who specifically volunteer for such service. . . .

I have added the last two lines, "excepting those troops who specifically volunteer for such service." Now, there may be men in the New England States, young men of valor and of vim, who desire to go to Europe, who desire to enter into this trench warfare and fight the Germans. Let them go if they wish. The boys of my district do not want to go. The boys of many of your districts do not want to go. There is going to be a conscription forced upon them. Their people do not want them to go to Europe, but they are willing to give every ounce of blood in their bodies in defense of America on American soil. . . .

If my amendment is added to this declaration of war it will give the country and Congress time to deliberate. We can not possibly recruit 500,000 or a million men in a year under volunteer service. It has got to be conscription, and in six or eight months from now you and I may feel that we do not want our boys to go against this awful slaughter. Suppose the near future should bring about the downfall of the Hohenzollerns in Germany and the Hapsburgs in Austria-Hungary, and the people of a new duo of republics arranged for a separate peace with the new Republic of Russia? Would you still feel inclined to send our troops into France or Salonika because England would not agree to a separate peace? Would you then favor sending our boys into the fertile fields of Mesopotamia in order to gratify England's wishes? Surely nothing can be further from your desires; and yet that very condition is as likely to occur as many others suggested on the floor of this House to-day. Military experts advise us that it takes three years to make a good soldier, and still a distinguished Member of the Senate suggested the other day that we ought to send 10,000 of our men at once to France—for the moral effect—at once. Send 10,000 of the finest specimens of American manhood to France at once to be slaughtered for the moral effect it will have on certain European nations now in a bloody death struggle. Are we too becoming war mad? The people of the country are against entering this war by a majority of from a hundred to a thousand to one. You owe it to the mothers, the sisters, the families of these boys to adopt my amendment.

Last Saturday I drove up Michigan Avenue and I saw some of our boys being taught to drive a bayonet through a ring of that size [indicating]. It was instruction in bayonet warfare. Do you know what that means? That means "going over the top" and landing on a human being and stabbing him with a bayonet. That is what our boys are practicing to-day in Chicago. It is not fair nor humane to send our soldiers up against those trained forces in Europe. It is like throwing a fine greyhound into a pit for a death struggle with a trained bulldog who has seen many victories. . . .

D

SOCIAL REFORMER JANE ADDAMS ON THE
LONELINESS OF THE PACIFIST IN TIME OF WAR

*"Solitude has always had its demons, harder to withstand than the
snares of the world, and the unnatural desert into which the pacifist
was summarily cast out seemed to be peopled with them. We sorely
missed the contagion of mental activity. . . ."*

From the very beginning of the great war, as the members of our group
gradually became defined from the rest of the community, each one
felt increasingly the sense of isolation which rapidly developed after the
United States entered the war into that destroying effect of "aloneness,"
if I may so describe the opposite of mass consciousness. We never ceased
to miss the unquestioning comradeship experienced by our fellow citizens
during the war, nor to feel curiously outside the enchantment given to
any human emotion when it is shared by millions of others. The force
of the majority was so overwhelming that it seemed not only impossible
to hold one's own against it, but at moments absolutely unnatural, and
one secretly yearned to participate in "the folly of all mankind." Our
modern democratic teaching has brought us to regard popular impulses
as possessing in their general tendency a valuable capacity for evolu-
tionary development. In the hours of doubt and self-distrust the question
again and again arises, has the individual or a very small group, the right
to stand out against millions of his fellow countrymen? Is there not a
great value in mass judgment and in instinctive mass enthusiasm, and
even if one were right a thousand times over in conviction, was he not
absolutely wrong in abstaining from this communion with his fellows?
The misunderstanding on the part of old friends and associates and the
charge of lack of patriotism was far easier to bear than those dark periods
of faint-heartedness. We gradually ceased to state our position as we
became convinced that it served no practical purpose and, worse than
that, often found that the immediate result was provocative. . . .

The pacifist was constantly brought sharply up against a genuine
human trait with its biological basis, a trait founded upon the instinct to

---

Jane Addams, *Peace and Bread in Time of War*. New York: King's Crown Press, 1945,
140–151. Reprinted by permission.

dislike, to distrust and finally to destroy the individual who differs from the mass in time of danger. Regarding this trait as the basis of self-preservation it becomes perfectly natural for the mass to call such an individual a traitor and to insist that if he is not for the nation he is against it. To this an estimated nine million people can bear witness who have been burned as witches and heretics, not by mobs, for of the people who have been "lynched" no record has been kept, but by order of ecclesiastical and civil courts.

There were moments when the pacifist yielded to the suggestion that keeping himself out of war, refusing to take part in its enthusiasms, was but pure quietism, an acute failure to adjust himself to the moral world. Certainly nothing was clearer than that the individual will was helpless and irrelevant. We were constantly told by our friends that to stand aside from the war mood of the country was to surrender all possibility of future influence, that we were committing intellectual suicide, and would never again be trusted as responsible people or judicious advisers. Who were we to differ with able statesmen, with men of sensitive conscience who also absolutely abhorred war, but were convinced that this war for the preservation of democracy would make all future wars impossible, that the priceless values of civilization which were at stake could at this moment be saved only by war? But these very dogmatic statements spurred one to alarm. Was not war in the interest of democracy for the salvation of civilization a contradiction of terms, whoever said it or however often it was repeated?

Then, too, we were always afraid of fanaticism, of preferring a consistency of theory to the conscientious recognition of the social situation, of a failure to meet life in the temper of a practical person. Every student of our time had become more or less a disciple of pragmatism and its great teachers in the United States had come out for the war and defended their positions with skill and philosophic acumen. There were moments when one longed desperately for reconciliation with one's friends and fellow citizens; ... Solitude has always had its demons, harder to withstand than the snares of the world, and the unnatural desert into which the pacifist was summarily cast out seemed to be peopled with them. We sorely missed the contagion of mental activity, for we are all much more dependent upon our social environment and daily newspaper than perhaps any of us realize....

The consciousness of spiritual alienation was lost only in moments of comradeship with the like minded, which may explain the tendency of the pacifist in war time to seek his intellectual kin, his spiritual friends, wherever they might be found in his own country or abroad.

It was inevitable that in many respects the peace cause should suffer in public opinion from the efforts of groups of people who, early in the war, were convinced that the country as a whole was for peace and who tried again and again to discover a method for arousing and formulating the sentiment against war. . . .

We also read with a curious eagerness the steadily increasing number of books published from time to time during the war, which brought a renewal of one's faith or at least a touch of comfort. These books broke through that twisting and suppressing of awkward truths, which was encouraged and at times even ordered by the censorship. Such manipulation of news and motives was doubtless necessary in the interest of war propaganda if the people were to be kept in a fighting mood. . . .

On the other hand there were many times when we stubbornly asked ourselves, what after all, has maintained the human race on this old globe despite all the calamities of nature and all the tragic failings of mankind, if not faith in new possibilities, and courage to advocate them. Doubtless many times these new possibilities were declared by a man who, quite unconscious of courage, bore the "sense of being an exile, a condemned criminal, a fugitive from mankind." Did every one so feel who, in order to travel on his own proper path had been obliged to leave the traditional highway? The pacifist, during the period of the war could answer none of these questions but he was sick at heart from causes which to him were hidden and impossible to analyze. He was at times devoured by a veritable dissatisfaction with life. Was he thus bearing his share of blood-guiltiness, the morbid sense of contradiction and inexplicable suicide which modern war implies? We certainly had none of the internal contentment of the doctrinnaire, the ineffable solace of the self-righteous which was imputed to us. No one knew better than we how feeble and futile we were against the impregnable weight of public opinion, the appalling imperviousness, the coagulation of motives, the universal confusion of a world at war. There was scant solace to be found in this type of statement: "The worth of every conviction consists precisely in the steadfastness with which it is held," perhaps because we suffered from the fact that we were no longer living in a period of dogma and were therefore in no position to announce our sense of security! We were well aware that the modern liberal having come to conceive truth of a kind which must vindicate itself in practice, finds it hard to hold even a sincere and mature opinion which from the very nature of things can have no justification in works. The pacifist in war time is literally starved of any gratification of that natural desire to have his own decisions justified by his fellows.

That, perhaps, was the crux of the situation. We slowly became aware that our affirmation was regarded as pure dogma. We were thrust into the position of the doctrinnaire, and although, had we been permitted, we might have cited both historic and scientific tests of our so-called doctrine of Peace, for the moment any sanction even by way of illustration was impossible.

It therefore came about that ability to hold out against mass suggestion, to honestly differ from the convictions and enthusiasms of one's best friends did in moments of crisis come to depend upon the categorical belief that a man's primary allegiance is to his vision of the truth and that he is under obligation to affirm it. . . .

WORLD WAR II

The Second World War has been called America's only "consensus" war in that criticism of the interventionist policies of President Franklin D. Roosevelt in 1937–1941 ended abruptly with the Japanese attack on Pearl Harbor on December 7, 1941. Until the surrender of Japan on August 14, 1945 (Germany surrendered on May 7, 1945), there was in the United States virtual unanimity of opinion on the immediate origins of the conflict and on the war aims of the nation.

Not surprisingly, the President's War Message of December 8 was a cry of outrage. The Pacific Fleet had been caught napping at its docks and moorings the day before and had been blown out of the water by the carrier air forces of the Imperial Japanese Navy. Casualties were high: 2403 Americans killed and 1178 wounded. Higher still was the hurt and embarrassment of an American defeat effected with such apparent ease by an enemy 4000 miles away. The United States would, said Roosevelt in his War Message, "make very certain that this form of treachery shall never endanger us again." Such was the beginning of what might be called the "Pearl Harbor Syndrome" that many Americans would carry with them into the Cold War. Indeed, the main slogan of the war was "Remember Pearl Harbor!"

So unanimous and intense was the conviction that the Axis powers had "caused" the war, and were bent on world conquest, that panicky Americans lost sight of the elementary civil liberties of Japanese-Americans who resided in the United States. In the confused months that followed the disaster at Pearl Harbor, these gentle citizens were herded into detention camps like so many cattle. Like the German-Americans of World War I, they were presumed guilty of disloyalty on the basis of their ethnic origins. There was, however, not one single incident of Japanese-American disloyalty during the conflict. Indeed, a Nisei combat infantry unit was formed after some of the "enemy-within" hysteria had subsided. It performed heroically in Italy against the Germans.

World War II was also a consensus war in an ideological sense. In the retrospect of three decades the ideological dimensions still seem clear. The brutal Naziism of Adolph Hitler and the Greater East Asia Co-Prosperity Sphere expansionism of Imperial Japan have attracted few American apologists since 1945. Germany, it has generally been agreed, ran amok under Hitler and his notorious Third Reich. So too did Japan under its military extremists. Thus, while there has been much scholarly argument over the nature and degree of German "war guilt" in 1914, there has been little debate over basic German responsibility for the holocaust of 1939–1945. Scholarly contention has been confined largely to whether Hitler's aggressive territorial ambitions were European, Eurasian, or world-wide in scope, and why the German people allowed themselves to be gulled by Hitler in the first place. It has also centered on the degree to which Anglo-French appeasement in the 1930s influenced Hitler's ambitions and the timing of the Nazi decision for war. There has been considerable scholarly disagreement as well over the motives and intent of the Japanese adhesion to the German-Italian alliance, and the extent to which Roosevelt's steadfast refusal to accept a Japanese conquest of China compromised peace in the Pacific in 1941. But there has been little disagreement on the inhumane philosophical and political principles for which the Axis Powers stood.

These antidemocratic, imperialist, and militarist principles were first brought forcibly to the attention of the American people by Roosevelt in his famous "Quarantine Speech" in Chicago in October, 1937, delivered at a time when Japan had extended its 1931–1932 invasion and absorption of Manchuria to a full-scale military attack on China. Italy had but recently invaded and annexed helpless Ethiopia, and Hitler was even at that moment preparing the occupation of Austria. In Spain, General Francisco Franco's Fascists were systematically snuffing out democracy in that unhappy land. As Roosevelt phrased it in Chicago, "The landmarks and traditions which have marked the progress of civilization toward a condition of law, order and justice are being wiped away." This warning fell on deaf ears and did little more than persuade nationalist and isolationist critics of the New Deal in the United States to redouble their efforts to keep America out of the approaching war—as it had not been kept out in 1917.

Nor was isolationist and nationalist sentiment against American involvement in Europe's problems stilled by Hitler's occupation of Austria, his absorption of Czechoslovakia, his unprovoked attack on Poland, and his blitzkrieg and occupation of Norway, Denmark, Holland, Belgium, Luxembourg, France, Yugoslavia, and Greece. By the beginning of 1941 Hitler, like Napoleon before him, stood astride Europe and was preparing his all-conquering legions for the invasion of Russia. Only Britain continued to resist him, and Britain stood alone.

It was at this critical juncture that Roosevelt again attempted to put the European war into historical perspective. For his increasingly concerned countrymen (severely shaken as millions of them were by the fall of France), he linked the ideological issues he thought were involved with his decision to increase American aid to Britain in its continuing resistance to Nazi aggression. This was the "Four Freedoms Speech" of January 6, 1941. In this address, the President defined the nature of human freedom and argued that "the happiness of future generations of Americans may well depend upon how effective and how immediate we can make our aid [to Britain] felt." Similarly, the *New York Times*, in an April 30, 1941, editorial headed "Let Us Face the Truth," flatly stated that isolation was no longer either physically possible or intellectually defensible.

The battle of the Anglophile interventionists against isolation and the isolationists in America was a bitter one. It was waged by those wholly convinced, as one sympathizer put it, that the "democratic way of life . . . which had made America the hope of the world during the preceding one hundred and fifty years, could not be allowed to die."[1] Roosevelt, however, was constantly wary of isolationist political influence throughout the 1939–1941 period. Nevertheless, he cautiously pursued policies designed to assist Britain and China, policies that led, and perhaps could lead, only to an undeclared naval war in the Atlantic against Nazi Germany in the summer of 1941 and to a confrontation with Imperial Japan a few months later. Herbert Feis has emphasized Roosevelt's dilemmas and options as it became increasingly apparent to him that Japan was preparing a renewed round of military aggression in Southeast Asia in October-November, 1941. One tangential prong of that attack struck sleepy Pearl Harbor on December 7.

Thanks to the Pearl Harbor disaster, the nationalist-isolationist-Fortress America viewpoint was overnight stripped naked and discredited. Indeed, the nation was instantly, fiercely, and patriotically united by Japan's "sneak" attack. Roosevelt's radio address to the American people on December 9 breathed defiance, outrage, hope, confidence, and moral certitude—as have all presidential war statements.

What we have learned [said the President] is this. There is no such thing as security for any nation—or any individual—in a world ruled by the principles of gangsterism . . . . We are now in the midst of a war, not for conquest, not for vengeance, but

---

1 Walter Johnson, *The Battle Against Isolation* Chicago: Univ. Chicago Press, 1944, 228.

for a world in which this Nation, and all this Nation represents, will be safe for our children. . . . We are going to win the war and we are going to win the peace that follows . . . . the vast majority of the members of the human race are on our side. . . . For in representing our cause, we represent theirs as well—our hope and their hope for liberty under God.

That Germany and Japan had adopted policies of imperialist expansion and military aggression was apparent to some trained American observers as early as 1934. Douglas Miller, writing in Berlin in April, 1934, predicted the broad thrust of Nazi foreign policy for the remainder of the decade with an accuracy barely short of clairvoyance. And according to the Hossbach Memorandum, by November, 1937, Adolph Hitler had indeed planned a specific program and timetable of aggression in Europe. Ambassador Joseph Grew, writing from Tokyo in December, 1934, saw Japan bent on nothing less in Asia than the achievement of "Pax Japonica." It was not until July, 1941, however, that Japan made the final policy decisions that, short of outright American appeasement on the "China Incident" question, would launch her military forces throughout Southeast Asia and the Southwest Pacific in December.

Surprising as it may seem in retrospect, few of the activities, the invasions, or the threats of the Axis nations much impressed American isolationist opinion during the 1934–1941 period. The concept of collective security was not one that the isolationists embraced. To them the League of Nations was little more than a cruel and dangerous joke. Beginning with the basic premise that the United States had somehow been euchred into a needless and unnecessary war in 1917, the isolationists wanted to make certain that history would not repeat itself. By the mid-1930s the emergence of a "revisionist" historiography on World War I had also demonstrated to the satisfaction of many Americans that Imperial Germany had not been primarily responsible for the outbreak of hostilities in 1914, and that America in 1917 had been lied into that war by Wilson, Wall Street, and the munitions makers (the so-called "Merchants of Death"). This was conspiracy thesis pure and simple.

To a large extent, therefore, opposition to responsible internationalism in the 1930s was both a reflection and extension of opposition to Wilsonism in 1914–1920. Republican Senator Gerald P. Nye of North Dakota best expressed the broad outlines of the conspiracy theme in May, 1935, and took the lead in pushing through Congress various neutrality acts belatedly designed to keep the United States out of World War I. In similar vein, Senator Robert A. Taft of Ohio vigorously opposed Roosevelt's attempts to sustain Britain's otherwise lonely war against Hitler's Germany. In what was probably the most effective isolationist speech delivered in the prewar years, Taft marshalled the full range of Fortress America arguments and hurled them against Roosevelt's proposed Lend-Lease Bill.

Isolationist sentiment took its most extreme political form, however, in the America First movement. Speaking under the auspices of America First, the distinguished Colonel Charles A. Lindberg told Americans in April, 1941, that Britain had already lost the war and that the United States had no military prospects of defeating Germany even should America enter actively on the British side. In sum, Nazi Germany had won the conflict and had reduced Britain to but one option—to sue for the best peace terms possible. Meanwhile, said Lindberg, interventionist warmongers in America were misleading their countrymen with specious arguments that Britain could be saved through American aid and that Berlin posed a genuine military threat to the United States. An isolationist Fortress America, Lindberg maintained, had nothing to fear from Nazi Germany.

It is well to point out that while many of the America Firsters were Anglophobes, the movement was not pro-Nazi. It was instead pro-peace, peace at virtually any price, and it took the consistent position that America should resign from the international state system before again being dragged into a European war. Leaders of the organization also argued that America should effect this withdrawal regardless of any humanitarian considerations that were said to be at stake in Europe.

The America First movement, and all isolationist opinion, died a sudden death at Pearl Harbor. Nevertheless, the notion that Roosevelt, like Wilson before him, had participated in a conscious conspiracy against peace in 1940–1941 was resurrected soon after the war by a group of scholars who launched a "revisionist" interpretation of pre-war events. This school, led principally by historian Charles A. Beard, argued that Roosevelt, in his eagerness and desire to join Britain in the shooting war against Hitler in Europe, had actually provoked the peace-loving Japanese into the attack on Pearl Harbor and had criminally exposed the Pacific Fleet to that attack as bait. This "back-door-to-war" thesis has been most vigorously argued by Professor Charles C. Tansill. It has been denied with equal fervor by other historians and the scholarly controversy on this point continues.

Americans, in sum, were not agreed before the war on America's proper course in response to German and Japanese aggression. Nor after the war could American scholars agree on what actually had happened in American foreign policy in 1937–1941. But unlike American experience in all other of its major wars, pre-war critics and crusaders were firmly united during the conflict. There was almost no domestic peace movement to be confused with pro-Naziism and no civil libertarian attacks on the critics by the crusaders. This, at least, could be counted a gain—whatever might be said about the tragic and senseless persecution of the hapless Nisei.

WORLD WAR II

I
THE CRUSADERS AND THE SCHOLARS:
AMERICAN

A

*THE WAR MESSAGE: PRESIDENT FRANKLIN D. ROOSEVELT
DECEMBER 8, 1941*

> *"Yesterday, December 7, 1941—a date which will live in infamy—the United States of America was suddenly and deliberately attacked by naval and air forces of the Empire of Japan. . . . No matter how long it may take us to overcome this premeditated invasion, the American people in their righteous might will win through to absolute victory."*

Yesterday, December 7, 1941—a date which will live in infamy—the United States of America was suddenly and deliberately attacked by naval and air forces of the Empire of Japan.

The United States was at peace with that nation and, at the solicitation of Japan, was still in conversation with its Government and its Emperor looking toward the maintenance of peace in the Pacific. Indeed, 1 hour after Japanese air squadrons had commenced bombing in Oahu, the Japanese Ambassador to the United States and his colleague delivered to the Secretary of State a formal reply to a recent American message. While this reply stated that it seemed useless to continue the existing diplomatic negotiations, it contained no threat or hint of war or armed attack.

It will be recorded that the distance of Hawaii from Japan makes it obvious that the attack was deliberately planned many days or even

---

Congressional Record, 77th Congress, 1st Session, Vol. 89 (December 8, 1941), 9504–9505.

weeks ago. During the intervening time the Japanese Government has deliberately sought to deceive the United States by false statements and expressions of hope for continued peace.

The attack yesterday on the Hawaiian Islands has caused severe damage to American naval and military forces. Very many American lives have been lost. In addition American ships have been reported torpedoed on the high seas between San Francisco and Honolulu.

Yesterday the Japanese Government also launched an attack against Malaya.

Last night Japanese forces attacked Hong Kong.

Last night Japanese forces attacked Guam.

Last night Japanese forces attacked the Philippine Islands.

Last night the Japanese attacked Wake Island.

Last night the Japanese attacked Midway Island.

Japan has therefore undertaken a surprise offensive extending throughout the Pacific area. The facts of yesterday speak for themselves. The people of the United States have already formed their opinions and well understand the implications to the very life and safety of our Nation.

As Commander in Chief of the Army and Navy I have directed that all measures be taken for our defense.

Always will we remember the character of the onslaught against us.

No matter how long it may take us to overcome this premeditated invasion, the American people in their righteous might will win through to absolute victory.

I believe I interpret the will of the Congress and of the people when I assert that we will not only defend ourselves to the uttermost but will make very certain that this form of treachery shall never endanger us again.

Hostilities exist. There is no blinking at the fact that our people, our territory, and our interests are in grave danger.

With confidence in our armed forces—with the unbounded determination of our people—we will gain the inevitable triumph, so help us God.

I ask that the Congress declare that, since the unprovoked and dastardly attack by Japan on Sunday, December 7, a state of war has existed between the United States and the Japanese Empire.

B
PRESIDENT FRANKLIN D. ROOSEVELT WARNS AMERICA
THAT AGGRESSORS ARE ON THE MARCH
OCTOBER 5, 1937

"If those things come to pass in other parts of the world let no one imagine that America will escape, that it may expect mercy, that this Western Hemisphere will not be attacked, and that it will continue tranquilly and peacefully to carry on the ethics and the arts of civilization."

... The political situation in the world, which of late has been growing progressively worse, is such as to cause grave concern and anxiety to all peoples and nations who wish to live in peace and amity with their neighbors.

Some 15 years ago the hopes of mankind for a continuing era of international peace were raised to great heights when more than 60 nations solemnly pledged themselves not to resort to arms in furtherance of their national aims and policies. The high aspirations expressed in the Briand-Kellogg Peace Pact and the hopes for peace thus raised have of late given away to a haunting fear of calamity. The present reign of terror and international lawlessness began a few years ago.

It began through unjustified interference in the internal affairs of other nations or the invasion of alien territory in violation of treaties and has now reached a stage where the very foundations of civilization are seriously threatened. The landmarks and traditions which have marked the progress of civilization toward a condition of law, order, and justice are being wiped away.

Without a declaration of war and without warning or justification of any kind, civilians, including women and children, are being ruthlessly murdered with bombs from the air. In times of so-called peace ships are being attacked and sunk by submarines without cause or notice. Nations are fomenting and taking sides in civil warfare in nations that have never done them any harm. Nations claiming freedom for themselves deny it to others.

Peace and War: United States Foreign Policy, 1931–1941. Washington: Government Printing Office, 1943, 383–387.

Innocent peoples and nations are being cruelly sacrificed to a greed for power and supremacy which is devoid of all sense of justice and humane consideration.

To paraphrase a recent author, "perhaps we foresee a time when men, exultant in the technique of homicide, will rage so hotly over the world that every precious thing will be in danger, every book and picture and harmony, every treasure garnered through two millenniums, the small, the delicate, the defenseless—all will be lost or wrecked or utterly destroyed."

If those things come to pass in other parts of the world let no one imagine that America will escape, that it may expect mercy, that this Western Hemisphere will not be attacked, and that it will continue tranquilly and peacefully to carry on the ethics and the arts of civilization.

If those days come "there will be no safety by arms, no help from authority, no answer in science. The storm will rage till every flower of culture is trampled and all human beings are leveled in a vast chaos."

If those days are not to come to pass—if we are to have a world in which we can breathe freely and live in amity without fear—the peace-loving nations must make a concerted effort to uphold laws and principles on which alone peace can rest secure.

The peace-loving nations must make a concerted effort in opposition to those violations of treaties and those ignorings of humane instincts which today are creating a state of international anarchy and instability from which there is no escape through mere isolation or neutrality.

Those who cherish their freedom and recognize and respect the equal right of their neighbors to be free and live in peace, must work together for the triumph of law and moral principles in order that peace, justice, and confidence may prevail in the world. There must be a return to a belief in the pledged word, in the value of a signed treaty. There must be recognition of the fact that national morality is as vital as private morality. . . .

There is a solidarity and interdependence about the modern world, both technically and morally, which makes it impossible for any nation completely to isolate itself from economic and political upheavals in the rest of the world, especially when such upheavals appear to be spreading and not declining. There can be no stability or peace either within nations or between nations except under laws and moral standards adhered to by all. International anarchy destroys every foundation for peace. It jeopardizes either the immediate or the future security of every nation, large or small. It is, therefore, a matter of vital interest and concern to the people of the United States that the sanctity of international treaties and the maintenance of international morality be restored.

The overwhelming majority of the peoples and nations of the world today want to live in peace. They seek the removal of barriers against trade. They want to exert themselves in industry, in agriculture, and in business, that they may increase their wealth through the production of wealth-producing goods rather than striving to produce military planes and bombs and machine guns and cannon for the destruction of human lives and useful property.

In those nations of the world which seem to be piling armament on armament for purpose of aggression, and those other nations which fear acts of aggression against them and their security, a very high proportion of their national income is being spent directly for armaments. It runs from 30 to as high as 50 percent.

The proportion that we in the United States spend is far less—11 or 12 percent.

How happy we are that the circumstances of the moment permit us to put our money into bridges and boulevards, dams and reforestation, the conservation of our soil, and many other kinds of useful works rather than into huge standing armies and vast supplies of implements of war.

I am compelled and you are compelled, nevertheless, to look ahead. The peace, the freedom, and the security of 90 percent of the population of the world is being jeopardized by the remaining 10 percent, who are threatening a breakdown of all international order and law. Surely the 90 percent who want to live in peace under law and in accordance with moral standards that have received almost universal acceptance through the centuries, can and must find some way to make their will prevail.

The situation is definitely of universal concern. The questions involved relate not merely to violations of specific provisions of particular treaties; they are questions of war and of peace, of international law, and especially of principles of humanity. It is that they involve definite violations of agreements, and especially of the Covenant of the League of Nations, the Briand-Kellogg Pact, and the Nine Power Treaty. But they also involve problems of world economy, world security, and world humanity.

It is true that moral consciousness of the world must recognize the importance of removing injustices and well-founded grievances; but at the same time it must be aroused to the cardinal necessity of honoring sanctity of treaties, of respecting the rights and liberties of others, and of putting an end to acts of international aggression.

It seems to be unfortunately true that the epidemic of world lawlessness is spreading.

When an epidemic of physical disease starts to spread, the community approves and joins in a quarantine of the patients in order to protect the health of the community against the spread of the disease.

It is my determination to pursue a policy of peace and to adopt every practicable measure to avoid involvement in war. It ought to be inconceivable that in this modern era, and in the face of experience, any nation could be so foolish and ruthless as to run the risk of plunging the whole world into war by invading and violating in contravention of solemn treaties the territory of other nations that have done them no real harm and which are too weak to protect themselves adequately. Yet the peace of the world and the welfare and security of every nation is today being threatened by that very thing.

No nation which refuses to exercise forbearance and to respect the freedom and rights of others can long remain strong and retain the confidence and respect of other nations. No nation ever loses its dignity or good standing by conciliating its differences and by exercising great patience with and consideration for the rights of other nations.

War is a contagion, whether it be declared or undeclared. It can engulf states and peoples remote from the original scene of hostilities. We are determined to keep out of war, yet we cannot insure ourselves against the disastrous effects of war and the dangers of involvement. We are adopting such measures as will minimize our risk of involvement, but we cannot have complete protection in a world of disorder in which confidence and security have broken down.

If civilization is to survive the principles of the Prince of Peace must be restored. Shattered trust between nations must be revived.

Most important of all, the will for peace on the part of peace-loving nations must express itself to the end that nations that may be tempted to violate their agreements and the rights of others will desist from such a cause. There must be positive endeavors to preserve peace.

America hates war. America hopes for peace. Therefore, America engages in the search for peace.

C

PRESIDENT FRANKLIN D. ROOSEVELT DEFINES THE FOUR
FREEDOMS FOR WHICH THE UNITED STATES STANDS
JANUARY 6, 1941

> *"We must all prepare to make the sacrifices that the emergency—as*
> *serious as war itself—demands. Whatever stands in the way of*
> *speed and efficiency in defense preparations must give way to the*
> *national need."*

... The happiness of future generations of Americans may well depend
upon how effective and how immediate we can make our aid [to Britain]
felt. No one can tell the exact character of the emergency situations that
we may be called upon to meet. The Nation's hands must not be tied
when the Nation's life is in danger.

We must all prepare to make the sacrifices that the emergency—as
serious as war itself—demands. Whatever stands in the way of speed and
efficiency in defense preparations must give way to the national need.

A free nation has the right to expect full cooperation from all
groups. A free nation has the right to look to the leaders of business,
of labor, and of agriculture to take the lead in stimulating effort, not
among other groups but within their own groups.

I have called for personal sacrifice. I am assured of the willingness
of almost all Americans to respond to that call.

A part of the sacrifice means the payment of more money in taxes.
In my Budget message I recommend that a greater portion of this great
defense program be paid for from taxation than we are paying today.
No person should try, or be allowed, to get rich out of this program;
and the principle of tax payments in accordance with ability to pay
should be constantly before our eyes to guide our legislation.

If the Congress maintains these principles, the voters, putting patriotism ahead of pocketbooks, will give you their applause.

In the future days, which we seek to make secure, we look forward
to a world founded upon four essential human freedoms.

Peace and War: United States Foreign Policy, 1931–1941, Washington: Government
Printing Office, 1943, 610–611.

The first is freedom of speech and expression—everywhere in the world.

The second is freedom of every person to worship God in his own way—everywhere in the world.

The third is freedom from want—which, translated into world terms, means economic understandings which will secure to every nation a healthy peacetime life for its inhabitants—everywhere in the world.

The fourth is freedom from fear—which, translated into world terms, means a world-wide reduction of armaments to such a point and in such a thorough fashion that no nation will be in a position to commit an act of physical aggression against any neighbor—anywhere in the world.

That is no vision of a distant millennium. It is a definite basis for a kind of world attainable in our own time and generation. That kind of world is the very antithesis of the so-called new order of tyranny which the dictators seek to create with the crash of a bomb.

To that new order we oppose the greater conception—the moral order. A good society is able to face schemes of world domination and foreign revolutions alike without fear.

Since the beginning of our American history we have been engaged in change—in a perpetual peaceful revolution—a revolution which goes on steadily, quietly adjusting itself to changing conditions—without the concentration camp or the quick-lime in the ditch. The world order which we seek is the cooperation of free countries, working together in a friendly, civilized society.

This Nation has placed its destiny in the hands and heads and hearts of its millions of free men and women; and its faith in freedom under the guidance of God. Freedom means the supremacy of human rights everywhere. Our support goes to those who struggle to gain those rights or keep them. Our strength is in our unity of purpose.

To that high concept there can be no end save victory.

D
A NEW YORK TIMES *EDITORIAL ON THE NECESSARY END OF ISOLATIONISM AND AN ISOLATED AMERICA APRIL 30, 1941*

"There is no isolation. There are only lines of defense. Distance is vanishing. Strategy is everything. And strategy in this year of grace has become the art and science of survival: survival in the personal sense, survival of ideas, survival of culture and tradition, survival of a way of life."

In New York Harbor, on an island close to the steamship lanes, stands the most famous statue in the world. It is not the most beautiful statue, but to many millions of passengers coming up the bay it has seemed to be. It stands for one of the dearest dreams in human history—Liberty.

The millions who pursued that dream began to come before there was a statue to greet them. They came first when the shores were lined with solemn woods. They came in sailing ships when the voyage required two months or more. They came in crowded steamship steerage under hardships not much less. They came to Plymouth Rock and to Ellis Island.

They came for one reason, escape; escape from religious or political persecution, from caste systems, from overcrowding and from lack of opportunity. But the hope of leaving all of the Old World behind could not be realized. Their hearts and heads forbade it. Their roots in its culture ran too deep. And the sea itself grew ever narrower. Express steamers began to cross it long ago in less than a week. Airplanes can span it now in less than a day. The wireless leaps it in less than a second. Emotion, ideas, even physical force can now move around the world more effectively than they could cross the tiniest country a century and a half ago.

There is no isolation. There are only lines of defense. Distance is vanishing. Strategy is everything. And strategy in this year of grace has become the art and science of survival: survival in the personal sense,

---

"Let us Face the Truth," *New York Times* Editorial, April 30, 1941. Reprinted by permission.

survival of ideas, survival of culture and tradition, survival of a way of life.

Those who tell us now that the sea is still our certain bulwark, and that the tremendous forces sweeping the Old World threaten no danger to the New, give the lie to their own words in the precautions they would have us take.

To a man they favor an enormous strengthening of our defenses. Why? Against what danger would they have us arm if none exists? To what purpose would they have us spend these almost incredible billions upon billions for ships and planes, for tanks and guns, if there is no immediate threat to the security of the United States? Why are we training the youth of the country to bear arms? Under pressure of what fear are we racing against time to double and quadruple our industrial production?

No man in his senses will say that we are arming against Canada or our Latin-American neighbors to the south, against Britain or the captive states of Europe. We are arming solely for one reason. We are arming against Hitler's Germany—a great predatory Power in alliance with Japan.

It has been said, times without number, that if Hitler cannot cross the English Channel he cannot cross three thousand miles of sea. But there is only one reason why he has not crossed the English Channel. That is because forty-five million determined Britons in a heroic resistance have converted their island into an armed base from which proceeds a steady stream of sea and air power. As Secretary Hull has said: "It is not the water that bars the way. It is the resolute determination of British arms. Were the control of the seas by Britain lost, the Atlantic would no longer be an obstacle—rather, it would become a broad highway for a conqueror moving westward."

That conqueror does not need to attempt at once an invasion of continental United States in order to place this country in deadly danger. We shall be in deadly danger the moment British sea power fails; the moment the eastern gates of the Atlantic are open to the aggressor; the moment we are compelled to divide our one-ocean Navy between two oceans simultaneously.

The combined Axis fleets outmatch our own; they are superior in numbers to our fleet in every category of vessel, from warships and aircraft-carriers to destroyers and submarines. The combined Axis air strength will be much greater then our own if Hitler strikes in time and when has he failed to strike in time? The master of Europe will have at his command shipways that can outbuild us, the resources of twenty conquered nations to furnish his materials, the oil of the Middle East to stoke his engines, the slave labor of a continent—bound by no union rules, and not working on a forty-hour week—to turn out his production.

Grant Hitler the gigantic prestige of a victory over Britain, and who can doubt that the first result, on our side of the ocean, would be the prompt appearance of imitation Nazi regimes in a half-dozen Latin-American nations, forced to be on the winning side, begging favors, clamoring for admission to the Axis? What shall we do then? Make war upon these neighbors: send armies to fight in the jungles of Central or South America; run the risk of outraging native sentiment, and turning the whole continent against us? Or shall we sit tight while the area of Nazi influence draws ever closer to the Panama Canal and a spreading checkerboard of Nazi airfields provides ports of call for German planes that may choose to bomb our cities?

But even if Hitler gave us time, what kind of "time" would we have at our disposal?

There are moral and spiritual dangers for this country as well as physical dangers in a Hitler victory. There are dangers to the mind and heart as well as to the body and the land.

Victorious in Europe, dominating Africa and Asia through his Axis partners, Hitler could not afford to permit the United States to live an untroubled and successful life, even if he wished to. We are the arch-enemy of all he stands for: The very citadel of that "pluto-democracy" which he hates and scorns. As long as liberty and freedom prevailed in the United States there would be a constant risk for Hitler that our ideas and our example might infect the conquered countries which he was bending to his will. In his own interest he would be forced to harry us at every turn.

Who can doubt that our lives would be poisoned every day by challenges and insults from Nazi politicians; that Nazi agents would stir up anti-American feeling in every country they controlled; that Nazi spies would overrun us here; that Hitler would produce a continual series of lightning diplomatic strokes—alliances and "non-aggression pacts" to break our will; in short, that a continuous war of nerves, if nothing worse, would be waged against us?

And who can doubt that, in response, we should have to turn our own nation into an armed camp, with all our traditional values of culture, education, social reform, democracy and liberty subordinated to the single, all-embracing aim of self-preservation? In this case we should indeed experience "regimentation." Every item of foreign trade, every transaction in domestic commerce, every present prerogative of labor, every civil liberty we cherish, would necessarily be regulated in the interest of defense.

But the most tragic aspect of this attempt to survive, alone on our continent, is that it would amount at best merely to sustaining life in a charnel-house. With Britain gone, with the bright lamp of English liberty extinguished, with all hope of resurrection denied to the little democracies that have contributed so generously to our civilization and our culture, with the hobnailed boots of an ignorant and obscene barbarism echoing in every capital from London to Athens, we should live in a new world, changed beyond all recognition.

In this downfall of democracy outside the United States there would come, for many of our own people, a loss of faith in our own democratic system. Our confidence would be undermined, our vision dimmed, our ranks divided. In a dark, uncertain world we should stand alone, deriving from no other country the sustaining strength of a common faith in our democratic institutions.

What would it profit us to achieve, at last, this perfect isolation?

The Statue of Liberty in New York Harbor has looked down across the bay at many men who have crossed the ocean to find freedom. It stands now as a silent witness to the fact that we are already locked in mortal combat with the German system.

American courage and American idealism, together with the sound common sense of the American people, summon us to the defense both of our physical security and of those moral and spiritual values which alone make life worth living. This defense means many things. It means, in the first instance, a clear recognition that the most dangerous of all courses we could follow in this hour of decision is a policy of drift; of do-nothing while there is still time to act effectively; of letting hesitancy ripen into disagreement, and disagreement curdle into factions which will split the country.

It means strong leadership in Washington; a willingness to forego the methods of indirection and surprise and veiled hints and innuendo, and to state the plain facts of the situation boldly. It means leadership which is as generous as it is strong; leadership which is willing to forget old quarrels, ready to bring into positions of high power and into the innermost confidence of the Government the accredited spokesmen of the opposition party; leadership which is at last prepared to delegate all necessary authority to the engineers of American production.

It means a genuinely firm insistence that strikes or lockouts in defense industries will no longer be tolerated by public opinion. It means more immediate aid to the brave people who are now fighting in the front line of our defense. It means encouragement to American aviators who are ready to fly our own planes in the battle over Britain. It means a determination to see that our vital supplies reach England, under the protection of our own guns. Above all else it means a decision to avoid the same mistake that the democracies have made over and over again— the mistake of "too little and too late."

There is no escape in isolation. We have only two alternatives. We can surrender or we can do our part in holding the line. We can defend, with all the means in our power, the rights that are morally and legally ours. If we decide for the American tradition, for the preservation of all that we hold dear in the years that lie ahead, we shall take our place in the line and play our part in the defense of freedom.

E
HISTORIAN HERBERT FEIS ON ROOSEVELT AND THE FINAL DAYS BEFORE PEARL HARBOR

"Japan . . . was left not only to strike the first blow, but to decide, as well, whether and in what way the issue of war or peace was brought before the United States. This course lessened the risk of blunder and costly confusion at the instant hour. But it caused the growth, as the American people learned more of what had taken place before the Japanese attack, of a sense that they had been led in ignorance."

During the last few days of somber waiting the President faced three entwined questions. First: should he promise the British and Dutch that the United States would join them if Japanese forces attacked their ter-

---

Herbert Feis, *The Road to Pearl Harbor*, Princeton: Princeton University Press, 1950, 333–341. Reprinted by permission.

ritories or crossed certain bounds? Second: should he so warn Japan—openly or secretly? Third: should he inform Congress about the fast-coming crisis and the action he proposed to take?

The President, at one time or another, was on the point of doing each or all of these things. After listening, to Hull most especially, he did none of them. His mind could not settle on any program that seemed to fit the many uncalipered angles of the situation. Until the objects of the Japanese military movement that was under way became clear, it was hard to know what action was essential, and what Congress and the people would approve. And in the event that Japan struck at the Philippines, Guam, or Hawaii, he would not have to argue with those who still believed that the United States should take no part in foreign wars. It was best, he concluded, to wait until the event itself dramatized the danger and marked the response.

Japan, in other words, was left not only to strike the first blow, but to decide, as well, whether and in what way the issue of war or peace was brought before the United States. This course lessened the risk of blunder and costly confusion at the instant hour. But it caused the growth, as the American people learned more of what had taken place before the Japanese attack, of a sense that they had been led in ignorance.

Behind the scenes there was hurried suspense—intent reading of the news of Japanese ship movements, grim talk as to whether and how American forces should be engaged, anxious uncertainty over when and what to tell the country and Congress.

The Japanese envoys continued to drive down each day from the Embassy on Massachusetts Avenue to the State Department. They still bowed as they entered Hull's office. But no chance of change any longer attached to their visits. They had been told, it was known, to keep on talking in order to make military surprise the more complete. Hull listened only for clues to the Japanese program of action, and to keep the record straight.

On the 28th [of November] the War Council, meeting with the President, agreed (in accord with the Stark-Marshall memo) that if the Japanese attacked British or Dutch territories, or if they rounded the southern point of Indo-China and landed in the Gulf of Siam, and the British fought, the United States would have to fight. It favored the issuance of a warning to that effect. When the group dispersed it was understood that the President would send a private message to the

Emperor. This was to be at once a friendly expression of the wish for peace and a warning. He was also to "deliver a special message to Congress reporting on the danger and reporting what we would have to do if the danger happened."

The State Department was put to work at once on these two messages, using material and ideas sent by Stimson and Knox. There was no time to be lost, for Congress was going to meet on Monday (December 1) and unless held together would adjourn almost at once. The President left for Warm Springs, remarking to reporters that the Japanese situation might bring him back any time. Stimson rushed such drafts as he had written down to him by plane on the 29th. Then he and Knox again worked over with Hornbeck the message for the Emperor. "This was in the shape of a virtual ultimatum to Japan that we cannot permit her to take any further steps of aggression against any of the countries of the Southwest Pacific, including China."

During these same days (November 27–December 1) the British government again tried its utmost to get a definition of our intentions. On the 30th Halifax asked Hull what the American government would do if the British resisted a Japanese attempt to establish base on the Kra Isthmus. Hull answered that he would submit the question to the President, who would be back in Washington the next morning. Later that day a message came from Churchill, urging a declarative warning.

"It seems to me," this read, "that one important method remains unused in averting war between Japan and our two countries, namely a plain declaration, secret or public as may be thought best, that any further act of aggression by Japan will lead immediately to the gravest consequences."

About this and other messages to the same effect the sceptical mind can still play. Ever since learning of Hull's decision to discard the truce counter-offer, the British, Australian, and Dutch Ambassadors in every visit to the State Department expressed regret and stressed a desire for more time to prepare. It is hard to believe that Churchill thought a warning could now halt Japan; that the Japanese government had not already taken American entry in the war into full account.

Churchill commented later about this message, "I did not know that the die had already been cast by Japan or how far the President's resolves had gone." Besides, at a hazard, his pen may have been touched by a wish to bring the President to the point of final decision; to have him say, through the warning, whether or not the United States would fight at once even if its lands were not attacked. This was an answer to which the British felt themselves entitled.

In any case, the President, on Hull's advice, postponed the warning message to the Emperor until the attack had all but begun. Of the reasons which caused him to do so, I have found no convincing record or account.

Hull had also been poring over drafts of the message to Congress. This, too, he concluded, had better be reserved "until the last stage of our relations, relating to actual hostility, has been reached." He so advised the President. For this counsel, Hull, then and later, gave two reasons. A full account of the situation, he thought, would give material to Japanese advocates of war with which to rouse their people against us. Further it would cause excitement in Congress where isolationist feeling was still strong, stir division within the United States. This might be taken as a sign of weakness and bring on the war crisis sooner than otherwise.

Who is to know whether that is how, and how far, his mind and the President's along with his, travelled? There is reality, sad reality, in the fact that a revelation of the whole situation probably would have produced a serious, even though brief, division in the country. Old fights would have been fought again. Old and bitter charges would have been heard again. Even old slurs against the foreign countries with which now, more closely than ever, the United States would have to stand. But there is little reality in the thought that this quarrel might have hastened the war crisis or made a difference in Japanese morale. The attack was known to be actually in motion—though the points of attack were not spotted.

Whatever the inner core of thought and purpose, the message to Congress was also deferred. The President went down the road a little longer by himself. He told Hull (December 1) to query Nomura again about the meaning of the reported large troop movements into Indo-China. He asked for a copy for his own private files on the intercept of the cable sent on November 30 by the Japanese Foreign Minister, Togo, to the Japanese Ambassador in Berlin, Oshima. One passage, at least, of this message for Hitler and Ribbentrop, will return to the reader's mind: "that there is an extreme danger that war may suddenly break out between the Anglo-Saxon nations and Japan through some clash of arms and that the time of the start of this war may be quicker than anyone dreams."

The next three days (December 1–4) thus passed without any new American initiative. On the 4th Congress adjourned for a long weekend.

The signs that the end was close became as plain as though they were written on a blackboard for children. "Magic" produced more telltale cables. One from Tokyo (the 5th, Tokyo time) ordered most of the members of the Japanese Embassy staff to leave Washington by plane within the next couple of days. Another from Nomura (the 5th, Washington time) informed Tokyo, "We have completed destruction of codes . . ."

The President now decided (on the 6th) that the time had come for the last-minute note to the Emperor. It said nothing that had not been said before. Washington knew that it was being addressed to a throne that rested on weak silence.

Whether or not it was truly expected that an answer, a significant answer, would be received before some first clash, somewhere in the Pacific, is not to be known from the records in hand. Probably a wan hope, nothing more. How could there have been more?

From the Far East and London reports came that two large fleets of Japanese cruisers, destroyers, and transports were moving around the southern point of Indo-China. Cambodia Point is about 250 miles from Kota Bharu (where the Japanese landed first in Malaya) and about 500 miles from Singapore.

The Dutch and British were still asking to be told what we would do if the expeditions at sea landed in the Indies, Malaya, or Thailand. To the Dutch, Admiral Stark, after consulting the President, had given advice (on the 4th) that Japan might be warned that if its ships entered certain waters close to the Indies, it would be considered an act of war. But he had given no promise that the American government would, for its part, so regard it.

The British government was similarly holding back from any warning or anticipatory measures. Thus on December 6 the President was informed, via Harriman and Hopkins, that it was Churchill's belief that "it would be the policy of the British to postpone any action—even though this delay might involve some military sacrifice—until the President has taken such action as, under the circumstances, he considers best."

On that same evening (the 6th, Washington time) the Navy and Army Departments received the report of the arrangements worked out among Admiral Hart, Commander of the Asiatic Fleet, General MacArthur and Admiral Phillips. MacArthur cabled Marshall: "Complete coordination and cooperation most satisfactorily accomplished." Hart cabled Stark: "Am sending Glassford to command TF [Task Force] 5. Recommend you empower me to pull all or part of the command under British strategic direction or even direct command . . ." Hart was so sure of approval, and so sure the battle was about to start that he began to carry the arrangement into effect without waiting for the answer. On the evening of the 6th (Manila time), as recorded by Morison, he told Admiral Phillips: "I have just ordered my destroyers at Balik-papan [Borneo] to proceed to Batavia on the pretext of rest and leave. Actually they will join your force."

In the War Department, too, some lights burned late on this night of the 6th. Ships with important military supplies for the Philippines were on the ocean; and a flight of big bombers had just left the West Coast for Hawaii, en route to the Philippines.

After dinner the awaited message to Nomura was taken out of the air. The assistant to the Naval Aide hurried to put before the President the first thirteen (of fourteen) sections of this final answer from Japan. The President read them, and to Hopkins, pacing back and forth, said, in effect, "This means war." War from the east. He would still wait, and not because of secret knowledge begin it. The roles of disturber and of resister must not be confused in the last minute.

In private houses and on the streets of Washington, the morning of the 7th seemed like any other quiet Sunday morning. Even the readers of "Magic" did not greatly change their routine or manner.

The last of the fourteenth part of the note which Japan was about to present had been caught and deciphered. It was in the President's hands soon after breakfast. Japan was saying that all talk was at an end, and bitterly placing the blame upon us. The Japanese intent seemed clear; even before seeing this last section of its answer the President had concluded Japan was about to take some action that would mean war. But would it make some further declaration? And when?

In one way or another we soon learn, the President must have thought. For a little later the carrier of the "Magic" messages brought another. This informed that the Japanese government had ordered its envoys to present its answer to Hull at one o'clock that day—little more than two hours off. The President waited to let events instruct. He may well, though it is not of record, have spent part of that time in study of the text of a joint warning of Japan—submitted by Churchill.

In the Pentagon building Marshall and his staff fumbled with and over a last minute alert to the commanders at the outposts—the Philippines and Hawaii. In the Navy building Stark and his staff discussed Hart's reports of the arrangements he had made with Phillips.

At half-past ten Stimson and Knox went to Hull's office. Soon after, his secretary entered to say that the Japanese Embassy was on the telephone asking for an engagement for Nomura and Kurusu at one o'clock. With the flimsies of the last two "Magic" messages in mind, but out of sight, Hull agreed to the hour. It would be early dawn over the Pacific islands. The three cabinet officers stayed together till past noon, wondering where the action would start and going over plans for what should be said or done. "We three," Stimson recorded in his diary, "all thought we must fight if the British fought." They were ready so to argue before Congress and the nation with all the authority of their office.

At twelve-thirty the President received the Chinese Ambassador, Hu Shih, who had shuttled back from New York on learning that he was sought. With an air of leisure and gusto Roosevelt read aloud the text of his note to the Mikado. Now and again he paused to explain why he used such and such a phrase. When Mrs. Roosevelt came in to remind that time was getting on (and a big family luncheon assembling), he motioned to the Ambassador to resume his seat, and went on to the last word.

The President then told his thoughts of the moment. In Hu Shih's present memory these remain very much alive in words believed to be close to the original. "This is," Hu Shih recalls his saying at the end of the reading, "my last effort for peace." And then, "I am afraid it may fail." The President went on to say that if he got no reply to his message by the evening of the 8th, the American government would publish its text. But he added that he had just learned that "those fellows" (his term for Nomura and Kurusu) had asked for an urgent appointment with Hull. The Japanese government, he thought, was probably hurrying its answer to our last note (of November 26). In this hurry, the President went on to state he expected "foul play"; he had a feeling that within forty-eight hours something "nasty" might happen in Thailand, Malaya, the Dutch Indies, and "possibly" the Philippines.

Hu Shih took his leave at 1:10.

Undetected, a Japanese task force was coming upon Hawaii. Over the flagship *Akagi* flew the flag which had been displayed on the battleship *Mikasa* when, in 1905, the Japanese fleet moved into battle against the Russians in Tsushima Straits. The planes were leaving the decks of the carriers. Their errand, each crew had been told, was to destroy the power of the United States to cheat Japan out of its deserved place on the earth.

In the Japanese Embassy a great scurry was going on. The code clerks had selected trivial messages to decipher before the fourteenth part. A diplomatic secretary was doing over pages his awkward fingers had wrongly typed. There were a few last-minute revisions from Tokyo to be made. Nomura and Kurusu could have snatched what was ready and kept their one o'clock engagement with Hull. But they put it off till the typed message was in fair shape. The Ambassadors arrived at the State Department at two. They were shown into Hull's room at twenty minutes past two. This was about two and a half hours after the landing at Kota Bharu (British Malaya) had begun; an hour after the first bomb fell on Pearl Harbor. American battleships were settling in the sand.

The envoys sat awkwardly in the deep black leather chairs. Nomura gave over the accusing paper. Hull made a show of looking at it. Both refrain and phrases were familiar; Japan had sought only to bring stability to East Asia and peace to the world; the United States had failed to grasp its true intentions. With quickened voice, Hull called it false and distorted in every line. The envoys made no answer. Now enemies, they opened the door for themselves. The elevator was waiting, empty, to take them to the street. As they walked across the sidewalk to their car, the light but gleaming structure of the White House stood before them. The President was talking on the telephone to Hull. The clasp of war was closed. . . .

F

PRESIDENT FRANKLIN D. ROOSEVELT EXPLAINS THE ORIGINS OF THE WAR TO THE AMERICAN PEOPLE DECEMBER 9, 1941

"The course that Japan has followed for the past 10 years in Asia has paralleled the course of Hitler and Mussolini in Europe and Africa. Today, it has become far more than a parallel. It is collaboration so well calculated that all the continents of the world, and all the oceans, are now considered by Axis strategists as one gigantic battlefield."

The sudden criminal attacks perpetrated by the Japanese in the Pacific provide the climax of a decade of international immorality.

Powerful and resourceful gangsters have banded together to make war upon the whole human race. Their challenge has now been flung at the United States of America. The Japanese have treacherously violated the long-standing peace between us. Many American soldiers and sailors have been killed by enemy action. American ships have been sunk; American airplanes have been destroyed.

The Congress and the people of the United States have accepted that challenge.

Together with other free peoples, we are now fighting to maintain our right to live among our world neighbors in freedom and in common decency, without fear of assault.

I have prepared the full record of our past relations with Japan, and it will be submitted to the Congress. It begins with the visit of Commodore Perry to Japan 88 years ago. It ends with the visit of two Japanese emissaries to the Secretary of State last Sunday, an hour after Japanese forces had loosed their bombs and machine guns against our flag, our forces, and our citizens.

I can say with utmost confidence that no Americans today or a thousand years hence need feel anything but pride in our patience and our efforts through all the years toward achieving a peace in the Pacific

Peace and War: United States Foreign Policy, 1931–1941. Washington: Government Printing Office, 1943, 842–848.

which would be fair and honorable to every nation, large or small. And no honest person, today or a thousand years hence, will be able to suppress a sense of indignation and horror at the treachery committed by the military dictators of Japan, under the very shadow of the flag of peace borne by their special envoys in our midst.

The course that Japan has followed for the past 10 years in Asia has paralleled the course of Hitler and Mussolini in Europe and Africa. Today, it has become far more than a parallel. It is collaboration so well calculated that all the continents of the world, all the oceans, are now considered by the Axis strategists as one gigantic battlefield.

In 1931, Japan invaded Manchukuo—without warning.

In 1935, Italy invaded Ethiopia—without warning.

In 1938, Hitler occupied Austria—without warning.

In 1939, Hitler invaded Czechoslovakia—without warning.

Later in 1939, Hitler invaded Poland—without warning.

In 1940, Hitler invaded Norway, Denmark, Holland, Belgium, and Luxembourg—without warning.

In 1940, Italy attacked France and later Greece—without warning.

In 1941, the Axis Powers attacked Yugoslavia and Greece and they dominated the Balkans—without warning.

In 1941, Hitler invaded Russia—without warning.

And now Japan has attacked Malaya and Thailand—and the United States—without warning.

It is all of one pattern.

We are now in this war. We are all in it—all the way. Every single man, woman and child is a partner in the most tremendous undertaking of our American history. We must share together the bad news and the good news, the defeats and the victories—the changing fortunes of war.

So far, the news has all been bad. We have suffered a serious setback in Hawaii. Our forces in the Philippines, which include the brave people of that Commonwealth, are taking punishment, but are defending themselves vigorously. The reports from Guam and Wake and Midway Islands are still confused, but we must be prepared for the announcement that all these three outposts have been seized.

The casualty lists of these first few days will undoubtedly be large. I deeply feel the anxiety of all families of the men in our armed forces and the relatives of people in cities which have been bombed. I can only give them my solemn promise that they will get news just as quickly as possible.

This Government will put its trust in the stamina of the American people, and will give the facts to the public as soon as two conditions have been fulfilled: first, that the information has been definitely and officially confirmed; and, second, that the release of the information at the time it is received will not prove valuable to the enemy directly or indirectly.

Most earnestly I urge my countrymen to reject all rumors. These ugly little hints of complete disaster fly thick and fast in wartime. They have to be examined and appraised.

As an example, I can tell you frankly that until further surveys are made, I have not sufficient information to state the exact damage which has been done to our naval vessels at Pearl Harbor. Admittedly the damage is serious. But no one can say how serious until we know how much of this damage can be repaired and how quickly the necessary repairs can be made.

I cite as another example a statement made on Sunday night that a Japanese carrier had been located and sunk off the Canal Zone. And when you hear statements that are attributed to what they call "an authoritative source", you can be reasonably sure that under these war circumstances the "authorative source" was not any person in authority.

Many rumors and reports which we now hear originate with enemy sources. For instance, today the Japanese are claiming that as a result of their one action against Hawaii they have gained naval supremacy in the Pacific. This is an old trick of propaganda which has been used innumerable times by the Nazis. The purposes of such fantastic claims are, of course, to spread fear and confusion among us, and to goad us into revealing military information which our enemies are desperately anxious to obtain.

Our Government will not be caught in this obvious trap—and neither will our people.

It must be remembered by each and every one of us that our free and rapid communication must be greatly restricted in wartime. It is not possible to receive full, speedy, accurate reports from distant areas of combat. This is particularly true where naval operations are concerned. For in these days of the marvels of radio it is often impossible for the commanders of various units to report their activities by radio, for the very simple reason that this information would become available to the enemy and would disclose their position and their plan of defense or attack.

Of necessity there will be delays in officially confirming or denying reports of operations, but we will not hide facts from the country if we know the facts and if the enemy will not be aided by their disclosure.

To all newspapers and radio stations—all those who reach the eyes and ears of the American people—I say this: you have a most grave responsibility to the Nation now and for the duration of this war.

If you feel that your Government is not disclosing enough of the truth, you have every right to say so. But—in the absence of all the facts, as revealed by official sources—you have no right to deal out unconfirmed reports in such a way as to make people believe they are gospel truth.

Every citizen, in every walk of life, shares this same responsibility. The lives of our soldiers and sailors—the whole future of this Nation—depend upon the manner in which each and every one of us fulfils his obligation to our country.

Now a word about the recent past—and the future. A year and a half has elapsed since the fall of France, when the whole world first realized the mechanized might which the Axis nations had been building for so many years. America has used that year and a half to great advantage. Knowing that the attack might reach us in all too short a time, we immediately began greatly to increase our industrial strength and our capacity to meet the demands of modern warfare.

Precious months were gained by sending vast quantities of our war material to the nations of the world still able to resist Axis aggression. Our policy rested on the fundamental truth that the defense of any country resisting Hitler or Japan was in the long run the defense of our own country. That policy has been justified. It has given us time, invaluable time, to build our American assembly lines of production.

Assembly lines are now in operation. Others are being rushed to completion. A steady stream of tanks and planes, of guns and ships, of shells and equipment—that is what these 18 months have given us.

But it is all only a beginning of what has to be done. We must be set to face a long war against crafty and powerful bandits. The attack at Pearl Harbor can be repeated at any one of many points in both oceans and along both our coast lines and against all the rest of the hemisphere.

It will not only be a long war, it will be a hard war. That is the basis on which we now lay all our plans. That is the yardstick by which we measure what we shall need and demand; money, materials, doubled and quadrupled production—ever-increasing. The production must be not only for our own Army and Navy and Air Forces. It must reinforce the other armies and navies and air forces fighting the Nazis and the war-lords of Japan throughout the Americas and the world.

I have been working today on the subject of production. Your Government has decided on two broad policies.

The first is to speed up all existing production by working on a seven-day-week basis in every war industry, including the production of essential raw materials.

The second policy, now being put into form, is to rush additions to the capacity of production by building more new plants, by adding to old plants, and by using the many smaller plants for war needs.

Over the hard road of the past months, we have at times met obstacles and difficulties, divisions and disputes, indifference and callousness. That is now all past—and, I am sure, forgotten.

The fact is that the country now has an organization in Washington built around men and women who are recognized experts in their own fields. I think the country knows that the people who are actually responsible in each and every one of these many fields are pulling together with a teamwork that has never before been excelled.

On the road ahead there lies hard work—gruelling work—day and night, every hour and every minute.

I was about to add that ahead there lies sacrifice for all of us.

But it is not correct to use that word. The United States does not consider it a sacrifice to do all one can, to give one's best to our Nation, when the Nation is fighting for its existence and its future life.

It is not a sacrifice for any man, old or young, to be in the Army or the Navy of the United States. Rather is it a privilege.

It is not a sacrifice for the industrialist or the wage-earner, the farmer or the shopkeeper, the trainman or the doctor, to pay more taxes, to buy more bonds, to forego extra profits, to work longer or harder at the task for which he is best fitted. Rather is it a privilege.

It is not a sacrifice to do without many things to which we are accustomed if the national defense calls for doing without.

A review this morning leads me to the conclusion that at present we shall not have to curtail the normal articles of food. There is enough food for all of us and enough left over to send to those who are fighting on the same side with us.

There will be a clear and definite shortage of metals of many kinds for civilian use, for the very good reason that in our increased program we shall need for war purposes more than half of that portion of the principal metals which during the past year have gone into articles for civilian use. We shall have to give up many things entirely.

I am sure that the people in every part of the Nation are prepared in their individual living to win this war. I am sure they will cheerfully help to pay a large part of its financial cost while it goes on. I am sure they will cheerfully give up those material things they are asked to give up.

I am sure that they will retain all those great spiritual things without which we cannot win through.

I repeat that the United States can accept no result save victory, final and complete. Not only must the shame of Japanese treachery be wiped out, but the sources of international brutality, wherever they exist, must be absolutely and finally broken.

In my message to the Congress yesterday I said that we "will make very certain that this form of treachery shall never endanger us again." In order to achieve that certainty, we must begin the great task that is before us by abandoning once and for all the illusion that we can ever again isolate ourselves from the rest of humanity.

In these past few years—and, most violently, in the past few days— we have learned a terrible lesson.

It is our obligation to our dead—it is our sacred obligation to their children and our children—that we must never forget what we have learned.

And what we all have learned is this:

There is no such thing as security for any nation—or any individual—in a world ruled by the principles of gangsterism.

There is no such thing as impregnable defense against powerful aggressors who sneak up in the dark and strike without warning.

We have learned that our ocean-girt hemisphere is not immune from severe attack—that we cannot measure our safety in terms of miles on any map.

We may acknowledge that our enemies have performed a brilliant feat of deception, perfectly timed and executed with great skill. It was a thoroughly dishonorable deed, but we must face the fact that modern warfare as conducted in the Nazi manner is a dirty business. We don't like it—we didn't want to get in it—but we are in it, and we're going to fight it with everything we've got.

I do not think any American has any doubt of our ability to administer proper punishment to the perpetrators of these crimes.

Your Government knows that for weeks Germany has been telling Japan that if Japan did not attack the United States, Japan would not share in dividing the spoils with Germany when peace came. She was promised by Germany that if she came in she would receive the complete and perpetual control of the whole of the Pacific area—and that means not only the Far East, not only all of the islands in the Pacific, but also a strangle-hold on the west coast of North, Central and South America.

We also know that Germany and Japan are conducting their military and naval operations in accordance with a joint plan. That plan considers all peoples and nations which are not helping the Axis powers as common enemies of each and every one of the Axis powers.

That is their simple and obvious grand strategy. That is why the American people must realize that it can be matched only with similar grand strategy. We must realize for example that Japanese successes against the United States in the Pacific are helpful to German operations in Libya; that any German success against the Caucasus is inevitably an assistance to Japan in her operations against the Dutch East Indies; that a German attack against Algiers or Morocco opens the way to a German attack against South America.

On the other side of the picture, we must learn to know that guerilla warfare against the Germans in Serbia helps us; that a successful Russian offensive against the Germans helps us; and that British successes on land or sea in any part of the world strengthen our hands.

Remember always that Germany and Italy, regardless of any formal declaration of war, consider themselves at war with the United States at this moment just as much as they consider themselves at war with Britain and Russia. And Germany puts all the other republics of the Americas into the category of enemies. The people of the hemisphere can be honored by that.

The true goal we seek is far above and beyond the ugly field of battle. When we resort to force, as now we must, we are determined that this force shall be directed toward ultimate good as well as against immediate evil. We Americans are not destroyers—we are builders.

We are now in the midst of a war, not for conquest, not for vengeance, but for a world in which this Nation, and all that this Nation represents, will be safe for our children. We expect to eliminate the danger from Japan, but it would serve us ill if we accomplished that and found that the rest of the world was dominated by Hitler and Mussolini.

We are going to win the war and we are going to win the peace that follows.

And in the dark hours of this day—and through dark days that may be yet to come—we will know that the vast majority of the members of the human race are on our side. Many of them are fighting with us. All of them are praying for us. For, in representing our cause, we represent theirs as well—our hope and their hope for liberty under God.

WORLD WAR II

II
THE CRUSADERS:
GERMAN AND JAPANESE

A
DIPLOMAT DOUGLAS MILLER PREDICTS THE PROBABLE
FUTURE COURSE OF GERMAN FOREIGN POLICY
APRIL 17, 1934

*"The Nazis are not satisfied with the existing map of Europe. They
are at heart belligerent and aggressive . . . the more completely their
experiments succeed the more certain is a large-scale war in Europe
some day."*

The fundamental purpose is to secure a greater share of the world's
future for the Germans, the expansion of German territory and growth
of the German race until it constitutes the largest and most powerful
nation in the world, and ultimately, according to some Nazi leaders,
until it dominates the entire globe.

The German people suffering from a traditional inferiority complex, smarting from their defeat in the war and the indignities of the
post-war period, disillusioned in their hopes of a speedy return to
prosperity along traditional lines, inflamed by irresponsible demagogic
slogans and flattered by the statement that their German racial in-
heritance gives them inherent superior rights over other peoples, have
to a large measure adopted the National Socialist point of view for the
time being.

Douglas Miller, Memorandum to Consul General George S. Messersmith, (Berlin),
April 17, 1934, in *Peace and War: United States Foreign Policy, 1931–1941.* Washington:
Government Printing Office, 1943, 211–214.

There are two other purposes subsidiary to the main purpose. Germany is to be made the economic center of a self-sustaining territorial block whose dependent nations in Central and Eastern Europe will look to Berlin for leadership. This block is to be so constituted that it can defy wartime blockade and be large enough to give the peoples in it the benefits of free trade now enjoyed by the 48 American States. In accordance with this purpose, an agricultural self-sufficiency program has been adopted, foreign foodstuffs are being rigorously excluded or the imported supply secured in increasing quantities from Central and Southeastern Europe. A hereditary peasantry has been set up, firmly attached to the soil through the prohibition of the sale or mortgaging of the peasants' land or crops. An increasing number of commodities have been placed under Government monopolies with fixed prices to consumers and producers, the principle of the *numerus clausus* or fixed number of persons engaged in any occupation has been increasingly adopted. The National Socialist conception of the correct or Government-fixed price instead of the price fixed by supply and demand has been introduced.

The second subsidiary purpose is the welding of all individuals in the present and future Greater Germany into a homogeneous racial family, gladly obedient to the will of its leader, with class and cultural differences inside the country eliminated, but a sharp line drawn between Germans and the foreign world outside. In carrying out this purpose, the Jews are to be entirely eliminated, the Slavic or eastern elements in the population to be minimized and eventually bred out of the race. A national religion is in process of organization; trade unions, political parties and all social, political, cultural, trade or other organizations not affiliated with the National Socialist party, have been abolished; the individual's rights have been largely taken away. In the future the nation is to count for everything, the individual for nothing. Germany is to engage in a gigantic struggle with the rest of the world to grow at the expense of its neighbors. The German population owes the nation the patriotic duty of supporting it and bringing forward all necessary sacrifices to reach the common goal.

To these long-distance objectives must be added the fourth and most important purpose of all, namely to retain control at all costs. The National Socialist party may compromise on distant objectives, if necessary, but cannot compromise on a question of retaining its absolute hold on the German people. This control had been gained by making most irresponsible and extravagant promises; by the studied use of the press, the radio, public meetings, parades, flags, uniforms, and all methods of working on popular psychology and finally by the use of force. This control once lost, could never be regained. It is absolutely necessary for the party to continue to make a show of success and to keep popular enthusiasm and fanaticism alive. There must be no open criticism or grumbling, even discussion of the future form of the State, the form in which industry is to be organized, or the laws regarding the hereditary peasantry is prohibited. Since the German public is politically inept and unusually docile, the Nazi movement has been able to dominate the situation for the past year, but the hard facts of the economic situation are beginning to be felt by the more intelligent Germans, particularly bankers, business men, professional men and persons who have touch with the outside world.

The Nazis are not satisfied with the existing map of Europe. They are at heart belligerent and aggressive. True, they desire nothing more than a period of peace for several years in which they can gradually re-arm and discipline their people. This period may be 5 years, 10 years, or longer, but the more completely their experiments succeed the more certain is a large-scale war in Europe some day.

In estimating the aims and purposes of the National Socialist movement, we must not make the mistake of putting too much reliance on public statements designed for consumption abroad which breathe the spirit of good peace and will and assert the intention of the Government to promote the welfare of the German people and good relations with their neighbors. Nor should we imagine that the present Government leaders will feel and act as we would in their circumstances, namely think only of Germany's welfare. The real emotional drive behind the Nazi program is not so much love of their own country as dislike of other countries. The Nazis will never be content in merely promoting the welfare of the German people. They desire to be feared and envied by foreigners and to wipe out the memory of 1918 by inflicting humiliations in particular upon the French, the Poles, the Czechs and anybody else they can get their hands on.

A careful examination of Hitler's book and his public speeches reveals the fact that he cannot be considered as absolutely sane and normal on this subject. The same is true of many other Nazi leaders. They have capitalized the wounded inferiority complex of the German people, and magnified their own bitter feelings into a cult of dislike against the foreign world which is past the bounds of ordinary good sense and reason. Let us repeat this fact and let it sink in, the National Socialist movement is building a tremendous military machine, physically very poorly armed, but morally aggressive and belligerent. The control of this machine lies in the hands of narrow, ignorant and unscrupulous adventurers who have been slightly touched with madness from brooding over Germany's real or imagined wrongs, as well as the slights and indignities thrown in their own individual way as they attempted to organize the movement. Power of this kind concentrated in hands like these is dangerous. The Nazis are determined to secure more power and more territory in Europe. If this is voluntarily given to them by peaceful means, well and good, but if not, they will certainly use force. That is the only meaning behind the manifold activities of the movement in Germany today.

B
GERMAN COLONEL FREIDRICH HOSSBACH RECORDS ADOLPH HITLER'S PLANS FOR AGGRESSIVE WAR IN EUROPE
BERLIN, NOVEMBER 5, 1937

"The German question can be solved only by way of force, and this is never without risk. . . . For the improvement of our military political position it must be our first aim, in every case of entanglement by war, to conquer Czechoslovakia and Austria, simultaneously, in order to remove any threat from the flanks in case of a possible advance Westwards."

The Fuehrer stated initially that the subject matter of today's conference was of such high importance, that its detailed discussion would certainly in other states take place before the Cabinet in full session. However, he, the Fuehrer, had decided not to discuss this matter in the larger circle of the Reich Cabinet, because of its importance. His subsequent statements

---

Col. Freidrich Hossbach, Notes on a Conference in Berlin, November 5, 1937, Document No. 386–PS. In U.S. Department of State, *Nazi Conspiracy and Aggression.* Washington: Government Printing Office, 1946–1948, 377-380.

were the result of detailed deliberations and of the experiences of his four and a half years in government; he desired to explain to those present his fundamental ideas on the possibilities and necessities of expanding our foreign policy and in the interests of a far-sighted policy he requested that his statements be looked upon in the case of his death as his last will and testament.

The Fuehrer then stated: The aim of German policy is the security and the preservation of the nation and its propagation. This is consequently a problem of space. The German nation comprises eighty-five million people, which, because of the number of individuals and the compactness of habitation, form a homogeneous European racial body, the like of which can not be found in any other country. On the other hand it justifies the demand for larger living space more than for any other nation. If there have been no political consequences to meet the demands of this racial body for living space then that is the result of historical development spread over several centuries and should this political condition continue to exist, it will represent the greatest danger to the preservation of the German nation at its present high level. An arrest of the deterioration of the German element in Austria and in Czechoslovakia is just as little possible as the preservation of the present state in Germany itself.

Instead of growth, sterility will be introduced, and as a consequence, tensions of a social nature will appear after a number of years, because political and philosophical ideas are of a permanent nature only as long as they are able to produce the basis of the realization of the actual claim of existence of a nation. The German future is therefore dependent exclusively on the solution of the need for living space. Such a solution can be sought naturally only for a limited period, about one to three generations.

Before touching upon the question of solving the need for living space, it must be decided whether a solution of the German position with a good future can be attained, either by way of an autarchy or by way of an increased share in universal commerce and industry. . . .

The only way out, and one which may appear imaginary, is the securing of greater living space, an endeavor which at all times has been the cause of the formation of states and of movements of nations. It is explicable that this tendency finds no interest in Geneva and in satisfied states. Should the security of our food situation be our foremost thought, then the space required for this can only be sought in

Europe, but we will not copy liberal capitalist policies which rely on exploiting colonies. It is not a case of conquering people, but of conquering agriculturally useful space. It would also be more to the purpose to seek raw material-producing territory in Europe directly adjoining the Reich and not overseas, and this solution would have to be brought into effect for one or two generations. What would be required at a later date over and above this must be left to subsequent generations. The development of great world-wide national bodies is naturally a slow process and the German people, with its strong racial root [Volksstamm] has for this purpose the most favorable foundations in the heart of the European Continent. The history of all times—Roman Empire, British Empire—has proved that every space expansion can only be effected by breaking resistance and taking risks. Even setbacks are unavoidable; neither formerly nor today has space been found without an owner; the attacker always comes up against the proprietor. . . .

The question for Germany is where the greatest possible conquest could be made at lowest cost.

German politics must reckon with its two hateful enemies, England and France, to whom a strong German colossus in the center of Europe would be intolerable. Both these states would oppose a further reinforcement of Germany, both in Europe and overseas, and in this opposition they would have the support of all parties. . . .

Nevertheless, we have to take the following into our political consideration as power factors:

Britain, France, Russia and the adjoining smaller states.

The German question can be solved only by way of force, and this is never without risk. The battles of Frederick the Great for Silesia, and Bismarck's wars against Austria and France had been a tremendous risk and the speed of Prussian action in 1870 had prevented Austria from participating in the war. If we place the decision to apply force with risk at the head of the following expositions, then we are left to reply to the questions 'when' and 'how'. In this regard we have to decide upon three different cases.

Case 1. Period 1943–1945: After this we can only expect a change for the worse. The rearming of the Army, the Navy and the Air Force, as well as the formation of the Officers' Corps, are practically concluded.

Our material equipment and armaments are modern; with further delay the danger of their becoming out-of-date will increase. In particular the secrecy of 'special weapons' cannot always be safeguarded.

Enlistment of reserves would be limited to the current recruiting age groups and an addition from older untrained groups would be no longer available.

In comparison with the rearmament, which will have been carried out at the time by other nations, we shall decrease in relative power. Should we not act until 1943–1945, then, dependent on the absence of reserves, any year could bring about the food crisis, for the countering of which we do not possess the necessary foreign currency. This must be considered as a 'point of weakness in the regime.' Over and above that, the world will anticipate our action and will increase counter-measures yearly. Whilst other nations isolate themselves we should be forced on the offensive.

What the actual position would be in the year 1943–1945 no one knows today. It is certain, however, that we can wait no longer.

On the one side the large armed forces, with the necessity for securing their upkeep, the aging of the Nazi movement and of its leaders, and on the other side the prospect of a lowering of the standard of living and a drop in the birth rate, leaves us no other choice but to act. If the Fuehrer is still living, then it will be his irrevocable decision to solve the German space problem no later than 1943–1945. The necessity for action before 1943–1945 will come under consideration in cases 2 and 3.

Case 2. Should the social tensions in France lead to an internal political crisis of such dimensions that it absorbs the French Army and thus renders it incapable for employment in war against Germany, then the time for action against Czechoslovakia has come.

Case 3. It would be equally possible to act against Czechoslovakia if France should be so tied up by a war against another State that it cannot 'proceed' against Germany.

For the improvement of our military political position it must be our first aim, in every case of entanglement by war, to conquer Czechoslovakia and Austria, simultaneously, in order to remove any threat from the flanks in case of a possible advance Westwards. In the case of a conflict with France it would hardly be necessary to assume that Czechoslovakia would declare war on the same day as France. However, Czechoslovakia's desire to participate in the war will increase proportionally to the degree to which we are being weakened. Its actual participation could make itself felt by an attack on Silesia, either towards the North or the West.

Once Czechoslovakia is conquered—and a mutual frontier, Germany-Hungary is obtained—then a neutral attitude by Poland in a German-French conflict could more easily be relied upon. Our agreements with Poland remain valid only as long as Germany's strength remains unshakeable; should Germany have any setbacks then an attack by Poland against East Prussia, perhaps also against Pomerania, and Silesia, must be taken into account.

Assuming a development of the situation, which would lead to a planned attack on our part in the years 1943 to 1945, then the behaviour of France, England, Poland and Russia would probably have to be judged in the following manner:

The Fuehrer believes personally, that in all probability England and perhaps also France, have already silently written off Czechoslovakia, and that they have got used to the idea that this question would one day be cleaned up by Germany. The difficulties in the British Empire and the prospect of being entangled in another long-drawn-out European War, were decisive factors in the nonparticipation of England in a war against Germany. The British attitude would certainly not remain without influence on France's attitude. An attack by France, without British support, is hardly probable assuming that its offensive would stagnate along our Western fortifications. Without England's support, it would also not be necessary to take into consideration a march by France through Belgium and Holland, and this would also not have to be reckoned with by us in case of a conflict with France, as in every case it would have as a consequence, the enmity of Great Britain. Naturally we should in every case, have to bar our frontier during the operation of our attacks against Czechoslovakia and Austria. It must be taken into consideration here that Czechoslovakia's defence measures will increase in strength from year to year, and that a consolidation of the inside values of the Austrian Army will also be effected in the course of years. Although the population of Czechoslovakia, in the first place is not a thin one, the embodiment of Czechoslovakia and Austria would nevertheless constitute the conquest of food for five to six million people, on the basis that a compulsory emigration of two million from Czechoslovakia, and of one million from Austria could be carried out. The annexation of the two States to Germany, militarily and politically, would constitute a considerable relief, owing to shorter and better frontiers, the freeing of fighting personnel for other purposes, and the possibility of reconstituting new armies up to a strength of about twelve Divisions, representing a new Division per one million population.

No opposition to the removal of Czechoslovakia is expected on the part of Italy; however, it cannot be judged today what would be her attitude in the Austrian question, since it would depend largely on whether the Duce were alive at the time or not.

The measure and speed of our action would decide Poland's attitude. Poland will have little inclination to enter the war against a victorious Germany, with Russia in the rear.

Military participation by Russia must be countered by the speed of our operations; it is a question whether this needs to be taken into consideration at all, in view of Japan's attitude.

Should Case 2 occur—paralyzation of France by a Civil War— then the situation should be utilized *at any time* for operations against Czechoslovakia, as Germany's most dangerous enemy would be eliminated.

The Fuehrer sees Case 3 looming near; it could develop from the existing tensions in the Mediterranean, and should it occur, he has firmly decided to make use of it any time, perhaps even as early as 1938.

Following recent experiences in the course of events of the war in Spain, the Fuehrer does not see an early end to hostilities there. Taking into consideration the time required for past offensives by Franco, a further three years duration of war is within the bounds of possibility. On the other hand, from the German point of view, a one hundred per cent victory by Franco is not desirable; we are more interested in a continuation of the war and preservation of the tensions in the Mediterranean. Should Franco be in sole possession of the Spanish Peninsula, it would mean the end of Italian intervention and the presence of Italy on the Balearic Isles. As our interests are directed towards continuing the war in Spain, it must be the task of our future policy to strengthen Italy in her fight to hold on to the Balearic Isles. However, a solidification of Italian positions on the Balearic Isles can not be tolerated either by France or by England and could lead to a war by France and England against Italy, in which case Spain, if entirely in white [Franco's] hands, could participate on the side of Italy's enemies. A subjugation of Italy in such a war appears very unlikely. Additional raw materials could be brought to Italy via Germany. The Fuehrer believes that Italy's military strategy would be to remain on the defensive against France on the Western frontier and carry out operations against France from Libya, against the North African French colonial possessions.

As a landing of French-British troops on the Italian coast can be discounted, and as a French offensive via the Alps to Upper Italy would be extremely difficult, and would probably stagnate before the strong Italian fortifications, French lines of communication by the Italian fleet will to a great extent paralyze the transport of fighting personnel from North Africa to France, so that at its frontiers with Italy and Germany, France will have, at its disposal, solely the metropolitan fighting forces.

If Germany profits from this war by disposing of the Czechoslovakian and the Austrian questions, the probability must be assumed that England—being at war with Italy—would not decide to commence operations against Germany. Without British support, a warlike action by France against Germany is not to be anticipated.

The date of our attack on Czechoslovakia and Austria must be made independent of the course of the Italian-French-English war and would not be simultaneous with the commencement of military operations by these three States. The Fuehrer was also not thinking of military agreements with Italy, but in complete independence and by exploiting this unique favorable opportunity, he wishes to begin to carry out operations against Czechoslovakia. The attack on Czechoslovakia would have to take place with the speed of lightning. . . .

Fieldmarshal von Blomberg and Generaloberst von Fritsch in giving their estimate on the situation, repeatedly pointed out that England and France must not appear as our enemies, and they stated that the war with Italy would not bind the French Army to such an extent that it would not be in a position to commence operations on our Western frontier with superior forces. Generaloberst von Fritsch estimated the French forces which would presumably be employed on the Alpine frontier against Italy to be in the region of twenty divisions, so that a strong French superiority would still remain on our Western frontier. The French would, according to German reasoning, attempt to advance into the Rhineland. We should consider the lead which France has got in mobilization, and quite apart from the very small value of our then existing fortifications—which was pointed out particularly by Generalfieldmarshal von Blomberg—the four motorized divisions which had been laid down for the West would be more or less incapable of movement. With regard to our offensive in a Southeasterly direction, Fieldmarshal von Blomberg drew special attention to the strength of the Czechoslovakian fortifications, the building of which had assumed the character of a Maginot Line and which would present extreme difficulties to our attack.

Generaloberst von Fritsch mentioned that it was the purpose of a study which he had laid on for this winter to investigate the possibilities of carrying out operations against Czechoslovakia with special consideration of the conquest of the Czechoslovakian system of fortifications; the Generaloberst also stated that owing to the prevailing conditions, he would have to relinquish his leave abroad, which was to begin on the 10 November. This intention was countermanded by the Fuehrer, who gave as a reason that the possibility of the conflict was not to be regarded as being so imminent. In reply to statements by Generalfieldmarshal von Blomberg and Generaloberst von Fritsch regarding England and France's attitude, the Fuehrer repeated his previous statements and said that he was convinced of Britain's non-participation and that consequently he did not believe in military action by France against Germany. Should the Mediterranean conflict already mentioned, lead to a general mobilization in Europe, then we should have to commence operations against Czechoslovakia immediately. If, however, the powers who are not participating in the war should declare their disinterestedness, then Germany would, for the time being, have to side with this attitude.

In view of the information given by the Fuehrer, Generaloberst Goering considered it imperative to think of a reduction or abandonment of our military undertaking in Spain. The Fuehrer agreed to this, insofar as he believed this decision should be postponed for a suitable date.

C

AMBASSADOR JOSEPH C. GREW PREDICTS THE PROBABLE FUTURE COURSE OF JAPANESE FOREIGN POLICY DECEMBER 27, 1934

"Their aim is to obtain trade control and eventually predominant political influence in China, the Philippines, the Straits Settlements, Siam and the Dutch East Indies, the Maritime Provinces and Vladivostok, one step at a time, as in Korea and Manchuria, pausing intermittently to consolidate and then continuing as soon as the intervening obstacles can be overcome by diplomacy or force."

... The thought which is uppermost in my mind is that the United States is faced, and will be faced in future, with two main alternatives. One is to be prepared to withdraw from the Far East, gracefully and gradually perhaps, but not the less effectively in the long run, permitting our treaty rights to be nullified, the Open Door to be closed, our vested economic interests to be dissolved and our commerce to operate unprotected. There are those who advocate this course, and who have advocated it to me personally, on the ground that any other policy will entail the risk of eventual war with Japan. ... In their opinion, "the game is not worth the candle" because the United States can continue to subsist comfortably even after relinquishing its varied interests in the Far East, thereby eliminating the risk of future war.

The other main alternative is to insist, and to continue to insist, not aggressively yet not the less firmly, on the maintenance of our legitimate rights and interests in this part of the world and, so far as practicable, to support the normal development of those interests constructively and progressively.

There has already been abundant indication that the present Administration in Washington proposes to follow the second of these alternatives. For purposes of discussion we may therefore, I assume, discard the hypothesis of withdrawal and examine the future outlook with the assurance that our Government has not the slightest inten-

---

Joseph Grew to Department of State, Tokyo, December 27, 1934 in *Peace and War: United States Foreign Policy, 1931–1941.* Washington: Government Printing Office, 1943, 237–241; 244.

tion of relinquishing the legitimate rights, vested interests, non-discriminatory privileges for equal opportunity and healthful commercial development of the United States in the Far East....

The administration of that policy from day to day becomes a matter of diplomacy, sometimes delicate, always important, for much depends on the method and manner of approach to the various problems with which we have been, are, and will continue to be faced. With the ultra-sensitiveness of the Japanese, arising out of a marked inferiority complex which manifests itself in the garb of an equally marked superiority complex, with all its attendant bluster, chauvinism, xenophobia and organized national propaganda, the method and manner of dealing with current controversies assume a significance and importance often out of all proportion to the nature of the controversy....

It is difficult for those who do not live in Japan to appraise the present temper of the country. An American Senator, according to reports, has recently recommended that we should accord parity to Japan in order to avoid future war. Whatever the Senator's views may be concerning the general policy that we should follow in the Far East, he probably does not realize what harm that sort of public statement does in strengthening the Japanese stand and in reinforcing the aggressive ambitions of the expansionists. The Japanese press of course picks out such statements by prominent Americans and publishes them far and wide, thus confirming the general belief in Japan that the pacifist element in the United States is preponderantly strong and in the last analysis will control the policy and action of our Government. Under such circumstances there is a general tendency to characterize our diplomatic representations as bluff and to believe that they can safely be disregarded without fear of implementation. It would be helpful if those who share the Senator's views could hear and read some of the things that are constantly being said and written in Japan, to the effect that Japan's destiny is to subjugate and rule the world, and could realize the expansionist ambitions which lie not far from the surface in the minds of certain elements in the Army and Navy, the patriotic societies and the intense nationalists throughout the country. Their aim is to obtain trade control and eventually predominant political influence in China, the Philippines, the Straits Settlements, Siam and the Dutch East Indies, the Maritime Provinces and Vladivostok, one step at a time, as in Korea and Manchuria, pausing intermittently to consolidate and then continuing as soon as the intervening obstacles can be overcome by diplomacy or force. With such dreams of empire cherished by many, and with an army and navy capable of taking the bit in their own teeth and running away with it regardless of the restraining influence of the saner heads of Government in Tokyo (a risk which unquestionably exists and of which we have already had ample evidence in the Manchurian affair), we would be reprehensibly somnolent if we were to trust to the security of treaty restraints or international comity to safeguard our own interests or, indeed, our own property.

I may refer here to my despatch No. 608 of December 12, 1933, a re-reading of which is respectfully invited because it applies directly to the present situation. That despatch reported a confidential conversation with the Netherlands Minister, General Pabst, a shrewd and rational colleague with long experience in Japan, in which the Minister said that in his opinion the Japanese Navy, imbued as it is with patriotic and chauvinistic fervor and with a desire to emulate the deeds of the Army in order not to lose caste with the public, would be perfectly capable of descending upon and occupying Guam at a moment of crisis or, indeed, at any other moment, regardless of the ulterior consequences. I do not think that such an insane step is likely, yet the action of the Army in Manchuria, judged from the point of view of treaty rights and international comity, might also have been judged as insensate. The important fact is that under present circumstances, and indeed under circumstances which may continue in future (although the pendulum of chauvinism throughout Japanese history has swung to and fro in periodic cycles of intensity and temporary relaxation) the armed forces of the country are perfectly capable of over-riding the restraining control of the Government and of committing what might well amount to national "hara-kiri" in a mistaken conception of patriotism.

When Japanese speak of Japan's being the "stabilizing factor" and the "guardian of peace" of East Asia, what they have in mind is a Pax Japonica with eventual complete commercial control, and, in the minds of some, eventual complete political control of East Asia. While Ambassador Saito may have been misquoted in a recent issue of the Philadelphia Bulletin as saying that Japan will be prepared to fight to maintain that conception of peace, nevertheless that is precisely what is in the minds of many Japanese today. There is a swashbuckling temper in the country, largely developed by military propaganda, which can lead Japan during the next few years, or in the next few generations, to any extremes unless the saner minds in the Government prove able to cope with it and to restrain the country from national suicide.

The efficacy of such restraint is always problematical. Plots against the Government are constantly being hatched. We hear, for instance, that a number of young officers of the 3rd Infantry Regiment and students from the Military Academy in Tokyo were found on November 22 to have planned to assassinate various high members of the Government, including Count Makino, and that students of the Military Academy were confined to the school area for a few days after the discovery of that plot, which had for its object the placing in effect at once of the provisions of the now celebrated "Army pamphlet" (see despatch No. 1031 of November 1, 1934). A similar alleged plot to attack the politicians at the opening of the extraordinary session of the Diet—another May 15th incident—is also said to have been discovered and nipped in the bud. Such plots aim to form a military dictatorship. It is of course impossible to substantiate these rumors, but they are much talked about and it is unlikely that so much smoke would materialize without some fire. I wish that more Americans could come out here and live here and gradually come to sense the real potential risks and dangers of the situation instead of speaking and writing academically on a subject which they know nothing whatever about, thereby contributing ammunition to the Japanese military and extremists who are stronger than they have been for many a day. The idea that a great body of liberal thought lying just beneath the surface since 1931 would be sufficiently strong to emerge and assume control with a little foreign encouragement is thoroughly mistaken. The liberal thought is there, but it is inarticulate and largely impotent, and in all probability will remain so for some time to come.

At this point I should like to make the following observation. From reading this despatch, and perhaps from other reports periodically submitted by the Embassy, one might readily get the impression that we are developing something of an "anti-Japanese" complex. This is not the case. One can dislike and disagree with certain members of a family without necessarily feeling hostility to the family itself. For me there are no finer people in the world than the type of Japanese exemplified by such men as ... and a host of others. I am rather inclined to place ... in the same general category; if he could have his way unhampered by the military I believe that he would steer the country into safer and saner channels. One of these friends once sadly remarked to us: "We Japanese are always putting our worst foot foremost, and we are too proud to explain ourselves." This is profoundly true. Theirs has been and is a "bungling diplomacy". They habitually play their cards badly.

Amau's statement of April 17 was a case in point. The declaration of the oil monopoly in Manchuria at this particular juncture, thereby tending to drive Great Britain into the other camp at a moment when closer Anglo-Japanese cooperation was very much in view, was another. While it is true that the military and the extremists are primarily responsible for the "bungling diplomacy" of Japan, the Japanese as a race tend to be inarticulate, more at home in action than with word. . . .

Theodore Roosevelt enunciated the policy "Speak softly but carry a big stick". If our diplomacy in the Far East is to achieve favorable results, and if we are to reduce the risk of an eventual war with Japan to a minimum, that is the only way to proceed. Such a war may be unthinkable, and so it is, but the spectre of it is always present and will be present for some time to come. It would be criminally short-sighted to discard it from our calculations, and the best possible way to avoid it is to be adequately prepared, for preparedness is a cold fact which even the chauvinists, the military, the patriots and the ultra-nationalists in Japan, for all their bluster concerning "provocative measures" in the United States, can grasp and understand. The Soviet Ambassador recently told me that a prominent Japanese had said to him that the most important factor in avoiding a Japanese attack on the Maritime Provinces was the intensive Soviet military preparations in Siberia and Vladivostok. I believe this to be true, and again, and yet again, I urge that our own country be adequately prepared to meet all eventualities in the Far East.

The Counselor, the Naval Attaché and the Military Attaché of this Embassy, having separately read this despatch, have expressed to me their full concurrence with its contents both in essence and detail.

D
JAPAN CASTS THE DIE FOR WAR—TOKYO
JULY 2, 1941

"First of all, the plans which have been laid with reference to French Indo-China and Thai will be prosecuted, with a view to consolidating our position in the southern territories. In carrying out the plans outlined in the foregoing article, we will not be deterred by the possibility of being involved in a war with England and America."

An Outline of the Policy of the Imperial Government in View of Present Developments

(Decision reached at the Conference held in the Imperial Presence on July 2)

I. Policy

1. The Imperial Government is determined to follow a policy which will result in the establishment of the Greater East Asia Co-Prosperity Sphere and world peace, no matter what international developments take place.

2. The Imperial Government will continue its effort to effect a settlement of the China Incident and seek to establish a solid basis for the security and preservation of the nation. This will involve an advance into the Southern Regions and, depending on future developments, a settlement of the Soviet Question as well.

3. The Imperial Government will carry out the above program no matter what obstacles may be encountered.

U.S. Congress, *Joint Committee on the Investigation of the Pearl Harbor Attack, Hearings.* . . . Washington: Government Printing Office, 1946, Part 20, 4018–4019.

II. Summary

1. Steps will be taken to bring pressure on the Chiang Regime from the Southern approaches in order to bring about its surrender. Whenever demanded by future developments the rights of a belligerent will be resorted to against Chungking and hostile concessions taken over.

2. In order to guarantee national security and preservation, the Imperial Government will continue all necessary diplomatic negotiations with reference to the southern regions and also carry out various other plans as may be necessary. In case the diplomatic negotiations break down, preparations for a war with England and America will also be carried forward. First of all, the plans which have been laid with reference to French Indo-China and Thai will be prosecuted, with a view to consolidating our position in the southern territories.

In carrying out the plans outlined in the foregoing article, we will not be deterred by the possibility of being involved in a war with England and America.

3. Our attitude with reference to the German-Soviet War will be based on the spirit of the Tri-Partite Pact. However, we will not enter the conflict for some time but will steadily proceed with military preparations against the Soviet and decide our final attitude independently. At the same time, we will continue carefully correlated activities in the diplomatic field.

. . . In case the German-Soviet War should develop to our advantage, we will make use of our military strength, settle the Soviet question and guarantee the safety of our northern borders. . . .

4. In carrying out the preceding article all plans, especially the use of armed forces, will be carried out in such a way as to place no serious obstacles in the path of our basic military preparations for a war with England and America.

5. In case all diplomatic means fail to prevent the entrance of America into the European War, we will proceed in harmony with our obligations under the Tri-Partite Pact. However, with reference to the time and method of employing our armed forces we will take independent action.

6. We will immediately turn our attention to placing the nation on a war basis and will take special measures to strengthen the defenses of the nation.

7. Concrete plans covering this program will be drawn up separately. . . .

E

NAZIISM IN FULL FLOWER:
GERMAN ENGINEER HERMAN GRABE DESCRIBES A
GERMAN MASSACRE OF JEWS IN THE UKRAINE
OCTOBER 5, 1942

"Some of the people shot were still moving. Some were lifting their arms and turning their heads to show that they were still alive. The pit was already two-thirds full. I estimated that it already contained about 1,000 people. I looked for the man who did the shooting. He was an S.S. man, who sat at the edge of the narrow end of the pit, his feet dangling into the pit. He had a tommy-gun on his knees and was smoking a cigarette."

On 5th October, 1942, when I visited the building office at Dubno my foreman told me that in the vicinity of the site, Jews from Dubno had been shot in three large pits, each about 30 metres long and 3 metres deep. About 1,500 persons had been killed daily. All the 5,000 Jews who had still been living in Dubno before the pogrom were to be liquidated. As the shooting had taken place in his presence he was still much upset.

Thereupon I drove to the site accompanied by my foreman and saw near it great mounds of earth, about 30 metres long and 2 metres high. Several trucks stood in front of the mounds. Armed Ukrainian militia drove the people off the trucks under the supervision of an S.S. man. The militiamen acted as guards on the trucks and drove them to and from the pit. All these people had the regulation yellow patches on the front and back of their clothes, and thus could be recognized as Jews.

My foreman and I went directly to the pits. Nobody bothered us. Now I heard rifle shots in quick succession from behind one of the earth mounds. The people who had got off the trucks—men, women and children of all ages—had to undress upon orders of an S.S. man, who carried a riding or dog whip. They had to put down their clothes in fixed places, sorted according to shoes, to clothing and underclothing. I saw a heap of shoes of about 800 or 1,000 pairs, great piles of under linen and clothing.

International Military Tribunal at Nuremberg, *The Trial of German Major War Criminals*, Document PS 2992. London: His Majesty's Stationery Office, 1946–1952, XIX, 457.

Without screaming or weeping these people undressed, stood around in family groups, kissed each other, said farewells, and waited for a sign from another S.S. man, who stood near the pit, also with a whip in his hand. During the 15 minutes that I stood near I heard no complaint or plea for mercy. I watched a family of about eight persons, a man and a woman both about 50 with their children of about 1, 8, and 10, and two grown up daughters of about 20–29. An old woman with snow-white hair was holding the one-year-old child in her arms and singing to it and tickling it. The child was cooing with delight. The couple were looking on with tears in their eyes. The father was holding the hand of a boy about 10 years old and speaking to him softly; the boy was fighting his tears. The father pointed to the sky, stroked his head, and seemed to explain something to him.

At that moment the S.S. man at the pit shouted something to his comrade. The latter counted off about 20 persons and instructed them to go behind the earth mound. Among them was the family which I have mentioned. I well remember a girl, slim and with black hair, who, as she passed close to me, pointed to herself and said "23." I walked around the mound and found myself confronted by a tremendous grave. People were closely wedged together and lying on top of each other so that only their heads were visible. Nearly all had blood running over their shoulders from their heads. Some of the people shot were still moving. Some were lifting their arms and turning their heads to show that they were still alive. The pit was already two-thirds full. I estimated that it already contained about 1,000 people. I looked for the man who did the shooting. He was an S.S. man, who sat at the edge of the narrow end of the pit, his feet dangling into the pit. He had a tommy-gun on his knees and was smoking a cigarette. The people, completely naked, went down some steps which were cut in the clay wall of the pit and clambered over the heads of the people lying there, to the place to which the S.S. man directed them. They lay down in front of the dead or injured people; some caressed those who were still alive and spoke to them in a low voice.

Then I heard a series of shots. I looked into the pit and saw that the bodies were twitching or the heads lying motionless on top the bodies which lay before them. Blood was running away from their necks. I was surprised that I was not ordered away but I saw that there were two or three postmen in uniform nearby. The next batch was approaching already. They went down into the pit, lined themselves up against the previous victims and were shot. When I walked back round the mound

I noticed another truckload of people which had just arrived. This time it included sick and infirm persons. An old, very thin woman with terribly thin legs was undressed by others who were already naked, while two people held her up. The woman appeared to be paralyzed. The naked people carried the woman around the mound. I left with my foreman and drove in my car back to Dubno.

On the morning of the next day, when I again visited the site, I saw about 30 naked people lying near the pit—about 30–50 metres away from it. Some of them were still alive; they looked straight in front of them with a fixed stare and seemed to notice neither the chilliness of the morning nor the workers of my firm who stood around. A girl of 20 spoke to me and asked me to give her clothes and help her escape. At that moment we heard a fast car approach and I noticed that it was an S.S. detail. I moved away to my site. Ten minutes later we heard shots from the vicinity of the pit. The Jews alive had been ordered to throw the corpses into the pit, then they had themselves to lie down in it to be shot in the neck.

WORLD WAR II

III
THE CRITICS AND THE SCHOLARS:
AMERICAN

A

SENATOR GERALD P. NYE ON
STAYING OUT OF THE NEXT EUROPEAN WAR
MAY 28, 1935

"But since wars are for economic causes basically. . . . It is useless
to pretend that our isolation from foreign political entanglements
means anything if we open wide the gates to foreign loans and credits
for munitions and spread out a network of munition ships that will
be ignition points of another war."

. . . If Europe is to again blow up in our very face, America can avoid
being dragged into a repetition of other days if America but possesses
the intelligence to permit experience to be its light.

Do we have that intelligence? Sometimes I wonder. I cannot forget
that it was only 17 years ago that found us giving thanks for the end of
that conflict which had left on every hand wreckage, wastage, debt,
despair, heartache. We found our consolation and compensation quite
alone in the thought that ours had been a successful effort to make the
world safe for democracy, and in the further thought that we had
engaged with success in a war to end war. We swore then with greatest
fervor that we would never, never let that experience be visited upon
this earth again.

Congressional Record, 74th Congress, 1st Session, Vol. 79 (May 28, 1935),
8338–8339.

But look upon ourselves today, so shortly after that engagement to save democracy and end war. Democracy has never been upon thinner ice than since then. There is more actual threat and danger of more war now than was true a few days before the World War came.

Do we have the intelligence to stay out of another such war? Again I wonder. For I see mad things being done. I see the world spending more money getting ready for more war than it ever spent in peace time, and I see America annually spending more money in preparation for more war than is being spent by any nation on earth and wonder if experience, after all, has meant anything. I see my country engaged in fighting the depression that war gave us with large appropriations for public works, and then note that the very first allocation from these funds is hundreds of millions of dollars to the Navy to be used in building more ships to be ready for more war, to be followed by more depression so that we can have another public-works program through which to build more ships and make ready for still more war. . . .

Then again do I wonder if we do have the intelligence that will let us permit experience to be our guide in the future.

This past year has witnessed the most intensive inquiry into the questions of arms traffic, munitions, war profits, and profits from preparedness for war that the world ever saw undertaken. It has been my privilege to work with six other Members of the United States Senate in this study. I am happy tonight to say that it grows increasingly evident that our labors have not been in vain and that truly worth-while legislation will be forthcoming to meet the frightful challenge which the inquiry disclosures have [shown]. Largely because the people have shown tremendous interest in the subject, I am sure that substantial legislation is on the way to restrain those racketeers who find large profit in breeding hate, fear, and suspicion as a base for large preparedness programs, and who have learned that while there is large profit in preparing for war, there is larger profit for them in war itself.

But out of this year of study has come tremendous conviction that our American welfare requires that great importance be given the subject of our neutrality when others are at war.

Tonight I think we will do well to give some thought to causes behind our entry into the Great War. Those causes as well as the results which have since followed are an experience we should not soon forget.

Nineteen hundred and fourteen found America just as determined, just as anxious for peace as it is now. But less than 3 years later we were in the greatest of all wars, creating obligations and burdens which even to this day bend our backs. What was it that took us into that war in spite of our high contrary resolve?

To me there is something sinister involved in using the language of 1914 in this present pre-war year of 1935. There is, I fear, danger that the soft, evasive, unrealistic, untrue language of 21 years ago will again take root and then rise up and slay its millions as it did then, both during and after a war.

Let me make this clear. If the people of the world are told again that the next war is a political war for the noblest possible ideals, those same people will be the ones to suffer not only during the war, but also when the war is over and the peace signed on the basis of the crude, economic struggle.

Did the English or the Germans or the French in 1914 know that they were fighting the battle of commercial rivalries? No. Did the American people know that they were fighting to save the skins of the bankers who had coaxed the people into loaning $2,000,000,000 to the Allies? No. They all thought that they were fighting for national honor, for democracy, for the end of war.

It was only after the war that President Wilson confessed that he knew what it was all about. He said at St. Louis in 1919:

> Why, my fellow citizens, is there any man here or any women, let me say is there any child here, who does not know that the seed of war in the modern world is industrial and commercial rivalry? The real reason that the war that we have just finished took place was that Germany was afraid her commercial rivals were going to get the better of her, and the reason why some nations went into the war against Germany was that they thought Germany would get the commercial advantage of them. The seed of the jealousy, the seed of the deep-seated hatred was hot, successful commercial and industrial rivalry. This war in its inception was a commercial and industrial war. It was not a political war.

Ah, the rulers of the world, the foreign offices, the state departments, the presidents and kings and czars and kaisers, knew what the war was about all the time. It was only afterward that the people were informed why they had been fighting. There was fraud perpetrated by the governments of the world in hiding from their people the economic causes for which they were fighting. . . .

The fraud of pretending that wars are political—involve national honor—when they are essentially for economic causes—leads to friction when the wars are over. Fraud and friction go hand in hand.

Let us be as frank before the next war comes as Wilson was frank after the last war was over. Let us know that it is sales and shipments of munitions and contraband, and the lure of the profits in them, that will get us into another war, and that when the proper time comes and we talk about national honor, let us know that simply means the right to go on making money out of a war.

Let us have done with all the fraud, and we will have done with all the post-war friction.

There are many who have tried to keep us from being involved in entangling foreign political alliances. But since wars are for economic causes basically, it is as important to avoid becoming involved in entangling foreign economic alliances. That is the crux of the matter. It is useless to pretend that our isolation from foreign political entanglements means anything if we open wide the gates to foreign loans and credits for munitions and spread out a network of munition ships that will be ignition points of another war. . . .

B
SENATOR ROBERT A. TAFT OPPOSES ROOSEVELT'S LEND-LEASE POLICY FEBRUARY 22, 1941

"Lending war equipment is much like lending chewing gum. We certainly do not want the same gum back. . . . The very title of the bill is a fraud."

Mr. TAFT. Mr. President, the bill before the Senate is neither a lease bill nor a lend bill. It is a bill to determine for the next year, and perhaps for many years to come, the fundamental nature of the foreign policy of the United States. It may well determine within a short time whether or not we enter the war.

We have just held a national election, in which both great national parties adopted a definite position on foreign policy and the same position. There has been no substantial change in the position in Europe since November, and no reason that I know of why any Republican or Democrat should depart from the position taken by his party. That policy was a policy in favor of aid to England, but only to the extent that it did not involve us in war or impair the defense of this country. . . .

From what I have said, with what will follow, I think the Senator [Lucas] can very clearly conclude that, in my opinion, both President Roosevelt and Mr. Willkie, in their advocacy of the lend-lease bill, are departing from the position which they took before the people of the United States in November 1940. . . .

I ask whether all sincerity and honesty have disappeared from American political life. Are promises made to the people by parties and by candidates merely scraps of paper?

The present bill goes far beyond aid to Britain. Congress is asked to authorize the President to pursue a policy of intervention in foreign disputes against his own declaration. Congress is asked to authorize the President to impair our own defense to the extent of things which may aid Britain. This bill would, if enacted, be a repudiation of the promises of the Democratic Party, and a repudiation of the promises of the Republican Party. . . .

I have introduced a substitute bill which extends credits to Great Britain in the sum of $2,000,000,000, which I believe would be sufficient until the first of next January, although the amount could be increased practically overnight by the passage of a joint resolution increasing the amount and authorizing the sale of Army and Navy equipment to the extent that it is consistent with our own defense.

The other powers given by the bill before us seem to me wholly irrelevant to the question of aid to Britain. They go beyond anything justified in the past campaign. If the bill is to be voted upon in substantially its present form, I intend to vote against it, even though some features of it provide for aid to Great Britain. . . .

The pending bill undoubtedly gives the President power to lease and lend American Army and Navy equipment, which he may not do now; but of all the foolish plans, this seems to me the most asinine. I doubt if it will ever be used by the President himself. Are we to send

American guns to Europe stamped, like a refrigerator sold on credit, "This is the property of the United States Government, to be returned after the war"? Are the fields of England and the deserts of Africa to be littered with worn-out equipment the property of the United States Government? There is some merit in taking a promise to repay in kind instead of in money, and I have provided for such considerations in my substitute; but lending war equipment is much like lending chewing gum. We certainly do not want the same gum back. [Laughter.] Not one word is contained in the testimony before the House or Senate committees in justification of any plan of lending or leasing. The very title of the bill is a fraud. . . . .

The bill authorizes the President to sell, transfer, exchange, lease, lend, or give away our entire Army and Navy, except the men. The only limitation is that equipment already acquired or appropriated for can be given away only to a valuation of $1,300,000,000. Today a battleship costs about $100,000,000. On battleships the President could certainly put a second-hand valuation of $25,000,000 or $50,000,000. Most of those battleships are fairly old and we have had them for many years. Within this limitation the President could certainly give away every battleship and cruiser in the American Navy. There can be no question in my mind that the bill contains this extraordinary grant of power.

I do not know what this imaginary doctrine of sovereignty is, under which it is claimed that we cannot give the President power to give away the Navy. There is no such principle in American constitutional law. The bill is perfectly definite. The bill provides that the President may sell, transfer, exchange, lease, lend, or otherwise dispose of any defense article. There is no way by which anyone can affirm that this provision does not permit the President to give away the Navy. Under the terms of the bill, of course, he can give away the Navy.

The power conferred by the bill is, in my opinion, a power to which no Congress, except a rubber-stamp Congress, could possibly agree. The Constitution imposes upon Congress the power to raise and support armies, and undoubtedly Congress has the duty to raise and support both an army and a navy sufficient for this country's defense. Congress cannot abdicate that power by authorizing the President to give away the Army and Navy. The only answer to the question is, of course, that the President would be crazy to think of giving away our battleships, cruisers, airplanes, and guns; but, if he would not think of using the power, why give it to him? No one can tell what an individual subjected to pressure and perhaps unsound advice may do. The President did transfer 50 destroyers at a time when it was admitted that even with those destroyers our Navy was inadequate. Today many persons think our frontier is the English Channel. The very theory of this bill is that our defense ought to be in Europe, and that if we do not send men we should at least send ships. Perhaps the President might agree with that view. We have no right to give him the power to give away the Army and Navy of the United States. . . .

We face a deficit of $10,000,000,000 next year without this bill and $15,000,000,000 with it. We can finance Britain only by borrowing money from our own banks and our own institutions. Surely these other governments have just as much interest as we have in the outcome of the war and can finance their exports to Britain by borrowing from their own citizens.

Britain has $14,000,000,000 of property all over the world. Why should we pay for British purchases in the countries where they have that property? Why should we pile up our debt?

This bill suggests that the United States take over the financing of the entire war; and modern war is crushingly expensive. Either we shall have to levy additional taxes on our citizens to pay for this British aid or we shall have dangerously to inflate our indebtedness and our bank deposits to a point where after the war we shall face either bankruptcy or, at the best, the worst depression and unemployment we have ever seen.

This bill might well be called a bill to make Uncle Sam the best and biggest Santa Claus the world has ever seen. . . .

We are giving the President the power to carry out this kind of a lend-lease measure and to transfer materials on American vessels to England, if he sees fit to do so, and to transfer them to England, without any limitations, so far as I can see. That means that American vessels may carry passengers and articles and materials to a belligerent state of Europe except for use in the war zone. If a few such ships were sunk and Americans were drowned, we would have a repetition of the very causes which took us into the World War. . . . So in my opinion we should discuss here and now the question whether there are circumstances under which we desire to intervene in the European war.

There are many in the United States today who openly urge such intervention, including the distinguished Senator from Virginia, the president of Harvard University, a number of great magazines and newspapers, several bishops of the Episcopal Church, and a number of influential individuals. Many others claim to be for peace who, in my opinion, are actually in favor of war, because the only logical conclusion of their own arguments is that we should enter the war if it in any way will assist Britain in repelling invasion. The distinguished majority leader, in his opening statement on the bill, explained that he was not for war because he did not think it would assist England, but implied that he might be if he thought it would assist England.

It is obvious to me that our actual entrance into the war would be of assistance to Britain. Evidently, Mr. Hitler thinks so, because he is very anxious to avoid our entrance into the war. He has studiously disregarded the unneutral acts in which our Government has already engaged. It would be unquestionably of assistance to Britain if our Navy took over the whole patrol of the Atlantic, and gave direct assistance at least in the Mediterranean. . . .

The William Allen White committee advocates the repeal of the Neutrality Act; the convoying of vessels to Europe; the opening of our bases to the British Fleet; the repeal of laws which prohibit recruiting and enlistments for the British armies. These are acts of war, and the kind of acts of war which inevitably will produce the collisions which mean war. . . .

Secretary Knox and Secretary Stimson assert that the defeat of Britain would mean an immediate attack by Germany on the United States, likely to be successful. I utterly disagree with them, but if that is their belief, the only logical course is for us to enter the war now. The truth is these gentlemen have always been for war. Secretary Knox has been in favor of convoying American ships through the war zone ever since the war started, in September 1939. If his policies had been followed, we would be in the war now. Secretary Stimson advocated convoys and the use of American bases by the British Fleet, in June 1940. The truth is that both these gentlemen were appointed because they were Republicans for war. . . .

Mr. President, this country is being flooded by propaganda, stirring the people up to the kind of emotion which is the necessary prerequisite of war. . . .

The attacks on appeasers are an attempt to suppress and strangle the voices of those opposed to war. There is here no question of appeasement. Appeasement means the yielding to demands with the hope that such yielding will prevent further aggression. Germany has made no demands on the United States; has made no attack on the United States. We are considering the question whether we shall go to war with a country which has taken no hostile step in the direction of the United States and whose violent language has only matched our own. The American appeasers are those who are vainly striving to satisfy Britain with money and materials in the hope that they may avoid the sending of men.

Many men are privately admitting today that they are in favor of entering the war, but they still publicly protest their peaceful intentions because they are afraid that public opinion is not yet sufficiently softened up for an outright war policy. Many men are still protesting their peaceful intentions only because they feel than an open advocacy of war today will create an adverse effect on the peace-loving American people.

In short, the time has come when the Nation should face the issue of war and openly debate it. Let us not drift into war by mistake and find later that a majority of the people were fooled into a course of action the end of which they did not understand. That is not the democratic way; nor is it the way to win a war.

The bill before the Senate raises directly the question whether we wish to go to war or not. If we really are for aid to Britain short of war, then the extension of a loan, and permission to buy the equipment manufactured for our own Army and air force are adequate. There is no need for the vast additional powers given in this bill. There is no need to authorize the President to participate actively in the war. If we are opposed to entering the war, then we should vote for the substitute which I advocate. . . .

The argument most strongly urged [for war] is that the possible defeat of Britain would be fatal to this country because it would mean an immediate military attack. Hitler, it is said, will invade the United States either directly across the ocean or by way of South America. This is asserted as a fact by reckless interventionists like Secretary Knox and implied by the President himself. How it can possibly be done is never spelled out. To my mind it is utterly impossible if we maintain and increase our defense forces. I notice a tendency today to shy away from the theory that Hitler can make a direct attack on the United States.

In the first place, it is extremely unlikely that Hitler would attempt any such expedition. The alarmists picture a unified Europe cooperating with Germany against the United States. As a matter of fact, Hitler will be badly tangled in trying to govern a dozen different races in Europe, none of them pleased with his rule. He has tremendous areas and turbulent peoples to police, including his own allies, who will not easily obey their own rulers, much less the Germans, whom they hate. No man and no race has ever succeeded in ruling Europe for long. Look at the matter for a moment from Hitler's point of view. He may be mad, but there has always been method in his madness. To set out for America with the flower of the German Army and leave a smoldering volcano behind him is not a thing any reasonable man would do. Napoleon's expedition to Moscow was nothing to such an enterprise.

Hitler would have little to gain by such an expedition, and all to lose. If he should win the war, the markets of the world will be open to him, and there are no raw materials which we have which he could not obtain elsewhere. As for our own surpluses, they will certainly be available at reasonable prices to European countries, even to Germany herself. The picture of a vast armada seeking the gold stored in the hills of Kentucky, as Cortez sought gold in the mountains of Mexico, must be too fantastic even for the advocates of this bill.

In the second place, a successful invasion of the United States is impossible. We have heard a good deal about a direct attack on the United States, across the Atlantic Ocean, stopping for ice in Greenland, and fish in Newfoundland. [Laughter.] That theory now seems to be abandoned. . . .

Direct attack being impossible, the favorite excitement now is an invasion through South America, via Dakar and Brazil. I wish some of the alarmists would look at this situation realistically, as Mr. Hitler would have to look at it. Think of the difficulty of organizing an expeditionary force of a million men—and a million men would not be enough for any such expedition—and transporting it first from Germany 3,000 miles to Dakar, a desert port in Africa. From Dakar, it is said, it is only 1,600 miles to Brazil. An airplane can fly it in a day. What has that got to do with the transportation of a million men, across an ocean in which there exists a strongly unified hostile fleet, to a country as bitterly opposed to invasion as the United States itself? Then after this German Army of a million men has gone 5,000 miles it is still just as far from the United States as it was when it started.

It has still to advance through the jungles and forests of the Amazon. It has to cross great mountain ranges, its lines of supply growing constantly longer and longer and more difficult to protect against the American Navy and the South American peoples that such an invasion has antagonized. Finally the army reaches the north shore of South

America. From that point, up through Central America and Mexico, is another 2,000 miles through trackless mountain forests, where today there are no roads. Central America certainly would be easy to defend from a land attack. An attack across the Caribbean Sea, in complete control of our own Navy, would be 10 times as difficult as it is to get across the English Channel. An invasion of the United States by the German Army is as fantastic as would be the invasion of Germany today by the American Army, and as unlikely to be undertaken. In all the months such an expedition would require to be organized and carried out we should have plenty of time to add to the defenses which we already have. . . .

For many years we have been building up the standard of living of our people. We have been trying to provide happiness for more people in greater amount. We have adopted all kinds of devices; but the general purpose has been to improve the material happiness of millions of families. Two years of war will wipe out all the progress we have made. We may retain social-security laws, and the like, but the general reduction in standard of living and the burden of taxation which inevitably result from war will more than balance any benefit those laws can give. War has always in the end wrecked finance and trade. There may be a short artificial boom, but it is bound to be followed by depression and hardship and unemployment. The petty difficulties of foreign trade would be a drop in the bucket compared to a few years of war at $50,000,000,000 a year.

It is said that we are to go to war to preserve freedom and the democratic way of life throughout the world. Nothing will destroy democracy so quickly as will war. We see today in this very bill a demand for powers more arbitrary than any President has ever asked. Already the Government has power to draft men and to draft industry. If war is once declared, it can take over the railroads, the telegraph, the radio, and the utilities. In short, it can establish a completely socialistic state, and there are plenty of persons in Washington who would like to use these powers for that purpose. Certainly the present administration is more likely to use them than was that of Woodrow Wilson.

The World War was fought to make the world safe for democracy. It resulted in more dictatorships than the world had seen for 100 years. England today is necessarily almost a socialistic state. The best opinion is that it will continue to be so after the war. In the meantime, in this country we would vastly increase Government activity. We would put the

Government into every business. . . . I have no question that a long war—and this would be a long war—would end the American way of life as we have known it.

If we enter the war today only in order to save the British Empire, we shall be involved in war for many years to come. It is difficult to see how Britain and ourselves together can produce more than a stalemate in Europe. Certainly it will take many years before a force can be landed on the Continent to overwhelm Hitler, as the shouters for war seem to think they can do within a year. Their only war aim is to lick Hitler. On the other hand, even if we should enter the war, Britain might still collapse in spite of all our aid, for that aid in 1941 cannot be very material. That would leave us holding the bag, engaged in war with all the military and naval forces of the earth. It is easy to get into war. It is not so easy to get out.

Furthermore, we should be in and out of war for hundreds of years to come. If the great British Empire cannot stand without our aid, we shall have to be forever bolstering that Empire. If we admit that the English Channel is our frontier, the British Isles becomes forever an outpost of our defenses. The English Channel is not a strong defensive position under the conditions of modern air warfare. Even if Germany is repulsed today, there will be a constant temptation to renew the attack. The weak position of maintaining a vulnerable outpost 2,500 miles from the United States would be a constant invitation to war. If we place our boundary at the English Channel, and take on this war as our war, it will inevitably involve us in operations on the Continent of Europe. . . .

This war is not our war. We did not start it. We were not asked for our opinion. We have not been told what the ultimate aims of the people are after Hitler is defeated. There is only one policy which can keep this country a peaceful country. That policy is to recognize the Atlantic and Pacific Oceans as our boundaries, and to defend those oceans. We can defend the Atlantic Ocean far more easily than we can defend the English Channel. Furthermore, the difficulty of attacking us across the Atlantic Ocean is so great that no enemy will consider attacking us if we maintain a strong Navy and air force.

The alarmists picture the ideology of fascism spreading over the world by the mere strength of the ideas contained in it. It is said that the world cannot be half democratic and half autocratic. Why not? The world has always been half democratic and half autocratic. Different ways of life have existed since the beginning of time. We have never had anything in common with the ideals of India, or China, or Russia, or many parts of Europe. When I think of the people back on the farms and in the cities of Ohio, I cannot imagine their accepting the ideals of fascism simply because Hitler is victorious in Europe. If our democracy is not based on a sounder foundation and more profound conviction than that, it does not deserve to survive. The very victories of Hitler will make fascism more repulsive to the American people.

In short, Mr. President, war is a vain policy, except a war fought at home to establish or preserve the freedom of a nation. War cannot bring peace, but only breeds more wars. War defeats its own ends. A war for democracy destroys democracy. A war for trade costs more than the trade is worth; and finally peace must be made perhaps in no way different from that which could have been made in the beginning; or it may be a peace like that made at Versailles, containing only the seeds of future war. War cannot impose on other peoples forms of government which they do not want. It cannot make other people happy. It never has attained and never will attain the four objectives stated by the President in his address on January 6.

War will never spread freedom of speech and expression anywhere in the world. War will never bring freedom from want anywhere in the world. No; it will bring only poverty and hardship and suffering. War will never bring freedom from fear or disarmament or national security. If we wish to bring about the objectives which the President always states so well, if we wish to preserve democratic government in the world, then war is the most futile means to that end.

We can only spread democracy as we did it in the nineteenth century—by the example of our own success. If we can show the people of the world that a democratic government can itself retain freedom of speech and of religion, freedom from want, and freedom from fear, then there is some hope that the other peoples of the world will rise against their dictators, and establish the form of government which has brought freedom and happiness to millions in this country. By assistance and encouragement and friendship and cooperative action we can increase the force of our example. . . .

C
COLONEL CHARLES A. LINDBERG AND THE
SPIRIT OF FORTRESS AMERICA
APRIL 23, 1941

". . . from the standpoint of aviation. . . I have been forced to the conclusion that we cannot win this war for England, regardless of how much assistance we send. . . . But they have one last desperate plan remaining. They hope that they might be able to persuade us to send another American Expeditionary Force to Europe and to share with England militarily, as well as financially, the fiasco of this war."

There are many viewpoints from which the issues of this war can be argued. Some are primarily idealistic. Some are primarily practical. One should, I believe, strive for a balance of both. But, since the issues that can be covered in a single address are limited, tonight I shall discuss the war from a viewpoint which is primarily practical. It is not that I believe ideals are unimportant, even among the realities of war; but if a nation is to survive in a hostile world, its ideals must be backed by the hard logic of military practicability. If the outcome of war depended upon ideals alone, this would be a different world than it is today.

I know I will be severely criticized by the interventionists in America when I say we should not enter a war unless we have a reasonable chance of winning. That, they will claim, is far too materialistic a standpoint. They will advance again the same arguments that were used to persuade France to declare war against Germany in 1939. But I do not believe that our American ideals and our way of life, will gain through an unsuccessful war. And I know that the United States is not prepared to wage war in Europe successfully at this time. We are no better prepared today than France was when the interventionists in Europe persuaded her to attack the Siegfried Line.

I have said before, and I will say again, that I believe it will be a tragedy to the entire world if the British Empire collapses. That is one of the main reasons why I opposed this war before it was declared, and

Speech Given under Auspices of America First Committee, April 23, 1941. *New York Times*, April 24, 1941. Reprinted by permission.

why I have constantly advocated a negotiated peace. I did not feel that England and France had a reasonable chance of winning. France has now been defeated and, despite the propaganda and confusion of recent months, it is now obvious that England is losing the war. I believe this is realized even by the British Government. But they have one last desperate plan remaining. They hope that they may be able to persuade us to send another American Expeditionary Force to Europe and to share with England militarily, as well as financially, the fiasco of this war.

I do not blame England for this hope, or for asking for our assistance. But we now know that she declared a war under circumstances which led to the defeat of every nation that sided with her from Poland to Greece. We know that in the desperation of war England promised to all these nations armed assistance that she could not send. We know that she misinformed them, as she has misinformed us, concerning her state of preparation, her military strength, and the progress of the war.

In time of war, truth is always replaced by propaganda. I do not believe we should be too quick to criticize the actions of a belligerent nation. There is always the question whether we, ourselves, would do better under similar circumstances. But we in this country have a right to think of the welfare of America first, just as the people in England thought first of their own country when they encouraged the smaller nations of Europe to fight against hopeless odds. When England asks us to enter this war, she is considering her own future, and that of her empire. In making our reply, I believe we should consider the future of the United States and that of the Western Hemisphere.

It is not only our right, but it is our obligation as American citizens to look at this war objectively and to weigh our chances for success if we should enter it. I have attempted to do this, especially from the standpoint of aviation; and I have been forced to the conclusion that we cannot win this war for England, regardless of how much assistance we send.

I ask you to look at the map of Europe today and see if you can suggest any way in which we could win this war if we entered it. Suppose we had a large army in America, trained and equipped. Where would we send it to fight? The campaigns of the war show only too clearly how difficult it is to force a landing, or to maintain an army, on a hostile coast.

Suppose we took our Navy from the Pacific, and used it to convoy British shipping. That would not win the war for England. It would, at best, permit her to exist under the constant bombing of the German air fleet. Suppose we had an air force that we could send to Europe. Where could it operate? Some of our squadrons might be based in the British Isles; but it is physically impossible to base enough aircraft in the British Isles alone to equal in strength the aircraft that can be based on the Continent of Europe.

I have asked these questions on the supposition that we had in existence an Army and an air force large enough and well enough equipped to send to Europe; and that we would dare to remove our Navy from the Pacific. Even on this basis, I do not see how we could invade the Continent of Europe successfully as long as all of that Continent and most of Asia is under Axis domination. But the fact is that none of these suppositions are correct. We have only a one-ocean Navy. Our Army is still untrained and inadequately equipped for foreign war. Our air force is deplorably lacking in modern fighting planes because most of them have already been sent to Europe.

When these facts are cited, the interventionists shout that we are defeatists, that we are undermining the principles of democracy, and that we are giving comfort to Germany by talking about our military weakness. But everything I mention here has been published in our newspapers, and in the reports of congressional hearings in Washington. Our military position is well known to the governments of Europe and Asia. Why, then, should it not be brought to the attention of our own people?

I say it is the interventionist in America, as it was in England and in France, who gives comfort to the enemy. I say it is they who are undermining the principles of deomocracy when they demand that we take a course to which more than 80 per cent of our citizens are opposed. I charge them with being the real defeatists, for their policy has led to the defeat of every country that followed their advice since this war began. There is no better way to give comfort to an enemy than to divide the people of a nation over the issue of foreign war. There is no shorter road to defeat than by entering a war with inadequate preparation. Every nation that has adopted the interventionist policy of depending on some one else for its own defense has met with nothing but defeat and failure.

When history is written, the responsibility for the downfall of the democracies of Europe will rest squarely upon the shoulders of the interventionists who led their nations into war uninformed and unprepared. With their shouts of defeatism, and their disdain of reality, they have already sent countless thousands of young men to death in Europe. From the campaign of Poland to that of Greece, their prophesies have been

false and their policies have failed. Yet these are the people who are
calling us defeatists in America today. And they have led this country,
too, to the verge of war.

There are many such interventionists in America, but there are more
people among us of a different type. That is why you and I are assembled
here tonight. There is a policy open to this nation that will lead to success—a policy that leaves us free to follow our own way of life, and to
develop our own civilization. It is not a new and untried idea. It was
advocated by Washington. It was incorporated in the Monroe Doctrine.
Under its guidance, the United States has become the greatest nation in
the world.

It is based upon the belief that the security of a nation lies in the
strength and character of its own people. It recommends the maintenance
of armed forces sufficient to defend this hemisphere from attack by any
combination of foreign powers. It demands faith in an independent
American destiny. This is the policy of the America First Committee
today. It is a policy not of isolation, but of independence; not of defeat,
but of courage. It is a policy that led this nation to success during the most
trying years of our history, and it is a policy that will lead us to success
again.

We have weakened ourselves for many months, and still worse, we
have divided our own people by this dabbling in Europe's wars. While
we should have been concentrating on American defense we have been
forced to argue over foreign quarrels. We must turn our eyes and our
faith back to our own country before it is too late. And when we do this,
a different vista opens before us. Practically every difficulty we would face
in invading Europe becomes an asset to us in defending America. Our
enemy, and not we, would then have the problem of transporting millions of troops across the ocean and landing them on a hostile shore.
They, and not we, would have to furnish the convoys to transport guns
and trucks and munitions and fuel across three thousand miles of water.
Our battleships and our submarines would then be fighting close to
their home bases. We would then do the bombing from the air and the
torpedoing at sea. And if any part of an enemy convoy should ever pass
our navy and our air force, they would still be faced with the guns of our
coast artillery and behind them the divisions of our Army.

The United States is better situated from a military standpoint than
any other nation in the world. Even in our present condition of un-
preparedness no foreign power is in a position to invade us today. If we

concentrate on our own defenses and build the strength that this nation should maintain, no foreign army will ever attempt to land on American shores.

War is not inevitable for this country. Such a claim is defeatism in the true sense. No one can make us fight abroad unless we ourselves are willing to do so. No one will attempt to fight us here if we arm ourselves as a great nation should be armed. Over a hundred million people in this nation are opposed to entering the war. If the principles of democracy mean anything at all, that is reason enough for us to stay out. If we are forced into a war against the wishes of an overwhelming majority of our people, we will have proved democracy such a failure at home that there will be little use fighting for it abroad.

The time has come when those of us who believe in an independent American destiny must band together and organize for strength. We have been led toward war by a minority of our people. This minority has power. It has influence. It has a loud voice. But it does not represent the American people. During the last several years, I have traveled over this country from one end to the other. I have talked to many hundreds of men and women, and I have letters from tens of thousands more, who feel the same way as you and I.

Most of these people have no influence or power. Most of them have no means of expressing their convictions, except by their vote which has always been against this war. They are the citizens who have had to work too hard at their daily jobs to organize political meetings. Hitherto, they have relied upon their vote to express their feelings; but now they find that it is hardly remembered except in the oratory of a political campaign. These people—the majority of hardworking American citizens, are with us. They are the true strength of our country. And they are beginning to realize, as you and I, that there are times when we must sacrifice our normal interests in life in order to insure the safety and the welfare of our nation.

D

PROFESSOR CHARLES C. TANSILL ON ROOSEVELT'S CONSPIRACY TO ENTER THE WAR AGAINST HITLER THROUGH THE PACIFIC BACK DOOR

". . . the President knew that the Japanese deadline for an end to the current negotiations was on November 29. He expressed a fear that Japanese armed forces might make an attack 'as soon as next Monday.' The main question was 'how we should maneuver them into the position of firing the first shot without allowing too much danger to ourselves.'"

. . . In the second week in November 1941 tension began to mount in Tokyo. On November 10 the Japanese Foreign Minister expressed to Grew the opinion that the "preliminary and exploratory conversations" in Washington had proceeded long enough. It was time for both countries to "enter into formal and official negotiations." The Japanese Government had "repeatedly made proposals calculated to approach the American point of view, but the American Government. . . had taken no step toward meeting the Japanese position." On this same day (November 10), Ambassador Nomura presented to President Roosevelt a further explanation of his Government's proposals. In the meantime the Japanese Foreign Office instructed Nomura that November 25 was the deadline. All negotiations would have to be concluded by that date. This deadline was repeated from Tokyo on November 11. Under pressure from the Foreign Office, Nomura was extremely anxious to secure an early answer to the Japanese proposals of November 7 and 10. While he was awaiting this answer, he noted the military preparations that were being rushed by the Roosevelt Administration: "They are contriving by every possible means to prepare for actual warfare." Tokyo replied to this cablegram by insisting that the deadline of November 25 was "an absolutely immovable one."

Secretary Hull knew of this deadline through intercepted Japanese instructions to Nomura, so on November 15 he handed to Nomura a long oral statement setting forth the bases of an agreement. He knew they would not be acceptable to Japan. Complete control over "its economic,

Charles C. Tansill, *Back Door to War: The Roosevelt Policy, 1933–1941*, Chicago: Henry Regnery, 1952, 645–652. Reprinted by permission.

financial and monetary affairs" should be restored to China, and Japan should abandon any thought of preserving in China, or anywhere else in the Pacific area, a "preferential position."

The abrupt tone of this note was a challenge that could easily lead to a break in diplomatic relations. Japan had long feared that such a break was inevitable, but in a final attempt to stave off such an emergency it had been decided to send to Washington another diplomat who would assist Nomura in the delicate negotiations that were hanging by a very slender thread. The new appointee, Saburo Kurusu, had served as consul in Chicago and New York and had recently been in Berlin as ambassador. His happy marriage to an American girl gave him a personal interest in maintaining friendly relations between Japan and the United States.

On November 17, Nomura and Kurusu had a talk with President Roosevelt, and then long, inconclusive conversations with Hull were carried on. To Kurusu it seemed that the President was "very much in earnest in regard to effecting an understanding between Japan and the United States." With Hull, little progress was made. This was particularly true with reference to a solution of the difficulties between China and Japan. Roosevelt seemed to have taken a liking to his old naval acquaintance, Nomura, and was not ready to push things. One day Lowell Mellett and Max Lowenthal paid a visit to the office of Senator Burton K. Wheeler to convey the information that "the President does not want to push America into the war." The Senator took this statement with a large grain of salt, but he remembered that at times Secretary Hull had been more belligerent than the President. This fact had been particularly evident during the sessions of the Democratic National Convention in 1940. When Wheeler was putting up a strong fight to write an antiwar plank in such specific terms that the President could not disregard it, "Jimmy" Byrnes confided to him that Hull was strongly against such a plank. It would prevent him from exerting maximum pressure upon Japan.

In November 1941 the Hull policy of pressure upon Japan was being implemented at full strength. On November 20, Kurusu discussed with Hull the matter of bringing to a close the hostilities between China and Japan. The Japanese Foreign Office believed this could be arranged if the United States would stop sending supplies to China. After stressing this point, Nomura then remarked: "If the tension between Japan and the United States can be relaxed, be it ever so little, particularly in the southwestern Pacific, and quickly clear the atmosphere, then I think we could go on and settle everything else." Kurusu pushed the idea of a *modus vivendi*, and President Roosevelt responded by outlining one that might be accepted. The fourth item in this Presidential proposal read as follows: "U.S. to *introduce* Japs to Chinese to talk things over but U.S. to take no part in their conversations. Later on Pacific agreements."

Japan met this show of conciliation with a concession of her own. The deadline in the negotiations was now extended from November 25 to November 29. But this was the final concession: "This time we mean it, that the deadline absolutely cannot be changed. After that things are automatically going to happen."

On the same day that this deadline was extended (November 22), Nomura and Kurusu once more met Hull in conference. It was soon apparent from his tone that there was small chance that Japanese conditions for a truce would be accepted: (1) a revocation of the American order of July 26 freezing Japanese credits in the United States and thereby stopping all shipments of oil from American ports; (2) American consent to a program aimed at increasing the export of oil and other commodities from the Netherlands East Indies to Japan; (3) American mediation between China and Japan so as to initiate negotiations between the two powers and the cessation of American assistance to Chiang Kai-shek. American consent to these conditions was out of the question even if Japan made far-reaching concessions in return.

During the conference on November 22, Hull acidly complained of the "threatening tone" of the Japanese press and then asked why some Japanese statesman did not start "preaching peace?" When Nomura remarked that he "did not have the slightest doubt that Japan desired peace," Hull scoffed at this statement and lamented that it was a pity that Japan "could not do just a few small things to help tide over the situation." He was particularly critical of the Japanese attitude towards Chiang Kai-shek.

Two days later (November 24), Hull had a conference with the diplomatic representatives of Australia, Britain, China, and the Netherlands. He quickly discovered that the Chinese Ambassador, Dr. Hu Shih, was not enthusiastic about a three months' truce with Japan. But Hull went ahead and drafted a *modus vivendi* which President Roosevelt regarded as a "fair proposition" but he was "not very hopeful" and thought there might be "real trouble very soon."

On the following morning (November 25), Hull showed to Secretaries Knox and Stimson this draft that provided for a three months' truce with Japan. But its terms were so drastic that Stimson believed that Japan would not accept it. That afternoon Secretaries Hull, Knox, and Stimson, along with General Marshall and Admiral Stark, went to the White House for a long conference with the President. From intercepted Japanese cablegrams to Nomura, the President knew that the Japanese deadline for an end to the current negotiations was on November 29. He expressed a fear that Japanese armed forces might make an attack "as soon as next Monday." The main question was "how we should maneuver them into the position of firing the first shot without allowing too much danger to ourselves."

When Hull returned to the Department of State he had a long talk with the Chinese Ambassador who handed him a telegram from Chungking: "After reading your [Hu Shih's] telegram the Generalissimo showed rather strong reaction. He got the impression that the United States Government has put aside the Chinese question in its conversations with Japan instead of seeking a solution and is still inclined to appease Japan at the expense of China." This impudent telegram placed Hull on the defensive. He frankly admitted that the conversation he had been carrying on with the Japanese envoys was merely a delaying action: "The official heads of our Army and Navy for some weeks have been most earnestly urging that we not get into war with Japan until they have an opportunity to increase further their plans and methods and means of defense in the Pacific area."

On the afternoon of November 25 there were more cablegrams from China. Mr. T. V. Soong handed Secretary Stimson another cablegram from Chiang Kai-shek in which the Generalissimo urged the United States to be "uncompromising" in its attitude towards Japan. This pressure was increased by a communication from Owen Lattimore, the American adviser of Chiang Kai-shek, to Lauchlin Currie, administrative assistant to President Roosevelt: Any *"modus vivendi"* arrived at with Japan "would be disastrous to Chinese belief in America." For a week Currie was "terribly anxious" because he feared that "Hull was in danger of selling China and America and Britain down the river." In Chungking, Madame Chiang Kai-shek became "unrestrainedly critical" of the American Government for its failure to "plunge into the war" and thus aid China.

On the morning of November 26, Hull saw a telegram from Churchill to the President: "There is only one point that disquiets us. What about Chiang Kai-shek? Is he not having a very thin diet?" It was not long before Hull was nearly hysterical. During a telephone conversation with Secretary Stimson he remarked that he had just about made up his mind about the *modus vivendi*—he "would kick the whole thing over." A few moments later Stimson phoned to the President and informed him that a Japanese expeditionary force was moving south from Shanghai. The President promptly "blew up" and exclaimed that this fact "changed the whole situation because it was an evidence of bad faith on the part of the Japanese." But the leading officers of the American armed forces still counseled caution. On this same morning (November 26) there was a meeting of the Army-Navy Joint Board and Admiral Ingersoll presented a series of arguments "why we should not precipitate a war."

But Hull was tired of carrying on negotiations with Japan. He was not a master of diplomatic double talk and he squirmed under the direct questions of the Japanese envoys. As far back as January 23, 1941, he had listened without any real interest to the proposals that Bishop Walsh and Father Drought had brought from Matsuoka: "(1) an agreement to nullify their [Japanese] participation in the Axis Pact; (2) a guarantee to recall all military forces from China and to restore to China its geographical and political integrity." If he had rejected these unusually conciliatory proposals why should he be deeply concerned about recent ones that did not go nearly so far!

On the afternoon of November 26 he abandoned all thought of a truce with Japan and put into final shape a ten-point proposal. Both he and the President knew this program would be rejected by Japan. There was no thought of compromise or conciliation: "The Government of Japan will withdraw all military, naval, air and police forces from China and from Indochina." When Kurusu read the ten-point proposal of Secretary Hull he immediately inquired if this was the American answer to the Japanese request for a *modus vivendi* or truce. Was not the American Government interested in a truce? Hull merely replied that "we have explored that" but had arrived at no real decision. Kurusu could only reply that the Secretary's attitude "could be interpreted as tantamount to meaning the end." It was obvious that the next step was war.

On the morning of December 4, the Navy radio receiving station at Cheltenham, Maryland, intercepted a Japanese overseas news broadcast from Station JAP in Tokyo, in which there was inserted a false weather report, "east wind rain." On November 19 the Japanese Government had instructed its ambassador in Washington that such a weather forecast would indicate imminence of war with the United States. After intercepting this Japanese instruction the radio receiving stations of the American armed forces were on the alert for the "east wind rain" message. As soon as it was translated, Lieutenant Commander Kramer handed it to Commander Safford with the exclamation: "This is *it.*" Safford got in touch immediately with Rear Admiral Noyes who telephoned the substance of the intercepted message "to the naval aide to the President."

According to the testimony of Captain Safford [in 1941 a Commander], the

"winds" message and the change of the [Japanese] naval operations code came in the middle of the week: two days to Saturday and three days to Sunday. It was unthinkable that the Japanese would surrender their hopes of surprise by delaying until the week-end of December 13–14. This was not crystal-gazing or "intuition"—it was just the plain, common sense acceptance of a self-evident proposition. Col. Sadtler saw it, and so did Capt. Joseph R. Redman, U.S.N., according to Col. Sadtler's testimony in 1944.... The Japanese were going to start the war on Saturday, December 6, 1941, or Sunday, December 7, 1941.

For the next three days Commander Safford and Lieutenant Commander Kramer tried in vain to get some action out of their superior officers with regard to the implications of the "east wind rain" message. When they induced Captain McCollum to exert some pressure upon Admiral Stark he was given a sharp rebuke which so infuriated him that he later poured the whole story into the receptive ears of Admiral Kimmel. This disclosure led Kimmel to press for the Pearl Harbor investigations.

The unaccountable failure of high officers to convey a warning to Honolulu about the imminence of war was given additional highlights on the evening of December 6 when the Japanese reply to the American note of November 26 was sent secretly to Ambassador Nomura. It was intercepted by Navy receiving stations and decoded. When the President read the message to Nomura he at once exclaimed: "This means war!" He tried to get in touch with Admiral Stark but was informed that the chief of naval operations was at the National Theatre enjoying the delightful strains of *The Student Prince.* The next day the Admiral's ears would be assailed by the crashing echoes of the attack upon Pearl Harbor.

It would ordinarily be assumed that the President, after reading this intercepted Japanese message, would hurriedly call a conference of the more important Army and Navy officers to concert plans to meet the anticipated attack. The testimony of General Marshall and Admiral Stark would indicate that the Chief Executive took the ominous news so calmly that he made no effort to consult with them. Did he deliberately seek the Pearl Harbor attack in order to get America into the war? What is the real answer to this riddle of Presidential composure in the face of a threatened attack upon some American outpost in the faraway Pacific? This problem grows more complicated as we watch the approach of zero hour. At 9:00 A.M. on December 7, Lieutenant Commander Kramer delivered to Admiral Stark the final installment of the Japanese instruction to Nomura. Its meaning was now so obvious that Stark cried out in great alarm: "My God! This means war. I must get word to Kimmel at once." But he made no effort to contact Honolulu. Instead he tried to get in touch with General Marshall, who, for some strange reason, suddenly decided to go on a long horseback ride. It was a history-making ride. In the early hours of the American Revolution, Paul Revere went on a famous ride to warn his countrymen of the enemy's approach and thus save American lives. In the early hours of World II, General Marshall took a ride that helped prevent an alert from reaching Pearl Harbor in time to save an American fleet from serious disaster and an American garrison from a bombing that cost more than two thousand lives. Was there an important purpose behind this ride? This question looms constantly larger as we look further into the Pearl Harbor hearings.

When Colonel Bratton, on the morning of December 7, saw the last part of the Japanese instruction to Nomura he realized at once that "Japan planned to attack the United States at some point at or near 1 o'clock that day." To Lieutenant Commander Kramer the message meant "a surprise attack at Pearl Harbor today." This information was in the hands of Secretary Knox by 10:00 A.M., and he must have passed it on to the President immediately.

It was 11:25 A.M. when General Marshall returned to his office. If he carefully read the reports on the threatened Japanese attack (on Pearl Harbor) he still had plenty of time to contact Honolulu by means of the scrambler telephone on his desk, or by the Navy radio or the FBI radio. For some reason best known to himself he chose to send the alert to Honolulu by RCA and did not even take the precaution to have it stamped, "priority." As the Army Pearl Harbor Board significantly remarked: "We find no justification for a failure to send this message by multiple secret means either through the Navy radio or the FBI radio or the scrambler telephone or all three." Was the General under Presidential orders to break military regulations with regard to the transmission of important military information? Did he think that the President's political objectives outweighed considerations of national safety? Was the preservation of the British Empire worth the blood, sweat, and tears not only of the men who would die in the agony of Pearl Harbor but also of the long roll of heroes who perished in the epic encounters in the Pacific, in the Mediterranean area, and in the famous offensive that rolled at high tide across the war-torn fields of France? New cemeteries all over the world would confirm to stricken American parents the melancholy fact that the paths of military glory lead but to the grave.

But the President and Harry Hopkins viewed these dread contingencies with amazing equanimity. In the quiet atmosphere of the oval study in the White House, with all incoming telephone calls shut off, the Chief Executive calmly studied his well-filled stamp albums while Hopkins fondled Fala, the White House scottie. At one o'clock, Death stood in the doorway. The Japanese had bombed Pearl Harbor. America had suddenly been thrust into a war she is still fighting.

THE COLD WAR

For a quarter of a century American participation in the Cold War was managed by politicians, statesmen, and military officials who had observed at first hand the collapse of the collective security ideal that was the League of Nations, who had lived through the Hitler holocaust, and who remembered Pearl Harbor. These were men to whom the words "appeasement," "isolationism," "aggression," and "dictatorship" had a special and terrible meaning. Theirs was a scarred generation, one that had witnessed in 1931–1941 the rise of Nazi Germany, Fascist Italy, and Imperial Japan, and had watched the ruthlessness with which Joseph Stalin had imposed his special brand of totalitarian communism on Soviet Russia. They were a group of leaders who were determined that the chaotic history of 1920–1941 would not repeat itself, that freedom and democracy would not disappear from the face of the earth, and that America, having emerged from World War II as the world's leading power, would not lapse again into the isolationism that had encouraged the rise of Nazi Germany. There was a strong feeling among them in 1946–1947 that the United States would have to play in the post-war world the same stabilizing, humanizing, and peace-keeping role that Britain had played in the 1815–1914 period. Indeed, it was the collapse of Britain's traditional power position in the Eastern Mediterranean in 1947, exposing Greece and Turkey to Soviet absorption, that triggered the adoption of the containment policy.

Given this reading of recent world history and the accompanying mind-set against totalitarian expansion that such reading reinforced, it was not surprising that the leadership of the Truman Administration entered into a Cold War with the Soviet Union in 1947. The military might of Stalinist Russia had flowed quickly and decisively into Eastern and Central Europe, into power vacuums created by the victories of its armies over the Nazi invader. To many Americans, however, it appeared that Russia, motivated by an inherently expansionist communist ideology, had replaced Nazi Germany as a menace to world peace, and that Stalin was seeking to fasten a new form of totalitarianism on war-weary Europe. In China, at the same time, the communist forces of Mao Tse-Tung were overwhelming Chiang Kai-shek's Nationalists despite massive amounts of American military and economic aid to Chiang. It seemed that much of the postwar world was about to become communist.

It was in this context that the United States fired its first two volleys in the Cold War—the Truman Doctrine of March, 1947, and the Marshall Plan of June, 1947. The former supplied American military aid

to Greece and Turkey; the latter provided economic aid for the rebuild-
ing of a war-torn European economy thought to be amenable to the
blandishments of communism. As Representative John McCormack of
Massachusetts put it, "The issue is joined between the forces of democracy and communism."[1] At the same time, the State Department, in
the person of George F. Kennan, produced in July, 1947, a theoretical
justification of America's toughening anti-Soviet stance. This was the
"Containment Doctrine," a pragmatic blueprint for action that would
serve America throughout the Cold War as the basic intellectual rational-
ization of the peace-keeping role the United States was prepared to play
in post-war international politics. Its firmness helped carry Truman to
his surprise electoral victory in 1948 over Thomas E. Dewey and Henry
A. Wallace.[2]

As it became increasingly apparent that the veto provision of the
United Nations Charter condemned the UN to virtual ineptitude and in-
activity as an effective collective security mechanism, the United States
also moved toward the construction of a traditional defensive alliance
system. In 1949, the North Atlantic Treaty Organization (NATO) came
into existence, designed in part to effect the containment of the Soviet
Union in Europe. It marked the first participation of the United States
in a formal treaty arrangement since the Franco-American Alliance of
1778–1800. Russia eventually responded to NATO in 1955 with the
counterbalancing Warsaw Pact alliance; but this response came only
after the death of Stalin, the subsequent collapse of Moscow's mono-
lithic direction of the world communist movement, and the successful
American containment of communist expansion in Korea. By 1955, an
uneasy balance of power had returned to Europe, and Russia had turned
to the economic consolidation of its Eastern European empire.

The attack of Communist North Korea on South Korea in June,
1950, seemed clear evidence to many Americans that Stalin, contained
and frustrated in Europe, had shifted the arena of Soviet expansion to
the Far East. Because of the fortuitous absence from New York of the
Soviet representative on the UN Security Council, and the removal

---

1 Peter J. Kumpa, "Truman Doctrine: If It Hadn't Been There . . .," *Baltimore
Sunday Sun* (March 12, 1972), Kl.

2 The domestic political advantages of the Cold War issue in 1948 are discussed in
Robert A. Divine, "The Cold War and the Election of 1948," *The Journal of American
History*, LIX (June, 1972), 90–110.

thereby of the inevitable Russian veto, President Truman was able to dispatch American military force to beleaguered South Korea under the aegis of the United Nations. "The attack upon Korea," he said, "makes it plain beyond all doubt that communism has passed beyond the use of subversion to conquer independent nations and will now use armed invasion and war."

The Cold War had turned hot. Put another way, the American policy of containment, designed for Europe, was hastily extended to East Asia under the banner of the United Nations. It was also specifically extended to Indochina where Truman simultaneously directed "acceleration in the furnishing of military assistance to the forces of France" to meet the internal and external communist and nationalist challenge to French colonialism there.

Thanks to the subsequent military intervention of the People's Republic of China, the Korean War became a bloody and indecisive affair that ended in stalemate. American intervention did, however, preserve the political and territorial integrity of South Korea—but only at the cost of 50,000 American lives. If such intervention and sacrifice was historically unique as the first successful punishment of aggression by international collective action, it was fraught with future danger in that it projected American power and interests onto the Asian continent. Indeed, by 1954, it seemed to President Dwight D. Eisenhower that unless the United States remained in Asia to help contain the southerly expansion of Communist China, the weak little Indochinese successor states, especially South Vietnam, would soon topple over like so many dominoes. To prevent this from happening, the Southeast Asia Treaty Organization (SEATO) was brought into existence in September, 1954, and its protective features were soon extended to South Vietnam. As Massachusetts Senator John F. Kennedy noted in 1956, "Vietnam represents the cornerstone of the Free World in Southeast Asia, the keystone to the arch, the finger in the dike. . . . Vietnam represents a test of American responsibility and determination in Asia."[3]

It was no surprise, then, in 1962, that President Kennedy repeated the domino analogy used earlier by Eisenhower and embraced the employment of the containment principle in Southeast Asia. As it became

---

3 Speech to American Friends of Vietnam, Washington, D.C. June 1, 1956, in *A Symposium on American's Stake in Vietnam*. New York: American Friends of Vietnam, September, 1956, 10–11.

clear to him and his advisors that Communist North Vietnam (aided by Communist China and the Soviet Union) was employing both external aggression and internal subversion to conquer South Vietnam, Kennedy opened the SEATO umbrella. Initially, American military "advisers" were sent to Saigon to train and bolster the South Vietnamese armed forces. But by the time Kennedy was assassinated in November, 1963, American forces were openly, actively and directly involved in combat operations.

When it appeared in March, 1965, that North Vietnam was about to overrun South Vietnam and win a stunning military victory in the field, President Lyndon B. Johnson sharply escalated the level of American military involvement. "The first reality," he explained, "is that North Viet-Nam has attacked the independent nation of South Viet-Nam." Because the objective of North Vietnam was "total conquest," the United States, said Johnson, and no moral or legal choice but to intervene. Again the Cold War had become hot. As the State Department explained it, American obligations to South Vietnam under the SEATO pact demanded nothing less than "military assistance."

And so it was that the United States became enmeshed in a long, costly, distant, inconclusive, and unpopular war in the jungles of Vietnam, a war not unlike the guerrilla operation fought against the tenacious Filipinos in 1899–1902. In spite of repeated escalations of men and material (to the number of 560,000 troops), it was a war which the Pentagon could not win. Atrocities perpetrated by ill-trained and ill-led American conscript soldiers against Vietnamese civilians at My Lai in March, 1968, shocked American public opinion, rocked the Army to its foundations, and amplified the popular outcry that demanded an end to the continued expenditure of lives and treasure in defense of a South Vietnam said to be a corrupt military dictatorship willing only to fight to the last drop of American blood.

In early 1970, President Richard M. Nixon apparently decided that the better part of domestic political valor was to disengage American forces from the fray and turn the prosecution of the war over to the South Vietnamese themselves. To help effect this so-called "Vietnamization" of the struggle, Nixon ordered in April, 1970, a "surgical strike" into neutral Cambodia to knock out staging areas used by the North Vietnamese army there to facilitate its attacks on South Vietnam. This action, which appeared to some observers to be an expansion of the American military commitment in Southeast Asia, produced still another political explosion at home, one so powerful that it caused pundit Joseph Alsop to despair that America could ever play a decisive role in maintaining the peace and stability of the world. The indecisive agony of the Vietnam War and the increasingly negative public reaction to it, he felt, heralded the end of containment and augured the onset of a "new isolationism" in America.

Viewed from Moscow, Pyongyang, Peking, and Hanoi, the Cold War was conceived, plotted, and launched by aggressive American capitalist-imperialists who, brandishing their atomic bombs, were bent on destroying the peoples' democracy and socialism which could lead the post-war world into a communist utopia. Joseph Stalin pointed out in March, 1946, that the war-torn Soviet Union desired only an era of peace. He accused the West of anti-Soviet provocations, called attention to earlier Western intervention in the Bolshevik Revolution, explained the advent of communism in Eastern Europe as a "normal function" and as a working out of "the law of historical development." He also insisted that Eastern Europe contain only "governments whose relations to the Soviet Union are loyal." Similarly, Soviet Foreign Minister V. M. Molotov saw the 1947 Truman Doctrine-Marshall Plan as an expression of a rampant American imperialism designed to encircle and crush the peace-loving Soviet Union. Presumably to frustrate this American conspiracy, the Czech Communist Party, encouraged and supported by the proximity of Soviet arms, overthrew the democratic government of Eduard Beneš in February, 1948, and brought Czechoslovakia into the Russian orbit. Prague now had a government "loyal" to Moscow. Nor was that to be the end of it. With monotonous regularity Soviet tanks and troops lumbered westward to crush popular uprisings against communism in Russia's Eastern European satellite states—East Germany (1953), Czechoslovakia (1953), Poland (1955), Hungary (1956), Czechoslovakia (1968).[4]

After Stalin's death in 1953, however, there was less talk in Soviet circles about "capitalist encirclement" and much talk about "peaceful coexistence" with the West. But as Lenin had stated, "the strictest dedication to the ideas of communism must be combined with the ability to make all the necessary practical compromises, to 'tack', to make agree-

---

4 In somewhat similar fashion, American intervention in Guatemala (1954), Cuba (1961–1962), and the Dominican Republic (1965) was designed to protect America's traditional Caribbean sphere of influence from communist contagion.

ments, zigzags, retreats and so on."[5] Whether "peaceful coexistence" was but another of the many zigzags in Soviet foreign policy cannot yet be determined. It can be interpreted in a number of ways. In any event, by the late 1950s the Russian-American expression of the Cold War was moved to a back burner. Not so the Sino-American phase.

To prevent the triumph of capitalist-imperialism and to insure the survival, expansion, and ultimate victory of revolutionary socialism in East Asia, Mao Tse-Tung had earlier outlined the military-political strategy and tactics that would guide Chinese (as well as North Korean and North Vietnamese) foreign policy during the Cold War. Mao's revolutionary strategy emphasized abiding patience, internal ideological certainty and unity, flexibility of tactics, rapid escalations and deescalations of military effort, drumbeat propaganda, and constant pressure on the enemy of the moment; it included a sophisticated combination of covert subversion and overt pressure, sometimes vicarious, sometimes direct, against the capitalist enemy or his allies. Such were the main features of Mao's formula for "protracted war" against imperialism. "As a distant journey tests the strength of a horse and a long task proves the character of a man," he wrote, "[so] guerrilla warfare will demonstrate its enormous power in the course of a long and ruthless war."

The failure of overt force in Korea seemed to dictate the employment of covert subversion and guerrilla warfare in Vietnam. There Maoist aid, theory, tactics, and organization expelled the French in 1954, and gradually wore down the Americans in the 1960s. By 1972 the indefatigable Communists were still hard at work in their attempt to bring about the unification of North and South Vietnam by sword and mortar. Calculated North Vietnamese and Viet Cong atrocities against the civilian population of South Vietnam were part of a broad strategy of terror. In sum, Hanoi outwaited, outwitted, outfought, outbled, and outlasted the United States in Vietnam, just as Maoist revolutionary thought had advised and predicted. Mr. Nixon's surprise visit to Peking in March, 1972, in an effort to reduce Sino-American tension in East Asia, brought into serious question the continued usefulness and viability of America's containment policy in Indochina.

The length and complexity of the Cold War, together with its varying intensities, its geopolitical implications, and its shifting tactics,

---

5 Foreign Policy Research Institute of the University of Pennsylvania, *Khrushchev's Strategy and Its Meaning for America. . . .*, Committee on the Judiciary of the United States Senate, 86th Congress, 2nd Session. Washington: GPO, 1960, 1–29.

produced a quarter of a century of vigorous criticism of American policies. This home-grown opposition stemmed from the nationalist right, the pacifist left, and the concerned center. Critics of Korea became crusaders in Vietnam and vice versa. Politicians shifted their stances over the years in their searches for votes.

The bitterness of the Cold War debate among Americans also effectively blocked the emergence of Cold War scholarship. Thanks in part to the noncooperation of the United States government, historical detachment was virtually impossible to achieve. News was "managed," relevant documents were stamped "secret," official spokesmen obscured the truth (the "Credibility Gap"), primary source material was revealed on a selective basis, and government archives were closed to historians. Instead, polemical historiography became a weapon in the Cold War debate as American scholars supported either the hawk or dove position with all the fury of their footnotes.

It should be pointed out, however, that most of the Cold War "scholarship" published by mid-1972 was generally hostile to the official government position, certainly so with regard to the American involvement in Vietnam. Indeed, a new "revisionist" history blamed the onset of the Cold War mainly on an imperialistic United States and emphasized America's "atomic blackmail" of Russia in 1945–1947. It also argued that Soviet foreign policy was no less moral or more brutal than that of the United States, and charged that America's fuzzy commitment to saving the "free peoples" of the world by containing the Communists led only to embarrassing entanglements with reactionary allied governments and eventually to the disaster in Vietnam. In general, the revisionist historians decided in various ways and to varying degrees that the Soviet Union and its allies were usually right in the Cold War and that the United States and its "free world" allies were usually wrong.

At the very outset of the Cold War, Walter Lippmann decreed that containment would not work. He felt that it was an overreaction to Soviet truculence and that its employment would "cause us to squander our substance and our prestige." He felt that American "satellite states and puppet governments are not good material out of which to construct unassailable barriers" to Soviet expansion, and recommended instead the creation of a new balance of power system in Europe.

Former Vice President Henry A. Wallace charged in 1948 that growing American-Russian tension was largely the fault of United States capitalist interests, that the security-conscious Soviet Union had been provoked by the West into filling the post-war power vacuum in Eastern and Central Europe, and that rising anticommunist sentiment in the United States was but a cloak behind which American racism, anti-unionism, facism, and reaction were secreted. His left-leaning Progressive Party, heavily infiltrated by the CPUSA, polled some 1,000,000 votes in the 1948 presidential election.

Critical thunder from the left was matched in intensity on the right when American troops became bogged down in 1951 on the Korean Peninsula. The notion of fighting a major war on a limited scale for limited containment and collective security goals was an idea wholly foreign to many Americans. General Douglas McArthur addressed this frustration when he charged the Truman Administration with spinelessness, with appeasement of Communist China, and with indecision in Korea. He demanded an all-out military effort in East Asia to crush the communist enemy. Similarly, Senator Joseph R. McCarthy of Wisconsin saw a communist clique within the State Department nefariously plotting to lose the war in Korea and to sell out the entire free world to Sino-Soviet communism. He also charged the Truman "conspirators" with having purposely "lost" China to the Communists in 1946–1948. Even California Senator Richard M. Nixon, later a Vietnam crusader, assailed the Truman Administration in July, 1951, for its "no win" policy in Korea and for harboring "communists" within the government.[6] On the other hand, leftist college students in the United States attacked Truman's "fascist aggression" in Korea and supported communist propaganda charges that the American military systematically employed "germ warfare" there against the heroic Chinese and North Korean armies.

The deepening American involvement in the Vietnam War produced even sharper domestic political tensions than had the earlier debate on Korea, coupled as it was with the broadly-based civil rights movement of the 1960s. Once again, however, conspiracy thesis often dominated the analyses of critics and crusaders on both the right and left.

Centering initially on college campuses, among young professional people, and among those dedicated to the "counterculture" and to radical new "life styles," the peace movement grew rapidly in the period from 1965 to 1970. As one dimension of a broader and many-faceted social protest movement, the peace crusade of the late 1960s was in in-

---

6 *Congressional Record*, 82nd Congress, 1st Session (July 3, 1951), Vol. 97, Pt. 13, Appendix, A4107–A4110.

tensity unlike anything of its kind in American history. Leaders of "The Movement," as it was called, vigorously and variously demanded equal social, political, and economic rights for American Negroes, for women, for Mexican-Americans and for American Indians. They insisted on ecological and environmental reforms, "relevance" in education, votes for 18-year-olds, the liberalization of laws relating to abortion, divorce, and homosexuality, the legalization of marijuana, the abolition of military conscription, and, in general, an end to the control of American life by its so-called "capitalist establishment." Thousands of young American men, mostly college students, fled in exile to Canada rather than serve in the armed forces of the United States in Vietnam. Other thousands took to violent demonstrations in their cities and on their campuses to call attention to their demands. Protest marches on Washington became commonplace.

Disparate as The Movement otherwise was, it was solidly unified in unbending hostility to American participation in the Vietnam War. Regarding the political situation in Vietnam as a local civil war in which a reactionary United States had intervened to conceal serious inadequacies and shortcomings in American society, anti-war critics openly cheered North Vietnam-Viet Cong victories in the field and condemned as "imperialist aggression" the resulting escalation of the American military involvement. Carl Oglesby, spokesman for the radical, campus-based Students for a Democratic Society, blamed American involvement in the war on aging New Deal "liberals" who blindly equated their just war against Hitler with an unjust war against the Viet Cong revolutionaries in Vietnam. Their revolution, he maintained, was "as honest a revolution as you can find anywhere in history."

This attack on American policy produced in turn a sharp and continuing patriotic reaction on the right. Representative John Bell Williams of Mississippi was but one of many conservative Americans who saw the peace and civil rights movement as a Negro conspiracy, as a "highly organized Communist plot, designed to embarrass us in the eyes of the world, and to encourage Red China to redouble its efforts to push us out of Vietnam." In the words of Joseph J. Lombardo, former national commander of the Veterans of Foreign Wars, "No period in our history has produced so many dissenters against law and order and lawfully constituted authority and in open support of our enemies."[7]

---

7 Speech to 52nd Annual Convention, Maryland Veterans of Foreign Wars, Baltimore, Md., June 24, 1972. *Baltimore Sunday Sun*, June 25, 1972, A20.

Whatever the origin or nature of the Vietnam war, the inability of the American command to bring it speedily to a conclusion in the field, despite repeated escalations of military effort, produced growing frustration among Americans—not only among right and left crusaders and critics, but among increasing numbers of American moderates. As the casualties mounted to 55,000 American dead, the situation was ripe for political exploitation.

Arkansas Senator J. William Fulbright, earlier a strong supporter of the Kennedy-Johnson policy of containment in Southeast Asia, emerged in 1966 as the leading antiwar critic of President Lyndon B. Johnson. Charging that the President had usurped the war-making power of the Congress, Fulbright praised the idealism and partriotism of antiwar dissenters, condemned America's "fatal arrogance of power" in world politics, and demanded total disengagement from the nation's military commitment to the corrupt Saigon government. Similarly, Minnesota Senator Eugene McCarthy emerged from virtual political obscurity to forge and lead a peace faction within the Democratic Party. His youth-oriented 1968 presidential primary campaign (the "Children's Crusade") was based on the proposition that the United States had lost the war in Vietnam, had no business being there in the first place, and could do little more than negotiate the terms of its withdrawal from the contest.

Eugene McCarthy failed to capture the Democratic nomination in 1968, however, and failed to incorporate his peace views into the Democratic platform. But his stunning victory in the New Hampshire presidential primary in March, 1968, drove incumbent President Johnson from the field, marshalled the antiwar sentiment of The Movement and hundreds of thousands of other war-weary Americans behind his candidacy, and split the Democratic Party on the war issue.

Former Republican Vice President Richard M. Nixon, barely defeated in his bid for the White House in 1960 by John F. Kennedy, narrowly won the election of 1968. Nixon won in part on the pledge that he would end American participation in the war in Vietnam by gradually turning over its continued prosecution to the South Vietnamese, and in part because the Democratic nominee, Vice President Hubert H. Humphrey, attempted to carry water on both shoulders on the war question. As one student peace activist in the campaign later put it, "There was a tremendous emotion in the '68 elections. People had worked months and months, and we felt if we worked long enough and hard enough, we'd get something. What we got was Richard Nixon. It took us until 1970 to realize that."[8]

Whatever Nixon's intentions about ending the war (as distinct from his campaign stance on it), control of the issue began to pass from his hands in May, 1970. The public outcry that greeted his announcement of the punitive expedition into Cambodia was coupled with the tragedy at Kent State University. There student dissenters burned down the R.O.T.C. building and otherwise demonstrated against Nixon's Cambodian decision. Units of the Ohio National Guard were rushed to the campus to maintain order. In a confrontation with taunting students that followed, the ill-trained young guardsmen fired into the crowd. When the shooting ceased, four Kent State students lay dead.

For all practical purposes those shots ended direct American participation in the land war in Vietnam. Americans in all walks of life were aghast. Student protest riots and demonstrations swept the nation, closing down hundreds of universities and colleges across the land. At the sophisticated University of Oregon student editors demanded an immediate end to the war, called for the closing of the university as an act of propitiation and mourning, and noted ominously that "after five years of peaceful protests, thousands of concerned young people now feel their only alternative is to take up the gun." On the opposite coast, at unsophisticated little Washington College in rural Maryland, student editors bemoaned the isolation of their campus from the mainstream of American student activism, demanded that their faculty "provide information and discussion about contemporary affairs," and recommended the organization of "extracurricular lectures and seminars on such subjects as current international and national affairs, pollution and racism." At both institutions regular classes were briefly suspended as acts of protest. American troop withdrawals from Vietnam began soon after.

Historians critical of American involvement in Southeast Asia also came forward again to be heard. In March, 1971, the distinguished Henry Steele Commager summed up the historical and constitutional case against the continuation of American involvement in Vietnam. Selecting his supporting historical illustrations with care, Commager told the Senate Foreign Affairs Committee that America's military inter-

---

8 Phil Churner, quoted in *The Chronicle of Higher Education*, VI (March 13, 1972), 4.

vention in Southeast Asia was simply unconstitutional. He blamed the national malaise on the constitutional abuse of the war-making power of presidents over the past twenty years, and argued for speedy American withdrawal from the war. He concluded with the following thought.

> As we have greater power than any other nation, so we should display greater moderation in using it, greater humility in justifying it, and greater magnanimity in withholding it. We display neither moderation nor humility nor magnanimity, but that arrogance of power which your chairman [Fulbright] has so eloquently deplored. In the long run the abuse of executive power cannot be divorced from the abuse of national power. If we subvert world order and threaten world peace, we must inevitably subvert and threaten our own political institutions first. This we are in the process of doing.

Just what the implications of that observation would mean to America's self-proclaimed role in history as defender of human freedom and as "the last, best hope of earth" was not clear.

What soon became clear was that President Nixon was not listening to Commager, Fulbright, and The Movement with all the attentiveness at his command. Having gradually withdrawn some 500,000 American troops from Vietnam in 1970–1972 in response to mounting criticism of U.S. policy there, the President was suddenly presented with a massive, renewed invasion of northern South Vietnam on March 30, 1972 by more than 100,000 North Vietnamese soldiers fully equipped with tanks and mobile artillery. With his Saigon ally initially in full retreat and his "Vietnamization" policy in apparent disarray, the President decreed heavy American air attacks on the storage, staging, and transportation facilities of North Vietnam, announced the mining of Haiphong and other North Vietnamese harbors (through which substantial shipments of Russian and Chinese military equipment daily flowed to Hanoi), and slapped a naval blockade on the entire North Vietnamese coast. The 60,000 Americans remaining in South Vietnam were not combat troops and were of no value in the crisis. Nixon did not, however, call for a return of American combat infantry to Vietnam.

In a television address to the American people on the evening of May 8, 1972, the President argued, as Presidents Truman, Eisenhower, Kennedy, and Johnson had in substance argued before him, that abandoning our commitment in Vietnam here and now would mean turning 17,000,000 South Vietnamese over to Communist terror and tyranny. . . . An American defeat in Vietnam would encourage this kind of aggression all over the world— aggression in which smaller nations, armed by their major allies, could be tempted to attack neighboring nations at will. World peace would be in grave jeopardy. . . . In these circumstances, with 60,000 Americans threatened, any President who failed to act decisively would have betrayed the trust of his country and the cause of peace. . . . I ask you for the same strong support you have always **given** your President in difficult moments. . . . You want peace. I want peace. But you also want honor and not defeat. You want a genuine peace, not a peace that is merely a prelude to another war. . . . We Americans did not choose to resort to war. It has been forced upon us by an enemy that has shown utter contempt toward every overture we have made for peace. That is why tonight I ask for your support of this decision, a decision . . . to win the kind of peace that will last. With God's help and with your support we shall accomplish that great goal.

In spite of his accommodative visit to Peking in March, it was clear by mid-1972 that President Nixon was not willing wholly to abandon his SEATO ally to Asian Communism or to accept an American military humiliation in Vietnam. Whether he commanded the support of the American people in this view remained to be seen. If, however, the issue eventually came down to a question of American "honor" in Southeast Asia, there was no certainty that he would prevail. Such was the temper of the times.

THE
COLD WAR

I
THE CRUSADERS:
AMERICAN

A
DIPLOMAT GEORGE F. KENNAN
ON THE CONTAINMENT OF SOVIET IMPERIALISM
JULY, 1947

". . . the Kremlin has no compunction about retreating in the face of superior force. And being under the compulsion of no timetable, it does not get panicky under the necessity for such retreat. . . . In these circumstances it is clear that the main element of any United States policy toward the Soviet Union must be that of a long term, patient but firm and vigilant containment of Russian expansive tendencies."

The political personality of Soviet power as we know it today is the product of ideology and circumstances: ideology inherited by the present Soviet leaders from the movement in which they had their political origin, and circumstances of the power which they now have exercised for nearly three decades in Russia. There can be few tasks of psychological analysis more difficult than to try to trace the interaction of these two forces and the relative role of each in the determination of official Soviet conduct. Yet the attempt must be made if that conduct is to be understood and effectively countered.

It is difficult to summarize the set of ideological concepts with which

---

[George F. Kennan], "The Sources of Soviet Conduct," *Foreign Affairs*, XXV (July, 1947), 566–582. Reprinted by permission. Author identified as "Mr. 'X'."

the Soviet leaders came into power. Marxian ideology, in its Russian-Communist projection, has always been in process of subtle evolution. The materials on which it bases itself are extensive and complex. But the outstanding features of Communist thought as it existed in 1916 may perhaps be summarized as follows: (*a*) that the central factor in the life of man, the fact which determines the character of public life and the "physiognomy of society," is the system by which material goods are produced and exchanged; (*b*) that the capitalist system of production is a nefarious one which inevitably leads to the exploitation of the working class by the capital-owning class and is incapable of developing adequately the economic resources of society or of distributing fairly the material goods produced by human labor: (*c*) that capitalism contains the seeds of its own destruction and must, in view of the inability of the capital-owning class to adjust itself to economic change, result eventually and inescapably in a revolutionary transfer of power to the working class; and (*d*) that imperialism, the final phase of capitalism, leads directly to war and revolution.

The rest may be outlined in Lenin's own words: "Unevenness of economic and political development is the inflexible law of capitalism. It follows from this that the victory of Socialism may come originally in a few capitalist countries or even in a single capitalist country. The victorious proletariat of that country, having expropriated the capitalists and having organized Socialist production at home, would rise against the remaining capitalist world, drawing to itself in the process the oppressed classes of other countries." It must be noted that there was no assumption that capitalism would perish without proletarian revolution. A final push was needed from a revolutionary proletariat movement in order to tip over the tottering structure. But is was regarded as inevitable that sooner or later that push be given. . . .

Now it must be noted that through all the years of preparation for revolution, the attention of these men, as indeed of Marx himself, had been centered less on the future form which Socialism would take than on the necessary overthrow of rival power which, in their view, had to precede the introduction of Socialism. Their views, therefore, on the positive program to be put into effect, once power was attained, were for the most part nebulous, visionary and impractical. Beyond the nationalization of industry and the expropriation of large private capital holdings there was no agreed program. The treatment of the peasantry, which according to the Marxist formulation was not of the proletariat, had always been a vague spot in the pattern of Communist thought; and it remained an object of controversy and vacillation for the first ten years of Communist power. . . .

Now it lies in the nature of the mental world of the Soviet leaders, as well as in the character of their ideology, that no opposition to them can be officially recognized as having any merit or justification whatsoever. Such opposition can flow, in theory, only from the hostile and incorrigible forces of dying capitalism. As long as remnants of capitalism were officially recognized as existing in Russia, it was possible to place on them, as an internal element, part of the blame for the maintenance of a dictatorial form of society. But as these remnants were liquidated, little by little, this justification fell away; and when it was indicated officially than they had been finally destroyed, it disappeared altogether. And this fact created one of the most basic of the compulsions which came to act upon the Soviet regime: since capitalism no longer existed in Russia and since it could not be admitted that there could be serious or widespread opposition to the Kremlin springing spontaneously from the liberated masses under its authority, it became necessary to justify the retention of the dictatorship by stressing the menace of capitalism abroad. . . .

Of the original ideology, nothing has been officially junked. Belief is maintained in the basic badness of capitalism, in the inevitability of its destruction, in the obligation of the proletariat to assist in that destruction and to take power into its own hands. But stress has come to be laid primarily on those concepts which relate most specifically to the Soviet regime itself: to its position as the sole truly Socialist regime in a dark and misguided world, and to the relationships of power within it.

The first of these concepts is that of the innate antagonism between capitalism and Socialism. We have seen how deeply that concept has become imbedded in foundations of Soviet power. It has profound implications for Russia's conduct as a member of international society. It means that there can never be on Moscow's side any sincere assumption of a community of aims between the Soviet Union and powers which are regarded as capitalist. It must invariably be assumed in Moscow that the aims of the capitalist world are antagonistic to the Soviet regime and, therefore, to the interests of the peoples it controls. If the Soviet Government occasionally sets its signature to documents which would indicate the contrary, this is to be regarded as a tactical maneuver permissible in dealing with the enemy (who is without honor) and should be taken in the spirit of *caveat emptor*. Basically, the antagonism remains. It is postulated. And from it flow many of the phenomena which we find disturbing in the Kremlin's conduct of foreign policy: the secretiveness, the lack of frankness, the duplicity, the war suspiciousness, and the basic unfriendliness of purpose. These phenomena are there to stay, for the foreseeable future. There can be variations of degree and of emphasis. When there is something the Russians want from us, one or the other of these features of their policy may be thrust temporarily into the background; and when that happens there will always be Americans who will leap forward with gleeful announcements that "the Russians have changed," and some who will even try to take credit for having brought about such "changes." But we should not be misled by tactical maneuvers. These characteristics of Soviet policy, like the postulate from which they flow, are basic to the internal nature of Soviet power, and will be with us, whether in the foreground or the background, until the internal nature of Soviet power is changed.

This means that we are going to continue for a long time to find the Russians difficult to deal with. It does not mean that they should be considered as embarked upon a do-or-die program to overthrow our society by a given date. The theory of the inevitability of the eventual fall of capitalism has the fortunate connotation that there is no hurry about it. The forces of progress can take their time in preparing the final *coup de grâce*. Meanwhile, what is vital is that the "Socialist fatherland"—that oasis of power which has been already won for Socialism in the person of the Soviet Union—should be cherished and defended by all good Communists at home and abroad, its fortunes promoted, its enemies badgered and confounded. The promotion of premature, "adventuristic" revolutionary projects abroad which might embarrass Soviet power in any way would be an inexusable, even a counter-revolutionary act. The cause of Socialism is the support and promotion of Soviet power, as defined in Moscow.

This brings us to the second of the concepts important to contemporary Soviet outlook. That is the infallibility of the Kremlin. The Soviet concept of power, which permits no focal points of organization outside the Party itself, requires that the Party leadership remain in theory the sole repository of truth. For if truth were to be found elsewhere, there would be justification for its expression in organized activity. But it is precisely that which the Kremlin cannot and will not permit. . . . Once a given party line has been laid down on a given issue of current policy, the whole Soviet governmental machine, including the mechanism of diplomacy, moves inexorably along the prescribed path, like a persistent toy automobile wound up and headed in a given direction, stopping only when it meets with some unanswerable force. The individuals who are the components of this machine are unamenable to argument or reason which comes to them from outside sources. Their whole training has taught them to mistrust and discount the glib persuasiveness of the outside world. . . .

But we have seen that the Kremlin is under no ideological compulsion to accomplish its purposes in a hurry. Like the Church, it is dealing in ideological concepts which are of long term validity, and it can afford to be patient. It has no right to risk the existing achievements of the revolution for the sake of vain baubles of the future. The very teachings of Lenin himself require great caution and flexibility in the pursuit of Communist purposes. Again, these precepts are fortified by the lessons of Russian history: of centuries of obscure battles between nomadic forces over the stretches of a vast unfortified plain. Here caution, circumspection, flexibility and deception are the valuable qualities; and their value finds natural appreciation in the Russian or the oriental mind. Thus the Kremlin has no compunction about retreating in the face of superior force. And being under the compulsion of no timetable, it does not get panicky under the necessity for such retreat. Its political action is a fluid stream which moves constantly, wherever it is permitted to move, toward a given goal. Its main concern is to make sure that it has filled every nook and cranny available to it in the basin of world power. But if it finds unassailable barriers in its path, it accepts these philosophically and accommodates itself to them. The main thing is that there should always be pressure, increasing constant pressure, toward the desired goal. There is no trace of any feeling in Soviet psychology that that goal must be reached at any given time. . . .

In these circumstances it is clear that the main element of any United States policy toward the Soviet Union must be that of a long-term, patient but firm and vigilant containment of Russian expansive tendencies. It is important to note, however, that such a policy has nothing to do with outward histrionics: with threats or blustering or superfluous gestures of outward "toughness." While the Kremlin is basically flexible in its reaction to political realities, it is by no means unamenable to considerations of prestige. Like almost any other government, it can be placed by tactless and threatening gestures in a position where it cannot afford to yield even though this might be dictated by its sense of realism. The Russian leaders are keen judges of human psychology, and as such they are highly conscious that loss of temper and of self-control is never a source of strength in political affairs. They are quick to exploit such evidences of weakness. For these reasons, it is a *sine qua non* of successful dealing with Russia that the foreign government in question should remain at all time cool and collected and that its demands on Russian policy should be put forward in such a manner as to leave the way open for a compliance not too detrimental to Russian prestige.

In the light of the above, it will be clearly seen that the Soviet pressure against the free institutions of the Western world is something that can be contained by the adroit and vigilant application of counter-force at a series of constantly shifting geographical and political points, corresponding to the shifts and maneuvers of Soviet policy, but which cannot be charmed or talked out of existence. The Russians look forward to a duel of infinite duration, and they see that already they have scored great successes. . . .

But if ideology convinces the rulers of Russia that truth is on their side and that they can therefore afford to wait, those of us on whom that ideology has no claim are free to examine objectively the validity of that premise. The Soviet thesis not only implies complete lack of control by the West over its own economic destiny, it likewise assumes Russian unity, discipline and patience over an infinite period. Let us bring this apocalyptic vision down to earth, and suppose that the Western world finds the strength and resourcefulness to contain Soviet power over a period of ten to fifteen years. What does that spell for Russia itself?

The Soviet leaders, taking advantage of the contributions of modern technique to the arts of despotism, have solved the question of obedience within the confines of their power. Few challenge their authority; and even those who do are unable to make that challenge valid as against the organs of suppression of the state.

The Kremlin has also proved able to accomplish its purpose of building up in Russia, regardless of the interests of the inhabitants, an industrial foundation of heavy metallurgy, which is, to be sure, not yet complete but which is nevertheless continuing to grow and is approaching those of the other major industrial countries. All of this, however, both the maintenance of internal political security and the building of heavy industry, has been carried out at a terrible cost in human life and in human hopes and energies. It has necessitated the use of forced labor on a scale unprecedented in modern times under conditions of peace. It has involved the neglect or abuse of other phases of Soviet economic life, particularly agriculture, consumers' goods production, housing and transportation.

To all that, the war has added its tremendous toll of destruction, death and human exhaustion. In consequence of this, we have in Russia they once were to the magical attraction which Soviet power still radiates of the people are disillusioned, skeptical and no longer as accessible as they once were to the magical attraction which Soviet power still radiates to its followers abroad. The avidity with which people seized upon the slight respite accorded to the Church for tactical reasons during the war was eloquent testimony to the fact that their capacity for faith and devotion found little expression in the purposes of the regime.

In these circumstances, there are limits to the physical and nervous strength of people themselves. These limits are absolute ones, and are binding even for the cruelest dictatorship, because beyond them people cannot be driven. . . .

In addition to this, we have the fact that Soviet economic development, while it can list certain formidable achievements, has been precariously spotty and uneven. Russian Communists who speak of the "uneven development of capitalism" should blush at the contemplation of their own national economy. Here certain branches of economic life, such as the metallurgical and machine industries, have been pushed out of all proportion to other sectors of economy. Here is a nation striving to become in a short period one of the great industrial nations of the world while it still has no highway network worthy of the name and only a relatively primitive network of railways. Much has been done to increase efficiency of labor and to teach primitive peasants something about the operation of machines. But maintenance is still a crying deficiency of all Soviet economy. Construction is hasty and poor in quality. Depreciation must be enormous. . . .

It is difficult to see how these deficiencies can be corrected at an early date by a tired and dispirited population working largely under the shadow of fear and compulsion. And as long as they are not overcome, Russia will remain economically a vulnerable, and in a certain sense an impotent, nation, capable of exporting its enthusiasms and of radiating the strange charm of its primitive political vitality but unable to back up those articles of export by the real evidences of material power and prosperity.

Meanwhile, a great uncertainty hangs over the political life of the Soviet Union. That is the uncertainty involved in the transfer of power from one individual or group of individuals to others.

This is, of course, outstandingly the problem of the personal position of Stalin. We must remember that his succession to Lenin's pinnacle of preeminence in the Communist movement was the only such transfer of individual authority which the Soviet Union has experienced. That transfer took twelve years to consolidate. It cost the lives of millions of people and shook the state to its foundations, the attendant tremors were felt all through the international revolutionary movement, to the disadvantage of the Kremlin itself.

It is always possible that another transfer of preeminent power may take place quietly and inconspicuously, with no repercussions anywhere. But again, it is possible that the questions involved may unleash, to use some of Lenin's words, one of those "incredibly swift transitions" from "delicate deceit" to "wild violence" which characterize Russian history, and may shake Soviet power to its foundations. . . .

Thus the future of Soviet power may not be by any means as secure as Russian capacity for self-delusion would make it appear to the men in the Kremlin. That they can keep power themselves, they have demonstrated. That they can quietly and easily turn it over to others remains to be proved. Meanwhile, the hardships of their rule and the vicissitudes of international life have taken a heavy toll of the strength and hopes of the great people on whom their power rests. It is curious to note that the ideological power of Soviet authority is strongest today in areas beyond the frontiers of Russia, beyond the reach of its police power. . . .

It is clear that the United States cannot expect in the foreseeable future to enjoy political intimacy with the Soviet regime. It must continue to regard the Soviet Union as a rival, not a partner, in the political arena. It must continue to expect that Soviet policies will reflect no abstract love of peace and stability, no real faith in the possibility of a permanent happy coexistence of the Socialist and capitalist worlds, but rather a cautious, persistent pressure toward the disruption and weakening of all rival influence and rival power.

Balanced against this are the facts that Russia, as opposed to the Western world in general, is still by far the weaker party, that Soviet policy is highly flexible, and that Soviet society may well contain deficiencies which will eventually weaken its own total potential. This would of itself warrant the United States entering with reasonable confidence upon a policy of firm containment, designed to confront the Russians with unalterable counter-force at every point where they show signs of encroaching upon the interests of a peaceful and stable world.

But in actuality the possibilities for American policy are by no means limited to holding the line and hoping for the best. It is entirely possible for the United States to influence by its actions the internal developments, both within Russia and throughout the international Communist movement, by which Russian policy is largely determined. This is not only a question of the modest measure of informational activity which this government can conduct in the Soviet Union and elsewhere, although that, too, is important. It is rather a question of the degree to which the United States can create among the peoples of the world generally the impression of a country which knows what it wants, which is coping successfully with the problems of its internal life and with the responsibilities of a World Power, and which has a spiritual vitality capable of holding its own among the major ideological currents of the time. To the extent that such an impression can be created and maintained, the aims of Russian Communism must appear sterile and quixotic, the hopes and enthusiasm of Moscow's supporters must wane, and added strain must be imposed on the Kremlin's foreign policies. For the palsied decrepitude of the capitalist world is the keystone of Communist philosophy. Even the failure of the United States to experience the early economic depression which the ravens of the Red Square have been predicting with such complacent confidence since hostilities ceased would have deep and important repercussions throughout the Communist world.

By the same token, exhibitions of indecision, disunity and internal disintegration within this country have an exhilarating effect on the whole Communist movement. At each evidence of these tendencies, a thrill of hope and excitement goes through the Communist world; a new jauntiness can be noted in the Moscow tread; new groups of foreign supporters climb on to what they can only view as the band wagon of international politics; and Russian pressure increases all along the line in international affairs.

It would be an exaggeration to say that American behavior unassisted and alone could exercise a power of life and death over the Communist movement and bring about the early fall of Soviet power in

Russia. But the United States has it in its power to increase enormously the strains under which Soviet policy must operate, to force upon the Kremlin a far greater degree of moderation and circumspection than it has had to observe in recent years, and in this way to promote tendencies which must eventually find their outlet in either the break-up or the gradual mellowing of Soviet power. For no mystical, Messianic movement—and particularly not that of the Kremlin—can face frustration indefinitely without eventually adjusting itself in one way or another to the logic of that state of affairs. . . .

In the light of these circumstances, the thoughtful observer of Russian-American relations will find no cause for complaint in the Kremlin's challenge to American society. He will rather experience a certain gratitude to a Providence which, by providing the American people with this implacable challenge, has made their entire security as a nation dependent on their pulling themselves together and accepting the responsibilities of moral and political leadership that history plainly intended them to bear.

B
PRESIDENT HARRY S. TRUMAN PLEDGES AMERICAN AID TO FREE NATIONS STRUGGLING TO MAINTAIN THEIR FREEDOM IN THE FACE OF COMMUNIST AGGRESSION: THE TRUMAN DOCTRINE
MARCH 12, 1947

"I believe that it must be the policy of the United States to support free peoples who are resisting attempted subjugation by armed minorities or by outside pressures."

One of the primary objectives of the foreign policy of the United States is the creation of conditions in which we and other nations will be able to work out a way of life free from coercion. This was a fundamental issue in the war with Germany and Japan. Our victory was won

---

Public Papers of the President . . . Harry S. Truman. . . . 1947. Washington: GPO, 1963, 176–180.

over countries which sought to impose their will, and their way of life upon other nations.

To insure the peaceful development of nations, free from coercion, the United States has taken a leading part in establishing the United Nations. The United Nations is designed to make possible lasting freedom and independence for all its members. We shall not realize our objectives, however, unless we are willing to help free peoples to maintain their free institutions and their national integrity against aggressive movements that seek to impose upon them totalitarian regimes. This is no more than a frank recognition that totalitarian regimes imposed upon free peoples, by direct or indirect aggression, undermine the foundations of international peace and hence the security of the United States.

The peoples of a number of countries of the world have recently had totalitarian regimes forced upon them against their will. The Government of the United States has made frequent protests against coercion and intimidation, in violation of the Yalta agreement, in Poland, Rumania, and Bulgaria. I must also state that in a number of other countries there have been similar developments.

At the present moment in world history nearly every nation must choose between alternative ways of life. The choice is too often not a free one.

One way of life is based upon the will of the majority, and is distinguished by free institutions, representative government, free elections, guaranties of individual liberty, freedom of speech and religion, and freedom from political oppression.

The second way of life is based upon the will of a minority forcibly imposed upon the majority. It relies upon terror and oppression, a controlled press and radio, fixed elections, and the suppression of personal freedoms.

I believe that it must be the policy of the United States to support free peoples who are resisting attempted subjugation by armed minorities or by outside pressures.

I believe that we must assist free peoples to work out their own destinies in their own way.

I believe that our help should be primarily through economic and financial aid which is essential to economic stability and orderly political processes.

The world is not static, and the *status quo* is not sacred. But we cannot allow changes in the *status quo* in violation of the Charter of the United Nations by such methods as coercion, or by such subterfuges as political infiltration. In helping free and independent nations to maintain their freedom, the United States will be giving effect to the principles of the Charter of the United Nations. . . .

C
SECRETARY OF STATE GEORGE C. MARSHALL COMMITS THE UNITED STATES TO ASSISTANCE IN REBUILDING EUROPE'S WAR-TORN ECONOMY: THE MARSHALL PLAN
JUNE 5, 1947

"Our policy is directed not against any country or doctrine but against hunger, poverty, desperation, and chaos. . . . Governments, political parties, or groups which seek to perpetuate human misery in order to profit therefrom politically or otherwise will encounter the opposition of the United States."

. . . The truth of the matter is that Europe's requirements for the next 3 or 4 years of foreign food and other essential products—principally from America—are so much greater than her present ability to pay that she must have substantial additional help, or face economic, social, and political deterioration of a very grave character.

The remedy lies in breaking the vicious circle and restoring the confidence of the European people in the economic future of their own countries and of Europe as a whole. The manufacturer and the farmer throughout wide areas must be able and willing to exchange their products for currencies the continuing value of which is not open to question.

Aside from the demoralizing effect on the world at large and the possibilities of disturbances arising as a result of the desperation of the people concerned, the consequences to the economy of the United States should be apparent to all. It is logical that the United States should do

George C. Marshall, speech at Harvard University, June 5, 1947. *Congressional Record*, 80th Congress, 1st Session, Appendix, A 3248.

whatever it is able to do to assist in the return of normal economic health in the world, without which there can be no political stability and no assured peace. Our policy is directed not against any country or doctrine but against hunger, poverty, desperation, and chaos. Its purpose should be the revival of a working economy in the world so as to permit the emergence of political and social conditions in which free institutions can exist. Such assistance, I am convinced, must not be on a piecemeal basis as various crises develop. Any assistance that this Government may render in the future should provide a cure rather than a mere palliative. Any government that is willing to assist in the task of recovery will find full cooperation, I am sure, on the part of the United States Government. Any government which maneuvers to block the recovery of other countries cannot expect help from us. Furthermore, governments, political parties, or groups which seek to perpetuate human misery in order to profit therefrom politically or otherwise will encounter the opposition of the United States.

It is already evident that, before the United States Government can proceed much further in its efforts to alleviate the situation and help start the European world on its way to recovery, there must be some agreement among the countries of Europe as to the requirements of the situation and the part those countries themselves will take in order to give proper effect to whatever action might be undertaken by this Government. It would be neither fitting nor efficacious for this Government to undertake to draw up unilaterally a program designed to place Europe on its feet economically. This is the business of the Europeans. The initiative, I think, must come from Europe. The role of this country should consist of friendly aid in the drafting of a European program and of later support of such a program so far as it may be practical for us to do so. The program should be a joint one, agreed to by a number, if not all European nations.

An essential part of any successful action on the part of the United States is an understanding on the part of the people of America of the character of the problem and the remedies to be applied. Political passion and prejudice should have no part. With foresight, and a willingness on the part of our people to face up to the vast responsibility which history has clearly placed upon our country, the difficulties I have outlined can and will be overcome.

D

PRESIDENT HARRY S. TRUMAN EXPLAINS THE NEED FOR AMERICAN MILITARY INTERVENTION IN KOREA JUNE 27, 1950

"The attack upon Korea makes it plain beyong all doubt that communism has passed beyond the use of subversion to conquer independent nations and will now use armed invasion and war. . . . The United States will continue to uphold the rule of law."

In Korea, the Government forces, which were armed to prevent border raids and to preserve internal security, were attacked by invading forces from North Korea. The Security Council of the United Nations called upon the invading troops to cease hostilities and to withdraw to the 38th Parallel. This they have not done but, on the contrary, have pressed the attack. The Security Council called upon all members of the United Nations to render every assistance to the United Nations in the execution of this resolution. In these circumstances, I have ordered United States air and sea forces to give the Korean Government troops cover and support.

The attack upon Korea makes it plain beyond all doubt that communism has passed beyond the use of subversion to conquer independent nations and will now use armed invasion and war. It has defied the orders of the Security Council of the United Nations issued to preserve international peace and security. In these circumstances, the occupation of Formosa by Communist forces would be a direct threat to the security of the Pacific area and to United States forces performing their lawful and necessary functions in that area.

Accordingly, I have ordered the Seventh Fleet to prevent any attack upon Formosa. As a corollary of this action, I am calling upon the Chinese Government on Formosa to cease all air and sea operations against the mainland. The Seventh Fleet will see that this is done. The determination of the future status of Formosa must await the restoration of security in the Pacific, a peace settlement with Japan, or consideration by the United Nations.

U.S. Department of State, *American Foreign Policy, 1950–1955. Basic Documents.* Washington: GPO, 1957, II, 2539–2540.

I have also directed that United States forces in the Philippines be strengthened and that military assistance to the Philippine Government be accelerated.

I have similarly directed acceleration in the furnishing of military assistance to the forces of France and the Associated States in Indochina and the dispatch of a military mission to provide close working relations with those forces.

I know that all members of the United Nations will consider carefully the consequences of this latest aggression in Korea in defiance of the Charter of the United Nations. A return to the rule of force in international affairs would have far-reaching effects. The United States will continue to uphold the rule of law. . . .

E
PRESIDENT DWIGHT D. EISENHOWER AND THE "DOMINO THEORY" OF COMMUNIST AGGRESSION IN SOUTHEAST ASIA
APRIL 7, 1954

"Finally, you have broader considerations that might follow what you would call the 'falling domino' principle. You have a row of dominoes set up, you knock over the first one, and what will happen to the last one is the certainty that it will go over very quickly."

Robert Richards, Copley Press: Mr. President, would you mind commenting on the strategic importance of Indochina to the free world? I think there has been, across the country, some lack of understanding on just what it means to us.

The President: You have, of course, both the specific and the general when you talk about such things.

First of all, you have the specific value of a locality in its production of materials that the world needs.

Public Papers of the Presidents . . . Dwight D. Eisenhower . . . 1954. Washington: GPO, 1960, 382–383.

Then you have the possibility that many human beings pass under a dictatorship that is inimical to the free world.

Finally, you have broader considerations that might follow what you would call the "falling domino" principle. You have a row of dominoes set up, you knock over the first one, and what will happen to the last one is the certainty that it will go over very quickly. So you could have a beginning of a disintegration that would have the most profound influences.

Now, with respect to the first one, two of the items from this particular area that the world uses are tin and tungsten. They are very important. There are others, of course, the rubber plantations and so on.

Then with respect to more people passing under this domination, Asia, after all, has already lost some 450 million of its peoples to the Communist dictatorship, and we simply can't afford greater losses.

But when we come to the possible sequence of events, the loss of Indochina, of Burma, of Thailand, of the Peninsula, and Indonesia following, now you begin to talk about areas that not only multiply the disadvantages that you would suffer through loss of materials, sources of materials, but now you are talking really about millions and millions and millions of people.

Finally, the geographical position achieved thereby does many things. It turns the so-called island defensive chain of Japan, Formosa, of the Philippines and to the southward; it moves in to threaten Australia and New Zealand.

It takes away, in its economic aspects, that region that Japan must have as a trading area or Japan, in turn, will have only one place in the world to go—this is, toward the Communist areas in order to live.

So, the possible consequences of the loss are just incalculable to the free world.

F
PRESIDENT JOHN F. KENNEDY ON THE AMERICAN STAKE IN
SOUTHEAST ASIA
SEPTEMBER 9, 1963

"We can't make the world over, but we can influence the world. . . .
What I am concerned about is that Americans will get impatient and
say because they don't like events in southeast Asia or they don't
like the government in Saigon, that we should withdraw. That only
makes it easy for the Communists. I think we should stay."

Mr. Chet Huntley: Are we likely to reduce our aid to South Viet-Nam now?

The President: I don't think we think that would be helpful at this time. If you reduce your aid, it is possible you could have some effect upon the government structure there. On the other hand, you might have a situation which could bring about a collapse. Strongly in our mind is what happened in the case of China at the end of World War II, where China was lost, a weak government became increasingly unable to control events. We don't want that.

Mr. [David] Brinkley: Mr. President, have you had any reason to doubt this so-called "domino theory," that if South Viet-Nam falls, the rest of southeast Asia will go behind it?

The President: No, I believe it. I believe it. I think that the struggle is close enough. China is so large, looms so high just beyond the frontiers, that if South Viet-Nam went, it would not only give them an improved geographic position for a guerrilla assault on Malaya, but would also give the impression that the wave of the future in southeast Asia was China and the Communists. So I believe it. . . .

Mr. Brinkley: With so much of our prestige, money, so on, committed in South Viet-Nam, why can't we exercise a little more influence there, Mr. President?

The President: We have some influence. We have some influence, and we

---

Public Papers of the Presidents . . . John F. Kennedy . . . 1963. Washington: GPO, 1964, 658–660.

are attempting to carry it out. I think we don't—we can't expect these
countries to do everything the way we want to do them. They have
their own interest, their own personalities, their own tradition. We can't
make everyone in our image, and there are a good many people who
don't want to go in our image. In addition, we have ancient struggles
between countries. In the case of India and Pakistan, we would like to
have them settle Kashmir. That is our view of the best way to defend
the subcontinent against communism. But that struggle between India
and Pakistan is more important to a good many people in that area than
the struggle against the Communists. We would like to have Cambodia,
Thailand, and South Viet-Nam all in harmony, but there are ancient
differences there. We can't make the world over, but we can influence
the world. The fact of the matter is that with the assistance of the United
States, SEATO, southeast Asia and indeed all of Asia has been maintained independent against a powerful force, the Chinese Communists.
What I am concerned about is that Americans will get impatient and say
because they don't like events in southeast Asia or they don't like the
government in Saigon, that we should withdraw. That only makes it easy
for the Communists. I think we should stay. We should use our influence
in as effective a way as we can, but we should not withdraw.

G
PRESIDENT LYNDON B. JOHNSON
DEFENDS AMERICAN MILITARY ESCALATION IN VIETNAM
APRIL 7, 1965

*"We fight because we must fight if we are to live in a world where
every country can shape its own destiny. . . . The first reality is that
North Viet-Nam has attacked the independent nation of South Viet-
Nam. Its object is total conquest. . . . We will not be defeated. We
will not grow tired. We will not withdraw. . . ."*

Tonight Americans and Asians are dying for a world where each people
may choose its own path to change.

Public Papers of the Presidents . . . Lyndon B. Johnson . . . 1965. Washington: GPO,
1966, I, 394 399.

This is the principle for which our ancestors fought in the valleys of Pennsylvania. It is the principle for which our sons fight tonight in the jungles of Viet-Nam.

Viet-Nam is far away from this quiet campus. We have no territory there, nor do we seek any. The war is dirty and brutal and difficult. And some 400 young men, born into an America that is bursting with opportunity and promise, have ended their lives on Viet-Nam's steaming soil.

Why must we take this painful road?

Why must this Nation hazard its ease, and its interest, and its power for the sake of a people so far away?

We fight because we must fight if we are to live in a world where every country can shape its own destiny. And only in such a world will our own freedom be finally secure.

This kind of world will never be built by bombs or bullets. Yet the infirmities of man are such that force must often precede reason, and the waste of war, the works of peace.

We wish that this were not so. But we must deal with the world as it is, if it is ever to be as we wish.

The world as it is in Asia is not a serene or peaceful place.

The first reality is that North Viet-Nam has attacked the independent nation of South Viet-Nam. Its object is total conquest.

Of course, some of the people of South Viet-Nam are participating in attack on their own government. But trained men and supplies, orders and arms, flow in a constant stream from north to south. This support is the heartbeat of the war.

And it is a war of unparalleled brutality. Simple farmers are the targets of assassination and kidnapping. Women and children are strangled in the night because their men are loyal to their government. And helpless villages are ravaged by sneak attacks. Large-scale raids are conducted on towns, and terror strikes in the heart of cities.

Over this war—and all Asia—is another reality: the deepening shadow of Communist China. The rulers in Hanoi are urged on by Peking. This is a regime which has destroyed freedom in Tibet, which has attacked India, and has been condemned by the United Nations for aggression in Korea. It is a nation which is helping the forces of violence in almost every continent. The contest in Viet-Nam is part of a wider pattern of aggressive purposes.

Why are these realities our concern? Why are we in South Viet-Nam?

We are there because we have a promise to keep. Since 1954 every American President has offered support to the people of South Viet-Nam. We have helped to build, and we have helped to defend. Thus, over many years, we have made a national pledge to help South Viet-Nam defend its independence.

And I intend to keep that promise.

To dishonor that pledge, to abandon this small and brave nation to its enemies, and to the terror that must follow, would be an unforgivable wrong.

We are also there to strengthen world order. Around the globe, from Berlin to Thailand, are people whose well-being rests, in part, on the belief that they can count on us if they are attacked. To leave Viet-Nam to its fate would shake the confidence of all these people in the value of an American commitment and in the value of America's word. The result would be increased unrest and instability, and even wider war.

We are also there because there are great stakes in the balance. Let no one think for a moment that retreat from Viet-Nam would bring an end to conflict. The battle would be renewed in one country and then another. The central lesson of our time is that the appetite of aggression is never satisfied. To withdraw from one battlefield means only to prepare for the next. We must say in southeast Asia—as we did in Europe—in the words of the Bible: "Hitherto shalt thou come, but no further."

There are those who say that all our effort there will be futile—that China's power is such that it is bound to dominate all southeast Asia. But there is no end to that argument until all of the nations of Asia are swallowed up.

There are those who wonder why we have a responsibility there. Well, we have it there for the same reason that we have a responsibility for the defense of Europe. World War II was fought in both Europe and Asia, and when it ended we found ourselves with continued responsibility for the defense of freedom.

Our objective is the independence of South Viet-Nam, and its freedom from attack. We want nothing for ourselves—only that the people of South Viet-Nam be allowed to guide their own country in their own way.

We will do everything necessary to reach that objective. And we will do only what is absolutely necessary.

In recent months attacks on South Viet-Nam were stepped up. Thus, it became necessary for us to increase our response and to make attacks by air. This is not a change of purpose. It is a change in what we believe that purpose requires.

We do this in order to slow down aggression.

We do this to increase the confidence of the brave people of South Viet-Nam who have bravely borne this brutal battle for so many years with so many casualties.

And we do this to convince the leaders of North Viet-Nam—and all who seek to share their conquest—of a very simple fact:

We will not be defeated.

We will not grow tired.

We will not withdraw, either openly or under the cloak of a meaningless agreement. . . .

H
THE STATE DEPARTMENT EXPLAINS
WHY THE UNITED STATES FIGHTS IN VIETNAM
JUNE, 1967

"In Europe, the time we have bought through containment has worked changes on both sides of the Iron Curtain, permitting both sides to edge away from the threat of nuclear war. . . . In Asia, however, communism still acts in the belief that there is more profit in war than in peace. Asian communism still lives by the dogmas of Mao Tse-tung, who said . . . 'We can even say that the whole world can be reshaped only with the gun.'"

There Would Be No War Today If North Viet-Nam Had Kept Its Pledge

The paramount fact about the war in Viet-Nam is this:

If there had been no violation by North Viet-Nam of article 10 of the Geneva agreement, calling for total cessation of hostilities, there would be no war in Viet-Nam today.

United States Department of State, *Why We Fight in Vietnam*. Pamphlet, Office of Media Services, Bureau of Public Affairs, Department of State, No. 6, June, 1967.

The keystone of the 1954 Geneva Agreement on the Cessation of Hostilities in Viet-Nam is *article 10*, which provides that the commanders of forces on each side, "shall order and enforce the *complete* cessation of all hostilities in Viet-Nam by *all* armed forces under their control, including *all* units and personnel of the ground, naval and air forces."

Hostilities ceased in the North, but they never fully ceased in the South. The Communist North organized, directed, and supplied armed forces operating against the South, forcing the Government of South Viet-Nam to seek help in taking defensive measures. The Communist North, denying its responsibility for the attacks in the South, despite conclusive proof to the contrary, complained to the International Commission for Supervision and Control in Viet-Nam (ICC) that the South's *defensive* measures constituted a violation of the Geneva agreement.

Behind this smokescreen the aggression against the South was rapidly escalated.

Historical Background from 1954

The end of the French colonial era in Indo-china came with the signing of the Geneva accords in July 1954. Representatives of Cambodia, the Democratic Republic of (North) Viet-Nam, France, Laos, Communist China, the State of (South) Viet-Nam, the Soviet Union, Great Britain, and the United States met in Geneva and brought the long struggle between the forces of the French Union and the Communist-led Viet Minh and its allies to an end.

Four documents were produced: three agreements on the cessation of hostilities in Cambodia, Laos, and Viet-Nam; and one overall unsigned final declaration of the conference. The three agreements on the cessation of hostilities were signed on behalf of the commanders of the military forces opposing each other, the Vice Minister of Defense of the Democratic Republic of Viet-Nam signing in each case for the Communist-led forces.

Unsupervised Elections Provision Rejected by United States, South Viet-Nam

In addition, two unilateral declarations were issued:
- In one, the representative of the State of Viet-Nam stated his

government's unwillingness to be bound by any agreement between the other parties concerning the political future of the people of South Viet-Nam. Tran Van Do, the esteemed statesman then representing the State of Viet-Nam, protested that others had arrogated to themselves "the right, *without prior agreement from the delegation of the State of Viet-Nam,* to fix the date of the future elections despite the clearly political character of such a provision."

In his declaration to the conference Tran Van Do said:

> The delegation of the State of Viet Nam has put forward its proposals aimed at obtaining an armistice without partition, even temporary, of Viet Nam, by means of the disarmament of all the belligerent forces after their withdrawal into assembly areas as restricted as possible, and by the establishment of temporary control by the United Nations Organization over the whole of the territory until such time as the restoration of order and peace permits the Vietnamese people to decide its future by free election.
>
> The Vietnamese delegation . . . protests solemnly against the hasty conclusion of the armistice agreement by the French and Viet Minh (Communist) High Commands alone, in view of the fact that the French High Command only commands Vietnamese troops by delegation of the powers of the Chief of State of Viet Nam, and above all in view of the fact that several clauses of this agreement are of a nature to compromise gravely the political future of the Vietnamese people. . . .
>
> Consequently, the Government of the State of Viet Nam demands that it should be put on record that it protests solemnly against the way in which the armistice was concluded and against the conditions of this armistice, which takes no account of the profound aspirations of the Vietnamese people, and that *it reserves complete freedom of action* for safeguarding the sacred right of the Vietnamese people to territorial unity, independence, and freedom.

●In the other, the United States through its representative, Under Secretary Walter Bedell Smith, declared the United States unwillingness to join in the declaration of the conference. He repeated the U.S. position on free elections, saying:

In the case of nations now divided against their will, we shall continue to seek to achieve unity through free elections supervised by the United Nations to insure that they are conducted fairly.

With respect to the statement made by the representative of the State of Viet-Nam, the United States reiterates its traditional position that peoples are entitled to determine their own future and that it will not join in an arrangement which would hinder this.

The reason for the protest of the United States and the State of Viet-Nam was simple: Unless the proposed elections were held under U.N. supervision with full freedom of opposition, secret ballots, and impartial counting of the ballots, the people of South Viet-Nam, whatever their feelings might be, would be totally at the mercy of Communist government in the North. For in North Viet-Nam, the Communists held under absolute control slightly more than half the Vietnamese population.

As for the agreements reached between the other parties, Under Secretary Smith stated that the policy of the United States would be to refrain from force or the threat of force to disturb those agreements, and that the United States would view any renewal of aggression in violation of the agreements with grave concern and as seriously threatening international peace and security.

Neither the United States nor the State of Viet-Nam associated itself with the final declaration.

After the Conference an Exodus from the North

With regard to Viet-Nam, the Geneva agreement called for an end to all hostilities, provided for provisional division of the country at the 17th parallel, and for the withdrawal of the opposing forces into the two zones thus created, and gave over the civil administration of the two zones to the two parties withdrawing into them.

While the Communists quickly and ruthlessly consolidated their control of the North, the turmoil in the South was compounded by the need to accept a million refugees from the North into the South and by the withdrawal of the military forces of the French.

Prime Minister (later President) Ngo Dinh Diem, initially had to administer a nation whose economy was ruined, and whose political life was fragmented by rivalries of religious sects and powerful political factions. He was able during the next 9 years to eliminate the entrenched private armies of the sects; form a small, unified national army; and, with U.S. aid, make progress toward reconstructing the economy.

U.S. Assistance Since 1950

Support for the South-Vietnamese Government in the form of economic, technical, and military assistance had been provided by the United States since 1950. After the Geneva accords, the U.S. Military Assistance Advisory Group (MAAG) became the only outside source of military aid for the South Vietnamese Armed Forces. While the armed forces available to protect South Viet-Nam were greatly reduced when French Union Forces were dismantled following the Geneva conference, the North Vietnamese quickly built their army from seven to 20 divisions with supplies obtained from Communist powers.

SEATO

The United States, France, Great Britain, Thailand, Pakistan, Australia, New Zealand, and the Philippines signed the Southeast Asia Collective Defense Treaty (SEATO) on September 8, 1954. A protocol to the treaty included Laos, Cambodia, and South Viet-Nam under articles III and IV of the treaty which among other things provides for economic and military assistance, the latter in case of armed attack or indirect attack and only at the invitation or with the consent of the government concerned. The SEATO treaty reinforced the position taken by the United States earlier the same year at the Geneva conference that we would view any renewal of aggression in violation of the Geneva accords as a serious threat to international peace and security.

Assistance Program Developments
Under Three Administrations

President Eisenhower on October 1, 1954, in a letter to the President of Viet-Nam, stated that the policy behind U.S. aid was "to assist the Government of Viet-Nam in developing and maintaining a strong, viable state, capable of resisting attempted subversion or aggression through military means."

Following 5 years of clandestine preparation and activity, in 1959

Communists in the North came into the open with their calculated program of aggression against the people of the South. The Lao Dong (Communist) Party in Hanoi announced that the time had come to "liberate" the South. Over the next few years the aggression developed steadily and in 1962 brought the condemnation of the International Control Commission (see below).

In 1962 *President Kennedy*, at the request of the South Vietnamese Government, established the United States Military Assistance Command, sustained by modern airpower and antiguerrilla special forces.

Two days after the death of President Kennedy, in 1963, *President Johnson* reaffirmed the U.S. intention to continue its military and economic support of South Vient-Nam's struggle against aggression from the North.

U.S. Destroyers Attacked

On August 2 and 4, 1964, U.S. destroyers were attacked in international waters off the Vietnamese coast by North Viet-Nam torpedo boats. In the same period, intelligence was accumulating which proved the presence of regular North Vietnamese battle units in South Viet-Nam. The aggression had moved to a new stage of outright military invasion.

In a message to Congress on August 5, 1964, the President asked for a resolution "expressing the unity and determination of the United States in supporting freedom and in protecting peace in Southeast Asia." In its resolution approved on August 7 by a vote of 88–2 and 416–0 in the Senate and House of Representatives respectively, the Congress declared the United States was "prepared, as the President determines, to take all necessary steps, including the use of armed force, to assist any member or protocol state of the Southeast Asia Collective Defense Treaty requesting assistance in defense of its freedom."

"Why Are We There?"

In the following months it became obvious that a greater U.S. military effort was required if South Viet-Nam was to be saved. In his State of the Union message on January 5, 1965, President Johnson said:

Why are we there? We are there, first because a friendly

nation asked us for help against Communist aggression. Ten years ago we pledged our help. Three Presidents have supported that pledge. We will not break it. . . . Our goal is peace in Southeast Asia. That will come only when aggressors leave their neighbors in peace.

Aggression by North Viet-Nam Investigated and Verified by the ICC

The International Commission for Supervision and Control in Viet-Nam was established under the Geneva agreement to supervise the cease-fire and to investigate violations of the agreement. The Commission (India, Poland, Canada) recognized that *good-faith compliance with article 10 and its supporting articles is mandatory; otherwise the rest of the agreement becomes meaningless.*

Consequently, when the Government of South Viet-Nam presented evidence of aggression from the North, the ICC undertook an investigation of the charge. Because of Communist Poland's objections to the investigation, it was first necessary to reestablish the legal basis for the investigation. This was done through the Legal Committee of the Commission (the Polish member dissenting), which found that there was ample legal basis for the Commission's investigation. The Committee's report made the following points (emphasis supplied):

●Article 10 of the Geneva agreement called for *"the complete cessation of all hostilities in Viet-Nam."*

●Article 19 requires both sides to insure their zones "are not used *for the resumption of hostilities or to further aggressive policy."*

●Article 24 requires each side to respect the territory of the other, and "to commit no act and *undertake no operation against the other Party."*

●Article 27 specifies that the agreement applies to *all elements* of the military command. This would include regular, irregular, and guerrilla forces.

With the legal basis for investigation clearly established, the ICC's Legal Committee wrote:

Having examined the complaints and the supporting material sent by the South Vietnamese Mission, *the Committee has come to the conclusion that in specific instances there is evidence to show that armed and unarmed personnel, arms, munitions and other supplies have been sent from the Zone in the North to the Zone in the South with the object of supporting, organizing and carrying out hostile activities, including armed attacks, directed against the Armed Forces and Administration of the Zone in the South. These acts are in violation of Articles 10, 19, 24, and 27 of the Agreement on the Cessation of Hostilities in Viet-Nam.*

In examining the complaints and the supporting material, in particular documentary material sent by the South Vietnamese Mission, the Committee has come to the further conclusion that there is evidence to show that the *PAVN (Army of North Viet-Nam) has allowed the Zone in the North to be used for inciting, encouraging and supporting hostile activities in the Zone in the South, aimed at the overthrow of the Administration in the South.* The use of the Zone in the North for such activities is in violation of Articles 19, 24, and 27 of the Agreement on the Cessation of Hostilities in Viet-Nam.

The ICC report (the Polish member dissenting) adopted in full the conclusions reached by the Legal Committee. On June 2, 1962, the Commission reported *"that there is sufficient evidence to show beyond reasonable doubt"* aggression was committed by North Viet-Nam.

The Indian delegation disagreed with the Polish dissent and reiterated the finding of aggression. In response to the Polish dissent to the Commission's majority findings, the Indian delegation issued a special statement saying in part:

The Indian Delegation has considered the Statement of the Polish Delegation. It does not agree with many of the views expressed by the Polish Delegation in its Statement, nor with its interpretation of the Special Reports. *The Indian Delegation reiterates its stand and findings. . . .*

Viet-Nam Asks for More Free-World Help

Unfortunately, the ICC was powerless to halt the aggression. The tempo of aggression was escalated further with North Vietnamese regular forces reinforcing the guerrillas as organized and supported by Hanoi. *The Government of South Viet-Nam asked for additional help from the United*

States and others in the free world. The level of U.S. logistical and advisory support was raised first by President Kennedy and then by President Johnson.

Hanoi, however, believing the conquest of the South to be imminent, became more bellicose. In August, 1964, North Vietnamese torpedo boats without provocation attacked a U.S. Navy vessel in the Tokin Gulf.

This unprovoked act of war escalated the conflict to a new level. It was now plain to all that the Hanoi government was totally committed to the use of force as an instrument of policy....

"Containment" is the popular word for U.S. strategy since World War II. It stands for resistance to efforts by militant Communist powers to expand their territory and control by force or threat of force. The strategy of containment was adopted by this country and its allies in recognition of the grim lessons of the 1930's and the Second World War. It is rooted in the conviction that to tolerate aggression is to invite more and greater violence between nations which ultimately, today, could mean nuclear war.

In Europe, the time we have bought through containment has worked changes on both sides of the Iron Curtain, permitting both sides to edge away from the threat of nuclear war to a more productive course of coexistence—and even occasional cooperation.

In Asia, however, communism still acts in the belief that there is more profit in war than in peace. Asian communism still lives by the dogmas of Mao Tse-tung, who said:

> Some people ridicule us as advocates of the omnipotence of war; *yes, we are advocates of the omnipotence of revolutionary war, and* this is good, not bad.... We can even say that *the whole world can be reshaped only with the gun.* ...

What has been called a strategy of containment is designed to bring about peace and reconciliation in Asia as well as in Europe. In the U.S. view, only if violence is opposed will peace and reconciliation become possible. If aggression succeeds, the Asian Communists will have shown that Mao is right: The world can only be reshaped by the gun....

I

PVT. PAUL MEADLO DESCRIBES AMERICAN ATROCITIES
IN THE SOUTH VIETNAMESE VILLAGE OF MY LAI IN
MARCH, *1968*

*"Why did I do it? Because I felt like I was ordered to do it . . . at
the time I felt like I was doing the right thing, because like I said I
lost buddies. . . . So after I done it, I felt good, but later on that day,
it was getting to me."*

Following is a transcript of an interview with Paul Meadlo, Vietnam
veteran, by Mike Wallace on the Columbia Broadcasting System Radio
Network last night [Nov. 24, 1969].

MEADLO: Captain Medina had us all in a group, and oh, he briefed
us, and I can't remember all the briefing.

WALLACE: How many of them were you?   A. Well, with the mortar
platoon, I'd say there'd be about 60–65 people, but the mortar platoon
wasn't with us, and I'd say the mortar platoon had about 20–25—about
25 people in the mortar platoon. So we didn't have the whole company in
the Pinkville [My Lai], no we didn't.

Q. There weren't about 40–45—   A. . . . right. . . .

Q.—that took part in all of this?   A. Right.

Q. Now you took off from your base camp   A. . . . yes—Dolly.

Q. . . . Dolly. At what time?   A. I wouldn't know what time it
was. . . .

Q. . . . in the early morning . . .   A. . . . In the early morning. It
was—it would have been a long time ago.

Q. And what had you been briefed to do when you got to Pinkville?

A. To search and to make sure that there weren't no N.V.A. in the
village and expecting to fight—when we got there. . . .

Q. To expect to fight?   A. To expect to fight.

Q. Un-huh. So you took off and—in how many choppers?

Well, I'd say the first wave was about four of us—I mean four
choppers, and. . . .

Q. How many men aboard each chopper?

A. Five of us. And we landed next to the village, and we all got in line and we started walking toward the village. And there was one man, one gook in the shelter, and he was all huddled up down in there, and the man called out and said there's a gook over here.

Q. How old a man was this? I mean was this a fighting man or an older man?   A. An older man. And the man hauled out and said that there's a gook over here, and then Sergeant Mitchell hollered back and said shoot him.

Q. Sergeant Mitchell was in charge of the 20 of you?   A. He was in charge of the whole squad. And so then the man shot him. So we moved on into the village, and we started searching up the village and gathering people and running through the center of the village.

Q. How many people did you round up?   A. Well, there was about 40–45 people that we gathered in the center of the village. And we placed them in there, and it was like a little island, right there in the center of the village, I'd say. And—

Q. What kind of people—men, women, children?

A. Men, women, children.

Q. Babies?

A. Babies. And we all huddled them up. We made them squat down, and Lieutenant Calley came over and said you know what to do with them, don't you? And I said yes so I took it for granted that he just wanted us to watch them. And he left, and came back about 10 to 15 minutes later, and said, how come you ain't killed them yet? And I told him that I didn't think you wanted us to kill them, that you just wanted us to guard them. He said, no, I want them dead. So—

Q. He told this to all of you, or to you particularly?

A. Well, I was facing him. So, but, the other three, four guys heard it and so he stepped back about 10, 15 feet, and he started shooting them. And he told me to start shooting. So I started shooting, I poured about four clips into the group.

Q. You fired four clips from your . . . . A. M-16.

Q. And that's about—how many clips—I mean how many—

A. I carried seventeen rounds to each clip.

Q. So you fired something like 67 shots—   A. Right.

Q. And you killed how many? At that time?

A. Well, I fired them on automatic, so you can't—you just spray the area on them and so you can't know how many you killed 'cause they were going fast. So I might have killed ten or fifteen of them.

Q. Men, women and children?   A. Men, women and children.

Q. And babies?

A. And babies.

Q. Okay, then what?   A. So we started to gather them up, more people, and we had about seven or eight people, that we was gonna put into the hootch, and we dropped a hand grenade in there with them.

Q. Now you're rounding up more?

A. We're rounding up more, and we had about seven or eight people. And we was going to throw them in the hootch, and well, we put them in the hootch and then we dropped a hand grenade down there with them. And somebody holed up in the ravine, and told us to bring them over to the ravine, so we took them back out, and led them over to—and by that time, we already had them over there, and they had about 70–75 people all gathered up. So we threw ours in with them and Lieutenant Calley told me, he said, Meadlo, we got another job to do. And so he walked over to the people, and he started pushing them off and started shooting. . . .

Q. Started pushing them off into the ravine?

A. Off into the ravine. It was a ditch. And so we started pushing them off and we started shooting them, so altogether we just pushed them all off, and just started using automatics on them. And then—

Q. Again—men, women, children?   A. Men, women and children.

Q. And babies?

A. And babies. And so we started shooting them and somebody told us to switch off to single shot so that we could save ammo. So we switched off to single shot and shot a few more rounds. And after that, I just—we just—the company started gathering up again. We started moving out, and we had a few gooks that was in—as we started moving out, we had gooks in front of us that was taking point, you know.

Q. Uh-huh.   A.—and as we walked—

Q. Taking point. You mean out in front? To take any fire that might come.

A. Right. And so we started walking across that field. And so later on that day, they picked them up, and gooks we had, and I reckon they took them to Chu Lai or some camp that they was questioning them, so I don't know what they done with them. So we set up [indistinct] the rest of the night, and the next morning we started leaving, leaving the perimeter, and I stepped on a land mine next day, next morning.

Q. And you came back to the United States.   A. I came back to the United States, and lost a foot out of it.

Q. You feel—

A. I feel cheated because the V.A. cut my disability like they did, and they said that my stump is well healed, well padded, without tenderness. Well, it's well healed, but it's a long way from being well padded. And without tenderness? It hurts all the time. I got to work eight hours a day up on my foot, and at the end of the day I can't hardly stand it. But I gotta work because I gotta make a living. And the V.A. don't give me enough money to live on as it is.

Q. Veterans Administration.   A. Right. So—

Q. Did you feel any sense of retribution to yourself the day after? A. Well, I felt that I was punished for what I'd done, the next morning. Later on in that day, I felt like I was being punished.

Q. Why did you do it?   A. Why did I do it? Because I felt like I was ordered to do it, and it seemed like that, at the time I felt like I was doing the right thing, because like I said I lost buddies. I lost a damn good buddy, Bobby Wilson, and it was on my conscience. So after I done it, I felt good, but later on that day, it was getting to me.

Q. You're married?   A. Right.

Q. Children?   A. Two.

Q. How old?   A. The boy is two and a half, and the little girl is a year and a half.

Q. Obviously, the question comes to my mind . . . the father of two little kids like that . . . how can he shoot babies?   A. I didn't have the little girl. I just had a little boy at the time.

Q. Uh-huh. How do you shoot babies?   A. I don't know. It's just one of them things.

Q. How many people would you imagine were killed that day?   A. I'd say about 370.

Q. How do you arrive at that figure?   A. Just looking.

Q. You say, you think, that many people, and you yourself were responsible for how many of them?   A. I couldn't say.

Q. Twenty-five? Fifty?   A. I couldn't say . . . just too many.

Q. And how many men did the actual shooting?   A. Well, I really couldn't say that, either. There was other . . . there was another platoon in there and . . . but I just couldn't say how many.

Q. But these civilians were lined up and shot? They weren't killed by cross-fire? A. They weren't lined up . . . they [were] just pushed in a ravine or just sitting, squatting . . . and shot.

Q. What did these civilians—particularly the woman and children, the old men—what did they do? What did they say to you? A. They weren't much saying to them. They [were] just being pushed and they were doing what they was told to do.

Q. They weren't begging or saying, "No . . . no," or— A. Right, they were begging and saying, "No, no." And the mothers was hugging their children and, but they kept right on firing. Well, we kept right on firing. They was waving their arms and begging. . . .

Q. Was that your most vivid memory of what you saw? A. Right.

Q. And nothing went through your mind or heart? A. Many a times . . . many a times. . . .

Q. While you were doing it? A. Not while I was doing it. I just seemed like it was the natural thing to do at the time. I don't know . . . I was getting relieved from what I'd seen earlier over there.

Q. What do you mean? A. Well, I was getting . . . like the . . . my buddies getting killed or wounded or—we weren't getting no satisfaction from it, so what it really was, it was just mostly revenge.

Q. You call the Vietnamese "gooks?" A. Gooks.

Q. Are they people to you? Were they people to you?

A. Well, they were people. But it was just one of them words that we just picked up over there, you know. Just any word you pick up. That's what you call people, and that's what you been called.

Q. Obviously, the thought that goes through my mind—I spent some time over there, and I killed in the second war, and so forth. But the thought that goes through your mind is, we've raised such a dickens about what the Nazis did, or what the Japanese did, but particularly what the Nazis did in the second world war, the brutalization and so forth, you know. It's hard for a good many Americans to understand that young, capable, American boys could line up old men, women and children and babies and shoot them down in cold blood. How do you explain that?

A. I wouldn't know.

Q. Did you ever dream about all of this that went on in Pinkville? A. Yes, I did . . . and I still dream about it.

Q. What kind of dreams? A. About the women and children in my sleep. Some days . . . some nights, I can't even sleep. I just lay there thinking about it.

J
PRESIDENT RICHARD M. NIXON EXPLAINS
THE NECESSITY OF THE AMERICAN MILITARY INCURSION INTO
CAMBODIA
APRIL 30, 1970

"I would rather be a one-term President and do what I believe is right than be a two-term President at the cost of seeing America become a second-rate power and to see this nation accept the first defeat in its proud 190-year history."

Ten days ago, in my report to the Nation on Vietnam, I announced a decision to withdraw an additional 150,000 Americans from Vietnam over the next year. I said then I was making that decision despite our concern over increased enemy activity in Laos, in Cambodia, and in South Vietnam.

At that time, I warned that if I concluded that increased enemy activity in any of these areas endangered the lives of Americans remaining in Vietnam, I would not hesitate to take strong and effective measures to deal with that situation.

Despite that warning, North Vietnam has increased its military aggression in all these areas, and particularly in Cambodia.

After full consultation with the National Security Council, Ambassador Bunker, General Abrams and my other advisers, I have concluded that the actions of the enemy in the last ten days clearly endanger the lives of Americans who are in Vietnam now and would constitute an unacceptable risk to those who will be there after withdrawal of another 150,000.

To protect our men who are in Vietnam and to guarantee the continued success of our withdrawal and Vietnamization programs, I have concluded that the time has come for action.

Tonight, I shall describe the actions of the enemy, the actions I have ordered to deal with that situation, and the reasons for my decision.

Congressional Quarterly Almanac, 91st Congress, 2nd Session, 1970, Vol. XXVI. Washington: Congressional Quarterly Almanac, 1971, 87A–89A. Televised speech. Reprinted by permission.

Cambodia, a small country of seven million people, has been a neutral nation since the Geneva Agreement of 1954—an agreement, incidentally, which was signed by the government of North Vietnam.

American policy since then has been to scrupulously respect the neutrality of the Cambodian people. We have maintained a skeleton diplomatic mission of fewer than fifteen in Cambodia's capital, and that only since last August. For the previous four years, from 1965 to 1969, we did not have any diplomatic mission whatever in Cambodia. And for the past five years, we have provided no military assistance whatever and no economic assistance to Cambodia.

North Vietnam, however, has not respected that neutrality.

For the past five years—as indicated on this map that you see here—North Vietnam has occupied military sanctuaries all along the Cambodian frontier with South Vietnam. Some of these extend up to 20 miles into Cambodia. . . .

During my campaign for the Presidency, I pledged to bring Americans home from Vietnam. They are coming home.

I promised to end this war. I shall keep that promise.

I promised to win a just peace. I shall keep that promise.

We shall avoid a wider war. But we are also determined to put an end to this war. . . .

I have noted, for example, that a Republican Senator has said that this action I have taken means that my party has lost all chance of winning the November elections. And others are saying today that this move against the enemy sanctuaries will make me a one-term President. . . .

Whether I may be a one-term President is insignificant compared to whether by our failure to act in this crisis the United States proves itself to be unworthy to lead the forces of freedom in this critical period in world history. I would rather be a one-term President and do what I believe is right than to be a two-term President at the cost of seeing America become a second-rate power and to see this nation accept the first defeat in its proud 190-year history. . . .

The action I have taken tonight is indispensable for the continuing success of that withdrawal program.

A majority of the American people want to end this war rather than to have it drag on interminably. The action I have taken tonight will serve that purpose.

A majority of the American people want to keep the casualties of our brave men in Vietnam at an absolute minimum. The action I take tonight is essential if we are to accomplish that goal.

We take this action not for the purpose of expanding the war into Cambodia, but for the purpose of ending the war in Vietnam and winning the just peace we all desire. We have made and we will continue to make any possible effort to end this war through negotiations at the conference table rather than through more fighting on the battlefield. . . .

Tonight I again warn the North Vietnamese that if they continue to escalate the fighting when the United States is withdrawing its forces I shall meet my responsibility as Commander-in-Chief of our Armed Forces to take the action I consider necessary to defend the security of our American men.

This action that I have announced tonight puts the leaders of North Vietnam on notice that we will be patient in working for peace, we will be conciliatory at the conference table, but, we will not be humiliated. We will not be defeated. We will not allow American men by the thousands to be killed by an enemy from privileged sanctuaries.

The time came long ago to end this war through peaceful negotiations. We stand ready for those negotiations. We have made major efforts, many of which must remain secret. . . .

My fellow Americans, we live in an age of anarchy, both abroad and at home. We see mindless attacks on all the great institutions which have been created by free civilizations in the last 500 years. Even here in the United States great universities are being systematically destroyed. Small nations all over the world find themselves under attack from within and without.

If, when the chips are down, the world's most powerful nation, the United States of America, acts like a pitiful, helpless giant, the forces of totalitarianism and anarchy will threaten free nations and free institutions throughout the world.

It is not our power, but our will and character that is being tested tonight. . . .

With other nations, we shall do our best to provide the small arms and other equipment which the Cambodian army of 40,000 needs and can use for its defense. But the aid we will provide will be limited for the purpose of enabling Cambodia to defend its neutrality and not for purpose of making it an active belligerent on one side or the other.

Now confronted with this situation, we have three options. . . .

First, we can do nothing. Well, the ultimate result of that course of action is clear. Unless we indulge in wishful thinking, the lives of Americans remaining in Vietnam after our next withdrawal of 150,000 would be gravely threatened. . . .

Our second choice is to provide massive military assistance to Cambodia itself. Now unfortunately, while we deeply sympathize with the plight of seven million Cambodians whose country is being invaded, massive amounts of military assistance could not be rapidly and effectively utilized by the small Cambodian army against the immediate threat.

Our third choice is to go to the heart of the trouble. That means cleaning out major North Vietnamese and Viet Cong occupied territories, these sanctuaries which serve as bases for attacks on both Cambodia and American and South Vietnamese forces in South Vietnam. Some of these, incidentally, are as close to Saigon as Baltimore is to Washington.

This one [pointing to map], for example, is called the Parrot's Beak. It is only 33 miles from Saigon.

Now faced with these three options, this is the decision I have made.

In cooperation with the armed forces of South Vietnam, attacks are being launched this week to clean out major enemy sanctuaries on the Cambodian-Vietnam border.

A major responsibility for the ground operations is being assumed by South Vietnamese forces. For example, the attacks in several areas, including the Parrot's Beak that I referred to a moment ago, are exclusively South Vietnamese ground operations under South Vietnamese command, with the United States providing air and logistical support.

There is one area, however, immediately above Parrot's Beak, where I have concluded that a combined American and South Vietnamese operation is necessary.

Tonight, American and South Vietnamese units will attack the headquarters for the entire Communist military operation in South Vietnam. This key control center has been occupied by the North Vietnamese and Viet Cong for five years in blatant violation of Cambodia's neutrality.

This is not an invasion of Cambodia. The areas in which these attacks will be launched are completely occupied and controlled by North Vietnamese forces. Our purpose is not to occupy the areas. Once enemy forces are driven out of these sanctuaries and once their military supplies are destroyed, we will withdraw.

These actions are in no way directed to the security interests of any nation. Any government that chooses to use these actions as a pretext for harming relations with the United States will be doing so on its own responsibility, and on its on initiative, and we will draw the appropriate conclusions.

Now let me give you the reasons for my decision.

A majority of the American people, a majority of you listening to me, are for the withdrawal of our forces from Vietnam. . . .

These Communist occupied territories contain major base camps, training sites, logistics facilities, weapons and ammunition factories, air strips and prisoner of war compounds.

For five years, neither the United States nor South Vietnam has moved against those enemy sanctuaries because we did not wish to violate the territory of a neutral nation. Even after the Vietnamese Communists began to expand these sanctuaries four weeks ago, we counselled patience to our South Vietnamese allies and imposed restraints on our own commanders.

In contrast to our policy, the enemy in the past two weeks has stepped up his guerrilla actions and he is concentrating his main forces in these sanctuaries that you see on this map where they are building up to launch massive attacks on our forces and those of South Vietnam.

North Vietnam in the last two weeks has stripped away all pretense of respecting the sovereignty or neutrality of Cambodia. Thousands of their soldiers are invading the country from the sanctuaries; they are encircling the Capital of Phnom Penh, coming from these sanctuaries, as you see here. They have moved into Cambodia and are encircling the Capital.

Cambodia, as a result of this, sent out a call to the United States, to a number of other nations, for assistance, Because if this enemy effort succeeds, Cambodia would become a vast enemy staging area and a spring-board for attacks on South Vietnam along 600 miles of frontier— a refuge where enemy troops could return from combat without fear of retaliation.

North Vietnamese men and supplies could then be poured into that country, jeopardizing not only the lives of our own men, but the people of South Vietnam as well. . . .

K
COLUMNIST JOSEPH ALSOP FEARS THE ADVENT OF
A NEW ISOLATIONISM IN THE UNITED STATES
MAY 31, 1971

"This country's basic instincts are isolationist, and the American voters are clearly fed up, not only with the Vietnam war, but with the whole boring, expensive, dangerous business of being the world's No. 1 power. . . . There is a curious new flaccidity, a mysterious mushiness, about American life and thought that may be incurable."

Washington—In recent weeks—and last week especially—it has seemed more and more evident that the answer to a question Winston Churchill once asked, at the end of a long and bibulous lunch, is "No."

The year was 1948. I had been wandering about the Continent, and had run into Randolph Churchill, the great man's only son, who asked me to lunch at Chartwell. The lunch (which I described subsequently for the late lamented Saturday Evening Post) was at first an intimidating occasion. I had thought it would be a large gathering, and I could be as inconspicuous as a fly on the wall. Instead, there were only the great man, Randolph and myself.

Mr. Churchill (as he was then) appeared in a rumpled siren suit, and he looked like a grumpy old baby. When Randolph introduced me, his only response was a disapproving "Hrrumph." There were no cocktails. We sat down and drank our soup in nervous silence, broken only by an occasional "Hrrumph." Then in came a bottle of champagne, and then another. The effect on Mr. Churchill was that of the sun on a flower.

He began to talk, and he talked wonderfully well—wisely, wittily, and maliciously. Over the port and cigars, he talked about the then current scene, which he painted in gloomy colors, and with reason— Stalin had blockaded Berlin, and there had been the take-over attempts in Azerbaijan and Greece, the coup in Czechoslovakia, and much else. The United States had responded, at first with agonized reluctance, with Greek-Turkish aid, the Marshall plan, the beginnings of NATO.

"America," Mr. Churchill mused, puffing his cigar. "America. A

Joseph Alsop, "A Mysterious Mushiness," *Newsweek Magazine* (May 31, 1971), 88. Reprinted by permission.

great and powerful country, like a strong horse, pulling the rest of the world up behind it, towards peace and prosperity." Then he fixed me with an accusing stare. "But will America stay the course?"

I answered the question with a confident (and slightly intoxicated) "Yes." I would now answer the question with an almost equally unequivocal "No."

Times have changed, of course, since Mr. Churchill asked his question. Stalin is dead, and so is the Soviet monopoly of Communist power. In the post-Marshall-plan era, this country suffered from a Miss Fix-it complex, and our commitments were greatly overexpanded. The Europeans' contribution to Europe's defense has for twenty years been grossly inadequate, and the American military bureaucracy has never provided a fair return in combat power on its immense manpower and money investment. Above all, the Vietnam war has been a major national tragedy.

All this is true, but it is also true that Mr. Churchill's question remains the key question today, as it was when he asked it over the port. Churchill saw, with his genius for recognizing the obvious, that only American power could provide an effective counterbalance to Soviet power, and that if the United States ceased to behave like a "strong horse," Soviet power would ultimately prevail.

In intellectual circles here and abroad (except in Israel) this is now a most unfashionable view. The fashionable view is that the nuclear weapons have rendered the old concept of the balance of power obsolete, and that power is not therefore something to worry about. Unfortunately, this view is not shared in Moscow.

The U.S. reconnaissance satellites have brought back indisputable evidence of an immense Soviet effort to gain nuclear-missile superiority. There is equally hard evidence of a major Soviet effort to gain naval superiority, and the Soviets already enjoy decisive ground combat superiority on the Continent.

Meanwhile, this country, while still involved in a costly war, is spending less on national defense in terms of percentage of gross national product than before the Korean War, and much less on strategic weapons than in the Eisenhower era. Defense manpower is being cut back by 40 per cent and more, and if the draft ends we could soon have fewer men in uniform than before the second war.

The fashionable response to this contrast is to dismiss the hard evidence of the Soviet missile program as mere Pentagon propaganda—"The Annual Spring Scare," to quote the title of a recent New York

Times editorial. All the Democratic Presidential candidates but one favor further sharp cutbacks in defense. All the Democratic candidates but one are at best equivocal about the New Left demand that all logistic support for the South Vietnamese armed forces be ended, while the Russians and Chinese continue to supply the North Vietnamese with all the arms they need.

But perhaps the best evidence that the answer to Mr. Churchill's question is likely to be "No" was provided by last week's scare over the Mansfield amendment to cut the American troop commitment to NATO in half without hearings or prolonged debate. The amendment was given a very good chance of passing, with the support of the liberal Democrats. It was only defeated, with a big assist from Leonid Brezhnev, after the Administration had mustered all the elder statesmen of the "strong horse" period including old Harry S. Truman himself.

But this was a rear-guard action, and almost certainly the last. The elder statesmen represented the internationalist Democratic tradition of Roosevelt, Truman and John Kennedy. The liberals who now control the majority party have turned instead to the counter-tradition of "America first." Robert A. Taft is their unlikely hero.

There is no doubt that the liberal Democrats are onto a good thing politically. This country's basic instincts are isolationist, and the American voters are clearly fed up, not only with the Vietnam war, but with the whole boring, expensive, dangerous business of being the world's No. 1 power. This being a democracy, the voters will no doubt have their way, and the United States, after its brief period of primacy, will cease to be the world's No. 1 power. It will cease to be "a strong horse."

What will happen then? Perhaps Churchill was wrong, and the left-intellectuals are right, and the Russians having achieved primacy in both nuclear and conventional power, will choose not to exercise their power. Perhaps they will exercise it all too effectively. My guess, for what it is worth is that this country will suffer some sort of traumatic shock, something like the Cuban missile crisis in reverse, and that this will have the therapeutic effect that electric shock treatment sometimes has on the emotionally disturbed.

But I am not at all sure this is a good guess. There is a curious new flaccidity, a mysterious mushiness, about American life and thought that may be incurable. So the answer to Mr. Churchill's question is very probably "No."

THE
COLD WAR

II
THE CRUSADERS AND THE SCHOLARS:
COMMUNISTS

A
JOSEPH STALIN ON SOVIET SECURITY
AND THE HOSTILITY OF THE ANGLO-AMERICANS
MARCH 14, 1946

". . . what can be surprising in the fact that the Soviet Union, in a desire to ensure its security for the future, tries to achieve that these [Eastern European] countries should have government whose relations to the Soviet Union are loyal?"

Mr. Churchill maintains that Warsaw, Berlin, Prague, Vienna, Budapest, Belgrade, Bucharest and Sofia, all these famous cities and the populations of those areas, are within the Soviet sphere and are all subjected to Soviet influence and to the increasing control of Moscow.

Mr. Churchill qualifies this as the "boundless expansionist tendencies of the Soviet Union." It requires no special effort to show that Mr. Churchill rudely and shamelessly libels not only Moscow but also the above-mentioned States neighborly to the U.S.S R.

To begin with, it is quite absurd to speak of the exclusive control of the U.S.S.R. in Vienna and Berlin, where there are Allied control councils with representatives of four States, where the U.S.S.R. has only one-fourth of the voices.

"Stalin Interview with *Pravda* on Churchill [Iron Curtain Speech]," *New York Times*, March 14, 1946. Reprinted by permission.

It happens sometimes that some people are unable to refrain from libel, but still they should know a limit.

Secondly, one cannot forget the following fact: the Germans carried out an invasion of the U.S.S.R. through Finland, Poland, Rumania, Bulgaria and Hungary. The Germans were able to carry out the invasion through these countries by reason of the fact that these countries had governments inimical to the Soviet Union.

As a result of the German invasion, the Soviet Union has irrevocably lost in battles with the Germans, and also during the German occupation and through the expulsion of Soviet citizens to German slave labor camps, about 7,000,000 people. In other words, the Soviet Union has lost in men several times more than Britain and the United States together.

It may be that some quarters are trying to push into oblivion these sacrifices of the Soviet people which insured the liberation of Europe from the Hitlerite yoke.

But the Soviet Union cannot forget them. One can ask, therefore, what can be surprising in the fact that the Soviet Union, in a desire to ensure its security for the future, tries to achieve that these countries should have governments whose relations to the Soviet Union are loyal? How can one, without having lost one's reason, qualify these peaceful aspirations of the Soviet Union as "expansionist tendencies" of our Government?

Mr. Churchill further maintains that the Polish Government under Russian lordship has been spurred to an unjust and criminal spoliation against Germany. Here, every word is a rude and offensive libel. Contemporary democratic Poland is led by outstanding men. They have shown in deeds that they know how to defend the interests and worth of their homeland, as their predecessors failed to do.

What reason has Mr. Churchill to maintain that the leaders of contemporary Poland can submit their country to a lordship by representatives of any country whatever? Does Mr. Churchill here libel the Russians because he has intentions of sowing the seeds of discord between Poland and the Soviet Union?

Mr. Churchill is not pleased that Poland should have turned her policy toward friendship and alliance with the U.S.S.R. There was a time when in the mutual relations between Poland and the U.S.S.R. there prevailed an element of conflict and contradiction. This gave a possibility to statesmen, of the kind of Mr. Churchill, to play on these contradictions, to take Poland in hand under the guise of protection from the Russians, to frighten Russia by specters of a war between Poland and herself, and to take for themselves the role of arbiters.

But this time is past. For enmity between Poland and Russia has given place to friendship between them, and Poland, present democratic Poland, does not wish any longer to be a playing-ball in the hands of foreigners. It seems to be that this is just what annoys Mr. Churchill and urges him to rude, tactless outbursts against Poland. After all, it is no laughing matter for him. He is not allowed to play for other people's stakes.

As for Mr. Churchill's attack on the Soviet Union in connection with the extending of the western boundaries of Poland, as compensation for the territories seized by the Germans in the past, there it seems to me that he quite blatantly distorts the facts.

As is known, the western frontiers of Poland were decided upon at the Berlin conference of the three powers, on the basis of Poland's demands.

The Soviet Union repeatedly declared that it considered Poland's demands just and correct. It may well be that Mr. Churchill is not pleased with this decision. But why does Mr. Churchill, not sparing his darts against the Russians in the matter, conceal from his readers the fact that the decision was taken at the Berlin conference unanimously, that not only the Russians voted for this decision but also the English and Americans?

Why did Mr. Churchill have to delude people? Mr. Churchill further maintains that the Communist parties were very insignificant in all these Eastern European countries but reached exceptional strength, exceeding their numbers by far, and are attempting to establish totalitarian control everywhere; that police-government prevailed in almost all these countries, even up to now, with the exception of Czechoslovakia, and that there exists in them no real democracy.

As is known in Britain at present there is one party which rules the country—the Labor party. The rest of the parties are barred from the Government of the country. This is called by Churchill a true democracy, meanwhile Poland, Rumania, Yugoslavia, Bulgaria and Hungary are governed by several parties—from four to six parties. And besides, the opposition, if it is loyal, is guaranteed the right to participate in the Government. This, Churchill calls totalitarian and the Government of police.

On what grounds? Do you expect an answer from Churchill? Does he not understand the ridiculous situation he is putting himself in by such speeches on the basis of totalitarianism and police rule? Churchill would have liked Poland to be ruled by Sosnkowski and Anders, Yugoslavia by Mikhailovitch, Rumania by Prince Stirbey and Radescu, Hungary and Austria by some king from the House of Habsburg, and so on.

Mr. Churchill wants to assure us that these gentlemen from the Fascist servants' hall can ensure true democracy. Such is the Democracy of Mr. Churchill. Mr. Churchill wanders around the truth when he speaks of the growth of the influence of the Communist parties in eastern Europe. It should, however, be noted that he is not quite accurate. The influence of Communist parties grew not only in Eastern Europe but in almost every country of Europe where fascism has ruled before: Italy, Germany, Hungary, Bulgaria, Rumania, Finland, and in countries which have suffered German, Italian or Hungarian occupation. France, Belgium, Holland, Norway, Denmark, Poland, Czechoslovakia, Yugoslavia, Greece, the Soviet Union and so on.

The growth of the influence of communism cannot be considered accidental. It is a normal function. The influence of the Communists grew because during the hard years of the mastery of fascism in Europe, Communists showed themselves to be reliable, daring and self-sacrificing fighters against fascist regimes for the liberty of peoples.

Mr. Churchill sometimes recalls in his speeches the common people from small houses, patting them on the shoulder in a lordly manner and pretending to be their friend. But these people are not so simple-minded as it might appear at first sight. Common people, too, have their opinions and their own politics. And they know how to stand up for themselves.

It is they, millions of these common people, who voted Mr. Churchill and his party out in England, giving their votes to the Labor party. It is they, millions of these common people, who isolated reactionaries in Europe, collaborators with fascism, and gave preference to Left democratic parties.

It is they, millions of these common people, having tried the Communists in the fire of struggle and resistance to fascism, who decided that the Communists deserve completely the confidence of the people. Thus grew the Communists' influence in Europe. Such is the law of historical development.

Of course, Mr. Churchill does not like such a development of events. And he raised the alarm, appealing to force. But he also did not like the appearance of the Soviet regime in Russia after the First World War. Then, too, he raised the alarm and organized an armed expedition of fourteen states against Russia with the aim of turning back the wheel of history.

But history turned out to be stronger than Churchill's intervention and the quixotic antics of Chruchill resulted in his complete defeat. I do not know whether Mr. Churchill and his friends will succeed in organizing after the Second World War a new military expedition against eastern Europe. But if they succeed in this, which is not very probable, since millions of common people stand on guard over the peace, then one man confidently says that they will be beaten, just as they were beaten twenty-six years ago.

B
SOVIET FOREIGN MINISTER V. M. MOLOTOV CONDEMNS ANGLO-AMERICAN IMPERIALISM
NOVEMBER 7, 1947

"Reading of all these American plans for aid to Europe, aid to China, and so on, one might think that the domestic problems of the United States have long ago been solved, and that now it is only a question of America's putting the affairs of other states in order, dictating its policy to them and even the composition of their governments."

The Soviet Union has invariably carried out, and is carrying out, the policy of peace and international collaboration. Such are the relations of the Soviet Union with all the countries which evince a desire to collaborate.

The policy outlined by Comrade Stalin is opposed at present by another policy, based on quite different principles. Here we can talk first and foremost of the foreign policy of the United States, as well as

---

Excerpts from Molotov Speech Delivered on the 30th Anniversary of the Revolution. *New York Times*, November 7, 1947. Reprinted by permission.

that of Great Britain. Possibly there exists in the United States a program of economic development of the country for some period ahead. However, the press has not yet announced anything about this, although press conferences take place there quite frequently. On the other hand, much noise is being spread about various American projects, connected now with the Truman Doctrine, now with the Marshall plan.

Reading of all these American plans for aid to Europe, aid to China, and so on, one might think that the domestic problems of the United States have long ago been solved, and that now it is only a question of America's putting the affairs of other states in order, dictating its policy to them and even the composition of their governments.

In reality, matters are not like that. If the ruling circles of the U.S.A. had no cause for anxiety concerning domestic affairs, especially in connection with an approaching economic crisis, there would not be such a superfluity of economic projects of U.S.A. expansion, which in their turn are based on the aggressive military-political plans of American imperialism.

Now they no longer hide the fact that the United States of America, not infrequently together with Great Britain, is acquiring ever new naval and air bases in all parts of the globe, and even adapts whole states for such like aims, especially if closely situated to the Soviet Union.

Who does not complain about the pressure of American imperialism in that respect? Even if the governments of certain big states of Europe, Asia and America preserve a kind of solid silence in regard to this matter, it is clear that certain small states are faced by an absolutely intolerable position. Denmark, for instance, cannot achieve the restoration of her national sovereignty over Greenland, which the Americans do not want to leave after the end of the war. Egypt legitimately demands the withdrawal of British troops from her territory. Britain refuses to do that, and America supports the British imperialists in these matters also.

It is, however, clear that the creation of military bases in various parts of the world is not designed for defense purposes, but as a preparation for aggression. It is also clear that if, up to now, the combined British-American General Staff, created during the second World War, has been maintained, this is not being done for peace-loving purposes, but for the purpose of intimidating with the possibility of new aggression.

It would be a good thing for all this to be known to the American people, for under the so-called Western freedom of the press, when almost all newspapers and radio stations are in the hands of small cliques, the aggressive cliques of the capitalists and their servitors, it is difficult for the people to know the real truth.

It is interesting that in expansionist circles of the U.S.A. a new, peculiar sort of illusion is widespread—while having no faith in their internal strength—faith is placed in the secret of the atom bomb, although this secret has long ceased to exist.

Evidently the imperialists need this faith in the atom bomb which, as is known, is not a means of defense but a weapon of aggression. . . .

It is well known that the industry of the United States of America in the period between the two world wars has grown, although its development proceeded extremely unevenly and twice fell considerably below the level of 1913. For all that, during the second World War American industry grew rapidly, became inflated and began to yield enormous profits to the capitalists and state revenues, which American state monopoly capitalism is putting into circulation and applying to exert pressure everywhere in Europe and China, in Greece and Turkey, in South America and in the Middle East.

Certainly there are not a few who like to make use of a war situation. . . .

Today the ruling circles of the U.S.A. and Great Britain head one international grouping, which has as its aim the consolidation of capitalism and the achievement of the dominations of these countries over other peoples. These countries are headed by imperialist and anti-democratic forces in international affairs, with the active participation of certain Socialist leaders in several European states. . . .

As a result of post-war Anglo-American policy the British and American zones of occupation of Germany were united into a jointly administered bizonal territory—which has been given the name of "Bizonia" in the press—so that an Anglo-American policy could be unilaterally carried out there independently of the Control Council, in which representatives of all four occupying powers participate.

Our representatives in Germany are today virtually concerned only with the Soviet zone. A situation has arisen which cannot but produce alarm among the German people also, since, as the result of the Anglo-American policy, there exists the joint zone and other zones, but there is no Germany, no single German state.

The Soviet Union considers it necessary that the decisions of the Yalta and Potsdam conferences on the German question, decisions which provided for the restoration of Germany as a single democratic state, should be put into effect. Moreover, in the Soviet Union it is entirely understood that the joint zone is not Germany and that the German people has a right to the existence of its own state which, it goes without saying, must be a democratic state and must not create the threat of new aggression for other peace-loving states.

At the present time there exists the Anglo-American plan—by giving some aims to calm the population of the Anglo-American zone of Germany—for basing themselves here on the former capitalists who were recently the Hitlerite support, and for utilizing with their aid the joint zone with its Ruhr industrial basin as a threat against those countries which do not display slavish submissiveness with regard to the Anglo-American plans for domination in Europe.

But these adventurists' plans, based on Germany, will lead to nothing good and it goes without saying, will be rejected by democratic Europe.

From the example of the German question, one can see how widely present day Anglo-American principles diverge from the principles of the Soviet state, how Anglo-American principles are steeped in open imperialism, while the Soviet stands firmly on democratic positions.

The Soviet Union, in common with other democratic states, stands for peace and international collaboration on democratic principles. Under present conditions, this demands the uniting of all forces of the anti-imperialist and democratic camp in Europe and beyond the boundaries of Europe, so that an insurmountable barrier shall be created against imperialism, which is becoming more active, and against its new policy of aggression.

The rallying of democratic forces and courageous struggle against imperialism in its new plans for war adventures will unite the peoples into a powerful army, the equal of which cannot be possessed by imperialism, which denies the democratic rights of the people, infringing on the sovereignty of the nations and basing its plans on threats and adventures.

Uneasiness and alarm are growing in the imperialist ranks, since everybody sees that the ground is shaking under the feet of imperialism, while the forces of democracy and socialism are daily growing and consolidating.

What can the policy of imperialism offer people? Nothing but strengthening of oppression, the rebirth of the vestiges of hated fascism and imperialistic adventures.

It is necessary to open the peoples' eyes and to unite all the democratic and anti-imperialistic forces in order to foil any plans for the economic enslavement of nations and any new adventures on the part of the imperialists.

The historic experience of the Soviet Union has confirmed the justice of the great Lenin's words on the invincibility of the people which took power into their hands. Lenin said: "One can never conquer a people where the majority of workers and peasants have realized, sensed and seen that they are upholding their own sovereign power, the power of the working people, the victory of whose cause, if upheld, will secure for them and their children the possibility of enjoying all the benefits of culture, all the achievements of human labor."

The task of our time is to unite all the anti-imperialistic and democratic forces of the nations into one mighty camp, welded together by the unity of their vital interests against the imperialist and anti-democratic camp and its policy of enslavement of the peoples and new adventures.

A sober attitude to the matter shows simultaneously that in our time new imperialistic adventures constitute a dangerous game with destinies of capitalism.

C

PROFESSORS KATZENBACH AND HANNAHAN ON
THE REVOLUTIONARY STRATEGY OF MAO TSE TUNG:
AN AMERICAN VIEW
SEPTEMBER, 1955

"The Chinese Revolutionary Army was born in sublime poverty: no clothing, no guns, no cash, no food. Recognizing this as hard fact, Mao had to rerank the elements necessary to win a war. He pointed out that 'in studying the guiding laws of war of different historical stages, of different characters, of different places and of different nations, we must keep our eyes on their respective characteristics and their development, and must oppose a mechanical approach to the problem of war.'"

Edward L. Katzenbach, Jr., and Gene Z. Hannahan, "The Revolutionary Strategy of Mao Tse Tung," *Political Science Quarterly*, **70** (September, 1955), 322–338. Reprinted by permission.

Mao Tse-tung has done for war what Lenin did for imperialism and Marx for capitalism: he has given war "scientific" schemata. And as such his writings have been given a Communist-world-wide circulation. His work has been studied in Russia where it was used as the theoretical base of Russian guerrilla tactics, although, according to the Chinese, the Russians did not really understand the subject. In simplified form his writings are the military Bible of the Viet Minh in Indo-China, of the Huks in the Phillipines, and of the insurgents in Malaya.

Mao's military philosophy did not flow from his agile mind a finished product. His first important military piece, *The Struggle in the Chingkang Mountains* (1928), is dated. His most important work, *On the Protracted War* (1938), purports to be, and probably is, a classic and timeless. The first deals with a set of problems, the last with a set of premises. Mao, in other words, finally universalized his own experience. And that is why his work has become a primer for action for all those whose situation was and is in any way comparable.

In Mao's Communist cultural heritage there has been great interest in military affairs as well as some remarkable thinking. Marx, Engels, Lenin, Trotsky and Stalin agreed on the historical necessity of war as a concomitant of revolution. Hence all at one time or another expressed an interest in the special problems of a people's war. Their studies, however, were not systematized within an ideological framework, as are those of Mao. Mao claims to have applied to warfare the "immutable laws" that fellow-Communists have detected in socio-economic behavior. Essentially he discovered these for himself.

From his ideological forebears, most frequently from Lenin, Mao borrowed quotations—apparently more to give tone to his argument, like Biblical quotations to political orations, than for any other reason. And, of course, he borrowed an angle of sight, the notion that war is the midwife of revolution, and that war like revolution follows a course which is "scientifically ascertainable.". . .

Nor does Mao's thinking seem to have been extensively influenced by Western military thinkers. Mao read, as had Lenin and Trotsky and Stalin before him, some Clausewitz in Chinese translation as early as 1928. What he learned about Western military thought from Chu Te (now Commander-in-Chief of the Chinese People's Liberation Army and second only to Mao in the party hierarchy) who had Western military training is unknown. And some of Mao's later concepts are much like those expressed by Jomini in his study of *The Art of War*.

There can be no doubt of Mao's intimate acquaintance with the great military classics of Sun Tzu and lesser Chinese military thinkers. Yet, although much of his thinking is like theirs, direct influence is difficult to trace. He uses his military classics, however, as he uses his Marxist classics, simply as a mine of good examples and corroborative quotations for what appears to be his own independent thinking. . . .

The war which Mao Tse-tung fought from his early days as a peasant organizer and agitator in South China in 1927 was one in which the first rule was simple survival. So as the cornerstone of military planning Mao Tse-tung has placed a politico-revolutionary sense of time. Whereas Western military men have spent most of their lives considering the problems of the concentration of force *in time*, Mao has spent his life and thought on how to gain *time*. . . .

"The ten years' revolutionary war we have fought may be surprising to other countries, but for us it is only like the presentation, amplification and preliminary exposition of the theme in an . . . essay with many exciting paragraphs yet to follow," wrote Mao in 1936. Time, Mao believes, can be made to defeat technology. And unlimited time depends primarily on unlimited space. Unlike Western writers Mao does not concentrate on the problem of ending a war quickly. His problem is to keep it going. Again and again he returns to this theme: "Our War of Resistance cannot be quickly won and can only be a protracted war." Again, "as 'a distant journey tests the strength of a horse and a long task proves the character of a man,' [so] guerrilla warfare will demonstrate its enormous power in the course of a long and ruthless war. . . . "

Space in military terms may be described as square mileage plus obstacles minus a workable communications network. Thus ten square miles of mountainous jungle might be equal to a hundred square miles of rolling plain, and this in turn might be equal to a thousand square miles cut by roads and railroads. That space in China could be made to yield time, and time, revolutionary organization, and political cohesion, victory—this is the basis of Mao's optimism.

From the military point of view how then does Mao think that space can be made to yield time?

The Chinese Revolutionary Army was born in sublime poverty: no clothing, no guns, no cash, no food. Recognizing this as hard fact, Mao had to rerank the elements necessary to win a war. He pointed out that "in studying the guiding laws of war of different historical stages, of different characters, of different places and of different nations, we must keep our eyes on their respective characteristics and their development, and must oppose a mechanical approach to the problem of war." He told his readers that "[we had to] familiarise ourselves with all aspects of the enemy's situation as well as our own, to discover the laws of the actions of both sides, and to take these laws into account in our own actions."

Mao did not merely rethink but initially formulated a philosophy of war based on a reëstimate of strength ratios. Guns were few in the early days of the struggle and Mao, from necessity, found that arms were not the only effective tools in a revolution. "Weapons are an important factor in war but not the decisive one; it is man and not material that counts," he wrote. With neither military nor economic means he was forced to emphasize that "the ratio of strength is not only a comparison between military and economic strength, but also between manpower and the minds of men." Mao would scoff at the tale, which has at least the status of the apocryphal in the Western world, of the loss of the nail from the shoe of the horse, which lost the battle and then the empire. His theory is, in essence, a theory of substitution: substitution of propaganda for guns, subversion for air power, men for machines, space for mechanization, political for industrial mobilization. The theory was formed intuitively in day-to-day practice. Reflection then turned practice into a theory of war.

In his early pronouncements Mao stressed two points: the first, the necessity of political education; the second, the need for a "democratic" army. But those features of his democratic army which so impressed foreign military observers at first, such as complete equality between officers and men, tended to be less emphasized as the Red Army grew. And Mao's commentaries ceased to mention them. The emphasis on political education has, of course, remained, and with it that essential concomitant; the inculcation of "iron" discipline. It was political education which time was to yield. And it was political discipline which was to yield more time.

Political mobilization, Mao believes, "is the most fundamental condition for winning the war." And elsewhere he gives the reason in a simile, a form he dearly loves: "The people are like water and the army is like fish." "With the common people of the whole country mobilised, we shall create a vast sea of humanity and drown the enemy in it. . . ." Mao holds out military salvation, in a truly ideological sense, as a concomitant of political conversion.

Year after year Mao returned to the problems involved in creating a political revolution through a protracted armed struggle. . . .

Discouragement requires that war must be at once constantly successful and most cautiously fought. Losses must be kept at a minimum, and local successes must be continuous. The very price of survival is caution. Hence Mao's repetitive insistence on the necessity of local superiority: five and even ten against one is his formula. The political control necessary to maintain the formula undiluted in a situation in which revolutionary ardor is present is, of course, extraordinarily difficult. It accounts for Mao's insistence on absolute discipline.

Guerrilla warfare is the great timeserver of military strategy. Guerrilla operations are the muck, the quicksand in which military machinery bogs down in futility. And it is the cheapest kind of war to wage. It can also be the most futile, if left undirected. Like mud it can stave off defeat, but it cannot bring victory. Because he could not himself direct all operations, Mao outlined his doctrinal position on this type of war in a series of pamphlets: *Strategic Problems of China's Revolutionary War* (1936), *Strategic Problems in the Anti-Japanese Guerrilla War* (1938) and finally in *On the Protracted War* (1938).

Mao deals in one way or another with one central problem in all these works of his. The problem is one of combining dispersion with concentration. Local insurrection corps "armed with spears and fowling pieces," the "special feature," of revolution in agricultural China, had to be combined with the use of the regular Chinese Red Army. The local corps, by being dispersed, were to disperse the enemy. The army was to defeat said enemy in detail. There is nothing new certainly in this concept. What Mao did, however, was to set the concept in the context of time. In doing so, he plotted the course of war, as Marx had plotted the pattern of history, as thesis, antithesis, and victorious synthesis. . . .

"Is it not self-contradictory to fight heroically first and abandon territory afterwards?" he asks rhetorically. Rhetorically he answers with another question: "One eats first and then relieves oneself; does one eat in vain?"

The first stage is said to slip into the second for two interdependent reasons. In that the war is seen not to be over, a sense of futility creeps up both among the opponents' troops and on their home front where there is a "change for the worse" because of casualties, expense, and so forth. Communist morale by this very token begins to rise. When the see-saw of war reaches a state of equilibrium, the strategic stalemate, or stage two, has been reached.

An increase in guerrilla warfare, supplemented by mobile warfare fought by increasing numbers of regular Communist troops will then—despite defeatism, economic difficulties and "collaborators' subversive activities"—turn stage two into stage three. Finally, as this stage moves toward its culmination, guerrilla warfare becomes supplementary, and the more regular forms of warfare become once more the order of the day....

The outbreak of the civil war between the Communists and Nationalists in 1946 was a logical development of Mao's strategic plan. In fact, there was no essential shift or change in Communist strategy. This was a point which the Nationalists regrettably failed to grasp. Because the nature of the enemy had changed, the Communists reverted to Mao's first phase, i.e., to the strategic defensive. Nationalist advances were, territory-wise, nothing short of spectacular during the first year of the war. But, whether they knew it or not, they were fighting a war dictated by Communist military doctrine.

Mao was trading space for time and cities for men. In his "rear base," Manchuria, he was organizing, training and arming a strong force that was to remain uncommitted until the second phase, the stalemate, could be realized. Meanwhile, Chinese Communist military commanders in North China continued their policies of attrition of the enemy, capitalizing upon Chiang Kai-shek's habit of giving his commanders certain definite time limits for achieving their objectives. The "European-style" war fought by the Nationalists played into the hands of the Red strategists....

Maoist strategy paid off in late 1947 and early 1948 with the arrival of the military stalemate. The second phase was a brief one, largely because the Communists had laid their plans well. The war after 1948 was almost preordained. The Communists took full advantage of the overextended Nationalist armies, now wallowing deep in the Red-controlled areas. The Nationalists found themselves unable to take advantage of either time or space—both were now on the side of Mao.

The third and final stage was at hand when General Lin Piao led his Manchurian forces in the initial counter-offensive against the enemy. Pivoting from the Manchurian provinces, the Communist armies swept through the key Shanhai pass and into the vast North China plain. Joining up with other Red forces the Communist armies found little difficulty in breaking the back of the main Nationalist armies and eventually in completing the conquest of the China mainland. The civil war was a classic in Maoist strategy—a strategy clearly outlined over ten years previously, in 1938. The fact that neither the Nationalists nor the West took heed of the pronouncements of this prophetic strategist is attested to by the failure of the Nationalists and of the West to counter the advances made by Communist China since 1946.

The Korean conflict was a different type of war—with different objectives and conditions. And yet, we can see that much of Mao's doctrine obtained even there. Red military operations were largely those laid down by Mao in his study of the *Strategic Problems of China's Revolutionary War*—this despite the fact that China was engaged in its first "modern war" against the West. Mao's concept of time was aptly demonstrated in the protracted stalemate period when the Communists, seemingly indifferent to losses, conducted what appeared to United Nations observers as wasted military operations. But the Red high command had two very important reasons in mind. First, it was argued that the side which continued to be aggressive and held the initiative—despite the fact that peace was imminent and the truce lines were drawn—could be considered, at least propaganda-wise, the victor. In this way the Communists showed no aversion toward utilizing their men to gain a political or psychological victory through military action; even though in so doing they might take heavy losses. Such a means could never even be considered by United Nations forces. Secondly, the Communists hoped to learn more about positional (or trench) warfare at this time. Captured enemy documents reveal that the Red military leaders were willing to expend their manpower in learning this "Western-style" warfare. The Communists were preparing for the next war in the closing phases of the Korean conflict.

But the Communist high command knew that the campaign would be written as a whole, and not in terms of any one of its parts. Time and, indeed, setbacks were not only secondary, but could in fact be turned to the ultimate advantage of the Communists. In Maoist strategy, military victory in the field is valuable only in so far as it pertains to ultimate political success. And this latter is the only true criterion of victory in the Communist sense.

It need hardly be underlined that the war in North Vietnam likewise followed Mao's formula: stage one—1945–1948; stage two—1948–

1950; stage three—1950–1954. Conditions were, of course, virtually perfect from the Communist point of view. Because of a combination of jungle, mountain and swamp, the degree of mobility enjoyed by the armed forces depended directly on the degree to which they were *not* mechanized and motorized. Furthermore, radio communication in areas in which other means of communication were lacking gave partisans an opportunity to coordinate their activities so that concentration of local forces could be used to create diversion. It was almost as if the peninsula were being torn by groups of men dropped from an unseen plane to carry out a given mission of destruction, and then disappear. And politically, of course, the situation was as favorable to the Communists as it was geographically, for each defeat of the Franco-Vietnamese forces further disrupted their common front. Indeed, in retrospect, one of the more macabre aspects of that macabre war was the fact that each military defeat was in a sense a political victory for a fraction of the defeated. For, when Franco-Vietnamese forces were defeated, it gave the Vietnamese politicians an opportunity to press the more firmly for those political rights which the French granted only on the morrow of defeat.

It would seem undeniable that Mao's strategy, wherever applied, has been remarkably and tragically successful.

Indo-China was a graveyard for the reputations of fine and valiant French generals—for Valluy, Leclerc, Carpentier, Salan, Navarre. Each arrived on the field with a prophecy of victory, and left with words of despair. In Malaya such highly respected leaders as Sir Edward Gent, Major General Charles Boucher and Let. Gen. Sir Harold Briggs have been something less than brilliantly successful. The United States Secretary of Defense, Charles E. Wilson, admitted with his usual candor that the war in Indo-China was a failure not of arms but of strategy. The outcome of the war in Indo-China would not have been any different had the United States Army been "twice as big as it is, if the Navy [had] twice as many ships afloat, and the Air Force had [had] 200 wings," he said. The fact of past failure is amply documented.

Mao has always maintained that his is the last just war, the war to end wars, after which will emerge a historically unprecedented new era for mankind in which there will "no longer be any wars." There is, however, no indication that this war for a "new world of permanent peace and permanent light" will end before the world is made safe for communism. He believes that the willingness to compromise has a class basis, and that therefore compromise by its very origin cannot be successful. . . .

Mao's theory of war is based, as is any theory, on a set of postulates. And this structure is no stronger than its foundations. The first and most important of Mao's premises is that he and those who think like him have a monopoly on patience. This monopoly is comfortably cushioned, moreover, by the flexibility built into Mao's doctrine of the inevitability of ultimate victory. For the shift from one stage of war to the next is not always progressive. There may be setbacks depending on what in another society would be called "acts of God." . . .

Indeed, it is the faith of the Communists in Southeast Asia in their monopoly on patience that has made Mao's the ubiquitous gospel it is. . . .

The second premise, perhaps a corollary of the first, is that the anti-Communist front is committed to quick victory, and therefore cannot, and will not, underwrite a long-drawn-out war. . . .

It is in this connection that he believes that initial tactical self-sacrifice in the first stage of war is the necessary price of eventual victory. But the yeast of this process is, in the Communist view, the maintenance of the initiative after and even during the expected initial setbacks. In operational terms this means that local victories must be cheap and continuous. . . .

This leads to the third postulate: that the Communists can maintain the initiative from both a military and a political standpoint—if one can make the distinction. They reason that they can, largely because they know that a "people's war," operating under strict party discipline, has an enormously flexible arsenal. Communists understand, what is frequently forgotten, that it is not simply the weapons one has in one's arsenal that give one flexibility, but the willingness and ability to use them. Assassination, sabotage, ambush, "spontaneous uprisings," or mass attacks in fanatical waves, the more typical form of revolutionary warfare, are all a part of this arsenal. . . .

D

PROFESSOR DOUGLAS PIKE ON THE STRATEGY, TACTICS, AND IDEOLOGY OF THE VIET CONG

"The NLF and the people it influenced lived in a muzzy, myth-filled world of blacks and whites, good and evil, a simplistic world. . . . But it created a powerful external image for the Vietnamese immersed in the cause, restructuring his reality, providing him with a new identity and a boundless sense of unity."

Study of NLF [National Liberation Front, the political arm of the South Vietnamese Communist (Viet Cong) military effort] policy statements, inspection of its relations with those beyond the borders of Vietnam, and measuring its actions against its words leave one with a subjective impression of the general design of NLF goals and the parameters of those goals. These appear to be the following:

1. To achieve operative political control of South Vietnam; a willingness, but reluctance, to settle for some political power rather than all if it were clearly demonstrated that the alternative to some political power was either stalemate or total defeat.

2. To seek a South Vietnamese governmental policy of nonalignment in foreign affairs (but under a definition that would classify the DRV [Democratic Republic of Vietnam (North Vietnam)] as domestic rather than foreign), one that in operational terms would permit the reduction of American troops in exchange for the withdrawal of PAVN [North Vietnamese Army] forces from South Vietnam but with the proviso that this arrangement must be agreeable to the DRV.

3. To work for reunification of the two Vietnams through a step-by-step process, the time limits of which would be negotiable.

4. To forge a broad base of world support, one principally rooted in Communist-bloc nations and not tied too closely with any one foreign country. (Again, in NLF terms, relations with the DRV would be internal, not external.)

5. To vilify the United States, mobilize world opinion against it, and

Douglas Pike, *Viet Cong*. (Cambridge, Mass.: The M.I.T. Press, 1966, 370–371; 373–383. Reprinted by permission.

heighten its feelings of frustration and futility in its efforts in South Vietnam.

6. To exploit every American and GVN [Government of South Vietnam] weakness abroad regardless of how insignificant or transient any instance might appear to be.

7. With respect to the Sino-Soviet split, to contribute what little it could to healing the breach but not be forced into a position where it had to choose sides.

8. With respect to the DRV, to prevent itself from being submerged by Hanoi and to retain a bargaining position. Undoubtedly a schism existed: The majority of the politically acute NLF supporters realized that Northern and Southern interests were not identical. The cadres and the PRP [People's Revolutionary Party, the Southern branch of the North Vietnamese Communist Party which controlled the NLF] members within the NLF shared the DRV goals; they grew progressively stronger and virtually monopolized the hierarchy by 1965. The most divisive issue in this respect was reunification. The indigenous elements maintained that reunification meant annexation by the DRV and at any rate was opposed by too many forces within and outside of Vietnam ever to be possible; the loyalists maintained, as did the DRV, that reunification must remain the central long-range goal.

9. To strive for the withdrawal of American forces from South Vietnam, based on the calculation that the United States could be persuaded to accept a coalition neutral government if its position in South Vietnam became sufficiently untenable.

10. To avoid a "negotiated settlement" at an international conference on the ground that it would almost certainly amount to a sellout of the NLF. (But this did not preclude acceptance, as a tactic, of a coalition government.) In the event that a negotiated settlement might be required because complete victory was impossible or because outright defeat was a growing prospect, the conditions it hoped to achieve included (a) an authentic coalition government that would include elements of the NLF at the cabinet level; (b) an understanding that South Vietnam would pursue a nonaligned but China-leaning foreign policy on the model of Cambodia; (c) closer economic ties with the DRV; (d) amnesty for its followers, or opportunity for them to move to the DRV; and (e) withdrawal of most, but not necessarily all, American military forces. . . .

The basic characteristics of the NLF and its activities were the use of a united-front organization to establish a mass base of support; organization of the rural people, employing both rational appeals to self-interest and coercion, and then using the specially created social movements in antigovernmental activity; heavy use of various techniques for the communication of ideas to foment social strife; use of specialized military actions, selective in nature and psychological in intent; use of the Communist party *apparat*, and Communist doctrine among the leaders and full-time cadres, to establish orthodoxy and maintain discipline. The goal was control of the population and, through this control, organization of the people as a weapon against the government. But it was more than this. It was more than simply the inculcation of new beliefs or differing attitudes. The NLF's ultimate objective taken together with other activities was to create a new socialization pattern.

The NLF was concerned with the deepest social values. It sought to create a new system of formal and informal groupings by which the socialization was to be accomplished and behavior regulated. It manipulated economic activities, the base for all human activities, in such a way as to increase the degree of communalism or collectivization and thus to some degree alter the village means of production; it introduced a new political structure to keep internal order and to regulate contact within South Vietnam, particularly with respect to villagers hostile to the NLF; it manipulated educational and other intellectual activities within the village. It apparently attempted to substitute a disguised brand of Marxism for traditional religious beliefs, although in an oblique manner; and it introduced a new language terminology, social mythology, and folklore. In short, it attempted to work within the totality of village life and provide a new cultural focus....

In those areas of the country where it had firm and continuous social control the NLF was in effect a society within a society, with its own social structure, values, and coercive instruments. The NLF cadres made a conscious and massive effort to extend political participation, even if it was manipulated, on the local level so as to involve the people in a self-contained, self-supporting revolution. The functional liberation associations at the village level attempted to serve each individual member in terms of his own personal interests while at the same time developing a deep revolutionary consciousness. Ironically, as the result of increased coercion on the part of the NLF, as its popular support dwindled, its actual authority increased. What had been essentially a persuasive mechanism became basically a coercive one, not so much because of the failure of the original NLF social organization pattern as because of the arrival of Northern cadres who were unwilling to trust the original form because they felt in the long run that it would not serve the interests of the Party and indeed might become a threat to it. Once again, the not unfamiliar story of the revolution betrayed. But the organization at all times, whether persuasive or coercive, remained the central NLF activity in the village.

That the leaders of this enterprise were professionals must be evident from the structure they created. . . .

One of the most persistent questions asked about the NLF follower was "Why did he join?" The implication in the question is that for one or more rational or emotional reasons the individual Vietnamese decided to enlist in the cause, did so, and thus entered as a believer . . . almost the reverse was the case. The Vietnamese youth was first surrounded by a social organization that he had no hand in creating but to which he somehow belonged. Through a process of insinuation the youth came to realize that he was part of the NLF, never quite sure of how this happened and never with any overt choice presented to him. The process of glacially slow recruitment came first, the mystique was developed later. Or, as it has been aptly put, conversion followed subversion. Therefore not motives but circumstances must be considered in understanding the recruitment pattern and its contribution to the NLF mystique.

The most common answer given by a *guy chanh* to questions concerning the circumstances under which he became part of the NLF indicated that he was initially drawn into the organization and later recruited. He might first be asked to act as a messenger, or to take part in a struggle movement, or to deliver leaflets to an agent in the provincial capital. Then he would be urged to join his friends in a study group that might also be a literacy class. Then he would be asked to commit some act of violence; at this point, whether he knew it or not, he was in the net. When handled skillfully, subtly, and gradually, a teen-aged youth did not realize that he was involved until he was already enmeshed. This technique succeeded, for the most part, not in areas where the GVN was exerting itself but in the remote villages where the NLF and the Viet Minh before it were the only visible "government" the youth had ever known. And so the *guy chanh* would say, "Everyone seemed to think it was the correct thing to do," often adding plaintively, "There didn't seem to be any danger. The Saigon government was so far away I didn't think they would ever know about me." Of course a small minority actually sought out and joined the NLF. These included draft dodgers, military deserters, those who hated the government for some personal reason, opportunists, the ambitious who were seeking status, the rejected, the adventurers, and all the others in Eric Hoffer's categories of the True Believer.

For the most part, however, the supporters were recruited under circumstances where there was no alternative. Most recruitment was from among social groups such as the religious sects, with grievances against the government, and less effort was placed on the recruitment of individuals at random. At the same time the NLF sought to create situations that would give rise to grievances among such groups so as to facilitate recruitment. Once the youth was recruited, the training and indoctrination work supplied the rationale for belonging.

Americans and others often assumed that the NLF army members were fanatics. Because they performed well in combat, it was argued, they were highly motivated, which meant dedication to an ideological cause. Thus the search was for the essence of this belief. It proved elusive, largely because it did not exist. The best of the military units— the Main Force units—were highly effective because they were composed of professionals. These were not green young Vietnamese farmers, only recently introduced to the rifle, but experienced guerillas who had been fighting most of their adult lives. What impelled them was not ideology so much as professional competence, much like the United States Marine or the French Foreign Legionnaire. The men in the best of these units were very good; their discipline was superb; they knew how to use camouflage well, a requirement for survival; they were well skilled in small-unit tactics, especially the ambush in its many variations; they trained hard, rehearsed, and practiced attacks until letter perfect, and then they fought hard. Their mystique should be attributed chiefly to a unit *esprit de corps* that stemmed from the consensus that each man in the unit was a superior and vastly experienced professional. ...

The NLF and the people it influenced lived in a muzzy, myth-filled world of blacks and whites, good and evil, a simplistic world quite out of character with the one to which the Vietnamese was accustomed. But it created a powerful external image for the Vietnamese immersed in the cause, restructuring his reality, providing him with a new identity and a boundless sense of unity. The elements of this mystique were fourfold.

First, it was characterized by great moralism and was far more moral than ideological. Virtue was the golden word. The cause consisted of moral duties based on moral absolutes, guided by moral imperatives;

duty itself, under a virtuous leadership, was the highest value. Preoccupation with law and legality was not simply an effort to establish legitimacy but a justification of the moral correctness of the cause. Because he was virtuous, the NLF supporter was morally superior to the enemy and hence politically and militarily superior. The moralism manifested itself in a spirit of sincerity; the NLF surrounded its worlds and actions with an aura of sincerity.

Second, it was characterized by extreme romanticism. The NLF leaders, like Mao Tse-tung and Ho Chi Minh before them, were romantic rebels who saw themselves as idealists. Idealistic appeals abounded: the promise of the good life in utopian terms; the opportunity to revolt against all the evil, injustice, and inequity of this world; the chance to be part of a great crusade. But behind these was the romantic lure of the struggle itself; the means not the ends counted. There was more glory along the road than at its end. The clandestine organization made up of multitudes of inner groups, cults, and secret arrangements played on the Vietnamese individual's romantic love of the devious, and like Kim along the Grand Trunk Road he played The Game. (A psychiatrist visiting in Vietnam said it was actually a latent homosexual fear of penetration.) Yet in general the NLF mystique was less a positive cause than a negation. But this too had lure to the romantic—the lure of anarchy, beyond which, if it failed, lay the lure of martyrdom. The NLF in creating its mystique was acutely sensitive to the age-old Asian attitude of fatalism.

Third, its mystique was imitative and therefore militantly defensive, which probably should be counted as a weakness. The NLF leader was driven by a compulsive search for answers from elsewhere, anywhere. Examples were taken from other places and they were forced, and from other times and they were distorted. If the NLF was not slavishly copying Mao Tse-tung on the Long March, it was employing the Viet Minh's analysis of French Maginot Line thinking as it applied to the Americans, or calling on all cadres to repeat in a literal manner some victory scored a few months earlier in another part of Vietnam. The constant scanning of the horizon was part of a preoccupation with contemplation and self-analysis. Cadres, in a curious form of intellectualism, would explain the Revolution over and over to their most disinterested students—the rural Vietnamese. Copied though it was, it provided the supporter with a worldview that might not be understood but was satisfactory. Through indoctrination and even socialization he received needed psychological support and release from cultural tensions. (The same psychiatrist said the NLF was a father image led by Ho Chi Minh.)

And finally there was a will to believe, perhaps a characteristic of any mystique. It grew from the sense of universality of a movement representing Vietnam, the world, excluding not even a full social class (the enemies in Saigon and Washington). It was based on an assessment of the world environment that the NLF believed made Revolution in Vietnam irresistible and doomed GVN and U.S. prowess to steady deterioration. It was based on faith in the Vietnamese people's revolutionary capability, faith in the doctrinal approach, faith in revolutionary guerrilla warfare consisting of the combined armed and political struggle, and the infallible wisdom of the Party's leaders, who from long experience could divine the laws of history. . . .

Marxism-Leninism as filtered through first Chinese and then Vietnamese thought contributed much to the NLF mystique. . . .

A Communist condition had prevailed within the NLF from the start and was assumed as a matter of course by Vietnamese of all political shadings. With respect to the mystique the matter of communism's paramountcy became somewhat more complex. Partly it was a matter of definition.

If a Communist is one who believes that man's future is shaped by his tools of production, that history is dominated by a class struggle for control of those means of production, that capitalism must grow increasingly evil, and that a brotherhood of workers and farmers swearing allegiance to an international ideal must unite to seize power and build its own society led by the vanguard, the proletariat, and in turn by the vanguard of the vanguard, the Communist party—if this is a Communist, then there were few Communists among the NLF. If, however, a Communist is one who swears blind allegiance to the world movement whose loci of power are Moscow and Peking, from which in this instance via Hanoi he draws through a political umbilical cord sustenance and strength that he cannot, and does not want to, supply himself, then most of the NLF's leaders, cadres, and true believers were communists.

It was the difference between philosophic communism and alliance communism. For, in the first instance, to be a Communist meant mastering Marxism-Leninism, which NLF Vietnamese found notoriously difficult to understand since it is distinctly un-Vietnamese in nature and at variance with their most deeply ingrained views of the universe. (For example, it must have been indeed a Herculean task for a cadre to convince a Vietnamese that matter and not God or Spirit is the ultimate reality, or that nothing is inherently unknowable.) The second instance meant simply establishing identity and achieving unity in which an NLF supporter had only to approve of the powerful foreign forces that stood behind him and his cause. Only among the higher-echelon cadres, and even here not with total acceptance, was communism regarded as a new body of wisdom to be learned, understood, and put to use.

Thus the NLF was Communist not because it incorporated Communist doctrine but because it linked itself to foreign states that did. This distinction, or weakness, meant that the strengths that hold Communists and Communist movements together during dark days elsewhere were largely absent in Vietnam.

E
NORTH VIETNAMESE AND VIET CONG ATROCITIES IN THE SOUTH VIETNAM CITY OF HUÉ IN FEBRUARY, 1968

"Evidence indicated that many victims had been beaten to death, shot, beheaded or buried alive. Many bodies were found bound together in groups of 10 or 15, eyes open, with dirt or cloth stuffed in the mouth."

Saigon, South Vietnam, April 30. North Vietnamese and Vietcong slaughtered more than 1,000 South Vietnamese Government workers, priests and women in Hué during the Lunar New Year offensive, the United States mission asserted today.

In a grim report, United States officials said that 19 mass graves had been found in the Hué area. Evidence indicated that many victims had been beaten to death, shot, beheaded or buried alive. Many bodies were found bound together in groups of 10 or 15, eyes open, with dirt or cloth stuffed in the mouths.

New York Times, May 1, 1968, article by Bernard Weinraub. Reprinted by permission.

Although there had been rumors and reports that the North Vietnamese had executed scores of Hué's people, the United States mission withheld confirmation pending a detailed investigation. The report was the result of the investigation, made by the United States and South Vietnamese authorities. In listing the 19 graves, the mission issued detailed findings of the number of bodies found and the map coordinates of each site. The report also lists the locations—a high school, a primary school, a pagoda, the foot of a bridge and other sites in the ancient walled city.

At the Tang Quang Tu Pagoda United States and South Vietnamese officials found 67 bodies in 13 graves. All the victims had been shot.

A Buddhist monk in the Pagoda "heard nightly executions by pistol and rifle shots in a plowed field behind the pagoda during the first two weeks of February, with victims pleading for mercy," the United States mission said.

Among the victims were Nguyen Ngoc Ky, a leader of the Vietnam Nationalist party, a branch of the Vietnam Quomintang party. The splinter political group has been described as both anti-American and anti-Communist.

The founder of the party, Nguyen Thai Hug, was executed by the French in 1932.

Nearly half the victims in the graves around Hué were found in conditions indicating that they had been buried alive. The United States mission said that there was also evidence that many victims had been clubbed unconscious first.

At one grave, eight victims had been buried alive, including an 80-year-old teacher who had been accused of having a son in the army.

Near the imperial tombs area of the city, one of the largest graves was found with 201 bodies.

"Many victims buried alive here, including groups of 10 to 15 tied together," the report says. "Others shot. Victims included Father Urbain, 52, and Father Guy, 48, French priests from nearby Benedictine mission at Thienan.

"Father Urbain was bound hand and foot and buried alive with 10 others. Father Guy was forced to kneel and shot through the head."

The reasons Hué was selected by the enemy for large-scale executions puzzled American officials.

"Hué is the old capital and has always been independent and kind of aloof of the rest of the country," an American official said. "The feelings there have always been kind of intense, though, and some of the hates go back a long way. For many Vietnamese there are a lot of old scores to settle in Hué."

Another American official observed: "Don't forget that Hué was one of the few cities where the enemy stayed long enough to get organized. They seemed to do some very systematic slaughtering once they dug in."

In the savage fighting between the North Vietnamese and United States marines in Hué during the early weeks of February, 130 American servicemen were killed and 810 were wounded. About 2,000 civilians are believed to have died—either from North Vietnamese executions, the mortaring and shelling of the city by both sides, or American air strikes.

The executed victims of the North Vietnamese appeared in many cases to be Government employees or citizens linked to the South Vietnamese regime. Non-Vietnamese were also slain.

At one grave, where 77 bodies were found, the victims include three Koreans and one Hong Kong Chinese, a British citizen. All had been shot through the back of the head.

The bodies of four German members of the university medical faculty were found in a potato field. They had been shot.

Several Vietnamese bodies found in a grave near the south wall of the Hué Citadel, had been beheaded. At a slope near the river, 200 bodies were found, 40 to 50 of them women.

THE
COLD WAR

III
THE CRITICS:
AMERICAN

A
COLUMNIST WALTER LIPPMANN CHALLENGES
THE KENNAN CONCEPT OF CONTAINMENT
1947

*"I agree entirely that the Soviet power will expand unless it is pre-
vented from expanding because it is confronted with power, primarily American power, that it must respect. But I believe, and
shall argue, that the strategical conception and plan which Mr. X
[Kennan] recommends is fundamentally unsound, and that it cannot be made to work, and that the attempt to make it work will
cause us to squander our substance and our prestige. . . ."*

An anonymous article on "The Sources of Soviet Conduct" appeared in
the quarterly journal *Foreign Affairs* for July 1947 and shortly afterwards
it was republished by *Life* magazine. By its quality alone it would have
commanded wide attention. For it was manifestly the work of a man who
had observed the Soviet regime closely with a trained eye and an educated
mind, and had arrived at a theory as to why the conduct of the Soviet
government reflects "no abstract love of peace and stability, no real
faith in the possibility of a permanent happy co-existence of the socialist
and capitalist worlds, but rather a continuous, persistent pressure to-

Walter Lippmann, *The Cold War: A Study in U.S. Foreign Policy.* New York:
Harper, 1947, 9–13; 15–17; 20; 23–25; 29–30; 33–34; 38–39; 41; 43–45; 51–52;
54; 56–57; 62. Reprinted by permission.

wards the disruption and weakening of all rival influence and rival power."

Almost immediately several of the leading correspondents in Washington identified the author, who signed himself "X," as being Mr. George F. Kennan who, after a tour of duty at the Embassy in Moscow, had recently been appointed by Secretary Marshall to be the Director of the Policy Planning Staff of the Department of State. The attribution was not denied. After that Mr. X's article was no longer just one more report on the Soviet regime and what to do about it. It was an event, announcing that the Department of State had made up its mind, and was prepared to disclose to the American people, to the world at large, and of course also to the Kremlin the estimates, the calculations, and the conclusions on which the Department was basing its plans. . . .

My criticism, I hasten to say at once, does not arise from any belief or hope that our conflict with the Soviet government is imaginary or that it can be avoided, or ignored, or easily disposed of. I agree entirely with Mr. X that the Soviet pressure cannot "be charmed or talked out of existence." I agree entirely that the Soviet power will expand unless it is prevented from expanding because it is confronted with power, primarily American power, that it must respect. But I believe, and shall argue, that the strategical conception and plan which Mr. X recommends is fundamentally unsound, and that it cannot be made to work, and that the attempt to make it work will cause us to squander our substance and our prestige. . . .

I do not find much ground for reasonable confidence in a policy which can be successful only if the most optimistic prediction should prove to be true. Surely a sound policy must be addressed to the worst and hardest that may be judged to be probable, and not to the best and easiest that may be possible.

As a matter of fact, Mr. X himself betrays a marked lack of confidence in his own diagnosis. For no sooner had he finished describing the policy of firm containment with unalterable counterforce at every point where the Russians show signs of encroaching, when he felt he must defend his conclusions against the criticism, one might almost say the wise-crack, that this is a policy of "holding the line and hoping for the best." His defense is to say that while he is proposing a policy of holding the line and hoping for the best, "in actuality the possibilities for American policy are by no means limited to holding the line and hoping for the best." The additional possibilities are not, however, within the scope of the authority of the Department of State: "the aims of Russian communism must appear sterile and quixotic, the hopes and enthusiasms of Moscow's supporters must wane, and added strain must be imposed on the Kremlin's foreign policies" if "the United States can create among the peoples of the world generally the impression of a country which knows what it wants, which is coping successfully with the problems of its internal life and with the responsibilities of a world power, and which has a spiritual vitality capable of holding its own among the major ideological currents of the time."

This surely is a case of bolstering up the wishful thinking of "hoping for the best"—namely, the collapse of the Soviet power—by an extra strong dose of wishful thinking about the United States. There must be something deeply defective in Mr. X's estimates and calculations. For on his own showing, the policy cannot be made to work unless there are miracles and we get all the breaks. . . . Now the strength of the western world is great, and we may assume that its resourcefulness is considerable. Nevertheless, there are weighty reasons for thinking that the kind of strength we have and the kind of resourcefulness we are capable of showing are peculiarly unsuited to operating a policy of containment.

How, for example, under the Constitution of the United States is Mr. X going to work out an arrangement by which the Department of State has the money and the military power always available in sufficient amounts to apply "counterforce" at constantly shifting points all over the world? Is he going to ask Congress for a blank check on the Treasury and for a blank authorization to use the armed forces? Not if the American constitutional system is to be maintained. Or is he going to ask for an appropriation and for authority each time the Russians "show signs of encroaching upon the interests of a peaceful and stable world"? If that is his plan for dealing with the maneuvers of a dictatorship, he is going to arrive at the points of encroachment with too little and he is going to arrive too late. The Russians, if they intend to encroach, will have encroached while Congress is getting ready to hold hearings.

A policy of shifts and maneuvers may be suited to the Soviet system of government, which, as Mr. X tells us, is animated by patient persistence. It is not suited to the American system of government.

It is even more unsuited to the American economy which is unregimented and uncontrolled, and therefore cannot be administered according to a plan. Yet a policy of containment cannot be operated unless the Department of State can plan and direct exports and imports. For the policy demands that American goods be delivered or withheld at "constantly shifting geographical and political points corresponding to the shifts and maneuvers of Soviet policy."

Thus Mr. X and the planners of policy in the State Department, and not supply and demand in the world market, must determine continually what portion of the commodities produced here may be sold in the United States, what portion is to be set aside for export, and then sold, lent, or given to this foreign country rather than to that one. The Department of State must be able to allocate the products of American industry and agriculture, to ration the goods allocated for export among the nations which are to contain the Soviet Union, and to discriminate among them, judging correctly and quickly how much each nation must be given, how much each nation can safely be squeezed, so that all shall be held in line to hold the line against the Russians.

If then the Kremlin's challenge to American society is to be met by the policy which Mr. X proposes, we are committed to a contest, for ten or fifteen years, with the Soviet system which is planned and directed from Moscow. Mr. X is surely mistaken, it seems to me, if he thinks that a free and undirected economy like our own can be used by the diplomatic planners to wage a diplomatic war against a planned economy at a series of constantly shifting geographical and political points. He is proposing to meet the Soviet challenge on the ground which is most favorable to the Soviets, and with the very instruments, procedures, and weapons in which they have a manifest superiority. . . .

The Americans would themselves probably be frustrated by Mr. X's policy long before the Russians were. . . .

As a matter of fact this borderland in Europe and Asia around the perimeter of the Soviet Union is not a place where Mr. X's "unassailable barriers" can be erected. Satellite states and puppet governments are not good material out of which to construct unassailable barriers. A diplomatic war conducted as this policy demands, that is to say conducted indirectly, means that we must stake our own security and the peace of the world upon satellites, puppets, clients, agents about whom we can know very little. Frequently they will act for their own reasons, and on their own judgments, presenting us with accomplished facts that we did not intend, and with crises for which we are unready. The "unassailable barriers" will present us with an unending series of insoluble dilemmas. We shall have either to disown our puppets, which would be tantamount to appeasement and defeat and the loss of face, or must support them at an incalculable cost on an unintended, unforeseen and perhaps undesirable issue. . . .

The natural allies of the United States are the nations of the Atlantic community: that is to say, the nations of western Europe and of the Americas. The Atlantic Ocean and the Mediterranean Sea, which is an arm of the Atlantic Ocean, unite them in a common strategic, economic and cultural system. The chief components of the Atlantic community are the British Commonwealth of nations, the Latin states on both sides of the Atlantic, the Low Countries and Switzerland, Scandinavia and the United States.

The boundaries of the Atlantic community are not sharp and distinct, particularly in the case of the Germans and the western Slavs and the dependencies and the colonies of western Europe. But the nucleus of the Atlantic community is distinct and unmistakable, and among the nations that are indisputably members of the Atlantic community there exists a vital connection founded upon their military and political geography, the common traditions of western Christendom, and their economic, political, legal, and moral institutions which, with all their variations and differences, have a common origin and have been shaped by much the same historic experience.

Now the policy of containment, as described by Mr. X, is an attempt to organize an anti-Soviet alliance composed in the first instance of peoples that are either on the shadowy extremity of the Atlantic community, or are altogether outside it. The active proponents of the policy have been concerned immediately with the anti-Soviet parties and factions of eastern Europe, with the Greeks, the Turks, the Iranians, the Arabs and Afghans, and with the Chinese Nationalists. . . .

It will be evident, I am sure, to the reader who has followed the argument to this point that my criticism of the policy of containment, or the so-called Truman Doctrine, does not spring from any hope or belief that the Soviet pressure to expand can be "charmed or talked out of existence." I agree entirely with Mr. X that we must make up our minds that the Soviet power is not amenable to our arguments, but only "to contrary force" that "is felt to be too strong, and thus more rational in the logic and rhetoric of power."

My objection, then, to the policy of containment is not that it seeks to confront the Soviet power with American power, but that the policy is misconceived, and must result in a misuse of American power. For as I have sought to show, it commits this country to a struggle which has for its objective nothing more substantial than the hope that in ten or fifteen years the Soviet power will, as the result of long frustration, "break up" or "mellow." In this prolonged struggle the role of the United States is, according to Mr. X, to react "at a series of constantly shifting geographical and political points" to the encroachments of the Soviet power.

The policy, therefore, concedes to the Kremlin the strategical initiative as to when, where and under what local circumstances the issue is to be joined. It compels the United States to meet the Soviet pressure at these shifting geographical and political points by using satellite states, puppet governments and agents which have been subsidized and supported, though their effectiveness is meager and their reliability uncertain. By forcing us to expend our energies and our substance upon these dubious and unnatural allies on the perimeter of the Soviet Union, the effect of the policy is to neglect our natural allies in the Atlantic community, and to alienate them. . . .

The westward expansion of the Russian frontier and of the Russian sphere of influence, though always a Russian aim, was accomplished when, as, and because the Red Army defeated the German army and advanced to the center of Europe. It was the mighty power of the Red Army, not the ideology of Karl Marx, which enabled the Russian government to expand its frontiers. It is the pressure of that army far beyond the new frontiers which makes the will of the Kremlin irresistible within the Russian sphere of influence. It is the threat that the Red Army may advance still farther west—into Italy, into western Germany, into Scandinavia—that gives the Kremlin and the native communist parties of western Europe an abnormal and intolerable influence in the affairs of the European continent.

Therefore, the immediate and the decisive problem of our relations with the Soviet Union is whether, when, on what conditions the Red Army can be prevailed upon to evacuate Europe. . . .

For if, and only if, we can bring about the withdrawal of the Red Army from the Yalta line to the new frontier of the Soviet Union—and simultaneously, of course, the withdrawal of the British and American armies from continental Europe—can a balance of power be established which can then be maintained. For after the withdrawal, an attempt to return would be an invasion—an open, unmistakable act of military aggression. Against such an aggression, the power of the United States to strike the vital centers of Russia by air and by amphibious assault would stand as the opposing and deterrent force. And until treaties are agreed to which bring about the withdrawal of the Red Army, the power of the United States to strike these vital centers would be built up for the express purpose of giving weight to our policy of ending the military occupation of Europe.

All the other pressures of the Soviet Union at the "constantly shifting geographical and political points," which Mr. X is so concerned about—in the Middle East and in Asia—are, I contend, secondary and subsidiary to the fact that its armed forces are in the heart of Europe. It is to the Red Army in Europe, therefore, and not to ideologies, elections, forms of governments to socialism, to communism, to free enterprise, that a correctly conceived and soundly planned policy should be directed. . . .

The next question is whether the objective of obtaining the withdrawal of the Red Army is attainable. A certain answer to this question is, of course, impossible. We can only calculate the probabilities, and we can say that the objective I am contending for is concrete, substantial, intelligible to everyone, and a normal and universally accepted objective at the conclusion and settlement of a war. . . .

If the Kremlin really means to dominate Europe, it will not withdraw its armies which are halfway across Europe. Standing on the Elbe line in the middle of Europe and Austria, and on the vulnerable frontier of Italy, the Kremlin is in a far better position to advance farther west than it can be if it withdraws and stands on its own frontiers. The withdrawal of the army is, therefore, the acid test of Soviet conduct and purpose, incomparably clearer, more definite, more practical than whether or not they observe the Yalta Declaration in countries liberated from the Nazis but still occupied by the Red Army. Verbal agreements like the Yalta Declaration and the Atlantic Charter can be made the subject of endless tactical maneuvering. For agreements of this kind do not change the balance of power. But the evacuation of a continent would change the balance of power. . . .

Alien armies are, however, never well behaved: invariably they become corrupted. Thus we may count confidently upon a mounting popular support if we make it our mission to emancipate the ancient and proud continent of Europe from the military control of non-European powers. We shall be drawing upon the elemental and unifying passion of patriotism in Europe which, when it is aroused, is a much stronger passion than factionalism or any ideology. . . .

If, nevertheless, the Soviet government will not negotiate an agreement, if the price of a settlement is impossibly high, if the ransom is deliberately set in terms which mean that Russia does not intend to evacuate Europe, the situation will be no more dangerous than it is today. But our energies will be concentrated, not dispersed all over the globe, and the real issues will be much clearer. . . .

The contest between the Truman Doctrine on the one hand, the Marshall line and the support of U.N. on the other is the central drama within the State Department, within the Administration, within the government as a whole. The outcome is still undecided. . . . The Marshall proposal was not, as Mr. Molotov and many Americans who do not understand it have tried to make out, an extension to Europe as a whole of the experiment in Greece. Quite the contrary. In Greece we made an American plan, appropriated the money, entered Greece and are now trying to induce the Greek government to carry out our plan. In the Harvard speech Secretary Marshall reversed this procedure. He told the European governments to plan their own rehabilitation, and that then he would go to Congress for funds, and that then the European governments would have to carry out their plans as best they could with the funds he could persuade Congress to appropriate.

The difference is fundamental. The Truman Doctrine treats those who are supposed to benefit by it as dependencies of the United States, as instruments of the American policy for "containing" Russia. The Marshall speech at Harvard treats the European governments as independent powers, whom we must help but cannot presume to govern, or to use as instruments of an American policy. . . .

But there are reasons for thinking that the Russians will not be able to maintain the iron curtain and that we cannot construct western Europe as a containing wall. They are that the vital needs of the people of Europe will prevail; the economic interdependence of western and eastern Europe will compel the nations of the continent to exchange their goods across the military, political and ideological boundary lines which now separate them.

The great virtue of the Marshall proposal is that it has set in motion studies abroad and in this country which will demonstrate conclusively that the division of Europe cannot be perpetuated. And since the division of Europe came about because the Red Army and the Anglo-American armies met in the middle of Europe, the withdrawal of these armies is necessary if Europe is to be reunited. The Harvard speech calls, therefore, for a policy of settlement, addressed to the military evacuation of the continent, not for a policy of containment which would freeze the non-European armies in the heart of Europe.

The Marshall studies will show that the industrialized areas of western Europe cannot be supported, except to relieve their most pressing immediate needs, from North and South America. They must revive their trade with the agricultural regions of eastern Europe and with European Russia. If they do not do that, the cost of maintaining a tolerable standard of life in western Europe will be exorbitant, and the effort to meet it will require a revolutionary readjustment of the economic life of the whole Western Hemisphere.

At the same time studies made in Warsaw, Prague and in Moscow will show that the problems of eastern Europe are insoluble without increasing economic intercourse with western Europe. Thus from all quarters in eastern Europe and in western Europe, in Washington and in Moscow, the pressure will increase to reunite the divided economy of Europe—and perhaps to go on towards a greater unity than ever existed before. . . .

Until a settlement which results in withdrawal is reached, the Red Army at the center of Europe will control eastern Europe and will threaten western Europe. In these circumstances American power must be available, not to "contain" the Russians at scattered points, but to hold the whole Russian military machine in check, and to exert a mounting pressure in support of a diplomatic policy which has as its concrete objective a settlement that means withdrawal.

Then we shall know what we are trying to do. The Russians will know it. Europe will know it. We shall be trying to do a great thing which is simple and necessary: to settle the main actual consequences of this particular war, to put an end to the abnormal situation where Europe, one of the chief centers of civilization, though liberated from the Nazis, is still occupied by its non-European liberators.

We shall be addressing ourselves to an objective to which our own power is suited—be it in diplomacy or in war. We shall be seeking an end that all men can understand, and one which expresses faithfully our oldest and best tradition—to be the friend and the champion of nations seeking independence and an end to the rule of alien powers.

B

PROGRESSIVE PARTY PRESIDENTIAL CANDIDATE
HENRY A. WALLACE LINKS AMERICAN
ANTI-COMMUNISM ABROAD
WITH REACTION AND RACISM AT HOME
SEPTEMBER 10, 1948

"These men, Republicans and Democrats bound together by hate, are using every mechanism which bipartisan fear can suggest to defeat congressional candidates who stand for peace. . . . We are those who stand against the course which leads to war. We are those who protest a policy toward minority groups that is administered by a policeman's nightstick."

Just two years ago I spoke to many thousands of you who are here tonight. I said then and I say tonight that peace is the basic issue of the 1948 election campaign.

I say now that the first job of national defense, the most important job in maintaining the peace is the job of conquering hate here at home, the job of protecting the civil rights of all Americans.

This is a great American meeting.

It is a meeting in the best American tradition—a meeting of men and women of all races, of all creeds.

Last week—in smaller gatherings—we proved that such meetings can be held in the much-maligned Southern states. We proved that such meetings—meetings of all the people—can be held wherever men respect the Constitution of the United States; and wherever they respect the Christian principles of brotherhood on which so much of our modern civilization has been built.

The news reported from the South last week was news of eggs and tomatoes. It was news of violence and threats of violence.

Yes, and there were the ugly spewings of hate and prejudice; and the sad sight of men and women and children whose faces were contorted with hate.

But the significance of our trip south was not the dramatic proof

---

New York Times, September 11, 1948. Reprinted by permission.

that there are seeds of violence and fascism and deep prejudice in the Southern states. The significance was not in proving what is known.

No. The significance of our Southern trip lies in the two dozen completely unsegregated, peaceful meetings which we were able to hold. . . .

I had been South before—many times—and I thought I understood the plight of our Negro citizens.

But I discovered last week that my understanding was only the limited understanding: the sympathetic feeling of a friend for a man who is attacked.

To me, fascism is no longer a second-hand experience—a motion picture, a photograph or the deeply moving words of a great writer.

It is no longer a mere definition of an economic and political system in which freedom is stifled by private power; in which prejudices are bred and nourished; in which man is set against man for the profit of powerful and greedy forces.

No, fascism has become an ugly reality—a reality which I have tasted.

I have tasted it neither so fully nor so bitterly as millions of others. But I have tasted it.

And in tasting it I have reinforced my solemn resolution to fight it wherever and whenever it appears so long as I live. . . . I learned what prejudice and hatred can mean. I learned to know the face of violence, although I was spared the full force of violence. I saw the ugly reality of how hate and prejudice can warp good men and women: turn Christian gentlemen into raving beasts; turn good mothers and wives into Jezebels.

I didn't like that part of what I saw. I didn't like to see men and women fall victims to the catchwords of prejudice and the slogans of hate, even as the poor people of Germany were victimized by the catchwords and slogans of Hitler and Streicher.

I saw how a few hate mongers, carefully placed in a crowd of decent folks can set off a dangerous spark.

I saw a young college student—a Progressive party worker—who was severely cut across his chest and arms by the agents of hate. . . .

I heard Clark Foreman say so truthfully that "Down here, to believe in the Constitution means you are automatically called a Communist"; and I heard a young college student, a veteran, add: "It's like General Carlson said, 'To be called a Red here is a badge of honor.'"

I am confident that their spirit—the spirit of progressive South-
erners—will triumph in the South. I am hopeful that our trip helped
build their forces; helped rally new strength; helped along the movement which will free the South. Rich in resources—proud and courageous, the South must be—and will be—freed from the shackles in
which it has been held by huge corporations with headquarters only four
miles south of here—not in Virginia, not in Tennessee, but in Wall
Street.

The free South and the feudal South live side by side in the State
of Alabama. In one day we received courteous receptions and held free
meetings in the best American tradition in Decatur and Huntsville and
Gunthersville in the great TVA area; and on the same day we could not
hold meetings in Gadsden and Birmingham and Bessemer, cities which
are dominated by Northern-owned steel corporations. We did not hold
meetings because the police insisted on dividing Americans by the color
of their skins. We did not hold meetings because the constitutional right
to freely assemble and speak was denied by the police authorities of those
company towns.

Here—in Alabama—in a single day, we saw the economic basis of
hate and segregation.

In the steel towns it is profitable to keep labor divided.

North against South, race against race, farmer against worker—the
profits of the men who own the South are multiplied by keeping the
people divided.

But their days are numbered....

It is the owners of the mines and mills, the great plantations, and
newspapers who incite violence.

They don't personally engage in lynching either free speech or
human beings, just as they don't personally engage in fighting the wars
from which they profit.

But they inflame the passions of others. They have had others do
their dirty work. But the ranks of new recruits for their dirty work are
narrowing as more and more men and women of the South see how they
have been victimized by prejudice—as they see how it has profited the
few, and brought misery for themselves and their neighbors.

And the workers and farmers and independent business men of the
South are turning from the false leadership of those who have been styled
"Southern liberals"—they are turning from those who have preached
the tolerance of intolerance, tolerance of segregation; tolerance of

murderous Jim Crow. They are learning that such men are only slightly to the left of Hitler and Rankin.

They are learning that no man can believe in both segregation and democracy. . . .

In pledging to live by the Constitution, we have earned enemies. And we are proud of our enemies.

The men who stand for Jim Crow.

The men who stand for Taft-Hartley.

The men who support fascists in Greece and China.

The men who prefer an atmosphere of war, because they profit by it.

The men who hated Franklin Roosevelt and the New Deal and who now find their unity in hatred for the Progressive party.

These men, Republicans and Democrats bound together by hate, are using every mechanism which bipartisan fear can suggest to defeat congressional candidates who stand for peace. . . .

It is with great sadness that I note that the bipartisans have some new allies: fearful men who call themselves liberals and leaders of labor, men who cry out against Wall Street running the country and then ask workers to give dollar bills to keep President Truman and his Wall Street gang in Washington.

I say such action, such double talk, such duplicity is shameful, immoral, and corrupt.

These illiberal liberals, these labor leaders who fight monopoly with words, but whose actions support the candidates of monopoly, these men make possible the Truman double talk. They make it possible for Truman to condemn Taft-Hartley while using it to destroy unions and the Wagner Act; to call for civil rights, while maintaining segregation in the Armed Forces and conducting loyalty purges; to call for price controls after killing them, to call for peace while preparing for war.

The surest proof that we of the Progressive party are not impractical in our politics is in the alliances of hate which have been formed against us. . . .

We are those who stand against the course which leads to war.

We are those who protest a policy toward minority groups that is administered by a policeman's nightstick. We are those who feel attacked whenever the color of men's skin or the color of his political beliefs is the official excuse for brutality, whether in Mississippi or in Harlem, whether at home or abroad.

We must go now into every building of this city, into every suburban home, onto every street corner. We must tell the people who we are. We will stand up and take the jeers of hirelings.

We must work—we will work, so that on Nov. 2 Americans can clearly choose.

C
GENERAL DOUGLAS MacARTHUR ATTACKS
TRUMAN'S LIMITED WAR POLICY IN KOREA
APRIL 19, 1951

"But once war is forced upon us, there is no other alternative than to apply every available means to bring it to a swift end. War's very object is victory—not prolonged indecision. In war, indeed, there can be so substitute for victory."

... While I was not consulted prior to the President's decision to intervene in support of the Republic of Korea, that decision, from a military standpoint, proved a sound one [applause] as we hurled back the in-invaders and decimated his forces. Our victory was complete and our objectives within reach when Red China intervened with numerically superior ground forces. This created a new war and an entirely new situation—a situation not contemplated when our forces were committed against the North Korean invaders—a situation which called for new decisions in the diplomatic sphere to permit the realistic adjustment of military strategy. Such decisions have not been forthcoming. [Applause.]

While no man in his right mind would advocate sending our ground forces into continental China and such was never given a thought, the new situation did urgently demand a drastic revision of strategic planning if our political aim was to defeat this new enemy as we had defeated the old. [Applause.]

Apart from the military need as I saw it to neutralize the sanctuary protection given the enemy north of the Yalu, I felt that military neces-

Congressional Record, 82nd Congress, 1st Session, Vol. 97, Pt. 3, 4123–4125. Speech before joint session of the Congress.

sity in the conduct of the war made mandatory:

1. The intensification of our economic blockade against China;

2. The imposition of a naval blockade against the China coast;

3. Removal of restrictions on air reconnaissance of China's coast areas and of Manchuria [applause];

4. Removal of restrictions on the forces of the Republic of China on Formosa with logistical support to contribute to their effective operations against the common enemy. [Applause.]

For entertaining these views, all professionally designed to support our forces committed to Korea and bring hostilities to an end with the least possible delay and at a saving of countless American and Allied lives, I have been severely criticized in lay circles, principally abroad, despite my understanding that from a military standpoint the above views have been fully shared in the past by practically every military leader concerned with the Korean campaign, including our own Joint Chiefs of Staff. [Applause, the Members rising.]

I called for reinforcements, but was informed that reinforcements were not available. I made clear that if not permitted to destroy the build-up bases north of the Yalu; if not permitted to utilize the friendly Chinese force of some 600,000 men on Formosa; if not permitted to blockade the China coast to prevent the Chinese Reds from getting succor from without; and if there were to be no hope of major reinforcements, the position of the command from the military standpoint forbade victory. We could hold in Korea by constant maneuver and at an approximate area where our supply line advantages were in balance with the supply line disadvantages of the enemy, but we could hope at best for only an indecisive campaign, with its terrible and constant attrition upon our forces if the enemy utilized his full military potential. I have constantly called for the new political decisions essential to a solution. Efforts have been made to distort my position. It has been said, in effect, that I am a warmonger. Nothing could be further from the truth. I know war as few other men now living know it, and nothing to me is more revolting. I have long advocated its complete abolition as its very destructiveness on both friend and foe has rendered it useless as a means of settling international disputes. . . .

But once war is forced upon us, there is no other alternative than to apply every available means to bring it to a swift end. War's very object is victory—not prolonged indecision. [Applause.] In war, indeed, there can be no substitute for victory. [Applause.]

There are some who for varying reasons would appease Red China. They are blind to history's clear lesson. For history teaches with unmistakable emphasis that appeasement but begets new and bloodier war. It points to no single instance where the end has justified that means— where appeasement has led to more than a sham peace. Like blackmail, it lays the basis for new and successively greater demands, until, as in blackmail, violence becomes the only other alternative. . . .

The tragedy of Korea is further heightened by the fact that as military action is confined to its territorial limits, it condemns that nation, which it is our purpose to save, to suffer the devastating impact of full naval and air bombardment, while the enemy's sanctuaries are fully protected from such attack and devastation. Of the nations of the world, Korea alone, up to now, is the sole one which has risked its all against communism. The magnificence of the courage and fortitude of the Korean people defies description. [Applause.] They have chosen to risk death rather than slavery. Their last words to me were "Don't scuttle the Pacific.". . .

D

SENATOR JOSEPH R. McCARTHY
SEES A COMMUNIST CONSPIRACY
IN THE STATE DEPARTMENT TO TURN THE WORLD OVER
TO SOVIET RUSSIA AND RED CHINA
JUNE 14, 1951

"What is the objective of the great conspiracy? . . . . to diminish the United States in world affairs . . . [so] that we shall be contained, frustrated and finally fall victim to Soviet intrigue from within and Russian military might from without."

How can we account for our present situation unless we believe that men high in this Government are concerting to deliver us to disaster? This must be the product of a great conspiracy, a conspiracy on a scale so im-

Congressional Record, 82nd Congress, 1st Session, Vol. 97, Pt. 5, 6602–6603.

mense as to dwarf any previous such venture in the history of man. A conspiracy of infamy so black that, when it is finally exposed, its principals shall be forever deserving of the maledictions of all honest men.

Who constitutes the highest circles of this conspiracy? About that we cannot be sure. We are convinced that Dean Acheson, who steadfastly serves the interests of nations other than his own, the friend of Alger Hiss, who supported him in his hour of retribution, who contributed to his defense fund, must be high on the roster. The President? He is their captive. I have wondered, as have you, why he did not dispense with so great a liability as Acheson to his own and his party's interests. It is now clear to me. In the relationship of master and man, did you ever hear of man firing master? Truman is a satisfactory front. He is only dimly aware of what is going on.

I do not believe that Mr. Truman is a conscious party to the great conspiracy, although it is being conducted in his name. I believe that if Mr. Truman had the ability to associate good Americans around him, he would have behaved as a good American in this most dire of all our crises.

It is when we return to an examination of General Marshall's record since the spring of 1942 that we approach an explanation of the carefully planned retreat from victory. Let us again review the Marshall record, as I have disclosed it from all the sources available and all of them friendly. This grim and solitary man it was who, early in World War II, determined to put his impress upon our global strategy, political and military.

It was Marshall who, amid the din for a "second front now" from every voice of Soviet inspiration, sought to compel the British to invade across the Channel in the fall of 1942 upon penalty of our quitting the war in Europe.

It was Marshall who, after North Africa had been secured, took the strategic direction of the war out of Roosevelt's hands and who fought the British desire, shared by Mark Clark, to advance from Italy into the eastern plains of Europe ahead of the Russians.

It was a Marshall-sponsored memorandum, advising appeasement of Russia in Europe and the enticement of Russia into the far-eastern war, circulated at Quebec, which foreshadowed our whole course at Tehran, at Yalta, and until now in the Far East.

It was Marshall who, at Terhran, made common cause with Stalin on the strategy of the war in Europe and marched side by side with him thereafter.

It was Marshall who enjoined his chief of military mission in Moscow under no circumstances to "irritate" the Russians by asking them questions about their forces, their weapons, and their plans, while at the same time opening our schools, factories, and gradually our secrets to them in this country.

It was Marshall who, as Hanson Baldwin asserts, himself referring only to the "military authorities," prevented us having a corridor to Berlin. So it was with the capture and occupation of Berlin and Prague ahead of the Russians.

It was Marshall who sent Deane to Moscow to collaborate with Harriman in drafting the terms of the wholly unnecessary bribe paid to Stalin at Yalta. It was Marshall, with Hiss at his elbow and doing the physical drafting of agreements at Yalta, who ignored the contrary advice of his senior, Admiral Leahy, and of MacArthur and Nimitz in regard to the folly of a major land invasion of Japan; who submitted intelligence reports which suppressed more truthful estimates in order to support his argument, and who finally induced Roosevelt to bring Russia into the Japanese war with a bribe that reinstated Russia in its pre-1904 imperialistic position in Manchuria—an act which, in effect, signed the death warrant of the Republic of China.

It was Marshall, with Acheson and Vincent eagerly assisting, who created the China policy which, destroying China, robbed us of a great and friendly ally, a buffer against the Soviet imperialism with which we are now at war.

It was Marshall, who, after long conferences with Acheson and Vincent, went to China to execute the criminal folly of the disastrous Marshall mission.

It was Marshall who, upon returning from a diplomatic defeat for the United States at Moscow, besought the reinstatement of forty millions in lend-lease for Russia.

It was Marshall who, for 2 years suppressed General Wedemeyer's report, which is a direct and comprehensive repudiation of the Marshall policy.

It was Marshall who, disregarding Wedemeyer's advices on the urgent need for military supplies, the likelihood of China's defeat without ammunition and equipment, and our "moral obligation" to furnish them, proposed instead a relief bill bare of military support.

It was the State Department under Marshall, with the wholehearted support of Michael Lee and Remington in the Commerce Department, that sabotaged the $125,000,000 military-aid bill to China in 1948.

It was Marshall who fixed the dividing line for Korea along the thirty-eighth parallel, a line historically chosen by Russia to mark its sphere of interest in Korea.

It is Marshall's strategy for Korea which has turned that war into a pointless slaughter, reversing the dictum of Von Clausewitz and every military theorist since him that the object of a war is not merely to kill but to impose your will on the enemy.

It is Marshall-Acheson strategy for Europe to build the defense of Europe solely around the Atlantic Pact nations, excluding the two great wells of anti-Communist manpower in Western Germany and Spain and spurning the organized armies of Greece and Turkey—another case of following the Lattimore advice of "let them fall but don't let it appear that we pushed them."

It is Marshall who, advocating timidity as a policy so as not to annoy the forces of Soviet imperialism in Asia, had admittedly put a brake on the preparations to fight, rationalizing his reluctance on the ground that the people are fickle and if war does not come, will hold him to account for excessive zeal.

What can be made of this unbroken series of decisions and acts contributing to the strategy of defeat? They cannot be attributed to incompetence. If Marshall were merely stupid, the laws of probability would dictate that part of his decisions would serve this country's interest. If Marshall is innocent of guilty intention, how could he be trusted to guide the defense of this country further? We have declined so precipitously in relation to the Soviet Union in the last 6 years. How much swifter may be our fall into disaster with Marshall at the helm? Where will all this stop? That is not a rhetorical question: Ours is not a rhetorical danger. Where next will Marshall carry us? It is useless to suppose that his nominal superior will ask him to resign. He cannot even dispense with Acheson.

What is the objective of the great conspiracy? I think it is clear from what has occurred and is now occurring: to diminish the United States in world affairs, to weaken us militarily, to confuse our spirit with talk of surrender in the Far East and to impair our will to resist evil. To what end? To the end that we shall be contained, frustrated and finally fall victim to Soviet intrigue from within and Russian military might from without. Is that farfetched? There have been many examples in history of rich and powerful states which have been corrupted from within, enfeebled and deceived until they were unable to resist aggression.

The United States first ventured into world affairs a bare half century ago. Its rise to world leadership was almost unprecedentedly sudden. We call this a young country. It is in terms of the tenure of the settlement by Europeans on these lands. It is also in terms of the spirit and daring of its people. Yet the United States belongs to, is the last great example of, the farthest projection of an old culture. The vast and complicated culture of the west, which bloomed with the spread of the Gothic cathedrals and the universities which has carried science and technology and art and the humane values to lengths nowhere else dreamed of and whose sway covered the earth only a few years ago, is in manifest decay. We see the symptoms of decay in Western Europe. We find evidences of it here.

There is a rising power, not yet a culture; a power barbarous to us which has attracted many followers and devotees in the heart of the west. Why these men and women of the west are so attracted lies outside our interest at this moment. We know that these enemies of the west are here, we know they are at work among us, burrowing, mining, sapping ceaselessly; seeking to destroy our civilization. We know principally because we see the results of their work. We cannot always detect them at it. That is not an easy task as we have seen with the notorious case of Alger Hiss.

The enemies of our civilization, whether alien or native, whether of high or low degree, work in the dark. They are that way more effective. It is easy to single out, identify and isolate a frank and open Communist. The Communists openly among us are scarcely a problem at all. They have the aversion and contempt of all honest Americans. It is the clandestine enemy which taxes our ingenuity.

It is the great crime of the Truman administration that it has refused to undertake the job of ferreting the enemy from its ranks. I once puzzled over that refusal. The President, I said, is a loyal American; why does he not lead in this enterprise? I think that I know why he does not. The President is not master in his own house. Those who are master there not only have a desire to protect the sappers and miners—they could not do otherwise. They themselves are not free. They belong to a larger conspiracy, the world-wide web of which has been spun from Moscow. It was Moscow, for example, which decreed that the United States should execute its loyal friend, the Republic of China. The executioners were that well-identified group headed by Acheson and George Catlett Marshall.

How, if they would, can they break these ties, how return to simple allegiance to their native land? Can men sullied by their long and dreadful record afford us leadership in the world struggle with the enemy? How can a man whose every important act for years had contributed to the prosperity of the enemy reverse himself? The reasons for his past actions are immaterial. Regardless of why he has done what he did, he has done it and the momentum of that course bears him onward. This is his plight:

> I am in blood,
> Stepped in so far, that should I wade no more,
> Returning were as tedious as go o'er.

Can we foretell the next move on the timetable of the great conspiracy? It seems clearly indicated. Dean Acheson foreshadowed it the other day before the Russell committee when he expressed his desire to have a cease-fire negotiated with the Peiping Reds on the basis of the thirty-eighth parallel. A cease-fire leaving the enemy in command of Korea north of that imaginary line that has occasioned the spilling of so much blood. And then, after the cease-fire, to have our friends on Formosa delivered behind the iron curtain by a jury stacked with the friends of international communism and then have the question of the admission of Red China decided by the United Nations. While Acheson publicly proclaims he is opposed to the sell-out, but privately continues to encourage our "friends" in the United Nations to prepare to not only bury the Republic of China, but to heap refuse on its grave. If that is the best that the perfidious Red Dean can offer us, I say let him come again. After all, we need not take what he or the mayor of the palace or the weak Merovingian himself brings us.

The time has come to halt this tepid, milk-and-water acquiescence which a discredited administration, ruled by disloyalty, sends down to us. The American may belong to an old culture, he may be beset by enemies here and abroad, he may be distracted by the many words of counsel that assail him by day and night, but he is nobody's fool. The time has come for us to realize that the people who sent us here expect more than time-serving from us. The American who has never known defeat in war, does not expect to be again sold down the river in Asia. He does not want that kind of betrayal. He has had betrayal enough. He has never failed to fight for his liberties since George Washington rode to Boston in 1775 to put himself at the head of a band of rebels unversed in war. He is fighting tonight, fighting gloriously in a war on a distant American frontier made inglorious by the men he can no longer trust at the head of our affairs.

The America that I know, and that other Senators know, this vast and teeming and beautiful land, this hopeful society where the poor share the table of the rich as never before in history, where men of all colors, of all faiths, are brothers as never before in history, where great deeds have been done and great deeds are yet to do, that America deserves to be led not to humiliation or defeat, but to victory.

The Congress of the United States is the people's last hope, a free and open forum of the people's representatives. We felt the pulse of the people's response to the return of MacArthur. We know what it meant. The people, no longer trusting their executive, turn to us, asking that we reassert the constitutional prerogative of the Congress to declare the policy for the United States.

The time has come to reassert that prerogative, to oversee the conduct of this war, to declare that this body must have the final word on the disposition of Formosa and Korea. They fell from the grasp of the Japanese empire through our military endeavors, pursuant to a declaration of war made by the Congress of the United States on December 8, 1941. If the Senate speaks, as is its right, the disposal of Korea and Formosa can be made only by a treaty which must be ratified by this body. Should the administration dare to defy such a declaration, the Congress has abundant recourses which I need not spell out.

E

STUDENT RADICAL CARL OGLESBY OF STUDENTS FOR A DEMOCRATIC SOCIETY CONDEMNS AMERICA'S LIBERALISM AND THE WAR IN VIETNAM NOVEMBER 27, 1965

"This country, with its thirty-some years of liberalism, can send two hundred thousand young men to Vietnam to kill and die in the most dubious of wars, but it cannot get a hundred voter registrars to go into Mississippi. What do you make of it?"

We are here again to protest against a growing war. Since it is a very bad war, we acquire the habit of thinking that it must be caused by very bad men. But we only conceal reality, I think, to denounce on such grounds the menacing coalition of industrial and military power, or the brutality of the blitzkrieg we are waging against Vietnam, or the ominous signs around us that heresy may soon no longer be permitted. We must simply observe, and quite plainly say, that this coalition, this blitzkrieg, and this demand for acquiescence are creatures, all of them, of a government that since 1932 has considered itself to be fundamentally *liberal*.

The original commitment in Vietnam was made by President Truman, a mainstream liberal. It was seconded by President Eisenhower, a moderate liberal. It was intensified by the late President Kennedy, a flaming liberal. Think of the men who now engineer that war—those who study the maps, give the commands, push the buttons, and tally the dead: Bundy, McNamara, Rusk, Lodge, Goldberg, the President himself.

They are not moral monsters.

They are all honorable men.

They are all liberals.

But so, I'm sure, are many of us who are here today in protest. To understand the war, then, it seems necessary to take a closer look at this American liberalism. Maybe we are in for some surprises. Maybe we have here two quite different liberalisms: one authentically humanist, the other not so human at all.

Not long ago, I considered myself a liberal. And if someone had

Speech printed in Jacob and Saul Landau, *The New Radicals*, New York: Random House, 1966, 258–266.

asked me what I meant by that, I'd perhaps have quoted Thomas Jefferson or Thomas Paine, who first made plain our nation's unprovisional commitment to human rights. But what do you think would happen if these two heroes could sit down now for a chat with President Johnson and McGeorge Bundy?

They would surely talk of the Vietnam war. Our dead revolutionaries would soon wonder why their country was fighting against what appeared to be a revolution. The living liberals would hotly deny that it is one: there are troops coming in from outside, the rebels get arms from other countries, most of the people are not on their side, and they practice terror against their own. Therefore, *not* a revolution.

What would our dead revolutionaries answer? They might say: "What fools and bandits, sirs, you make then of us. Outside help? Do you remember Lafayette? Or the three thousand British freighters the French navy sank for our side? Or the arms and men we got from France and Spain? And what's this about terror? Did you never hear what we did to our own loyalists? Or about the thousands of rich American Tories who fled for their lives to Canada? And as for popular support, do you not know that we had less than one third of our people with us? That, in fact, the colony of New York recruited more troops for the British than for the revolution? Should we give it all back?"

Revolutions do not take place in velvet boxes. They never have. It is only the poets who make them lovely. What the National Liberation Front is fighting in Vietnam is a complex and vicious war. This war is also a revolution, as honest a revolution as you can find anywhere in history. And this is a fact which all our intricate official denials will never change.

But it doesn't make any difference to our leaders anyway. Their aim in Vietnam is really much simpler than this implies. It is to safeguard what they take to be American interests around the world against revolution or revolutionary change, which they always call Communism—as if that were that. In the case of Vietnam, this interest is, first, the principle that revolution shall not be tolerated anywhere, and second, that South Vietnam shall never sell its rice to China—or even to North Vietnam.

There is simply no such thing now, for us, as a just revolution—never mind that for two thirds of the world's people the twentieth century might as well be the Stone Age; never mind the terrible poverty and hopelessness that are the basic facts of life for most modern men;

and never mind that for these millions there is now an increasingly perceptible relationship between their sorrow and our contentment. . . .

To be sure, we have been most generous with our aid, and in Western Europe, a mature industrial society, that aid worked. But there are always political and financial strings. And we have never shown ourselves capable of allowing others to make those traumatic institutional changes that are often the prerequisites of progress in colonial societies. For all our official feeling for the millions who are enslaved to what we so self-righteously call the yoke of Communist tyranny, we make no real effort at all to crack through the much more vicious right-wing tyrannies that our businessmen traffic with and our nation profits from every day. And for all our cries about the international red conspiracy to take over the world, we take only pride in our six thousand military bases on foreign soil.

We gave Rhodesia a grave look just now—but we keep on buying her chromium, which is cheap because black slave labor mines it.

We deplore the racism of Verwoerd's fascist South Africa—but our banks make big loans to that country and our private technology makes it a nuclear power.

We are saddened and puzzled by random back-page stories of revolt in this or that Latin American state—but are convinced by a few pretty photos in the Sunday supplement that things are getting better, that the world is coming our way, that change from disorder can be orderly, that our benevolence will pacify the distressed, that our might will intimidate the angry.

Optimists, may I suggest that these are quite unlikely fantasies? They are fantasies because we have lost that mysterious social desire for human equity that from time to time has given us genuine moral drive. We have become a nation of young, bright-eyed, hard-hearted, slim-waisted, bullet-headed make-out artists. A nation—may I say it?—of beardless liberals.

You say I am being hard? Only think.

This country, with its thirty-some years of liberalism, can send two hundred thousand young men to Vietnam to kill and die in the most dubious of wars, but it cannot get a hundred voter registrars to go into Mississippi.

What do you make of it?

The financial burden of the war obliges us to cut millions from an already pathetic War on Poverty budget. But in almost the same breath,

Congress appropriates $140 million for the Lockheed and Boeing companies to compete with each other on the supersonic transport project—that Disneyland creation that will cost us all about $2 billion before it's done.

What do you make of it?

Many of us have been earnestly resisting for some years now the idea of putting atomic weapons into West German hands, an action that would perpetuate the division of Europe and thus the Cold War. Now just this week we find out that, with the meagerest of security systems, West Germany has had nuclear weapons in her hands for the past six years.

What do you make of it?

Some will make of it that I overdraw the matter. Many will ask: What about the other side? To be sure, there is the bitter ugliness of Czechoslovakia, Poland, those infamous Russian tanks in the streets of Budapest. But my anger only rises to hear some say that sorrow cancels sorrow, or that *this* one's shame deposits in *that* one's account the right to shamefulness.

And others will make of it that I sound mighty anti-American. To these, I say: Don't blame *me* for *that*! Blame those who mouthed my liberal values and broke my American heart. . . .

F

REPRESENTATIVE JOHN BELL WILLIAMS DEFINES THE PEACE MOVEMENT IN AMERICA AS A CONSPIRACY OF NATIVE RADICALS AND BLACKS
OCTOBER 22, 1965

"It is becoming increasingly evident that those trained in civil rights subversion are now turning their attention to the Communist-inspired goal—United States withdrawal from Vietnam."

. . . Mr. Speaker, a number of Members of this body have taken the floor in the last few days to express indignation over the current wave of demonstrations being waged in protest against American intervention in Vietnam. I, as much as any other Member of the Congress, deplore and resent these demonstrations. Surely, Mr. Speaker, at a time when Americans are fighting and dying to stop the enslavement of free people by predatory Communist forces, they need all the support that we can give them. Whatever mistakes may have been made in the past by those who formulate our foreign policies, the fact remains that we are in Vietnam; our boys are dying there, and our national honor and security are at stake. In the conduct of this mission, the President needs and deserves the support of every patriotic American citizen, and I, for one, am willing to give him my full support in this effort.

The wave of demonstrations and civil disobedience that spread throughout the country last weekend have all the earmarks of a highly organized Communist plot, designed to embarrass us in the eyes of the world, and to encourage Red China to redouble its efforts to push us out of Vietnam. These demonstrations, intended to serve the Communist cause by conveying a false picture of American disunity to the rest of the world, actually border on the side of treason.

These were not spontaneous, spur-of-the-moment manifestations of protest on the part of conscientious American citizens reacting to the danger of a war that might jeopardize the future security of our country. These demonstrations were obviously well planned in advance, well financed and well coordinated so as to gain for the demonstrators a maximum amount of publicity throughout the world. The participants were expert in the technique of civil disobedience through training and experience, as I will attempt to prove later in this dissertation.

To those of us who represent States and areas which have been subjected to the many massive so-called civil rights demonstrations during the last few years, Attorney General Katzenbach's recent public recognition of the role being played by Communists in these Vietnam demonstrations came as no surprise. What amazes many of us is the fact that General Katzenbach ignored this same Communist influence and participation in the wave of civil disobedience that lately has been going on in the name of civil rights. Those who, just a few weeks ago, were demonstrating for civil rights, are now in the forefront in trying to undermine our policies in southeast Asia. . . .

There is the high mogul of all racial demagogues and racketeers, the recipient of the now tarnished Nobel Peace Price, the most succesful money collector of them all, the grand high priest of civil disobedience, the Reverend Martin Luther King, Jr. This high and mighty emperor of discord, at whose feet worship thousands of cringing politicians, has publicly protested our war against Communist China's aggression, and has advocated the admission of Red China to the United Nations. That King should be parroting the party line comes as no shock to persons familiar with the background of support for pink-tinged causes and his association with known Communists, including participation in activities at pro-Communist Myles Horton's Highlander Folk School, the notorious Communist training school at Monteagle, Tenn.

It is becoming increasingly evident that those trained in civil rights subversion are now turning their attention to the Communist-inspired goal—United States withdrawal from Vietnam. . . .

Mr. Speaker, on July 28, the Freedom Democratic Party newsletter, circulated generally among Negroes throughout Mississippi in a continuing attempt to generate unrest among our people, contained an article exhorting Negroes to refuse to support our Government in its Vietnam effort. For the information of Members of the House, Mr. Speaker, I include the text of this article:

> Here are five reasons why Negroes should not be in any war fighting for America.
>
> 1. No Mississippi Negroes should be fighting in Vietnam for the white man's freedom, until all the Negro people are free in Mississippi.
>
> 2. Negro boys should not honor the draft here in Mississippi. Mothers should encourage their sons not to go.
>
> 3. We will gain respect and dignity as a race only by forcing the U.S. Government and the Mississippi government to come with guns, dogs and trucks to take our sons away to fight and be killed protecting Mississippi, Alabama, Georgia, and Louisiana.
>
> 4. No one has a right to ask us to risk our lives and kill other colored people in Santo Domingo and Vietnam, so that the white American can get richer. We will be looked upon as traitors by all the colored people of the world if the Negro people continue to fight and die without a cause.
>
> 5. Last week a white soldier from New Jersey was discharged from the Army because he refused to fight in Vietnam. He went on a hunger strike. Negro boys can do the same thing. We can write and ask our sons if they know what they are fighting for. If he answers "freedom," tell him that's what we

are fighting for here in Mississippi. And if he says "democracy" tell him the truth—we don't know anything about communism, socialism, and all that, but we do know that Negroes have caught hell here under this American democracy....

Mr. Speaker, this administration and those which have preceded it have ignored too long the root of the problem that has manifested itself in the Vietnam demonstrations. The time has arrived when the Communist influence in all massive protests and civil disobedience campaigns should be thoroughly investigated and exposed to public view.

G

SENATOR J. WILLIAM FULBRIGHT ON AMERICA'S ARROGANCE OF POWER IN WORLD POLITICS
APRIL 21, 1966

"The wisdom and productivity of the protest [peace] movement of students, professors, clergy and others may well be questioned, but their courage, decency and patriotism cannot be doubted. At the very least the student protest movement of the sixties is a moral and intellectual improvement on the panty raids of the fifties. In fact it is a great deal more: it is an expression of the national conscience and a manifestation of traditional American idealism."

The question that I find intriguing—the question which I have chosen as the theme of these lectures although I have no answer to it—is whether a nation so extraordinarily endowed as the United States can overcome that arrogance of power which has afflicted, weakened, and in some cases destroyed great nations in the past.

The causes of the malady are a mystery but its recurrence is one of the uniformities of history; power tends to confuse itself with virtue and a great nation is peculiarly susceptible to the idea that its power is a sign of God's favor, conferring upon it a special responsibility for other nations—to make them richer and happier and wiser, to remake them,

---

Congressional Record, 89th Congress, 2nd Session, Vol. 112, Pt. 7 (April 25, 1966), 8870–8873.

that is, in its own shining image. Power confuses itself with virtue and it also tends to take itself for omnipotence. Once imbued with the idea of a mission, a great nation easily assumes that it has the means as well as the duty to do God's work. The Lord, after all, surely would not choose you as His agent and then deny you the sword with which to work His will. German soldiers in the First World War wore belt buckles imprinted with the words: "Gott mit uns." It was approximately under this kind of infatuation—an exaggerated sense of power and an imaginary sense of mission—that the Athenians attacked Syracuse and Napoleon and then Hitler invaded Russia. In plain words, they overextended their commitments and they came to grief.

My question is whether America can overcome the fatal arrogance of power. My hope and my belief are that it can, that it has the human resources to accomplish what few if any great nations have ever accomplished before: to be confident but also tolerant and rich but also generous, to be willing to teach but also willing to learn, to be powerful but also wise. I believe that America is capable of all of these things: I also believe it is falling short of them. Gradually but unmistakably we are succumbing to the arrogance of power. In so doing we are not living up to our capacity and promise; the measure of our falling short is the measure of the patriot's duty of dissent.

The discharge of that most important duty is handicapped in America by an unworthy tendency to fear serious criticism of our Government. In the abstract we celebrate freedom of opinion as a vital part of our patriotic liturgy. It is only when some Americans exercise the right that other Americans are shocked. No one of course ever criticizes the right of dissent; it is always this particular instance of it or its exercise under these particular circumstances or at this particular time that throws people into a blue funk. I am reminded of Samuel Butler's observation that "People in general are equally horrified at hearing the Christian religion doubted, and at seeing it practiced.". . .

The second great advantage of free discussion to democratic policymakers is its bringing to light of new ideas and the supplanting of old myths with new realities. We Americans are much in need of this benefit because we are severely, if not uniquely, afflicted with a habit of policymaking by analogy: North Vietnam's involvement in South Vietnam, for example, is equated with Hitler's invasion of Poland and a parley with the Vietcong would represent another Munich. The treatment of slight and superficial resemblances as if they were fullblooded analogies, as instances, as it were, of history "repeating itself," is a substitute for thinking and misuse of history. The value of history is not what it seems to prohibit or prescribe but its general indications as to the kinds of policies that are likely to succeed and the kinds that are likely to fail, or, as one historian has suggested, its hints as to what is likely not to happen. . . .

There is a kind of voodoo about American foreign policy. Certain drums have to be beaten regularly to ward off evil spirits—for example, the maledictions which are regularly uttered against North Vietnamese aggression, the "wild men" in Peking, communism in general and President de Gaulle. Certain pledges must be repeated every day lest the whole free world go to rack and ruin—for example, we will never go back on a commitment no matter how unwise; we regard this alliance or that as absolutely "vital" to the free world; and of course we will stand stalwart in Berlin from now until Judgment Day. Certain words must never be uttered except in derision—the word "appeasement," for example, comes as near as any word can to summarize everything that is regarded by American policymakers as stupid, wicked and disastrous.

I do not suggest that we should heap praise on the Chinese Communists, dismantle NATO, abandon Berlin, and seize every opportunity that comes along to appease our enemies. I do suggest the desirability of an atmosphere in which unorthodox ideas would arouse interest rather than horror, reflection rather than emotion. As likely as not, new proposals, carefully examined, would be found wanting and old policies judged sound; what is wanted is not change itself but the capacity for change. Consider the idea of appeasement: In a free and healthy political atmosphere it would elicit neither horror nor enthusiasm but only interest in what precisely its proponent had in mind. As Winston Churchill once said: "Appeasement in itself may be good or bad according to circumstances. Appeasement from strength is magnanimous and noble and might be the surest and perhaps the only path to world peace. . . ."

While not unprecedented, protests against a war in the middle of the war are a rare experience for Americans. I see it as a mark of strength and maturity that an articulate minority have raised their voices against the Vietnamese war and that the majority of Americans are enduring this dissent, not without anxiety, to be sure, but with better grace and understanding than would have been the case in any other war of the 20th century.

It is by no means certain that the relatively healthy atmosphere in which the debate is now taking place will not give way to a new era of McCarthyism. The longer the Vietnamese war goes on without prospect of victory or negotiated peace, the war fever will rise; hopes will give way to fears and tolerance and freedom of discussion will give way to a false and strident patriotism. . . .

Past experience provides little basis for confidence that reason can prevail in an atmosphere of mounting war fever. In a contest between a hawk and dove the hawk has a great advantage, not because it is a better bird, but because it is a bigger bird with lethal talons and a highly developed will to use them. Without illusions as to the prospect of success we must try nonetheless to bring reason and restraint into the emotionally charged atmosphere in which the Vietnamese war is now being discussed. Instead of trading epithets about the legitimacy of debate and about who is and is not giving "aid and comfort" to the enemy, we would do well to focus calmly and deliberately on the issue itself, recognizing that all of us make mistakes and that mistakes can only be corrected if they are acknowledged and discussed, and recognizing further that war is not its own justification, that it can and must be discussed unless we are prepared to sacrifice our traditional democratic processes to a false image of national unanimity.

In fact the protesters against the Vietnamese war are in good historical company. On January 12, 1848, Abraham Lincoln rose in the U.S. House of Representatives and made a speech about the Mexican War worthy of Senator MORSE. Lincoln's speech was an explanation of a vote he had recently cast in support of a resolution declaring that the war had been unnecessary and unconstitutionally begun by President Polk. "I admit," he said, "that such a vote should not be given, in mere wantonness, and that the one given, is justly censurable, if it have no other, or better foundation. I am one of those who joined in that vote; and I did so under my best impression of the truth of the case."

That is exactly what the students and professors and politicians who oppose the Vietnamese war have been doing: they have been acting on their "best impression of the truth of the case." Some of our superpatriots assume that any war the United States fights is a just war, if not indeed a holy crusade, but history does not sustain their view. No reputable historian would deny that the United States has fought some wars which were unjust, unnecessary or both—I would suggest the War of 1812, the Civil War, and the Spanish-American War as examples. In an historical frame of reference it seems to me logical and proper to question the wisdom of our present military involvement in Asia.

The wisdom and productivity of the protest movement of students, professors, clergy and others may well be questioned, but their courage, decency, and patriotism cannot be doubted. At the very least the student protest movement of the sixties is a moral and intellectual improvement on the panty raids of the fifties. In fact it is a great deal more: it is an expression of the national conscience and a manifestation of traditional American idealism. I agree with the editorial comment of last October's very interesting issue of the Johns Hopkins magazine, in which it was suggested that the "new radical" movement "is not shallow and sophomoric, it is not based on the traditional formula of generational defiance, and it is not the result of an infusion of foreign ideologies. It is based instead on personal disenchantment and the feeling of these radicals that they must repudiate a corrupted vision of society and replace it with a purer one."

Protesters against the Vietnamese war have been held up to scorn on the ground that they wish to "select their wars," by which it is apparently meant that it is hypocritical to object to this particular war while not objecting to war in general. I fail to understand what is reprehensible about trying to make moral distinctions between one war and another, between, for example, resistance to Hitler and intervention in Vietnam. From the time of Grotius to the drafting of the United Nations Charter international lawyers have tried to distinguish between "just wars" and "unjust wars." It is a difficult problem of law and an even more difficult problem of morality, but it is certainly a valid problem and, far from warranting contempt, those who try to solve it deserve our sympathy and respect....

With due respect for the honesty and patriotism of the student demonstrations, I would offer a word of caution to the young people who have organized and participated in them. As most politicians discover sooner or later, the most dramatic expression of grievances is not necessarily the most effective. That would seem to be especially true in the United States, a country which, as I have pointed out, is easily and excessively alarmed by expressions of dissent. We are, for better or worse, an essentially conservative society; in such a society soft words are likely to carry more weight than harsh words and the most effective dissent is dissent that is expressed in an orderly, which is to say, a conservative manner.

For these reasons direct action such as the burning of draft cards probably does more to retard than to advance the views of those who take such action. The burning of a draft card is a symbolic act, really a form of expression rather than of action, and it is stupid and vindictive to punish it as a crime. But it is also a very unwise act, unwise because it is shocking rather than persuasive to most Americans and because it exposes the individual to personal risk without political reward. . . .

In recent years the Congress has not fully discharged its responsibilities in the field of foreign relations. The reduced role of the Congress and the enhanced role of the President in the making of foreign policy are not the result merely of President Johnson's ideas of consensus; they are the culmination of a trend in the constitutional relationship between President and Congress that began in 1940, that is to say, at the beginning of this age of crisis.

The cause of the change is crisis. The President has the authority and resources to make decisions and take actions in an emergency; the Congress does not. Nor, in my opinion, should it; the proper responsibilities of the Congress are to reflect and review, to advise and criticize, to consent and to withhold consent. In the last 25 years American foreign policy has encountered a shattering series of crises and inevitably—or almost inevitably—the effort to cope with these has been Executive effort, while the Congress inspired by patriotism, importuned by Presidents, and deterred by lack of information, has tended to fall in line behind the Executive. The result has been an unhinging of traditional constitutional relationships; the Senate's constitutional powers of advice and consent have atrophied into what is widely regarded—though never asserted—to be a duty to give prompt consent with a minimum of advice. The problem is to find a way to restore the constitutional balance, to find ways by which the Senate can discharge its duty of advice and consent in an era of permanent crisis.

Presidents must act in emergencies, especially when the country is at war, and of the last five Presidents only one has not had to wage a sizable war for at least a part of his period in office. Beset with the anxieties of a foreign crisis, no President can relish the idea of inviting opinionated and tendentious Senators into his high policy councils. His reluctance is human, but it is not in keeping with the intent of the Constitution. I believe that, as representatives of the people, Senators have the duty, not merely the right, to render advice, not on the day-to-day conduct of foreign policy, but on its direction and philosophy as these are shaped by major decisions. I conclude that, when the President, for reasons with which we can all sympathize, does not invite us into his high policy councils, it is our duty to infiltrate our way in as best we can....

How then can the Senate discharge its constitutional responsibilites of advice and consent in an age when the direction and philosophy of foreign policy are largely shaped by urgent decisions made at moments of crisis? I regret that I have no definitive formula to offer but I do have some ideas as to how both the Senate as an institution and an individual Senator can meet their constitutional responsibilities.

The Senate as a whole, I think, should undertake to revive and strengthen the deliberative function which it has permitted to atrophy in the course of 25 years of crisis. Acting on the premise that dissent is not disloyalty, that a true consensus is shaped by airing our differences rather than suppressing them, the Senate should again become, as it used to be, an institution in which the great issues of American politics are contested with thoroughness, energy, and candor. Nor should the Senate allow itself to be too easily swayed by executive pleas for urgency and unanimity, or by allegations of aid and comfort to the enemies of the United States made by officials whose concern may be heightened by a distaste for criticism directed at themselves.

In recent months, the Senate Committee on Foreign Relations has engaged in an experiment in public education. The committee has made itself available as a forum for the meeting of politicians and professors and, more broadly, as a forum through which recognized experts and scholars could help increase congressional and public understanding of the problems associated with our involvement in Vietnam and our relations with Communist China. It is my hope that this experiment will not only contribute to public education but will help to restore the Senate to its proper role as adviser to the President on the great issues of foreign policy.

I believe that the public hearings on Vietnam, by bringing before the American people a variety of opinions and disagreements pertaining to the war, and perhaps by helping to restore a degree of balance between the executive and the Congress, have done far more to strengthen the country than to weaken it. The hearings have been criticized on the ground that they conveyed an "image" of the United States as divided over the war. Since the country obviously is divided, what was conveyed was a fact rather than an image. As I have already indicated, I see no merit in the view that we should maintain an image of unity even though it is a false image maintained at the cost of suppressing the normal procedures of democracy....

H
SENATOR EUGENE McCARTHY'S
PLAN TO END AMERICAN MILITARY INVOLVEMENT
IN VIETNAM
AUGUST 17, 1968

"The war in Vietnam has been of enormous cost in human life and in material resources. It has diverted our energies from pressing domestic problems and impaired our prestige in the world. There is no foreseeable prospect of a military victory in Vietnam, or of a military solution to the conflict. Thus the only possibility of peace lies in a negotiated settlement. . . ."

A great party, like a great nation, must be willing to change its course when events and experience demonstrate that such a change is necessary to the welfare of the people it serves. This willingness to yield to the lessons of history is one of the great strengths of the Democratic party. Today the war in Vietnam is a most difficult test of that strength.

Certain lessons of that war are now clear:

(1) The war in Vietnam has been of enormous cost in human life and in material resources. It has diverted our energies from pressing domestic problems and impaired our prestige in the world.

(2) There is no foreseeable prospect of a military victory in Vietnam, or of a military solution to the conflict.

(3) Thus the only possibility of peace lies in a negotiated settlement between the four principal parties: 1. The South Vietnamese Government in Saigon, 2. the North Vietnamese Government, 3. the United States, 4. the National Liberation Front, or Vietcong.

(4) Any realistic settlement must be a compromise between the conflicting groups and forces in Vietnam. Since neither side is able to defeat the other, both must be prepared to yield some of their expressed objectives. In practical terms this means that any settlement which is both fair and realistic in light of the military situation must provide for a government in which all can have a share of power and responsibility. Any settlement which does not provide for this can only be won on the battlefield. For the composition of the future government of South

New York Times, August 18, 1968. Reprinted by permission.

Vietnam has been the principal stake and the spur of battle for all sides in the conflict.

(5) Any statement of principle or intention—either in speeches or in party platforms—which does not deal with the future government of South Vietnam in specific terms is an evasion of responsibility. Statements of general principle and policy, however well-intentioned, do not constitute a commitment to the concrete terms which are the only realistic foundation for peace. This is why the Republican platform does not contain any meaningful pledge to peace in Vietnam.

(6) The proposals of this platform, representing the present view of the Democratic party, are fully consistent with the expressed ideas of the late Senator Robert F. Kennedy.

There are three major elements in our approach to resolution of the conflict in Vietnam. First, we must begin serious negotiations about the terms of final settlement. Second, while those negotiations continue we must move to limit the conflict, and third, we must propose terms for a final settlement which include the general composition of the government of South Vietnam. Throughout, this process should avoid ideas and phrases which are politically attractive but which conceal fatal defects.

For example, the Republican party has proposed to turn much of the responsibility for the war over to the South Vietnamese. Yet almost all responsible observers agree that South Vietnam is not capable of an effective defense against the Vietcong. Therefore such a proposal involves only a token shift in responsibility and is meaningless, or it amounts to permitting a military victory for the Vietcong.

A new Democratic administration will take the following steps:

(1) We will immediately halt the bombing of North Vietnam and all other attacks by sea or artillery on the territory of North Vietnam. It is clear that such a step is an essential prelude to any fruitful negotiations. Certainly a great nation can make a generous gesture toward peace, especially when there is no evidence that a halt to the bombing will endanger our forces in the south.

(2) We will immediately reduce the level of conflict in the south, by halting the search-and-destroy operations and other offensive tactics by air and land which result in widespread destruction of the Vietnamese countryside.

(3) We will not further widen the war, either by increasing our forces or extending the conflict geographically.

(4) Whether or not there is agreement on a cease-fire or troop withdrawal to fixed locations, we will propose a two-stage process toward a final peace. Ultimately the government of South Vietnam should be freely chosen by all the people of that country. However, an agreement to hold such elections can only be realistically accepted when all parties are confident that (a) free elections will be held, and (b) those elected will be allowed to assume power. This will require a new governing structure in Saigon. Just as we would not trust the N.F.L. to hold free elections, they cannot be expected to rely on the good faith of the present military Government of South Vietnam.

(5) We will propose, therefore, to establish by negotiation a new government in South Vietnam containing all major elements of the population including substantial participation by the National Liberation Front. It will be the job of this government to prepare for elections, and international supervision and guarantees of the elections process will be invited. If the present leaders of South Vietnam refuse to agree to such a broadly based coalition we will then withdraw our support and our forces since an honorable peace will no longer be possible.

(6) Following the formation of a new government, elections will be held for a permanent government of South Vietnam. All groups, including the National Liberation Front and the Buddhists, will be permitted to organize parties, designate candidates and campaign throughout the country. Prior to such elections all American and North Vietnamese forces will have withdrawn from the country and there will be a general cease-fire under some form of international supervision.

(7) The government so selected will be free to determine the future course and relationships of South Vietnam, including its relations with North Vietnam.

With such a program we will have attained our only legitimate objective in South Vietnam: the self-determination of the Vietnamese people.

I

STUDENT EDITORIAL REACTIONS TO THE CAMBODIAN INCURSION AND THE TRAGEDY AT KENT STATE UNIVERSITY IN OHIO: THE UNIVERSITY OF OREGON AND WASHINGTON COLLEGE IN MARYLAND

MAY 6 and 8, 1970

"... the ultimate moral responsibility falls on the shoulders of Richard Nixon and his military advisors. They have expanded the war into Cambodia and persisted in escalation while pretending to be disengaging from the war. ... After Kent State [and] ... after five years of peaceful protests, thousands of concerned young people now feel their only alternative is to take up the gun. ... The faculty will be asked this afternoon to shut the University down. ..."

Oregon Daily Emerald, *University of Oregon, May 6, 1970*

The war has been brought home.

Four students protesting the war were murdered at Kent State University Monday by National Guardsmen. At universities across the nation, battle lines are being drawn, and the brutalities of Vietnam have come perilously close.

Legally, the responsibility for those four deaths and over a dozen casualties rests on the parties immediately involved. The responsibility falls upon the 1,000 students who burned down the Kent State ROTC facilities Saturday night, and stole the available fire hoses so that the fire could not be extinguished. They also responded to the presence of the National Guard that were called on the campus by throwing back tear gas cannisters, as well as rocks and sticks.

The legal responsibility, also falls upon the National Guard. Those weren't warning shots the Guard fired, they were aimed into the crowd. Although it is clear that the demonstrators had violated the law and could expect to be consequently deprived of certain rights, nothing warranted depriving them of their right to life.

The legal responsibility lies in great part with Gov. James Rhodes. When the National Guard is called up by the President, the regulations require that they not use live ammunition, unless so instructed by the

---

University of Oregon, *Oregon Daily Emerald*, May 6, 1970; Washington College in Maryland, *The Elm*, May 8, 1970. Both reprinted by permission.

Secretary of Defense. In this case, Rhodes called in the Guard, and apparently no such regulation existed.

President Nixon, commenting on the Kent State deaths, said, "When dissent turns to violence, it invites tragedy." Both the protestors who violently provoked the National Guard, and the Guardsmen and Gov. Rhodes, whose reactions were intolerably irresponsible, are to blame for this tragic occurrence.

But the ultimate moral responsibility falls on the shoulders of Richard Nixon and his military advisors. They have expanded the war into Cambodia and persisted in escalation while pretending to be disengaging from the war.

Nixon campaigned in 1968 to end the war and unify the country. Since in office, he has mired our military deeper in Southeast Asia, and expanded armed conflict into not only Cambodia and Laos, but Ohio.

After Kent State, there is no doubt that someday soon, when National Guard are called in somewhere in this country, they will not be the only ones shooting guns. For after five years of peaceful protests, thousands, of concerned young people now feel their only alternative is to take up the gun.

If Richard Nixon sincerely wishes to avoid further tragedies arising from violence in this country, he has only one alternative: end the war.

The faculty will be asked this afternoon to shut the University down, as a protest against an ever-expanding war in Asia, and the murder of students at Kent State University.

There is no question as to the course of action the faculty must take.

The University has a chance to join other institutions of higher education across this nation in demanding an end to the war. This is not a simple protest, but a mass refutation of a suicidal national policy.

The University, trying, as it has these many months, to remain neutral is now in a position where neutrality is idiocy, and the need for commitment greater than ever.

University President Robert Clark said Tuesday, "We must say to our young people, 'Give us your hands. You are ours. We are with you and are one of you. You shall not stand alone.'"

President Clark can prove the sincerity of his words by placing this University alongside Stanford, Columbia, Yale, Wisconsin, Washington and countless others, in demanding President Nixon change the course of American war policy.

To attempt to preserve the tarnished image of academic neutrality, through further shucking and jiving serves only to affirm the actions of the Nixon administration.

The Elm, *Washington College in Maryland, May 8, 1970*

President Nixon's decision to invade Cambodia, coupled with the tragic death of the four students at Kent State University, have initiated what may be the largest wave of student protest to date. The Washington College community faces the urgent and inescapable task of determining what will be their position in that wave of national concern.

America has through its history enjoyed a unique luxury; the luxury of being able to ignore the realities of war, the violence, the sorrow, the absurdity. Washington College has to an even greater extent enjoyed that luxury, by being shielded not only from the reality of foreign violence, but from domestic turmoil. We are now in a period where luxuries, for college or nation, can no longer be maintained. The very survival of this country as a democratic state may be in question. At such a time, no one can say that he is not committed or committed fully. The only question is how to transfer this commitment into realistic, effective action. It is because of this that Washington College finds itself in a unique position. The very purpose of the College is to create national, informed public citizens.

The College also possesses the facilities, the people and the knowledge to achieve this goal. These advantages are not now being used. At a time when college students are forced to involve themselves in the grave problems which face this nation, the College is providing neither the information nor the atmosphere in which to make a rational, informed decision.

It has been the College's position that it teaches the student to think logically and rationally. However, it is also the College's duty to provide information and discussion about contemporary affairs, the necessary information. One cannot think rationally in a rational decision vacuum.

One cannot say that the student should not be involved. By the student's very existence, he is involved. If the "older generation" decries their youth's present reaction to the problems and trends of today, then they must assume the responsibility of providing youth with the knowledge and capability to rationally influence their world, both morally and practically. It is all well and good to denounce irresponsibility in the young, but nothing is done to create responsibility and make it viable. The College is in a unique position to do this, and a failure to do so is not only morally wrong, but in a sense suicidal. . . .

The ELM, therefore, recommends that:

1. A permanent Student Committee be formed to arrange extra-curricular lectures and seminars on such subjects as current, international and national affairs, pollution and racism.

2. A series of intensive lectures, seminars and discussion groups be formed for the next three weeks to provide the information necessary to clear up the prevailing ignorance about the Indochinese war.

3. That any student who feels called upon to participate politically be given any and every opportunity to do so, even if only to validate our democratic system of government.

4. That the College should reevaluate its methods of achieving its time-honored goal of education to determine if they are truly educating people to take their place as an active and contributing member of society today and tomorrow.

In short, it is the duty of this college and every college to answer their students' cry for help in facing a difficult world. If this help is not given, they have no one to blame for the 'barbaric' actions of their students but themselves.

J

PROFESSOR HENRY STEELE COMMAGER ON EXECUTIVE USURPATION OF THE CONSTITUTIONAL POWER OF CONGRESS TO MAKE WAR
MARCH 8, 1971

"It is only in the last 20 years or so that presidents appear to have thrown caution and even consitutional scruples to the wind, as it were, and ventured, on their own authority, into military operations that were in fact acts of war, that were on a large scale, that were in distant parts of the globe, and that constituted 'commitments' whose vindication threatened the integrity of our political and constitutional system."

The constitution, as written in 1787 and as developed over a century and three quarters is of course a product of history, not the conclusion of a syllogism, and any consideration of the war powers must be rooted in history rather than in theory, and it is chiefly to history that I address myself. In this I shall be brief, for I am conscious that in your past campaigns you have marched over this terrain until you are familiar with every foot of it.

There is—as your own committee said four years ago—no ambiguity about the intent of the framers of the constitution. They proposed to make it impossible for a "ruler" to plunge the nation into war. In the old world monarchs had "the sole prerogative of making war and peace"—the phrase is from Blackstone Commentaries—and the founding fathers were determined that no American executive would have the power of a George III or a Frederick The Great ... "To that end, too," your committee continued, "they provided a pretty rigid separation of powers." This too was something new in history, for while philosophers of the old world recognized a "balance" of powers, none had imagined the kind of functional separation which Americans established in their state and their national constitutions. Separation of powers, as Justice

Testimony Before Senate Foreign Relations Committee, in *War Powers Legislation*. Hearings before the Committee on Foreign Relations, United States Senate, 92nd Congress, 1st Session on S.731, S.J.Res. 18 and S.J.Res. 59. Washington: GPO, 1972, 18–27.

Brandeis observed in a now classic obiter dicta "was adopted by the convention of 1787 not to promote efficiency but to preclude the exercise of arbitrary power. The purpose was not to avoid friction, but by means of the inevitable friction incident to the distribution of the governmental powers among three departments, to save the people from autocracy. . . ."

The constitution makers proposed to assign to the Legislature the power to declare war, e.g., to decide on war, and to the executive the power to make or conduct or direct the war. This is inescapably clear from the all-too-brief discussion of these words and phrases in the convention; it is sufficient to note here what is familiar enough: that the shift in terms from "make" to "declare" was designed to preserve to "the executive the power to repel sudden attacks": Sherman wanted to nail that down: The President should be able to repel *and not to commence war*, and as for the always cautious George Mason of Virginia "he was against giving the power of war to the executive because he was not to be trusted with it. . . . He was for clogging not for facilitating the making of war. . . ."

It is not necessary for me to detail here the many examples of executive use or abuse of war powers. In 1818, President Monroe authorized General Jackson to engage in "Hot pursuit" of the Seminole Indians into Spanish Florida: Always eager to smite the enemy Jackson showed perhaps excessive zeal, captured Spanish Forts, and hanged Arbruthnot and Ambrister, two British subjects. In 1845 [*sic*] President Polk ordered General Scott [*sic*] to occupy the disputed land between the Nueces and the Rio Grande; when the Mexicans advanced into the territory he engaged in battle—purely on Presidential authority. "American blood has been shed on American soil" Polk announced and only then asked for Congressional authority to fight. Polk earned the name "Polk the mendacious" but public opinion rejoiced in the fruits of the war. In 1854 Pres. Pierce authorized the bombardment of the city of Greytown, on the Mosquito Coast, and that act of quasi war rested exclusively on Presidential fiat. President Lincoln, as all know, raised armies, launched campaigns, declared a blockade and suspended the Writ of Habeas Corpus all on his own: More clearly than other executives who invoked the war powers, he was able to fall back upon the Constitutional obligation to see that the laws were faithfully executed, and we are still debating the thorny question whether the Civil War was a war within the meaning of the Constitution or not: certainly there was no declaration of war nor treaty of peace nor was there a "Foreign" enemy. Grant's escapade in

Santo Domingo in 1869 is notorious—and was embarrassing. McKinley launched an expeditionary force of 5,000 men into China—part of the Boxer Expedition—without bothering to obtain Congressional approval. Theodore Roosevelt's interventions in the Caribbean—as those, later, of Taft, Wilson, and Coolidge—were mostly without benefit of Congressional authorization. Wilson ordered the bombardment of Vera Cruz on his own, and so too the invasion of Mexico in pursuit of the elusive Pancho Villa, though here he went through the form of getting approval from Pres. Carranza of Mexico—an approval that speedily changed to disapproval.

It is all pretty impressive when summed up in this fashion. But it is relevant to note that in almost every instance in the 19th century, and in most in the first half of the 20th Presidential intervention was confined to the western hemisphere and even to contiguous territory of our *Mare Nostrum*, the Caribbean. President McKinley's astonishing participation in the Boxer Expedition came, with a symbolic appropriateness, in the year 1900. Yet even Franklin Roosevelt's executive agreements with Britain for a Destroyer—Bases exchange and with Denmark for the occupation of Iceland and Greenland, which pushed what was permissable to the furthest extreme, could be held, not implausibly, to be a legitimate part of hemispheric defense. It is only in the last twenty years or so that Presidents appear to have thrown caution and even constitutional scruples to the wind, as it were, and ventured, on their own authority, into military operations that were in fact acts of war, that were on a large scale, that were in distant parts of the Globe, and that constituted "commitments" whose vindication threatened the integrity of our political and constitutional system. . . .

Clearly the present crisis is a continuation of a long series of crises stretching from Washington's Proclamation of Neutrality to Truman's use of military and naval force in Korea and our current involvement in Southeast Asia. There are however new ingredients in the executive use of the war power which make earlier precedents if not irrevelant then far from conclusive and which greatly enhance the threat to the integrity of our constitutional system and to the peace of the world. Let me deal briefly with these:

First, our current presidential commitments—and if we cannot curb these, our future as well—are global rather than, as with Lincoln, domestic or, as with Monroe, Polk, Roosevelt and Wilson, hemispheric. They are not to be justified by invoking the Monroe Doctrine or its accumulated corollaries: they are justified rather by new doctrines such as that of "Vital Interest" or by the "Nixon Doctrine" of shared responsibility. Of both it can be said that their most conspicuous feature is the fog which enshrouds them.

Second, the unlimited power of the executive in foreign relations is no longer justified as an emergency power, but asserted to be a normal and almost routine exercise of executive authority. Lincoln pushed his authority to the outward limits of what was constitutionally permissible, but confessed, with characteristic humility that the emergency required him to do what he did, and asked Congress to give retroactive sanction to his acts. No such humility characterizes what we may call the Johnson-Nixon Theory of Executive Authority. Thus President Johnson asserted that he did not need the authority of the Tonkin Gulf Resolution to justify his bombardment of North Vietnam, for he already had that: thus President Nixon's Asst. Attorney General asserted that the President's authority to invade Cambodia *"must* be conceded by even those who read executive authority narrowly" (June 16, 1970). Why must it be? Certainly not because of the persuasive character of the arguments advanced by this distinguished counsel, for that character is wanting.

Third, the new commitments are not, as generally in the past, Ad Hoc and even fortuitous, but calculated and ideological. Thus we do not drop bombs on Vietnam or Laos because "American blood has been shed on American soil"—Polk's excuse, nor does the President respond to an imperative like the attack on Fort Sumter or even to U-boat warfare: nor do recent presidents presume to act—like President Truman—in response to a United Nations decision. Now presidents act to "contain communism" or to protect "vital interests 9000 miles away, or to fulfill "commitments" that are somehow never made clear and that other nations pledged to them just as solemnly somehow do not think require military fulfillment.

Fourth, we are a charter member of the United Nations whose function it is to settle international disputes peacefully yet Presidential Declarations of what they are prepared to do around the globe, blatantly by-pass the U.N. and The International Court of Justice and thus add to the undermining of our own Constitution the undermining of the United Nations.

Fifth, as power corrupts, the possession of great power encourages and even creates conditions in which it seems imperative to use it, and the concentration of that power vastly increases the risks of misuse. We had one example of that as early as 1846: what began as a simple vindication of a boundary line ended up as a war in which we tore Mexico in two. . . .

However we may balance the constitutional and legal arguments on the presidential power, it is highly improbable that those who have already made up their minds on the wisdom or the error of our involvement in Indochina are going to be persuaded or dissuaded by legal arguments. Those familiar with the arguments of state department spokesmen, witnesses before senate committees, law professors and others learned in the law, know how easy it is to construct impressive monuments out of the disjecta membra of legal precedents and judicial citations: each of us can say of the arguments of our critics and opponents what Finley Peter Dunne said of the arguments of corporation lawyers, that "what looks like a stonewall to a layman is a triumphant arch to a corporation lawyer.". . .

If we turn to the many examples of presidential war making in the past twenty years we are, I submit, impressed by the fact that in almost every instance the congress was actually in session and available for consultation: thus the Korean intervention, the landing of troops in Lebanon, the Bay of Pigs, the Occupation of the Dominican Republic by President Johnson, and the successive series of forays into Vietnam, Cambodia and Laos. . . .

There is one further observation that is relevant and may be instructive. Almost every instance of the use of presidential force in the past has been against small, backward, and distraught peoples: the situation today. Call the role of the victims of presidential application of force in the past: Spanish Florida, Honduras, Santo Domingo, Nicaragua, Panama, Haiti, Guatemala, a China torn by civil war, a Mexico distraught by civil war, a Russia and a Vietnam riven by war, it is a sobering fact that presidents do not thus rush in with the weapons of war to bring Britain, France, Italy, Russia, or Japan to heel. Would we have bombarded Southampton to collect a debt? Would we have sent an expedition into Rome to protect Americans against a threat from a fascist government? Would we have precipitated a war with Britain over a boundary dispute in Maine? Would we land marines in France if customs collectors did not behave themselves? Would we bomb Siberia for years if shots were fired—without any hits—at an American vessel? And does it really comport with the honor and dignity of a great nation to indulge its Chief Executive in one standard of conduct for the strong and another for the weak? . . .

Abuse of power by Presidents is a reflection, and perhaps a consequence, of abuse of power by the American people and nation. For two decades now we have misused our prodigious power. We misused our economic power, not least in associating economic with military assistance, and in imposing economic sanctions against Nations who did not see eye to eye with us about trade with our "enemies." We misused our our political power by trying to force neutrals onto our side in the cold war by bringing pressure on the Nations of Latin America to support our shortsighted policy of excluding China from the United Nations— surely the most egregious blunder in the history of modern diplomacy. We misued our political power by planting the CIA in some sixty countries to carry on what we chose to regard as National Defense but what was in the eyes of its victims the work of subversion. We misused our military power in forcing our weapons on scores of Nations throughout the globe, maintaining military alliances like NATO and SEATO and imposing our will upon these where we were able. We misused our international power by flouting the sovereign rights of neighboring Nations like Cuba and Guatemala and the Dominican Republic and violating our obligations under the OAS Treaty and the United Nations. And we are even now engaged in a monstrous misuse of power in waging war on a distant people that does not accept our ideology, or our determination of its future. Is it any wonder that against this almost lurid background, Presidents misuse their power?

As we have greater power than any other Nation, so we should display greater moderation in using it, greater humility in justifying it, and greater magnanimity in withholding it. We display neither moderation nor humility nor magnanimity, but that arrogance of power which your chairman has so eloquently deplored.

In the long run the abuse of the executive power cannot be divorced from the abuse of national power. If we subvert world order and threaten world peace, we must inevitably subvert and threaten our own political institutions first. This we are in process of doing.